THE HARDEST LOT OF MEN

C&C

CAMPAIGNS & COMMANDERS

GREGORY J. W. URWIN, SERIES EDITOR

THE HARDEST LOT OF MEN

The Third Minnesota Infantry in the Civil War

JOSEPH C. FITZHARRIS

UNIVERSITY OF OKLAHOMA PRESS : NORMAN

Publication of this book is made possible through
the generosity of Edith Kinney Gaylord.

Library of Congress Cataloging-in-Publication Data

Names: Fitzharris, Joseph C., 1946– author.
Title: The hardest lot of men : the Third Minnesota Infantry in the Civil War / Joseph C.
    Fitzharris.
Other titles: Third Minnesota Infantry in the Civil War
Description: First edition. | Norman, OK : University of Oklahoma Press, [2019] | Series:
    Campaigns and commanders ; volume 67 | Includes bibliographical references and index.
Identifiers: LCCN 2018058792 | ISBN 978-0-8061-6401-4 (hardcover) ISBN 978-0-8061-8601-6 (paper)
Subjects: LCSH: United States. Army. Minnesota Infantry Regiment, 3rd (1861–1865)—History.
    | Minnesota—History—Civil War, 1861–1865—Regimental histories. | United States—
    History—Civil War, 1861–1865—Regimental histories.
Classification: LCC E515.5 3rd . F58 2019 | DDC 973.7/476—dc23
LC record available at https://lccn.loc.gov/2018058792

The Hardest Lot of Men: The Third Minnesota Infantry in the Civil War is Volume 67 in the
Campaigns and Commanders series.

The paper in this book meets the guidelines for permanence and durability of the Committee on
Production Guidelines for Book Longevity of the Council on Library Resources, Inc. ∞

To my grandchildren,
Lexi, Tabren, Charles, and Kaden

Contents

ILLUSTRATIONS

Figures

Maps

PREFACE

This project began as a paper for the Twin Cities Civil War Round Table and grew beyond my expectations. Curiosity drove me to investigate the effects of surrender—being broken—on the men and the Third Minnesota Infantry and to look at the regiment's restoration as an effective unit. Research at the National Archives in Washington, D.C., led to my sitting with Dr. Thomas and Beverly Lowry, who introduced me to both military justice and to the riches found in the compiled military-service records. When I gave the resulting paper at the Society for Military History meeting in Quantico, Virginia, Dr. Gregory Urwin volunteered to read chapters of the book in progress—but there were no chapters for the book I had not realized I was researching.

Over the next twenty-plus years, my wife, Mary Fitzharris, found ways to fund travel and copying expenses and established the necessary deadlines to move the writing toward completion. I want to thank Mary for all her love, support, and deadlines. I am confident that no one is happier than she that this history of the Third Minnesota will finally be published. My sons, Scott and Keith Fitzharris, can barely remember a time when the regiment was not intruding. In addition, I received a grant from the Minnesota Humanities Commission and sabbatical leaves and support from the University of St. Thomas for travel to archives in Arkansas, Michigan, Tennessee, and Wisconsin and several trips to the National Archives. Dr. Ralph Pearson, vice president for academic affairs; Dr. Thomas Connery, dean of the College of Arts and Sciences; Dr. Michael Jordan, sometime dean and also chair of the History Department; and Dr. Robert Riley of Faculty Development were most helpful with funding. From the Quantico meetings onward, Dr. Urwin, Charles Rankin, and Adam Kane of the University of Oklahoma Press have been gracious, generous with advice, patient, and even longsuffering. All these people deserve special mention and have my deepest thanks.

Support comes in other forms too. My friends in the Twin Cities Civil War Round Table and the larger "Civil Warrior" community have offered nagging questions about how the book is coming along and things relevant to the Third that they encountered: burial records, photographs, and letters, among other things. My students have put up with comments drawn from "my little regiment," to steal Michael Musick's line, while my friends participating in the military-history sessions at the Northern Great Plains and Missouri Valley History Conferences have offered insights and critical comments on my papers—and encouragement.

No author works in isolation, each has librarians and archivists helping them, and I benefited from the help of superb Interlibrary Loan Librarians Faith Bonitz and JoAnne St. Aubin, who found the right haystacks containing the needles I thought I needed, a difficult task before the digitization of the National Union Catalog of Manuscripts. University Librarian Daniel Gjelten, Julie Kimlinger, and the O'Shaughnessy-Frey Library staff supported me and gave me library space for many years.

Regimental histories are a form of local history, and many surviving sources are in the hands of descendants or collectors, all of whom were most generous in allowing me access to and providing me copies of their letters, diaries, and photographs. Doug Larson and I had several good conversations while he worked on his article on Gales the undercook. Patrick Hill began a history of the Third and arranged for John LeVine to translate Carl Roos's "War Diary," allowing me then to use a St. Thomas grant to fund Henrik Nordstrom's translation of Col. Hans Mattson's wartime letters, written in Swedish.

Newell Chester was a constant source of encouragement and put me in touch with others who could help my project. Stephen E. Osman has been generous beyond measure, connecting me with people and materials, providing copies of materials in his own collections, and answering questions only a professional historian and reenactor could answer. He arranged for me to meet Brent Noll, a "digger" (artifact seeker) in Murfreesboro, who guided me to find past locations in the present, thus making references clear and solving the question of where the last camp of the Third was located. Wayne Jorgenson, J. David Johnson, and other collectors generously shared their photograph collections.

I want to thank all the people who supported me in this decades-long project; a major drawback to long gestation is that too many them have retired, died, moved, or became lost during the transition of notes from paper to digital and e-mails from system to system. I appreciate all their generosity of expertise, time, energy, and encouragement.

The staff of the University of Oklahoma Press, particularly Amy Hernandez and Stephanie Evans, are a delight to work with, and I appreciate all they did to make this book possible. Cartographer Erin Greb drew the maps that illuminate the regiment's travels. Copyeditor Kevin Brock, who (superbly) edited my earlier work, *Patton's Fighting Bridge Builders,* again managed to turn my manuscript into a far better book.

Of course, all errors, be they of omission or of commission, are mine alone.

THE HARDEST LOT OF MEN

INTRODUCTION

Authorizing the Regiment

On a cold and snowy night in 1994 before the Twin Cities Civil War Round-table's meeting, Vice Pres. Joan Shurlock approached me and asked, "You *will* give a paper next year, won't you?" The resulting presentation drew on the correspondence between James Madison Bowler, a soldier in the Third Minnesota Volunteer Infantry Regiment, and his fiancée and later wife, Lizzie Caleff. His lifelong angst at being surrendered on 13 July 1862 to Col. Nathan Bedford Forrest piqued my interest: were other men in the regiment similarly affected? Further research led to articles on the effects of surrender on unit integrity and on military justice, particularly field-officer courts—a very unknown replacement for regimental and garrison courts-martial. At this point the original paper had become a book project, despite my best intentions.[1]

The Third Minnesota was different from other regiments in significant ways. It took pride in its appearance, its discipline and good behavior, its precision in drill maneuvers, and its training. Broken by their surrender to Forrest at Murfreesboro in July 1862 and thinking that their beloved colonel, Henry C. Lester, had betrayed them in the doing, the Minnesotans were destroyed as a fighting force. Most surrendered regiments reorganized into weak placeholder outfits; the Third was both reconstituted and restored as a first-rate fighting unit. Most Civil War soldiers, both North and South, did not fight Indians, but the Third, led by its sergeants, did so against the Dakota Indians in defense of families, homes, and Minnesota. The public appreciation that resulted started the process of restoring the regiment, which was fully accomplished while fighting guerrillas. Arriving as provost guards in Little Rock with Maj. Gen. Frederick Steele's "Arkansas Expedition," the Minnesotans had returned to the proficiency first achieved under Colonel Lester in Murfreesboro. Mustered out late, on 2 September 1865, and sent home, the regiment was one of the last Minnesota units discharged. The Third has several marks of distinction: it was the third-largest Minnesota infantry unit (the Second and Fourth were larger), the most men die of disease (239), the third highest in numbers of desertions (the Second and Tenth having more); and the most men promoted as officers into U.S. Colored Troops units (82).[2]

A "band box" regiment, in the jargon of the day, the men of the Third, with their polished brass and white gloves, moved crisply on dress parade, consistently mistaken for a regular regiment by knowledgeable observers. They were equally well behaved day to day, according to the available general and field-officer courts-martial records. Those in other units called the Minnesotans foot cavalry as they, hardened by training, marched for miles at a ferocious pace. They did regular target practice, and most became marksmen. The soldiers became proficient at skirmisher drill, with the bayonet, and in street fighting. Their unit cohesion was such that at Murfreesboro, Tennessee (July 1862) and again at Fitzhugh's Woods in Arkansas (April 1864), they received and destroyed cavalry charges while in line of battle—infantry normally formed a bayonet-armed square.

Attacked by Forrest's cavalry brigade at Murfreesboro on Sunday, 13 July 1862, the Third's camp guards, sick, and teamsters repulsed two attacks by three to six times their number of rebels, led by Colonel Forrest himself, before being overrun. The main body of Minnesotans destroyed the Second Georgia Cavalry's charge in line of battle by rifle and artillery fire, according to Georgian Colonel Lawton. Unfortunately, the infantry's brigade commander, Col. William Duffield, wounded and Forrest's prisoner, surrendered his troops, ordering Colonel Lester to conduct a sham officers' council to surrender the regiment and successfully transferring the onus of defeat from the senior brigade officers with political futures to Lester and his Minnesotans.

An army court of inquiry later cleared Brig. Gen. Thomas Crittenden, the post commander, of wrongdoing, thereby creating an official history of the event contrary to the experiences of the men of the Third Minnesota as recorded in their letters home. But they did not challenge this at the time nor did veterans after the war take issue with Christopher C. Andrews's "Narrative of the Third Regiment," which modified the court's "official" history only enough to reflect the reality that the men had fought. Accepting these lies and half-truths as history meant adjusting their memories to accommodate both their knowledge and the "official" truth.[3] This apparent betrayal broke the regiment and destroyed the Minnesotans' cohesion, esprit de corps, and morale. The men wasted away in a prisoner of war camp until called forth to confront a different enemy from the Confederates.

Fighting the Dakota Indians, the Third was a force multiplier that blunted attacks at Fort Abercrombie and broke Chief Little Crow's band and its assault at Wood Lake. Observers noted the men's precision on parade but lack of discipline otherwise. The troops prematurely triggered Little Crow's ambush at Wood

Lake by their lack of cohesion, though they *fought* as a unit, goaded on by their shame from Murfreesboro and their anger at the Indians' torture and mutilation of captives. The sergeants commanding the regiment there were soon commissioned, and few company officers thereafter came from the "gentlemanly" parts of Minnesota society. Reorganized after foraging upon New Ulm and rioting in Saint Paul, the Third went south to Kentucky and the guerrilla-infested "Jackson Purchase" region along the Tennessee River.

At Fort Heiman Maj. Hans Mattson commanded the regiment and imposed a discipline reinforced by both nonjudicial punishments and field-officer courts-martial, drilled the men until they regained their presurrender polish and élan, and led them in successful scouts or expeditions. They were highly successful in antiguerrilla operations that aimed to destroy guerrilla bands; Cpl. Jesse Barrick received the Medal of Honor (in 1917, when standards were higher) for his single-handed capture of two prominent guerrilla leaders in May 1863.[4] Ordered to Vicksburg to serve with Maj. Gen. Ulysses S. Grant's siege forces, the restored regiment operated to the standards Colonel Lester had established for them the previous year.

One of the healthiest regiments in Steele's Arkansas Expedition, the Minnesotans' skirmisher and marksmanship skills were used to protect engineers laying a pontoon bridge for the cavalry to cross the Arkansas River and take Little Rock. Becoming the city's provost guard, the regiment exhibited skill at counterguerrilla operations, skills first learned in Nashville and honed in Murfreesboro. Transferred to Pine Bluff, the Third did guard and picket duty and conducted scouts and patrols as ordered, even though in this pit of disease on the river, they lacked medicines the entire summer of 1864. Consequently, the regiment suffered so many casualties that healthier units had to assist to bury its dead. Shifting station to DeVall's Bluff, a healthier posting, the Minnesotans recovered their health and their precision in drill. Kept in service on occupation duty after most regiments from their state went home, the troops had a brief few hours of mutinous behavior intended, as Mattson noted, to remind their superiors of their unhappiness. Finally mustered out and sent home for discharge, the men of the regiment pointedly refused to stop in Saint Paul for a grand reception, confounding both observers and most historians who could not figure out why they were so "uncivil."

The story of the Third Minnesota offers opportunities to examine how change occurs in a social unit or network. For example, enough documentation exists to gauge the effects of the surrender at Murfreesboro on the men's morale and esprit de corps (that is, their "brokenness"[5]) and to determine what the reorganized leadership did to reforge the unit. It also allows us to follow them in training, on antiguerrilla scouts, on picket duty, and in line of battle and see *their* world.

In the end, the historical evidence is available to correct injustices now 150-plus years old and finally tell the actual story of the Third Minnesota Infantry.

Regimental Histories

The first regimental histories of the Third Minnesota, written soon after the Civil War, celebrated the men and their achievements while ignoring the darker side of events. Charles W. Lombard of Company I, who enlisted in November 1862 and served to the final dress parade in September 1865, wrote a short pamphlet derived from his diary and published in 1869. He was unusually young, eighteen years old at discharge, to even be interested in writing such a chronicle. Most histories, such as Andrews's "Narrative of the Third," were written in the late 1880s and 1890s, when their authors were older and interested in renewing the campfire camaraderie and memories of youthful adventures.[6]

The children and grandchildren of the veterans wrote the next generation of unit histories, which extended into the 1930s. As the old soldiers faded away amid new wars, interest in the Civil War faded too. The centennial of the war in the 1960s produced a moderate revival of interest. Later, the Ken Burns *Civil War* series, shown on the Public Broadcasting System in 1990, caused a revival of interest that continues among both the public and scholars. Many of the resulting new regimental histories, often written by amateurs and reenactors, combine the vastly increased material available, especially online, with a modernized antiquarian style. Not too surprisingly, most historians regard regimental histories as "unmitigated trash" at the worst and, at best, hagiographic memorials in the "drums and cannon" school of ancestral celebration.[7]

Historical study underwent massive changes in the last third of the twentieth century, expanding into new topics such as masculinity, childhood, the home front, and the business of war while utilizing statistical methods (often erroneously) and various and sundry theoretical constructs borrowed from the "social science" disciplines (usually poorly specified and badly used). The broadening of topics, resources used, and questions asked and answered (the bright side of theory) affected military history, including Civil War studies.

The "new" regimental histories, including Salvatore Cilella's *Upton's Regulars* (2009) and Lesley Gordon's *Broken Regiment* (2014), recognize that a regiment was, as Gordon points out, the "building block" of the armies and thus was, as Michael Musick said, the "primary object of identification for the men who fought the war. . . . [A] unit meant neighbors, friends, and in many cases . . . blood relatives." The Third Minnesota and its fellow regiments serve as historical laboratories, where correctives to erroneous interpretations can first be essayed. These new histories combine questions, such as why soldiers joined a unit and went to war, how they responded to their first experience of combat, or how they reacted to discipline and the resulting military justice, with extensive use of the full range of primary sources, including some that are best used in the statistical aggregate. Regimental histories of this kind are the basis for examining larger issues, such as the consequences of surrender upon the men of a regiment or the exploration of the motives of soldiers and their reasons for going to war.[8]

The Historiography of the Third Minnesota

Twenty years after Lombard's early pamphlet, Andrews wrote the only full history of the unit, "Narrative of the Third Regiment," for the celebratory state publication *Minnesota in the Civil and Indian Wars* (1889). With full access to the documents held by the Minnesota Adjutant General's Office in Saint Paul, Andrews's history reported matters as interpreted by his memory of events. Thus, he blamed Colonel Lester for *wanting* to surrender the unit on 13 July 1862 without resolving the conflict between what he reported the regiment doing (for example, repulsing several assaults by Forrest's men) and the official story (that the Third did little or nothing). His version reflected the opinions typical of the (inexperienced) company commanders involved: that Lester's decisions and behavior were entirely flawed on that fatal day. In his later articles for the Military Order of the Loyal Legion of the United States, Andrews showed a more sophisticated appreciation of Lester's choices, though not of the quality one would expect from an experienced division commander.

The Civil War centennial brought renewed interest in the Third Minnesota. Most of these and subsequent articles focused upon the events of 13 July 1862, and all of them—including my own article on their surrender—are flawed in their dependence upon the same incomplete set of records and acceptance of the "official" narrative. In "Lester's Surrender at Murfreesboro" (1965), Walter Trenerry claimed that the colonel had partied with a Mrs. Maney the night before and was drunk, befuddled, indecisive, cowardly, and ultimately easily duped by Forrest into ignoring Colonel Duffield's advice to hold out. Trenerry depended upon archivists to search their holdings for him, and they (and therefore he) missed many relevant documents.[9]

In a colorfully inaccurate 1985 piece in *Military History* that repeated the exaggerated *Confederate Veteran* claims, William Brooksher and David Snider described Colonel Lester as a complacent garrison commander who separated his forces, allowing the rebels to overrun the Third in line of battle. Erroneously assuming that Lester still commanded the garrison, they also incorrectly identify the rebel units engaged.[10]

Utilizing materials found while researching his master's thesis on ethnic discrimination in Minnesota volunteer units, Kevin Weddle wrote "Disgraced at Murfreesboro," published in 1991 in *America's Civil War*. He accurately described the command situation and the units engaged, but his account of the Third's actions—that the regiment did nothing but wait for four hours while Hewitt's Union artillery "harassed the enemy with a desultory fire"—is flawed, and he wrongly labeled Lester "bewildered," his head swimming "with conflicting messages and emotions," and asserted that the actions of the colonel and his officers were "criminal." Weddle did not use the Confederate after-action reports (Forrest's stated who surrendered what to who) in the *Official Records* or seek out other accounts, depending solely upon the "official" history derived from the court of inquiry.[11]

Gerald Prokopowicz drew from his dissertation research examining unit cohesion and brigade identity in the Army of the Ohio to write "Disunion Equals Disaster" (2002), also published in *America's Civil War*. He claimed that the men of the Third Minnesota and the Ninth Michigan fought in the streets of Murfreesboro, reflecting the bitter quarrel between their commanders, Lester and Lt. Col. John Parkhurst respectively. He too missed the rebel after-action reports and took the court of inquiry findings and Andrews's history as givens, producing another flawed and inaccurate, though colorful, account.[12]

Curious about the effects of surrender upon the morale and cohesion of the Third Minnesota, I examined how the broken regiment was recreated as a first-rate unit in "'Our Disgraceful Surrender'" (2000), published in *Military History of the West*. Together with Trenerry, Brooksher and Snider, Weddle, and Prokopowicz, I utilized the court and Andrews narratives to describe the engagement and surrender. Fortunately, my analysis depended not upon the details of the surrender account being historically accurate, but instead upon their consistency with the later memories of the event held by the men.[13]

Four articles have dealt with the regiment's post-Murfreesboro experiences in Minnesota and Arkansas. Stephen Osman detailed the Third's service with Sibley's Indian Expedition, notably at the Battle of Wood Lake (23 September 1862), where their "audacity, skill, and firepower" disrupted Little Crow's plans and broke the chief's forces. Roy Johnson examined the battles for Fort Abercrombie (August–September 1862) and the role of Capt. Burger's relief force, which included a detachment from the Third. Don Simon reviewed the regiment's service in Arkansas, providing more detail than Andrews and bringing tactical knowledge (albeit that of a fresh second lieutenant) to bear on its operations, notably at Fitzhugh's Woods (1 April 1864). Mark Christ, writing on that battle, analyzed the contest between the outnumbered but successful Third and Brig. Gen. Dandridge McRae's rebel cavalry. These works have provided useful detail and analysis for significant events in the Third's history.[14]

Two final articles are Fitzharris's study of field-officer courts (that is, a court comprised of one field officer) and military justice, which used the Third's service records to provide the first explorations of these two subjects, and Doug Larson's look at Alfred Gales, a black undercook. Gales came "home" with the regiment for discharge in September 1865, leaving behind both slavery and his slave name, taking up residence in the state, and raising a family in Saint Paul. Both articles were pathbreakers, opening the way for additional work that is now available on both topics. For example, Lorien Foote's study of manhood and honor in the Union army, using field-officer and general courts-martial records, has revealed the arbitrary and capricious nature of sentencing, particularly the immediate "nonjudicial" punishments administered for minor offenses. In contrast, the officers of the Third administered a consistent military justice within the regiment, tempering justice with mercy; no letters or diaries from the unit refer to nonjudicial punishments like gagging.[15]

Key Questions

The secondary literature generated several questions, particularly relating to motivation, morale, cohesion, esprit de corps, and "brokenness." There is almost nothing written on how broken units were (or are) reconstituted, and almost nothing on units that were fully restored, as was the Third, which returned to its high standards of discipline and drill and performed superbly well in subsequent field operations. The clash between the letters and diaries and the "official history" of the Murfreesboro affair raises questions of truth—of who did what where and when—and about motive and about the workings of memory.

The history of the regiment reveals interesting relationships. Regularly, the men of the Third charmed rebel women they encountered into accepting the Union occupation of their community, in some cases to the point of conversion to Unionism. The men also developed close and lasting ties to Red Wing, Minnesota, and a great affection for the women of Portage, Wisconsin, and Louisville, Kentucky. In contrast, their regard for the citizens of Saint Paul, Minnesota, was such that they refused a welcome-home banquet and afterward held only three reunions in the capital city; the city press may have played a role in this disaffection. Lastly, their service in Little Rock illustrates that there were places and times when conditions favored overlaying the "hard hand of war" with a more conciliatory velvet glove.

Minnesota in 1861

After the opening debacle of the Civil War at Manassas Junction, Virginia (21 July 1861), when most still expected a short conflict, Minnesota governor Alexander Ramsey sought War Department permission to call for a third regiment of infantry. He never explained why he thought another one would be needed, especially when the state's second regiment was having serious trouble recruiting men. Secretary of War Simon Cameron, a corrupt Pennsylvania political boss, refused to grant approval. Undaunted, Ramsey raised the issue several more times until Cameron suddenly agreed.

Only three years in the Union by 1861, Minnesota remained a frontier state, its population settled mostly along the Mississippi and Minnesota Rivers and their major tributaries. The "native born" from New England dominated the state's economy and politics. Immigrants (59,000 people, or a third of the population) mostly came from the German states, Ireland, Sweden, and Norway. French Canadians and French-Indians (Métis) were the oldest group, mostly Roman Catholic, and distrusted. Protestants, particularly the Episcopal, Presbyterian, Methodist, and Congregational denominations, were numerous and powerful. Most residents lived on individual farmsteads or in small villages, these mostly south from Minneapolis and east of New Ulm, though settlement moved up the Saint Croix and the Mississippi into the Pineries (the pine forests then being logged).[16]

The two largest distinct American Indian tribes in the state were the Dakota (called the Sioux at the time) and the Ojibwe (Chippewa). The Dakota had reservations along the upper Minnesota River above New Ulm, and the Wahpeton, a related group, lived west of Minneapolis. The Dakota were culturally split between the traditionalists and those who thought adaptation was essential to their survival. The Ojibwe held huge swaths of forested land in the north above Little Falls that loggers had not yet invaded. These reservations resulted from a series of treaties negotiated from the 1830s to 1858; in 1862 further negotiations would be completed with the Ojibwe on the eve of the Dakota "Uprising."

Only 169,395 white people resided in the state, according to the 1860 federal census. The military-aged male population (those fifteen to thirty-nine years old) was small, only 40,733 men. On the eve of war in March 1861, the state militia had "147 officers and about 200 men," formed by law into regiments, brigades, and divisions covering the state, with generals, colonels, and staff officers. Although the militia was poorly armed, ill equipped, and badly organized, in 1859 then-Gov. Henry H. Sibley had mobilized it to quell disturbances. Its social purpose and anemic numbers, common to northern militias, is surprising given the potentially hostile Indians within the state.[17]

Minnesotans were proud of their first infantry regiment, and not just because of its good conduct in the battle at Manassas Junction. Ramsey was in Washington, D.C., on Sunday, 14 April, when news came of the firing on Fort Sumter. He had a meeting that day with Secretary Cameron to discuss patronage appointments, and he offered Cameron a volunteer regiment—the first one offered—for the Union cause; Ramsey carefully specified that the "General Government" would need to defray the state's expenses. His offer accepted, the governor telegraphed Minnesota adjutant general William Acker to issue the necessary proclamation.[18]

The cautious demand that the federal government pay expenses came because Minnesota lacked a revenue base adequate to finance raising regiments and had to borrow money to do so. Its "credit rating" was abysmal; the state had defaulted on territorial railway bonds during the Depression of 1857, which meant high interest payments on its bonds. The few banks in Minnesota all used nearly worthless state, university, or railway bonds to back their currency issues. Most Minnesotans consequently preferred notes issued by Wisconsin and Illinois banks, which were backed by southern state bonds. Following secession, however, the value of those bonds and the banknotes based on them became highly uncertain and fluctuated wildly against gold.[19]

As money became scarce in the secession spring, economic activity declined, and men lost jobs as sawmills closed, farmers reduced their spring planting, and the log-rafting firms reduced their crews. In addition, by 15 April, flooding was extensive, with the Mississippi River estimated to be three miles wide below Saint Paul. The steamboat *Favorite* reported sailing "across prairies and through forests without the slightest idea on a part of the officers where the channel was, excepting where she sighted towns and noted landmarks." Despite floods, the mud roads, and the cold, the First Minnesota filled with three-month men. When the War Department asked that the First be transformed to a three-year regiment, many in the ranks refused to reenlist since they thought the war would be over after one big battle. New recruits took their places, and the regiment filled again. It helped that patriotic fervor was matched with unemployment.[20]

The Democratic Party had welcomed immigrants as instant voters, while "Know-Nothing" nativists, many of whom joined the new Republican Party, hated and mistrusted them. A large number of Germans had settled in Stearns County, north of Minneapolis, along with a colony of southern migrants led by former territorial adjutant "general" Sylvanus Lowry. Both groups were Democratic in their sympathies, and Lowry's *St. Cloud Union* had become an influential newspaper. Raising a company for the First Minnesota, Ramsey's friend Stephen Miller feared that few Germans would enlist, costing Republicans votes in the county since soldiers then could not vote. Many also thought that the Irish, heavily Roman Catholic and the victims of both religious bigotry and ethnic discrimination; the Lutherans and Baptists; and the Scandinavians and central Europeans would all not be eager to enlist. Strangely, many Lutheran Scandinavians enlisted and also supported the Republican Party.[21]

Just one month after authorizing the First, Cameron called for a second three-year regiment from Minnesota. Suddenly, Ramsey had double the number of regimental positions to award, and regional and political factors came into play.

Distributing the largess of contracts and volunteer commissions was a longstanding American wartime principle. Although the editor of the *St. Paul Pioneer and Democrat* (a Democratic newspaper) argued that the governor should only use "military education and experience, sound judgment, unexceptionable facility, and unimpeachable loyalty" in making military appointments, he expected Ramsey (a Republican) to appoint a fair number of deserving Democrats like the First's Maj. William H. Dike.[22]

On 22 June the First Regiment left Fort Snelling on board the *War Eagle* and the *Northern Belle,* bound for the "seat of war" in Virginia. On the eve of 4 July, Christopher C. Andrews, copublisher (with Lowry) of the *St. Cloud Union,* visited the First at its "Camp Minnesota" outside Alexandria, Virginia. He heard about Col. Willis Gorman's unusual emphasis on target practice and complaints about his tough discipline, forbidding even officers to leave camp without permission. It is possible that the publisher met several company commanders, including Capt. Henry C. Lester of Winona's Company K. Returning home, Andrews dissolved his partnership with Lowry and, after the call for a third regiment, raised and became captain of Company I of the Third Minnesota; Lester would become the regiment's first colonel.[23]

With such a small and scattered military-age population, recruitment for the Second Minnesota was slowed because men could not be spared from the farms until after the harvest, when women and old men could thresh and bag the cereal grains and finish the fields. Even a "large patriotic meeting at the capital" in Saint Paul on 24 July did not stimulate enlistments. Secretary Cameron seemed quite unhappy at the delays. On 26 July Ramsey, obedient to Washington's call, issued an order calling for men to fill up the second regiment and intimated "that a Third and Fourth regiment may soon be called for from this state." When the new adjutant general, John Sanborn (Acker had resigned to become captain of Company C of the First back in April), traveled to Washington to meet with Cameron and army officials, Ramsey asked him to advocate for a third regiment. As partial justification for this request, the governor argued that the news and recruiters could travel easily and quickly, and men could complete their family tasks and respond to their nation's call before winter ended most travel. Administration officials seemed unable to comprehend that Minnesota was at the extreme western end of the settled nation, where there were no railroads and the rivers froze up during winter, making travel slow and costly (thus the need for expediency).[24]

Miller, now lieutenant colonel of the First, was commanding the unit since Colonel Gorman commanded their brigade. And since Major Dike also had resigned to run for governor, Miller was unhappy when he wrote Ramsey at the end of July. Seeking the colonelcy of the Third Minnesota, he wanted to "consult with you [Ramsey] in regard to the other field officers, I think that you will never had [*sic*] cause to regret it," adding later, "would it not get up something of an excitement to let the people know in advance that one or two of the field officers [of a Third Regiment] would be taken from those who fought at Bull Run."[25]

"If a vacancy occurs in the field officers of my Reg't," wrote Gorman to the governor on 21 August, "you should *by all means* appoint Capt. H. C. Lester and without the least hesitation"; Lester was the colonel's brigade adjutant. (Miller also supported Lester for appointment to the field.) The next day the men of Company K presented their captain with a sword as an indication of their "affection for" him, citing the "diligence you have ever manifested for their welfare, and their appreciation of your qualities as an efficient and worthy commander."[26]

Ramsey telegraphed Secretary Cameron on 20 August and again on the thirtieth, proposing to raise a third regiment. He stressed that there was still, just barely, time to raise the unit and send it south before the Mississippi River froze. By 3 September, the newspapers reported that the governor was seeking approval for a third infantry regiment as well as for several companies of cavalry, sharpshooters, and artillery "for the field," with four companies of home guards and a company of cavalry to garrison the frontier posts, all part of the expected call for "five hundred thousand men authorized to be raised at the late session of Congress."[27]

The ordnance sergeant at Fort Ridgely, John Jones, wrote Ramsey on 2 September seeking an appointment as a field officer in a new regiment, citing as grounds his prior service during the Mexican War and in the regular army. Jones was the first of many supplicants for position. Most people, knowing of Ramsey's friendship with Miller, assumed that the current lieutenant colonel would get the colonelcy of the new regiment and, like Sergeant Jones, sought a position as major or lieutenant colonel instead.[28]

Ramsey's diary makes no mention of his campaigning for reelection; instead, it notes that he was "busily engaged in disposing of military business." Ramsey expected to and did win the Republican nomination for governor. The Democrats were divided. The majority, led by "General" Lowry, favored a "peaceful" solution to the sectional divisions along pro-Southern lines and nominated Judge Edward O. Hamlin of Benton and Major Dike as their standard bearers. Men who would later become company commanders in the Third Minnesota, including Andrews (nominated for lieutenant governor), Isaac Taylor (who chaired the party's "Union Convention"), and Benjamin F. Rice, led the prowar Democrats.[29]

Taking ill, Colonel Miller went to Harrisburg, Pennsylvania, to recover, leaving the senior captain of the First in command. Expecting Ramsey to come east soon, he wrote that he could not take command of the Third Regiment if it left the state before the close of navigation. He mentioned the possibility of taking a fourth regiment, saying that they could "talk all these matters over" when Ramsey stopped in Harrisburg on his way to Washington, D.C. On 14 September Miller wrote, "You can tell our friends that the place was offered to me and declined because of protracted ill health, and I will confirm it." That day Ramsey telegraphed Cameron, again lobbying for permission to call up a third regiment, partly for the war and partly for frontier defense, adding that the state could not raise further units until it was reimbursed for the costs of raising the Second Minnesota.[30]

The "Birth" of the Regiment

Would-be officers began recruiting men for new regiments well before the War Department authorized their formation. Patriotism was the common theme in recruiting, though the pay and benefits attracted many men. Capt. John Preston began recruiting to fill the ranks of his Hastings Light Guards (which would become Company F of the Third), anticipating a new regiment, which rumor said would be a drafted unit. John Tourtellotte (who would become the second colonel of the Fourth Minnesota) was recruiting the Valley Sharpshooters. He observed that "the harvest is now over, and times hard, and there are still more who can do their country a service, and at the same time, help themselves." Lt. Cyrene Blakely began recruiting a company in Olmstead County. Benjamin Rice of Mankato, John Potters of Garden City, and Theodore Bowers of Vernon were all busily recruiting for the Minnesota Rangers of Blue Earth County; Bowers would not join Company H of the Third, but Potters became a corporal. Goodhue County auditor Hans Mattson, a leader of the Minnesota and national Swedish communities, wrote an appeal (in Swedish)—"Arise to Arms; Our Adopted County Calls"—published in the *Hemlandet,* a Swedish-language newspaper in Chicago, and translated as "To the Scandinavians of Minnesota" in the state papers. The *St. Paul Daily Press* observed, "These nationalities [Scandinavians] are moving in all parts of the State to enter the military service of their adopted country."[31]

On 17 September Ramsey again telegraphed Secretary Cameron: "Shall I call out a third regiment . . . ?" Cameron replied positively this time, authorizing the governor to "adopt measures to organize two more infantry regts at the earliest date possible" and to send the Second Minnesota direct to Washington. The next day, an "unusually hot day," Ramsey drove to Fort Snelling and set to work in the Commandant's Quarters, drafting the general order calling for two more regiments. The Third Minnesota Volunteer Infantry Regiment thus came into being.[32]

CHAPTER 1

Raising the Regiment

Raising a Civil War regiment was a large and complex task, especially in Minnesota's frontier society. By the time Secretary of War Cameron authorized the formation of the Third and Fourth Minnesota Regiments, Governor Ramsey and Adjutant General Sanborn had enough experience to know what they had to do. The biggest effort was to recruit the enlisted men, that is, the privates and the noncommissioned officers (corporals and sergeants). Finding the company (line) officers was more contentious. Selection of the regimental (field) officers and staff became a drawn-out political drama since Ramsey had not returned from Washington, D.C. Lt. Gov. Ignatius Donnelly and Sanborn could do many things, but neither man could commission officers.

A Civil War infantry regiment included ten companies, each led by a captain who was assisted by a first lieutenant and a second lieutenant. In combat these line officers would stand with their men in the line of battle. The orderly or first sergeant was the senior noncommissioned officer in a company, assisted by four other sergeants and four corporals. Sergeants served as guides and file closers who kept the men in their places in the line of battle. The rest of the soldiers were privates, teamsters, or musicians who played in one of the regimental bands. All regiments had a bugle, drum, and fife band (field music) used to signal commands at parades and in combat. Many volunteer units also had brass bands—trumpets, tubas, and the like—formed from professional musicians and often paid extra for their services. This band provided music for marching and entertainment, its members also serving as stretcher bearers and surgeon's assistants in combat. The Third lacked a proper brass band.[1]

The lieutenant colonel and the major, known as field officers, took station behind the line of battle to assist the colonel in his command of the regiment. The colonel had a staff of two officers: the adjutant, who was his executive officer and handled personnel matters, and the quartermaster, who supervised the regimental Quartermaster (supplies, equipment, clothing, forage for the animals)

The Third Minnesota's Civil War Area of Operations, 1861–1865.
Map by Erin Greb Cartography.

and Commissary (food for the men) Departments. The sergeant major was the senior noncommissioned officer in the regiment and assisted the adjutant in his duties. The quartermaster, ordnance, and commissary sergeants headed the noncommissioned-officer staffs of the relevant departments, supervising enlisted men assigned on daily duty to the kitchens, bakery, forge, wagon shop, and others. The surgeon and assistant surgeon, together with the hospital steward (the medic who supervised the men assigned daily as nurses in the regimental hospital), took position in the rear of the regiment, out of firing range, and set up their field hospital. Since the regular army only had chaplains assigned to a few major forts rather than to regiments, these men typically had no assigned combat duties, though good chaplains often found plenty to do during engagements by assisting the surgeons, helping the wounded immediately behind the line of battle, or carrying ammunition forward.

In combat formation the men lined up shoulder to shoulder in two ranks by company. Usually, one or two companies were sent forward as skirmishers, while the rest were placed in line of battle. The purpose of this formation was to bring as much firepower to bear on the enemy as possible. The companies at the ends of the line, the points of greatest danger from flanking (side) attack, held the "positions of honor." The regiments holding the ends of a brigade's line of battle similarly held positions of danger and honor. The names of the companies, A through K (no J to avoid confusion with I), reflected the relative dates of commission, and thus the seniority, of their commanders, with the captain of the company that filled its ranks first (A) being commissioned first. Similarly, the last company to fill was K, and its captain became the most junior of them all. A captain's seniority initially determined the positions of honor; over time this would change as the seniority of the captains changed and as colonels chose to encourage or reprimand a company.

Recruiting the Companies

Federal and state militia laws and the U.S. Army's Articles of War and Regulations governed the otherwise entrepreneurial recruiting process. Most men who began recruiting would-be soldiers for the Third Regiment expected to become lieutenants in or the captain of their company, depending on how many men they brought in. Federal legislation authorized the governor to appoint a recruiting officer with the temporary rank of second lieutenant, but any upstanding citizen seemed able to acquire a set of muster rolls from the Adjutant General's Office and establish himself as a recruiter.

No Minnesota city was large enough to provide a full company to any single regiment, making the company the county community at war; some counties also were too small and contributed platoons within a regional company. Ties to the home front were tight because so many of the men had known each other and their families back home. Usually, recruiters were men known and respected in their community. The recruits of each company would then elect their own officers, typically men of status and popularity, who were then commissioned by the governor under the militia law. After many officers in new regiments proved to be incompetent in the field or cowardly in combat, Congress soon authorized examining boards to purge the volunteer regiments of incompetent officers.[2]

The first company officers were gentlemen, by local standards, though neither status nor popularity ensured the quality and capabilities of these men. The officers of Company D, the Scandinavian Guards, certainly were gentlemen in a more European sense, though the deference this brought them in the immigrant community was already in decay. Hans Mattson was a member of the Swedish gentry class who had served as an artillery cadet in the royal army, experience that gave added weight to his appeal to his fellow immigrants to fight for their new country. State Representative Lars Aaker, elected first lieutenant under Mattson's captaincy, recruited at least a dozen of his fellow Norwegians for the company. Hans Eustrom, Mattson's friend and fellow artillery cadet, became second lieutenant. The company assembled at the Killehaus in Red Wing, where the men had a good dinner, heard speeches, and according to diarist Carl Roos, "became tipsy with the help of the honorable beer of the hotel." For his part, Roos claimed to be forty-four years old when he mustered in, though elsewhere he claimed a birthdate of 1802, which would have made him at least fifty-eight years of age. He was not only well over the maximum age for service but also the oldest man in what would become the Third Minnesota.[3]

Clinton Gurnee, a Red Wing lawyer, raised a second company from among the "native Americans" of Goodhue County while seeking appointment as a major from Governor Ramsey. He held patriotic meetings in area towns to encourage enlistments, drawing men from the rural parts of the county. Cannon Falls farmer William D. Hale, the twenty-five-year-old enrolling clerk in the state senate, was one of Gurnee's assistants, becoming a sergeant.[4]

Farther upriver at Hastings, Capt. John Preston of the Hastings Light Guards was recruiting a Dakota County company. Some of the men initially belonged to a militia company formed in May, with Lieutenant Governor Donnelly as its captain. Preston recruited several men who quickly deserted. Philip Miller, a thirty-year-old Canadian teamster from Stillwater (Washington County), drove Preston from Hastings to Fort Snelling on 8 October. The captain got him drunk and enticed him into signing the muster roll, though Miller carefully stated that he needed his wife's approval to enlist. When Mrs. Miller vigorously dissented, her husband informed Preston that he was not joining, thinking no more of the matter until the army arrested him for desertion on 24 November 1863. Preston also recruited thirty-three-year-old Alonzo Verrill, a farmer, who deserted eleven days after enlisting. Arrested in late 1863, while serving in Company F of the Eighth Minnesota, and charged with violating the Twenty-First Article of War for not having first been discharged from the Third, he was "returned" to his original unit at Pine Bluff, Arkansas, in June 1864.[5]

Recruiting proceeded across the settled part of the state. In Winona "Messers Upham and Peebles" called to "young men . . . [to] battle for your country." The *Winona Daily Republican* noted, "we have plenty of men who can leave their business, since the harvest is past, and fill up the ranks." The *Carver Transcript* expected the Third to fill quickly: "The war fever here seems to be reaching its crisis. The whole country back of here threatens to become depopulated by reason of enlistments for the war."[6]

Recruiter R. W. Dawley of Saint Charles, who was "an old hand at this fighting business, having served in the regular army during the Mexican War," told the *Winona Daily Republican* that he wanted "the 'hard-fisted' 'rough-and-tumbled' men of the country who can stand the brunt of the fare and life incident to soldiering. . . . We have got the best kind of timber in our country towns for soldiers, and we hope it will be made use of."[7]

Though recruiters wanted young men of military age—eighteen to about twenty-five years old—who were working the family farm (and wished to see more of the world than the back of a mule) or who were seasonal laborers facing an offseason of unemployment (the economy having nosedived after secession), a sizeable number of older, married men enlisted with the Third. Volunteers responded to the siren call of recruiters for different reasons. Beyond patriotism and fear of being labeled a coward, especially by the women; the opportunity to see the world; and the possibility of gaining glory in a short war lay other motives more attractive to family men, notably the pay. Joining the army meant eleven dollars per month with "room and board" in addition to the bounty of one hundred dollars from the Federal government, twenty-five dollars paid upon enlistment with the balance paid upon discharge. Some counties, towns, and occasional individuals offered bounties to fill up company ranks, and many communities promised to take care of the soldiers' families—some towns even followed through.[8]

Among the men signing up in early October was George Davis, a thirty-year-old Welsh immigrant who enrolled in Capt. Levi Butler's Minneapolis company. Davis and his wife came to America in 1855 on their wedding trip. They moved to Buffalo, Minnesota, in 1857 and had bought a new farm earlier in 1861. Now he was going soldiering. Butler, a Minneapolis physician, was quite energetic in his recruitment so that his unit filled first, becoming Company A and making him the senior captain in the Third. Peter Shippman, a "penniless immigrant . . . from north Germany," and Henry Timms, an immigrant from Holstein, Germany, "walked one hundred miles to Fort Snelling to enlist" in Capt. Christopher C. Andrew's Stearns County company (later Company I). Ezra Champlin and a friend decided to enlist in the Third rather than the Fourth Home Guards and began walking to the fort one night. They stopped about midnight at the home of two friends and learned that these men were also leaving for Snelling. In the morning the foursome journeyed on to war. John Berrisford, another English immigrant, worked in Baxter's bakery in Saint Paul, then quit and went to work in Mississippi, baking for a large group of men building levees. Upon secession, he had to quickly leave for the North, where he joined Capt. James Hoit's Washington County Rifles (Company B).[9]

Recruits came to the rendezvous at Fort Snelling, where confusion reigned. Positioned on the bluffs overlooking the junction of the Minnesota and Mississippi Rivers, the post was an impressive walled bastion that the army had first abandoned to the owls, bats, and rats, then sold to Franklin Steele, a real-estate speculator and former post sutler. Steele and his brother-in-law, Henry Hastings Sibley, a fur trader and the state's first governor, owned the two ferries that connected Snelling to Saint Paul and Mendota. The state seized the post for use as its recruiting rendezvous and constructed new warehouses. Once recruiting began for the new regiments, tents were pitched on the prairie west of the enclosure to house the companies that became the Second Minnesota.[10]

After the post surgeon, Dr. Thomas Potts, examined the enlistees to be sure they could fire a musket, Capt. Anderson Nelson, Tenth U.S. Infantry, first mustered in the various dribs and drabs to state militia service, then later mustered in entire units to federal service. Thomas Christie, who joined the First Minnesota Light Artillery Battery in November, described Nelson as an "old, severe man, administering the solemn oath to the enthusiastic volunteers with (apparently) the utmost indifference."[11]

The competition between recruiters to fill their companies and gain a commission was fierce. The first ten companies to fill would form the Third Regiment and go south to the war, the next ten would form the Fourth and guard the frontier over the winter, and the remainder would become artillerists. The soldiers of the Second Minnesota watched the "man trading" and "theft" with some amusement. D. B. Griffin of the Second noted the insults directed at those who would form the Fourth, the mildest of which included "'home cowards,' 'bloody fourths,' 'petticoat guards' and all the names they can think of," to encourage the volunteers to fill out the ranks of nearly complete units to become part of the Third. This stealing of men—"efforts to jump entire companies" as Lieutenant Governor Donnelly termed it—was complicated by the small groups of fifteen to twenty-five maintained by many recruiters with hopes of gaining a commission as second lieutenant.[12]

Not all recruiters achieved a rank. Christopher C. Andrews and George Sweet of Saint Cloud had brought in enough men to muster a company for the Third when combined with Joseph Swan's men; Sweet was not elected an officer by the combined men and left in disappointment. Lewis Hancock brought in fifty men for Foster's company (G) and was elected second lieutenant before the group left Red Wing. Introduced as the unit's drillmaster at Fort Snelling, John Devereaux proposed joining the company if he were "pretty well assured" that he would be elected second lieutenant. Although he lost the new election to Hancock, parties unspecified had already informed Donnelly and Adjutant General Sanborn that Devereaux should be commissioned regardless, which he was (Ramsey had left them signed blank commissions for company officers). Hancock understandably thought this quite unfair, but it could not be undone. George Bertram of Company H complained that he had been promised the second lieutenancy if he brought in seventeen men but had been passed over in favor of Isaac Taylor. The company supported Capt. Benjamin Rice, who said that Bertram had no votes at all in his support and Taylor was the company's choice.[13]

Other men sought posts in the regiment for either themselves or their constituents. A few, like William Shepard of Cannon City, who sought a first lieutenancy in a company whose captain was "American born," thought Ramsey would directly commission them company officers, but the governor and Donnelly appointed only those elected by their men, as the law provided. Others sought appointment as a band master, sutler, chaplain, or even major or lieutenant colonel.[14]

Every regiment had a drum, bugle, and fife as part of its ranks, and as a matter of pride most states additionally provided brass bands for their regiments. At Fort Snelling there was stiff competition among candidates to lead the Third's brass band. William F. Cross was "appointed Leader of the Band of the 3rd Regiment . . . [to] be obeyed and respected accordingly," on 7 October. A week later Gordon Cole of Faribault proposed replacing Cross with O. J. Hays Jr., who led the town band. In addition, Secretary of State David Blakely, brother of Cyrene Blakely, the Olmstead County company principal recruiter, informed Donnelly that brothers James and Charles Hubbard of Kalamazoo, Michigan, wanted "the two first-places" in the Third's band. He described them as "refined and high-toned gentlemen and scholars as well as musicians."[15]

Minnesota did appropriate some money for wind instruments for the Third and Fourth Regiments, but Sanborn managed to reserve all of these funds for his Fourth Regiment's band. The Third thus made do with "a brass and tallow" band, using the instruments the men brought with them to the fort. Many of these were "old and some of them badly cracked," wrote Cyrus (Frank) Redlon of Company A, one of the musicians, adding that some "had to be 'doctored' with candle grease to stop the leaks when going on guard mount or dress parade." Cross, later appointed "Drum Major" of the regimental (bugle, fife, and drum) band in May 1862, managed to make a good band despite these problems.[16]

Sen. David Heaton wrote Ramsey seeking a place for Erastus Hays as sutler— the civilian merchant of the regiment—saying, "you *will* have the power in your hands to do me *a most decided favor & that I trust you will exercise it.*" Hays, declared Heaton, was a *"true Republican"* and opposed to the Democratic "Steele clique." John Proctor of Stillwater recommended a Democrat, Elam Greeley, for wagon master, saying that he was "a good medical man a worthy citizen & that he is *poor enough,*" with a large family who needed more than the pay of a private. Neither man was appointed. Jane Grey Swisshelm, editor of the *St. Cloud Democrat,* a Republican newspaper, recommended William B. Mitchell for appointment as an assistant paymaster, though he was a minor and lacked an adult's physical strength and stamina. As it was, appointing paymasters, a position held normally by regular-army officers, was not one of Ramsey's perquisites.[17]

Several men applied for appointment as surgeon or assistant surgeon, but the army required that a board of surgeons examine the candidates, naming only the best men to these posts. Lieutenant Governor Donnelly appointed Doctors Gale of Minneapolis, Rener of Marine on Saint Croix, and Finch of Hastings as the board, without consulting them, saying time was of the essence since the regiment would leave soon. On 8 November the board reported that Captain Butler of Company A (whom some of the men favored), Francis Etheridge, and E. W. Cook were "fully capable of discharging the duties imposed upon Surgeons connected with the Army and would recommend Dr. H. B. Cole . . . competent to discharge the duties of an Assistant Surgeon." Three days later Butler mustered in as surgeon of the Third, with the rank of major, and 1st Lt. William W. Webster became captain of Company A in his place. Dr. Francis Milligan of Wabashaw, called "one of the most skillful surgeons, as well as successful physicians in the State," also passed his examination and was appointed assistant surgeon, with the rank of captain.[18]

The competition to become the major, an honorable position that paid well and appeared to demand little beyond an ability to ride a horse, was especially heated. Both Captains-to-be Gurnee and John Bennett wanted the golden oak leaves, though Jonathan Jones of Saint Paul protested that Bennett, a Democrat, was "not strong on the Union question." W. J. Howell of Fillmore County sought the majority of the Third, though he was not capable of marching on foot; he also admitted a lack of military knowledge but was confident that he could learn. As Robert McLaren of Red Wing (later commissioned into the Sixth) noted in his application, Ramsey had to achieve a regional balance in his field commissions, including a few Democrats among his Republicans, but with the governor out of the state, no appointments could be made.[19]

The competition to be chaplain was more heated and humorous than that for major. Northfield's Rev. John Scofield, two of whose three sons had enlisted in the regiment (Joseph and Andrew in Company B)—the third (Charles) would also soon join (in Company E)—applied, citing his "several years experience of camp life." Noting that both the Baptists and Presbyterians had furnished chaplains for earlier regiments, George Nourse thought it was time the Methodists and Congregationalists got their turns and recommended Rev. Asa Firk of the Plymouth Congregation of Saint Paul. Swisshelm, the Saint Cloud newswoman, recommended Rev. Mr. Phillips, the local Baptist pastor, though noting that "his command of language is not good, [and] his delivery very faulty. . . . Give him a happy influence over any body of men, [and] his humanity & care of the sick & wounded would be all right." Rev. Henry Elliot issued a circular extolling his virtues to the company officers, who then made the desired recommendation to the colonel. The *St. Paul Pioneer and Democrat* observed, "We can hardly bear to criticize such a fervent production." Elder Perkins of LeSeuer County was one of those who, as the *Mankato Record* noted, "have not resorted to electioneering and outside influence to promote his success" in gaining the chaplaincy, though he did write a tract to influence the officers.[20]

Ramsey was expected back from Washington, and the *St. Paul Weekly Pioneer* observed: "The hotels have been filling up with embryonic Colonels, Lieutenant Colonels, Majors, and Chaplains, for a week or two. . . . Some of the itinerant preachers intended to sleep with him between Winona and St. Paul and make a 'sure thing' of the 'pay of a Captain of Cavalry' for three years." The *Mankato Semi-Weekly Record* noted: "There are a sufficient number of applicants for the chaplaincies of the Third and Fourth regiments to fill a company to the minimum standard. We hope a company of chaplains will be organized forthwith."[21]

Would-be chaplains and majors campaigned, and officers stole men, but the volunteers themselves found time for urban relaxations, some in the ice cream saloons, but most in the other saloons. Illegal whiskey sellers tried to locate on the military reservation as close to Fort Snelling and their market as possible. One such establishment was in the quarry that had provided the stones used to build the fort. A patrol sent out by Col. Horatio Van Cleve (Second Minnesota) destroyed the still and the stock of whiskey and returned with four dozen pairs of uniform coats and trousers left by men of his regiment.[22]

On Sunday, 13 October, the Second held a "Grand Review" at dress parade, and many civilians came upriver from Saint Paul, riding the *City Belle* for twenty-five cents each. The men of the Third and Fourth Regiments enjoyed the excitement, hurry, and bustle. Drilling in the morning in their new companies, the recruits marched in dress parade despite their raw edges, ratty civilian clothes, and lack of guns. Reveille was at 4 A.M. on Monday, though many were up by 2 A.M.

since "the bonfires of old boxes and barrels found in and around camp made every object as plainly visible as in broad daylight." The Second was following the bad example of the First, which destroyed its furniture in a grand bonfire before departing. At about 9 A.M., with tents struck and gear packed, the Second marched down to the landing below the fort and boarded their steamboats. The men of the Third and Fourth saw them off, "swinging their hats and [with] loud cheering."[23]

Though a thousand men left the fort, it seemed as crowded as ever. Captain Butler of the Third became commander of the post in place of Colonel Van Cleve. Drill continued morning and afternoon; the men were becoming soldiers. "Military etiquette and subordination take the place of the free and independent style to which, in our former condition of sovereign citizens, we were all accustomed," wrote "K" to the *Faribault Northern Statesman.* "Obedience, first, last, and always, is the one lesson set before us, and discipline the one thing insisted on at every turn."[24]

Wearing now-shabby civilian clothes—for most the seats of their trousers were notable by their embarrassing absence—the men were, Sergeant Hale thought, "little better than a mob of men" and did not *look* like soldiers. When their clothing and equipment finally arrived at the Lower Landing from the New York Quartermaster Depot, it made an "immense pile of boxes" containing everything from pants to hats to "all the trimmings and ornaments—and everything necessary for service in the field, such as tents, cooking apparatus, musical instruments, etc." Swisshelm reported that the freight bill alone was two thousand dollars. But only a field officer could sign for the equipment, and with the departure of the Second Regiment, none were present. Lieutenant Governor Donnelly telegraphed Ramsey: "Men are dirty and sick for want of clothing. Name a field officer or come home and organize regiment." As late as 5 November the recruits had only received their shoes and blankets.[25]

In late October many of the companies received a short furlough. Both of the Goodhue County companies went home to Red Wing. The *Goodhue County Republican* ignored Mattson's Scandinavian Guards while praising Gurnee's company: "They do say the 'Red Wing Volunteers' is the crack company of the Minnesota Third." On Friday, 1 November, Gurnee's friends gathered at the Metropolitan Hotel to present him "a beautifully mounted sword . . . , expressing the deep interest felt for him and his gallant men, by the community that sent them forth." At a separate gathering, Florence Graham presented Mattson with a "very beautiful sword" from his many friends.[26]

Upon receiving Maj. Gen. Winfield Scott's order of 29 October to send the regiment to "report to Brig. Genl. Sherman when ready," Adjutant General Sanborn ordered that no more furloughs be granted the men of the Third and that all members should report to Fort Snelling by 4 November. Unsatisfied with their progress in drill, he appointed Col. William Crooks, who had attended the U.S. Military Academy for several years, as "General Drill Officer of the troops at Fort Snelling." A few days later Crooks became commander of the post, replacing newly appointed Surgeon Butler.[27]

Some of the visiting friends and family stayed in the boarding house in a former barracks just inside the gate. It "had the ordinary fare and appliances of a first class hotel," and the food was served on "white plate." Others stayed in Minneapolis or, more commonly, Saint Paul and came to the fort by carriage or steamboat. George Oakes chartered the *Jeannette Roberts* for an excursion to witness dress parade on Saturday, 2 November, leaving the Lower Levee at 1:20 P.M. for a fifty-cent roundtrip fare. This also included musical entertainment furnished by the Great Western Band of Saint Paul, which played for militia events.[28]

The Politics of Command

Governor Ramsey arrived in Saint Paul about 9:30 P.M. on Sunday, 3 November, and spent the next day "making apts [appointments] of field officers in 3d & 4th Infantry Regts." He appointed General Sanborn colonel of the Fourth but could not name his friend, Stephen Miller, as colonel of the Third due to the latter's poor health. Instead, Ramsey appointed Miller's protégé, Capt. Henry C. Lester of the First Regiment (Company K), recommended for the first available field appointment by both Cols. Willis Gorman and Napoleon Dana.[29]

Capt. Benjamin Smith, who raised a cavalry company from Blue Earth County, became lieutenant colonel of the Third. Present at Snelling, he took command of the regiment as soon as he completed the paperwork and took the commissioning oath. Since Smith's brother was senator-elect from the First District, pro-Democratic papers claimed that Ramsey's field-officer appointments were to garner support for his bid to replace Sen. Henry Rice, a Democrat, in the U.S. Senate.[30]

Rumors abounded that the governor would appoint John Hadley of Owatonna as the major of the Third. All the company officers jointly petitioned "His Excellency" on 3 November requesting that Hadley *not* receive the commission. Citing the ongoing failure of Federal arms (news of the recent defeat at Balls Bluff, Virginia, adding depth to their argument), the officers attributed this to "the want of Military Experience in leading officers" and opposed Hadley as incompetent and incapable. Imagine their horror when State Headquarters General Order 25 announced that Hadley would be their major, to "be obeyed and respected accordingly."[31]

The Regimental Council of Administration, composed of Major Hadley and the two senior captains, appointed Daniel Rohrer of Saint Paul, a former city treasurer and chair of the state Republican committee, as sutler. Minneapolis interests protested his appointment; in reply Ramsey's *St. Paul Daily Press* pointed out that Franklin Steele of Minneapolis, through his front men Eustis and Lamb, provided the subsistence for the fort and had "already made his $20,000 by the operation." The *Press* thought the choice of Rohrer, "a man too honorable to impose upon any human being," an excellent one. Senator Heaton, who championed Erastus Hays, was mightily disappointed. The post was of consequence since the sutler had a monopoly on supplying the regiment with sundries, treats, and the like, though the council set his prices and supervised his operations. Sutlers sold to the men on credit, since pay was often late, and got paid before the soldier on payday.[32]

Commissioned, Smith signed for the uniforms and equipment, enabling the men to draw their issue gear. Sergeant Hale, in the regimental quartermaster's department, described their "transformation from the most ragged & squalid set of men (a men mob) to a regular and fine appearing regiment." Uniformed and equipped, the soldiers moved out into tents, their camp organized along proper military lines. Many of the men, having drawn "a hat and brass fixings," had their "likenesses taken" by one or another local photographer. Their drill was improving too, and the regiment began to look like a military organization as they paraded in the snow in early November.[33]

"Orders were read on dress parade tonight [Sunday, 10 November] for us to be ready to start for Louisville, Ky the 14 inst.," noted Pvt. James Battey of Company E. The men of Company G met that evening and approved a resolution praising Thomas Moore of Wabashaw, who had provided a great supply of pins and needles and "did furnish us with huge quantities of Tobacco and Pipes, &c." Such exercises of democracy marked the volunteer military units of the Civil War, and good officers found positive ways to use it. The ladies of the First Baptist Church of Minneapolis presented each man in their Company A with "a handsome needle case."[34]

With the regiment's departure immanent, Swisshelm proudly reported that most of the men in Stearns County's Company I had "allotted $8 of their pay for the benefit of their families." Promoted by the new Sanitary Commission (a private organization providing advice and assistance to the army on questions of medical and general welfare), the allotment system offered a mechanism by which the married men could send part of their pay to their families. Minnesota's allotment officer, State Treasurer Charles Scheffer, would receive the funds collected at payday by the elected trustees of the regiment and then disburse the funds to the families. About a quarter of the men in the Third made such allotments, totaling about two thousand dollars per month.[35]

Departing to "the Seat of War"

After newspapers spread the word that the Third would depart on Friday, 15 November, friends and family traveled to Fort Snelling and the river-port towns to see the regiment pass—or to give the men one last hug if their boat stopped for a brief time. The troops were ready and celebrated their anticipated departure by lighting "a right proper bonfire . . . of our furnishings, chairs, benches and tables," as Pvt. Carl Roos of Company D noted, calling it "a vandalistic business of American mischieviousness [*sic*]."[36]

The boats did not arrive on schedule, so new orders revised the regiment's departure date to 16 November. That morning the men were "up at 3 A.M., had breakfast at 4, strap[ped] on our knapsacks at 5, [and] took our places in line at half-past 6." Companies A, B, and G boarded the *Northern Belle,* the only boat to arrive on time. The *City Belle* and *Frank Steele* were several hours late, and the companies still ashore went through company drill on the parade ground while they waited. Finally, all the boats were at the landing and took the men on board. Lieutenant Colonel Smith had the first and second divisions on the *Northern Belle,* while Captain Mattson commanded the third and fourth divisions—five companies—on the *City Belle.* Two companies of the Third and the companies of the First and Second Regiments now happily relieved from duty at Forts Abercrombie, Ridgely, and Ripley were aboard the *Frank Steele,* all under Major Hadley's command.[37]

The announcement of the appointment of Rev. Chauncey Hobart of Red Wing, a pioneer missionary in Minnesota and Wisconsin, as chaplain of the regiment seemed lost amid all the confusion of departure. The company officers had unanimously chosen Rev. Mr. Charles Woodward, an Episcopal minister from Rochester, and had informed him of their decision. Yet they had failed to consult the men first, as regulations required, and Smith refused to appoint Woodward. The soldiers, or "at least two thirds of those who had any respect for religion at all, were either members of the Methodist Church or had been brought up to believe in the particular tenets of that Church" and demanded a Methodist chaplain.[38]

The flotilla barely began its passage between Pike's Island and the "west," or Mendota, shore when one boat grounded on the Mendota sandbar, one of many exposed by the lower water level of the river each fall. It took several hours to free the vessel; the troops disembarked, marched downriver two miles, and reembarked. The men "ate hard bread and crackers on board above the city," according to Pvt. John Boxell, though "the hard bread was hard indeed, and the pork was stronger and worse looking than any I ever eat." Roos noted that the boats arrived at noon, late, at Saint Paul's Upper Landing. The Third Minnesota marched through the city, up Eagle Street to the Winslow House, over Third Street, and down Jackson to the Lower Landing, to "display our beautiful uniforms, which with elegance and substantiality, confessed our magnificence" before the crowds lining the sidewalks and buildings, many of whom had waited since 10 A.M. Back on board the boats, all the men received "their needle cases, spools of thread, etc., [these from the ladies of Saint Paul] all in due time, although there was no public parade about the matter."[39]

The men cheered as the boats backed into the Mississippi and waved as their boats steamed downriver. The editor of the *St. Anthony Falls State News* later wrote that one soldier "expresses disappointment at the reception with which the regiment was received at St. Paul and says that 'We embarked feeling as a Regiment that the people of that city were not heartily enthusiastic in giving God speed to the 'Third.'" The editor of the *Weekly Pioneer and Democrat* confirmed this impression: "the boys ... manifested much more enthusiasm than the crowd that witnessed their departure." Perhaps this was the origin of the considerable animus that developed over time among the veterans of the Third toward the capital city.[40]

About 4 P.M. "the whistles of the three steamers . . . announced that the long expected Regiment was approaching" Hastings. People cheered, and the men returned the greeting, as the boat with Company F sidled up to the landing. Captain Preston led his unit ashore to a rousing welcome; their sendoff was equally boisterous. The *Hastings Independent* said: "Many of the best men of the city and vicinity, composed the gallant Company. . . . [T]hey will do their whole duty."[41]

After grounding several times, the flotilla finally approached Red Wing at about seven or eight o'clock in the evening. The *Goodhue County Republican* reported that "each boat was greeted with cheers and a salute of guns, and upon the approach of the one containing the companies from Goodhue, an immense bonfire was lighted near the point of its landing." Ezra Champlin remembered that the *City Belle* had barely landed when "a rush was made for the loved ones who had been waiting the arrival. Fathers [and] mothers . . . clung to the boys with a love akin to desperation." The editor of the *St. Paul Weekly Press* observed: "The two Red Wing companies were literally taken to the hearts of the people of that patriotic town. After partaking of a bountiful collation, a beautiful flag was presented to the Scandinavia company." Private Roos proudly bore that American flag, which had "The Scandinavian Guards" embroidered on one of its red stripes. Despite the normal ethnic divisions in society, there was only one reception, not two separate ones, on the landing. During the joyous confusion, Pvt. Solon Bevans of Gurnee's company deserted, "suppos[ing] himself discharged." Mattson finally ordered the men back aboard, and with "gunshots, hurrahs, [and] whistles, the journey continued."[42]

Above La Crosse the men received "two days' rations of hard bread and *harder* meat," wrote "M," that "was furnished by one Eustice [Eustis and Lamb] at Fort Snelling. . . . It was of such quality that some of the boys immediately threw it into the river." "Hurbert" added, "We could eat pork in almost any form, but such a diversity of animals as he gave us we could not relish, for we found . . . a thousand animals within an animal, which immediately converted us into Jews for the present." From camp near Louisville, Kentucky, "G" later claimed that "a good share of the meat was perfectly raw. We threw away a great part of it, and the rest was condemned by the Surgeon after we got here." The consensus was that neither Eustis nor Lamb would be safe in camp and that their just rewards would come in the nether world.[43]

The convoy stopped at Lake City and at Wabashaw, where a party from Rochester boarded the *Frank Steele* to journey with Company K. Civilians occupied the cabins, so many soldiers slept on the decks between ports. The *City Belle* grounded below Wabashaw, and the *Northern Belle* helped it off the bar. Only the *Frank Steele* stopped at Winona, landing between 3 and 4 A.M. on Sunday so the men from the Winona and Rochester areas could meet their friends and families. The *Steele* was a fast boat and arrived in La Crosse several hours before the other vessels. The *Rochester Post* described the scene when most of the regiment landed about 7 A.M. on Sunday, 17 November, in La Crosse. The "soldiers were arrayed on the forward decks of the incoming boats, the flags waving in the breeze and the bands playing a lively air, the scene was an impressive one to behold."[44]

The companies on the *Northern Belle* had breakfast before landing. The other companies enjoyed apples provided by some of the citizens of the city. Roos mentioned that "some friends met them and 'they received some liquids out of our canteens,'" suggesting the state in which Company D began its service. Lieutenant Colonel Smith informed Governor Ramsey that "the captains of the steamboats received the hearty thanks of the whole regiment, for their personal efforts to make the trip pleasant and agreeable. Every soldier behaved as a gentleman, and everybody praised the fine and gallant appearance of our noble young men."[45]

At noon the regiment departed La Crosse on a train of twenty-five cars pulled by two locomotives. The officers and their families rode in "a very elegant and costly car, brought express from Milwaukee" by the general manager of the La Crosse and Milwaukee Railroad. (Officers' families often accompanied a regiment to its first posting.) It and the Northwestern Railroad worked together to move the regiment expeditiously at thirty miles an hour across Wisconsin, stopping only for water and fuel and to change crews at Portage, where the ladies of the town provided the Minnesotans a memorable supper. "Hurbert" noted in the *Daily Press*: "I must return the united thanks for the whole Regiment to the people of Portage City, Wis., who so bountifully supplied our wants with hot coffee, ham, chickens, bread and pies. Most heartily did we cheer and thank them, then hastened on our journey." Smith told Ramsey that the men offered "our thanks to the citizens of Portage . . . , who on our arrival invited us to a most sumptuous feast of eatables sufficient for twice our number."[46]

Upon arrival at the Chicago and Northwestern depot in Chicago at 6:30 A.M. on Monday, the "men were served with hot coffee and other necessaries and the officers provided for by the R. R. Company at the Sherman House." "Hurbert" said the coffee made the hard bread tastier but was not "strong enough to render palatable the meat furnished by friend Eusits." Roos reported that they "were escorted by the Chicago Light Guards Music Corps to the Michigan Central Depot." The *Chicago Times* took notice of the Swedes and Norwegians of Company D as well as the twelve men in Company A who were over six feet tall, while the *Chicago Tribune* observed that "the regiment is composed mainly of lumbermen, strong, able bodied, and inured to labor and danger. Their appearance was very soldierlike and elicited great praise."[47]

When the regiment, 900 officers and men, departed Fort Snelling, most if not all of the officers and a significant number of the enlisted men (mostly among the approximately 250 married members), were "gentlemen," to use historian Lorien Foote's term. Very few "roughs," or low-class troublemakers, can be identified using trial charges. Over a quarter of the regiment were immigrants (a third of Minnesotans were immigrants), and nearly half of them came from Sweden and Norway; Mattson's Company D consisted entirely of Scandinavians. At least 59 percent were farmers (compared to 52 percent of the state's labor force in 1860), and laborers composed only 2.5 percent of the regiment, compared to 10 percent of the state's population. Although the Chicago papers referred to lumbermen within the ranks, only 9 men listed that occupation (0.6 percent), though many farmers and farm laborers worked in the forests during the winter and some also worked the rafting crews in the spring to supplement their incomes. The older and married men were also more skilled in their trades, including printers (10), bakers (41), butchers (4), surveyors (3), "engineers" (3), carpenters (34), and blacksmiths (11). Perhaps 50 were merchants and professionals (including surgeons, physicians, druggists, lawyers, civil engineers, merchants, and teachers), many serving in the ranks. Wisconsin and Iowa regiments contained more farmers, merchants, and professional men, while Union forces on average had fewer farmers and laborers and more professionals and merchants than the Third.[48]

The military service records and the unit roster provided by the Minnesota Adjutant General's Office together provide age and date of enlistment information. The average age of a soldier in the Third Minnesota, based on 1,452 roster entries between 1861 and 1865, was 26.1 years old. Men in three companies—A, B, and D—were significantly older (D's average age was 28.2 years). The men in

Company K were the youngest, at an average of 24.7 years old. Year of enlistment has no significant effect on age distributions, which are rather uniform between companies for ages 21–28, and there were enough older men to give the regiment an air of "gravitas" that many others with more younger men (distributions skewed toward 18–22 years) lacked. This may be a factor in the better behavior of the Third compared to most regiments and historiographic expectations.[49]

Colonel Smith reported that the regiment included forty laundresses and thirty-four servants on strength, but no one noted on which of the twenty passenger coaches the laundresses rode as the Third left Chicago. (Enlisted men's wives usually accompanied the troops as laundresses, often because they had no place to live.) The train included three baggage cars, a sleeping car for the sick, and another for the officers and their families. William Hale wrote that, as their train departed Chicago, "for one half hour hurrah was returned by hurrah from the open windows of the cars, all the length of Lake Street." The route took them through Michigan City, New Albany, and Salem, past the "old Tippecanoe battlefield" into Lafayette, Indiana. There, the ladies gave the men "plenty of hot coffee and some cakes, pies, and apples. Some of the ladies were so devotedly patriotic," wrote "Hurbert," "that they nobly and boldly stepped up to their country's defenders and gave them a hearty kiss, and a 'God bless you,' and as good soldiers we wo'd not betray our country for a kiss, so we cheerfully gave it back." At Lafayette the train split. The portion Roos was on passed through Indianapolis at night; the baggage went by the Chicago, Burlington, and Quincy Railroad. Arriving in Jefferson, Indiana, at about 9 A.M. on Tuesday, 19 November, the soldiers gathered their baggage and waited for the steamboat to ferry them across the Ohio River to Louisville, Kentucky.[50]

CHAPTER 2

LEARNING THE
PROFESSION OF ARMS

About noon on Tuesday, 19 November, the regiment crossed the Ohio River on a ferryboat and marched through Louisville to the Louisville & Nashville Railroad depot, where the loyal citizens provided a welcoming meal of "hot coffee, boiled ham and bread, sweet and nice as ever could be—[it was] far better than we ever received at Fort Snelling." Pvt. Carl Roos of Company D described their route as "almost a continual welcome" amid flying and waving U.S. flags and handkerchiefs and "cordial expressions of sympathy" from large crowds. One "woman pok[ed] her head out of a window waving her handkerchief and hurrahing for Jeff Davis," who upon "receiving the scathing scream of the soldiers she very soon withdrew." Blacks enthusiastically exclaimed, "God bless you, kill a rebel for me!" Roos concluded, "Louisville is strong for the Union."[1]

Refreshed, the Minnesotans marched out the Oakland Turnpike to the old fairgrounds, now dubbed "Camp Todd," west of town, where, wrote Sgt. William Hale of Company E, they made camp in "three hours of confusion as bad as I ever knew. . . . [W]e are so very green in camp life." Wearing overcoats and blankets for warmth, the guards had, according to "Private," only their "Colt's Revolvers" (many of the men having bought revolvers before leaving Fort Snelling), "there being but two muskets in the Regiment. . . . [I]t rained and blew as though all 'secesh' was bound to be blown away and the 3d along with it." The next morning the regiment moved to a better part of the field and "encamped in regular order" according to regulations.[2]

Lieutenant Colonel Smith immediately reported to Brig. Gen. Don Carlos Buell, commanding the Department of Kentucky. He arranged to draw rations from the commissary stores in Louisville, imperative given the regiment's lack of edible meat, and requisitioned arms and accoutrements. A "board of survey" of company officers inspected and condemned the bad meat the men had received from Eustis. On Thursday, 21 November, Smith reported to Governor Ramsey, noting 1st Lt. Rollin Olin's good work as adjutant. He added that Major Hadley, encumbered by his family, was of no help in the "management of troops or in maintaining order and discipline," while most of the officers "demeaned themselves in a sober and gentlemanly manner." But 2nd Lt. Cyrene Blakely of Company K (one of Ramsey's political supporters) had left the regiment without permission during the journey (a violation of the 44th Article of War) and rejoined them shortly after they made camp.[3]

Pvt. John Boxell of Company G wrote his wife that the men had "good strong coffee twice a day, and plenty of sugar." Hard crackers, soup, pork, and bacon were the staples; fresh beef and warm bread were welcome changes. Several men were detailed daily to help each company cook. A sergeant supervised each of the four "messes" in a company, drawing their share of food from the cook and serving it out to the men, who ate where they pleased, be it in their tents or seated on stumps.[4]

General Buell placed Louisville and its surrounding area under martial law; "no one is allowed to enter or leave the city without a pass from Gen. Buell's office except military men," wrote Lieutenant Blakely. Pvt. Perry Honeywell of Company K added that their camp guards had "orders to fire upon any person who might attempt to pass the guard without the countersign . . . , no person being allowed to go outside the lines of the camp without a written pass from the Captain of their respective companies." Sergeant Hale was particularly annoyed at the restrictions that military law imposed on their liberties as citizens, saying "the range of liberty is *very very* small."[5]

The Third Minnesota became a part of Brig. Gen. Ormsby O. Mitchel's Sixteenth Brigade in Special Orders No. 16, Department of the Ohio, on 20 November. Mitchel, a famous astronomer, "knew everything about an army from the linch pin of a wagon to the most important implement of warfare," according to Buell, informing Maj. Gen. George McClellan that the general was just the man to "impress the firm hand of the military on raw recruits." Mitchel personally instructed the Minnesotans in everything from drill to military courtesy, with strict, standard hours for reveille, tattoo, lights out, drills, and dress parades. Officers began to learn their duties, including the manual of arms, so they could instruct their men, and guard mount, which required them to visit the guards day or night to ensure that they "understand and perform their duties." Orderlies had charge of each tent, "responsible for the neatness and good order" of the shelter and its occupants. Quartermasters and surgeons were tasked to identify the "deficiencies" of their departments and prepare the necessary requisitions to make them right. The men of the Third came to value Mitchel's opinion of them, Lieutenant Blakely even fearing that they would disappoint him in their drill.[6]

Cannon fired reveille at 5:45 A.M. Two hours of company drill in the morning and two hours of battalion drill in the afternoon, separated by dinner (lunch), and followed by dress parade at 4:30 P.M., supper, and another roll call. The men then had a little free time until the drums beat tattoo at 8 P.M. Candles fitted in the sockets of bayonets stuck in the ground provided light for reading, gambling, singing, or the opening of boxes of "good things," such as one package sent by the women of Wabashaw County, which the men received with "three cheers for the ladies." Several neighboring regiments had brass bands that would serenade the camp at night. "The negroes visit our camp every day," Honeywell wrote his father, entertaining "the Boys with their songs and comic maneuvers." He heard one black preacher claim that "an entire abolishment of slavery . . . [and the full advent of] freedom must follow" upon Union victory. The pastor added that "the presence of 30,000 *union* troops have dampened their ardor for cessiondom."[7]

Some men met friendly nearby residents who welcomed them into their homes. Private Boxell was the only known Mason in the regiment in 1861–62, and he regularly found neighboring brothers who invited him over for dinner, cared for him when he was sick, and generally made his life easier. Others found "neighbors" entirely too willing to sell them alcohol, leading Lieutenant Colonel Smith to threaten one man with a court-martial for his regular excesses; promising to reform, the soldier kept his freedom.[8]

All of this instruction and correction demanded an enormous amount of the drillmaster's time, which General Mitchel could not spend on one regiment exclusively. On 29 November, with Colonel Van Cleve's approval, Smith announced the appointment of 2nd Lt. William Woodbury, Company K, Second Minnesota, as drillmaster of the Third. "Lieut. W. is one of the very best drill officers that Minnesota has yet sent into service," wrote Lieutenant Blakely, "and under his tutorship, I trust, a reasonable improvement will be made in the condition of the regiment." Woodbury, who had helped drill the First and Second Regiments, began by requiring the officers and noncommissioned officers to study in the evenings to prepare for drill the next morning. One man wrote of this arrangement, "if we were Colonel, Lieut.-Col., or Major of a regiment, we should feel d—lish cheap to be obliged to borrow a Lieutenant from some other regiment to drill our men."[9]

The men began to reevaluate their officers as military leaders rather than as neighbors of substance. "American Boy" put it politely: "Our field officers, I think, have yet something to learn to qualify them for their high and responsible positions." Lieutenant Colonel Smith was "every inch a gentleman, and doubtless a brave man, but he is in the wrong pew. Our major is just what we all thought he was before we left Fort Snelling." Convinced that Major Hadley was not eager to do his duty with the troops since he spent most of his time with his family, Smith disciplined him, publicly ordering him to report in camp. This upset Hadley, who thought that "a Major was exempt from such restrictions, but," as

Smith wrote Ramsey, "on his arrival at camp, I would not permit him to carry his sword," the symbol of his authority as an officer. As a result of this reprimand, "the order and discipline of the camp is greatly improved."[10]

Several wives accompanied their soldier-husbands and served as laundresses or nurses for the regiment. Only one of the nurses is known by name: Sarah Strang, wife of Pvt. Jesse Barrick (later a Medal of Honor recipient), was employed until February 1862. We do not know if these women brought children with them, where in camp they slept, where they worked, or when they were sent home. Some officers' wives accompanied the unit and roomed in nearby houses; their husbands often stayed with them at night during this time. Any who remained in Kentucky by late November, however, did so in violation of Buell's general order prohibiting wives (and women generally) from being in camp or accompanying the regiments in the field.[11]

On 1 December Lieutenant Colonel Smith received weapons and accoutrements for the Third, which the company commanders issued to the men. These were "a cast off stock of Belgian muskets," wrote Lieutenant Blakely. "Such arms were never before furnished to men to fight with," having broken locks, corroded and bent barrels, and parts falling off. They were "unsafe for shooting, and in every respect wholly unfit for use." Many a man, on discharging his gun, had parts break, fly off, and hit him. "JHS" reported, "these weapons . . . will, I fear, prove quite as destructive for the men at the breach, as to the foe." Several officers favored marching into Louisville and "stacking the worthless things in front of the Adjutant General's office," which Blakely admitted would "be considered mutiny."[12]

These muskets were among the 18,000 bought in Liege, Belgium, by Marcellus Hartley, a Union purchasing agent. They were .69-caliber weapons, though varying between barrels, some of which were crooked; many were brittle and easily broken into pieces. In July 1862 former Secretary of War Joseph Holt and Robert D. Owens, both appointed commissioners to "audit contracts for ordnance," reported that, "as a result of negligence, ineptitude, etc., most imported weapons were guns of a very inferior quality," especially the Belgian and Austrian muskets reworked in Belgium.[13]

A couple of days later, the regiment received its camp equipment, mules, and wagons. Not long afterward, 2nd Lt. Samuel Ingman of Company F, finding the job too difficult and demanding, "declined to perform the duties" of regimental quartermaster. Col. Henry C. Lester assigned 2nd Lt. James Howlett of Company A in his place. In January 1862 Captain Gurnee of Company E tried to rectify his accounts and asked Howlett for copies of his company requisitions. The lieutenant had none at hand, requiring the captain to write to the state quartermaster (and adjutant) general to request copies, Ingman having sent all of his records to Saint Paul. Major Hadley and Lieutenant Ingman must have felt threatened when Buell, acting under section ten of the act of Congress of 8 August 1861, ordered the establishment of examining boards to weed out poor and incompetent officers from the volunteer regiments.[14]

Taking Post on the Louisville & Nashville Railroad

Two weeks after arriving at Camp Todd, now renamed Camp Jenkins, the regiment received orders to take station between Shepherdsville and Wilson's Creek along the route of the Louisville & Nashville Railroad, where they were to guard "against all injury through neglect or design the rail road and turnpike bridges." The men understood their mission. "JHS" wrote, "were these bridges that we are guarding day and night, to be destroyed (and there are many ready to do it if not overawed by soldiery) the entire transportation of troops and food to our army now gathering in force on Green river, would be cut off. [This is a position of] great responsibility; and until we get better guns we ought to hold a position that can be defended with clubs, as our muskets are little better." Needing to guard his supply lines, Buell used newer regiments with inferior arms for this essential but relatively less hazardous task.[15]

On Friday, 6 December 1861, the regiment marched through "ankle deep mud" into Louisville, halting for dinner on Broadway, before leaving south on the Shepherdsville Road, encamping about 3 P.M. in a "fine grass field" owned by a rebel sympathizer. The order of march had Company B as the advance guard and Company C as rear guard; ten men and two sergeants from each company were detailed "as guards or scouts on either side of the company." The baggage train followed the main body but ahead of the rear guard. At 4 A.M. on Saturday, the regiment had roll call and resumed the march at 6 A.M., arriving at Shepherdsville, "an old muddy hole" on the Salt River, at 4 P.M. Lieutenant Blakely thought there was "but one feature worth noticing . . . *Beautiful Ladies*." The men took shelter in a church, the courthouse, and other buildings for the night.[16]

Major Hadley's men of the second division took post at Shepherdsville along with the chaplain, the surgeon, and the sergeant major. Ordered to Lebanon Junction, the first division, Companies B, E, G, and H under Lieutenant Colonel Smith, marched twelve miles to Spring Garden on Sunday, wading "Crooked Creek a dozen or more times, sometimes knee deep," according to Pvt. James Battey of Company E, before arriving at the Second Minnesota's Camp Anderson at the junction in the rain on Monday afternoon. The camp was located between and just south of the main line and a spur to Lebanon, Kentucky, in an elevated field of clay surrounded by mixed forest.[17]

The Second welcomed their fellow Minnesotans, according to "Hubert," with "a good supper of soft bread, fresh beef, potatoes, coffee, &c.," then departed, leaving the men of the Third to make camp and pursue and capture "a porker of about 100 pounds" after considerable wallowing in the mud by all concerned. About 10:30 P.M. that night, firing followed by the beating of the long roll brought the troops out at the double quick. They formed up around the guardhouse and waited half an hour before being dismissed. Called out again at 1 A.M., they blamed the men of the Second for having fun with them.[18]

Captain Gurnee relieved Lt. Col. James George of the Second as provost marshal at Lebanon Junction. Having received instructions that Lester termed "not sufficient to guide him in a sensible discharge of his duties," the captain telegraphed Capt. James Fry, Buell's assistant adjutant general and effective chief of staff, on 9 December asking for guidance. A few days later some of the officers noticed people, thought "to be 'secesh,' surveying our camp." Lieutenant Colonel Smith ordered a detachment from Company B out to surround the hill and capture the suspicious party, which turned out to be Captain Webster and some men from his Company A (posted at Shepherdsville) who were seeking "a view of the country."[19]

Colonel Lester had joined the regiment on 4 December outside Louisville just before it departed, though he did not assume command at that time so he could first observe and get a feel for the unit and its officers. He was late arriving because Sen. Morton Wilkerson, who was to have informed him of his promotion, did not do so in a timely manner. Resigning his commission in the First Minnesota, Lester departed Camp Stone (in Virginia) on 15 November. Travel in winter was slow and delays common, thus he did not report to Governor Ramsey in Saint Paul until 25 November, when he was mustered in and commissioned as colonel. Lester left for the South three days later, going first to La Crosse and then taking the train through Chicago and on to Louisville.[20]

After taking post at Shepherdsville, Lester assumed command on Saturday, 7 December. In a series of orders over the next few days, he began to mold and discipline the regiment to his liking. He required that the company officers be present at all company and battalion drills, that the entire camp would be policed daily, and that "instead of drill on Saturday afternoon there will be a General Police of the Camp"; these notions of camp cleanliness became a hallmark of the Third. Lester emphasized "the necessity of a Strict observance of that Military Etiquette so necessary to the creation of good Soldiers" that promoted "in Soldiers that Self respect and dignity without which their duties become irksome drudgery and their education as soldiers impossible." In addition to cleanliness, he made clear the importance of camp security: "To sentinels in particular it is enjoined that every respect must be paid. . . . [T]hey are entitled to our highest consideration and any disrespect to them will be treated as a military offense."[21]

Reinforcing Lieutenant Woodbury's efforts, Lester began an evening school of instruction for the officers, teaching them tactics, the manual of arms, and other military subjects. Drill followed drill, officers and sergeants learning first before they then trained their men—and the colonel's standards were high. Writing Assistant Adjutant General Fry, he stated that he was "exceedingly anxious to give my regiment an opportunity to exercise in battalion maneuvers." Because of the colonel's leadership, training, and example, sergeants would later be able to effectively command companies—both in garrison at Benton Barracks, Missouri, and in battle at Fort Abercrombie and at Wood Lake, Minnesota—and Captain Andrews would be able to write his very well received *Hints to Company Officers on Their Military Duties* (and providing a view of Lester's standards and training tools; "A knowledge of picket and guard service is indispensable. This he [an officer] can derive from McClellan's 'Field Service for Cavalry'"). A veteran of the Army of the Potomac, Lester trained the Third Minnesota using McClellan's manual as Colonels Gorman and Dana had trained the First Minnesota, and to their standards, so that the regiment came to have "an unusually high degree of discipline and efficiency."[22]

Company commanders reported in the monthly "Record of Events" section of their muster rolls that discipline was "greatly improved," perhaps because of Lester's willingness to use both nonjudicial punishments (though there is no record of utilizing brutal punishments such as gagging) and courts-martial. One officer proudly declared to the *Winona Republican* that, "as a disciplinarian, Col. Lester stands preeminently above all other Minnesota officers, save perhaps, Gen. Dana." On 20 December Cpl. Richard Madden of Company C was reduced to the ranks for drunkenness, with Pvt. Francis Ide promoted in his place. Henry Wakefield of Company H deserted from Belmont Furnace between company and battalion drill. In addition, Cpl. Lyman Barris and Pvt. Theodore Miller from Company E went outside the lines with permission but then deserted. Miller had not been paid, and "his family were in a very destitute condition, without any means of support," so he returned home to support them; he later voluntarily joined the Sixth Minnesota. A regimental court-martial, consisting of Capt. John Preston of Company F and Lts. William Mills of Company C and Isaac Taylor of Company H, with Captain Mattson as the judge advocate, convened to try Pvt. James Montgomery of Company A. There is no record of the charges and specifications, but on 30 December his sentence, to be "fined half months pay," was read to the regiment.[23]

Andrews observed that the soldiers' developing unit pride, combined with the colonel's care for the men and "his uniformly just and dignified conduct, won for him [Lester] the admiration of officers and enlisted men alike." He established a regimental bakery to provide fresh bread, allowed the men to purchase "luxurious pies" from local women, and permitted visits to local families for tea. "M" thought Lester, whom most first saw at dress parade, was "a fine looking man, and I should judge would make an excellent officer." By 15 December he wrote that the colonel was known to be "using his best endeavors to secure an exchange of arms but has not succeeded as yet." On 22 December Cpl. James Bowler wrote his fiancée, Lizzie Caleff, that Company F, sent to Shepherdsville, named their "camp 'Lester' in honor of our respected Colonel."[24]

The regiment's initial headquarters was at Shepherdsville, a former state capital and center of a once-thriving salt trade, at the north end of its area of responsibility. It was "a low wet place, and after a heavy rain," according to "JHS," "boats might be used to advantage, as pedestrians find to their sorrow." Now, as Private Honeywell noted, Shepherdsville was "a deserted and almost abandoned town," with many buildings in an advanced state of decay. Sergeant Hale attributed this to "the curse of slavery." Colonel Boone's regiment and elements of other units were stationed there as well. This overcrowding interfered with Lester's training regimen, so he left two companies there (as required by Buell's orders) and moved the bulk of the Third and his headquarters south along the Louisville & Nashville to Belmont Furnace.[25]

The site of an ironworks run by German workers, who left when secession ended trade with the South and ruined the business, Belmont Furnace was "a pretty little hamlet of 40 houses" in a "snug little valley of Crooked Creek." Sergeant Hale noted that this was "a clear stream . . . , supplying plenty of water," and reported approvingly, "we are surrounded by high wood covered hills of all shapes." Field officers' quarters and headquarters were in the furnace's office building, while the men occupied the cottages. Camp Dana, named in honor of the First Minnesota's colonel, was "one mile back from the railroad, though in sight and hearing of the heavy trains running hourly, almost, laden with supplies and transportation for our legions before Bowling Green," as one soldier related to a newspaper back home.[26]

Camp life at Belmont Furnace and at the outposts centered on company and battalion drill. Private Boxell reported daily skirmish exercises. Target practice, though rarely mentioned, was also frequent. Capt. Everett Foster regularly took Company G for "practice firing after Guard Mount" and later certified, "on honor," the expenditure of two thousand rounds of ball cartridges for that purpose in December 1861 alone. In late February 1862 the companies at Camp Dana "commenced the bayonet exercise . . . for the first time, and succeeded so well that we bid fair to become perfect in a short time." The correspondent "American Boy" added, "We have learned thoroughly . . . the manual in regard to guarding railroads and bridges."[27]

Companies rotated between outposts at Colesburg, Wilson's Creek, Lebanon Junction, Bardstown Junction, Shepherdsville, and Belmont Furnace. At first Lester managed to keep six companies (the reserve for the outpost units) at headquarters, where the Minnesotans drilled, drilled, and drilled some more, then conducted target practice. Proficiency at drill was the best available measure of a regiment's potential combat effectiveness. By the end of December 1861, having effectively replaced four regiments guarding their section of the railroad, a fifth company went on outpost duty, leaving the regiment overextended and threatened. Battey noted in his diary that a guard reported a rumor of "secessionists 350 men going to burn the bridges and destroy our camp. Sent out 40 scouts and picket guards."[28]

Conditions at the outposts, shaped by the physical environment, neighbors—both friendly and threatening—disease, and their various duties, were poor at first and only slowly improved. Pvt. Curtis B. Ames of Company A was one of many who contracted rheumatism from exposure and sleeping on the ground at Lebanon Junction. Guard duty often occupied half of the detachment in each twenty-four-hour cycle, leaving only the off-duty men to drill and perform camp duties. While posted at Camp Scandia at Bardstown Junction in mid-December, the men of Company D were on half-rations and "commenced cursing Uncle Sam a little." Captain Mattson wrote his wife that he "asked them at our evening prayer tonight to be patient and to learn how to starve if necessary, and still not grumble and I think they will do so—they are such good boys." Lester proudly noted that "the men perform this arduous service with cheerfulness and would close with alacrity if our arms were ever respectable but we have the most wretched arms in the service."[29]

Outpost Duty on the Louisville & Nashville Railroad

The experiences of the men of the Third while on duty at the various outposts along the railroad varied with each location. At Colesburg the Minnesotans established their main camp near a creek that was clear, lined with sugar maples and other timber, and hillsides sporting grape vines and chestnuts. It was "a great place for peaches and all kinds of fruits," observed Boxell, along with petrified worms, lizards, and snakes. There was "good water, and whiskey in every house," he added, "and the boys had a good time. The rules are very strict about getting drunk, and the company kept pretty straight except one Peter LeClaire, a Sioux half breed." A railroad tunnel three-quarters of a mile long, carved through the solid rock of Muldrow's Hill, and a trestle bridge were two miles south of Colesburg, with another bridge a mile farther south. Detachments of the company of the Third assigned to Colesburg established a guard post at each site, encamping nearby. The bridge nearest the tunnel was 95 feet high and 500 feet long, according to Corporal Bowler, so its guards camped at the base of the span near the creek at the bottom of the steep-sided gorge.[30]

In contrast, at Bardstown Junction in early January 1862, Company D's conditions and camp were both deplorable. Private Roos recorded that they had "a half ration of corn porridge because rations were reduced and last morning only weak coffee." Supper was cooked pork and coffee. On one occasion Roos and others chose to visit the sutler's store for sausages. Thirsty afterward, he looked for fresh water, but all the streams had overflowed their banks, leaving their water a "red-brown mixture which only cattle could possibly use." Camp sanitation was unknown, and with the junction on flatter ground, Roos noted, "the exercise and parade ground . . . was strewn with mankind's excrement."[31]

Conditions at Bardstown junction favored typhoid fever, dysentery, and diarrhea, which increased almost as the caseload from measles, mumps, and chickenpox declined. Sickness stalked the Minnesotans no matter where the men camped, since most were from isolated small towns (including Saint Paul) and farms with little or no exposure to such childhood diseases. By the end of February, several hundred men, including Captains Foster and Gurnee, were sick with measles. Earlier that month, Pvt. James Liberty Fisk wrote his wife that he was suffering from chickenpox, adding, "All of us having been recently vaccinated [for smallpox] and the working thereof makes one feel slightly uncomfortable." Pvt. Joseph Abel of Company E contracted measles, then typhoid fever, and became the first man to die in the regiment. He was "buried . . . with military honors," wrote Mattson. "My Co and Gurnee's formed the procession. . . . I was very sad to leave him here in this strange country away from his parents and friends."[32]

Pvts. Oliver Shurtliff (Company G) and C. M. Wood (Company B) were next. Shurtliff was "interred with martial honors, preceded by an escort with arms reversed, followed by the mourning company, and the band with muffled drums. Arriving at the grave, there was prayer by the chaplain, the coffin lowered, [and] three volleys fired by the escort." The men of Company G, led by "Sergt L. S. Hancock . . . , erected the slab" over Shurtliff's grave, with Perry Martin delivering a few remarks. At the end of February, Dexter Chaddock, also of Company G, died, leaving behind "a wife and child, who was dependent on his care for support." The correspondent from the company suggested to the editor of the *Lake City Times*, "that in her [the widow's] afflication [sic] she has claims upon the generous consideration of her friends by whom she is surrounded." As they had earlier for Shurtliff, the enlisted men of the company met and resolved to "tender to his [Chaddock's] wife and parents our unfeigned sympathy."[33]

Local citizens, both Unionist and pro-Southern, invited several men to tea. Boxell spent Christmas with "Squire Carpenter, a fellow Mason," who provided "a dinner of roast turkey, pudding, peaches and cream." At the same time, "G" noted, "the lines are very distinctly drawn through that section between the Unionists and Seseshers. The feeling is very bitter; they seem to hate each other with a bitter hatred." "R" concurred: "It is impossible to write correctly the sentiments of the citizens in this vicinity . . . as a hundred thousand bayonets are apt to effect a great change in public opinion. Almost all pretend to be 'Union men,' and you would believe from their stories that they have been martyred for their patriotism. We take all of these for what they are worth."[34]

Captain Mattson noted that "the people around us all look like Horsethiefs, they try to put on sober airs and say they love the Union, and I say I believe it, but I know too much for them." He and other outpost commanders had lists of residents, "made by spies and police officers," usually created using blank regimental descriptive books, "with every mans and womans names, for 5 miles around," including height, complexion, eye and hair color, and other identifying features. "I also know who are enemies and I mean to keep watch of everyone of the rascals." Mattson thought that the people did not know how much the army knew about them, telling his wife that the records were "part of the evils and necessities of war."[35]

The men understood that they had "greater responsibilities that [sic] the whole 2nd Rgmt (Minn) had before us," Mattson believed. "Should one of them [the bridges the Third guarded] be burned by the rebels it would stop the supply to over 100,000 men in advance of us." The Minnesotans duties also included mastering their new profession of arms and trying to convert rebels to Unionism, a task that included administering the oath of allegiance to "sympathizers with the rebels" who often expressed their loyalties more directly. Discovering that three men were sneaking up to burn the bridge at Bardstown Junction, Company F soldiers guarding the bridge responded energetically: Frank Colby's gun would not fire, Page Howe's gun fired "without effect," and Henry Allen also fired but from too far away. Howe again tried his weapon, which discharged, but he missed. According to Bowler, Colby and Howe threw down their guns and "drew their Revolvers and rushed into the woods after them, but returned after firing three or four shots without any apparent effect."[36]

Such threats usually lacked the comedy of Bowler's account. First Lt. Isaac Tichenor of Company F noted that the pickets were fired upon every night. On one occasion a squad under Lt. Damon Greenleaf of Company I went out to investigate after such an alarm. Hearing the patrol advancing in the stygian darkness, Boxell hailed them, and "the Lieutenant in his hurry came with such force against my bayonet that but for his clothing it must have run into him." Giving the countersign, Greenleaf's squad went out at the double quick but found nothing.[37]

The troops spent considerable time making their outpost camps and regimental headquarters habitable and building winter quarters. Hale resigned as a sergeant in Company E the day after Christmas, replaced by Cpl. John Graham, who in turn was replaced by Pvt. Benjamin Densmore. Hale kept his post as quartermaster clerk and was "pleasant[ly] situated" in a cabin with a stone fireplace and "blackened rafters." Writing to his family, he mentioned the regiment's hope to gain enough experience to take "a position in the grand advance" in the spring. Hale also reported on a "contraband" who entered their camp fleeing "his mistress whom he had offended and she was going to give him 300 lashes in the morning. He is inside the line awaiting decision on his and like case from headquarters."[38]

A few days later Boxell wrote to his wife about the same contraband, "a poor slave boy 17 years old . . . trying to run away from his mistress." Some of the Minnesotans tormented the poor lad, saying blacks "ought to be slaves. . . . The officer of the Guard and most of the men sympathize with him." The growing problem of runaways crossing into Union lines led to efforts to keep them out and force their return to their local masters. General army policy, set by General McClellan and followed by his friend General Buell, was consistent with the limited war aims of restoring the Union as it was (with slavery intact) and Kentucky's loyal status and the protection of its citizens' property, including slaves. In regimental General Orders no. 27, Colonel Lester limited camp access by "colored persons . . . [to only those] servants of officers having passes"; all others were to be "placed forthwith outside of the lines."[39]

At some point in late December, in one of the towns in the Third's area of responsibility, there was a "slave auction for 1 year of service, women fetched $30 to 50, men twice that. . . . It was a sad spectacle to behold, there were slave women much whiter than their masters, with babes in their arms whiter still, on the platform. . . . Many of my boys went up to look at the auction," wrote Mattson, "and they all asked for a chance to disperse the crowd, at that time 50 of my men would have whipped 500 slave traders if I had given them a chance." In the West soldiers like Mattson's men saw slavery unadorned. The *Louisville Daily Journal* regularly carried advertisements for escaped slaves. No one saw a need to hide the labor system that made Kentucky rich and the state's loyalty important to the Union cause. William Sipes of the Seventh Pennsylvania Cavalry wrote that the soldiers of his regiment were far from abolitionists at first, "but contact with the institution, as exhibited by owners and slaves, soon revolutionized its views." Many western soldiers came to see slavery as *the essence* of the South's economic, political, and social order and favored abolition as a practical way to reduce the Confederacy's war-making capabilities.[40]

In September 1861 Corporal Bowler wrote his fiancée that he hoped the war would "continue until all traitors to our government are thoroughly conquered and not a slave shall be found in our country." He kept such "desires of my heart" to himself, adding that many men "do not know what they are fighting for and . . . have little idea what this war is to bring forth." In contrast, Lt. James Hoit, Cpl. Giles Fowler, Pvts. Andrew and Joseph Scofield, and other men from Newport were, according to Private Boxell, the "most bitter pro-slavery men I ever knew." They hated abolitionists, defining all who opposed slavery as such, which may explain some of Hoit's animus toward Boxell, who was transferred into Company B from Company G on 7 December.[41]

This animus would appear after Boxell became ill during the company's march from Belmont Furnace to Camp Anderson near Lebanon Junction on Friday, 27 December. Having crossed Crooked Creek several times, at one place Hoit made his men wade the creek rather than use a plank bridge. "Lieut Hoit, who was already on the plank himself, called out in his nasal tone, 'keep in ranks, *keep in ranks, keep in ranks*! Your very 'fraid of a little water.' . . . The gallant Lieutenant came back off the plank and waded through the Creek like a hero." His boots kept Hoit dry, but Boxell noted that his own "shoes and the bottoms of my trousers were frozen stiff in the tent" that night.[42]

On New Year's Eve 1861, Boxell developed chills and swelling on the left side of his face. With the company's captain, Chauncy Griggs, away at headquarters, the soldier took it upon himself to go to Harvey Wells's "Junction Hotel," within military lines. Wells and his assistant, Bob Samuels, were Masons who had taken the oath of loyalty, and "the slaves give Harvey a good name." He took the ailing man in and gave him "an excellent supper including oyster soup." Boxell had left home with only eighty-five cents in his pocket, which was long gone, and the regiment remained unpaid; he was fortunate that Wells was willing to give credit for the stay. When Griggs returned after New Year's Day, he ordered Boxell to the regimental hospital in Belmont. "It is in a little church up stairs, the doctors occupying the rooms downstairs. . . . Dr. Butler came in. He observed that I had no bedding. . . . The doctor cast his eyes at my swelled face, remarked that it came perhaps from an affected tooth and said no more. He soon after went to supper." There was only bedding enough for the dozen men already admitted with mumps, measles, and typhoid fever, so when the doctor returned, Boxell asked if he could go to the home of a friend named Carpenter one mile away. Butler replied: "We don't admit men of your stripe [that is, antislavery] into the hospital. . . . I will be over and investigate your case between this and bed time, . . . his language being very insulting and ungentlemanly." Boxell told the guard and hospital steward that he was going to his friend's home anyway—without permission. Carpenter provided him with a soft feather bed and eggnog to drink. Soon after this incident, Mattson sent Roos to the regimental hospital; the doctors gave him some pills and sent him back to his tent, there being no room for him in the hospital either.[43]

Pvt. George Brookins of Company I was hospitalized during this time as well and wrote his brother Thurman in Vermont that he had been moved out into "a house used as a 2nd grade hospital for those who can wait on themselves. . . . The Dr is afraid of the Inflammatory Rheumatism & very careful of me." Brookins, who knew Dr. Butler before the war, thought the surgeon was "very kind & attentive. . . . I had first [class] as far as nurses & pleasant comfortable room was concerned. The beds were pretty hard." The differences in attitude and levels of treatment between Boxell, Roos, and Brookins, due apparently to prior acquaintance or whim, may be part of the reason Lester would reprimand Butler in June 1862 and why the doctor clearly disliked the colonel. Neither Boxell, at thirty-four one of the older and more refined men in the regiment, nor Roos, who was the eldest man in the Third, would have agreed with Brookins's description of care or with Chaplain Hobart's claim, "Our surgeons are very competent and attentive to their duties."[44]

When Corporal Fowler came with gun and bayonet to take Boxell back to camp, Boxell refused to go, adding that he "did not consider Captain [G]riggs my superior in anything but military rank." Lieutenant Hoit then charged him with being absent without leave. After returning to camp and after meeting both the adjutant and the chaplain, Boxell went before Lester. He said that he looked as bad as he felt and told the colonel that he was willing to accept the appropriate punishment. Lester dispensed justice tempered with mercy. Boxell wrote: "Colonel Lester told me that it was irregular, but that he considered the circumstances of the case excused me. Mr. Boxell, said he, 'Your countenance is enough to convince me that you did not intend to do anything wrong.'" He thought Griggs seemed ashamed of his part in the affair, but "Hoit was very bitter."[45]

In mid-January Buell ordered the establishment of a general hospital at Belmont. Around one hundred men from the Third Minnesota were sick at this time, most afflicted with measles, and probably being cared for by comrades in company quarters. The able-bodied of the regiment moved into tents and began cleaning the designated cottages for their new purpose as convalescent wards. Private Fisk optimistically wrote his wife, "I shall soon take charge of the affairs of the General Hospital fitting up," though ultimately he was not detailed as a hospital clerk. By mid-February Bowler termed this compound the "general hospital for all the sick of the Kentucky army," adding that "if I were a girl I should offer my services to nurse the sick soldiers of our Army." He may have thought women nurses would bring some humanity to the wards, something Hale thought severely lacking from the current staff. He wrote his family that in the hospitals there was "no care totally insufficient medicine, and when poor emaciated fellows breathe the last, they are buried like dogs." Family members often came to tend to their sick soldiers; the home of a Dr. McClelland in Louisville took in one "soldier's wife from Minnesota" who had come south to tend her husband and needed income and housing until he was discharged.[46]

The Minnesotans' tent camp at Belmont Furnace was properly arranged, fronting on the parade ground where orders and the articles of war were read to the men, promotions and court-martial punishments were announced, and every day began and ended with roll call. Tents were in line on either side of a company street, perpendicular to the color line, where each company stacked its arms in line with the regimental flags (hence the name), ten paces in front of the first tents. Behind the shelters were the "the cook tents, with the large cheerful fires in close proximity." Everything was ditched for water runoff.[47]

Private Fisk, whose aspirations to be a hospital clerk were thwarted, really wanted to be an officer. George Bertram of Company H and Lewis Hancock of Company G were among those who also sought shoulder straps. Governor Ramsey, for his part, had men he wanted to reward. The paymaster, however, would only pay the twenty lieutenants authorized for the regiment, so Lester finessed the issue, advising Ramsey to seek War Department authority for more officers: "I am exceedingly anxious to have these promotions made if it can be done." When fifty-two-year-old Capt. John Bennett of Company C resigned while home on furlough—his wife had died, and he had "a large and helpless family of children" needing his care—Lester made clear his norms for promotion. Since none of those seeing advancement were in Company C and had no claim for promotion, he decided to be "guided by my views of the best interests of the Regiment after full consultation with the Officers interested."[48]

On 12 March Lester recommended the commissioning of Pvt. Joseph R. Putnam of Company A as a second lieutenant in Company K, passing over its sergeants "in accordance with the earnest request of his company officers and my own convictions of his superior qualifications." Writing Lieutenant Governor Donnelly a few days later, Corporal Bowler pungently termed Putnam a "miserable individual," adding: "If Col. Lester is going to disregard the wishes of the members of the companies and commission Gov R's pets to the disparagement of true merit, bitter will be the day when a reckoning shall come." Normally, sergeants obtained shoulder straps in order of seniority, but not all sergeants were fit to be line officers.[49]

Though Ramsey rarely interfered in the running of the regiment, Lester felt the need to accede to some of the governor's requests. Thus, appointing Lieutenant Blakely of Company K as adjutant, an administrative post offering an intimate understanding of how the regiment and the army worked, meant returning Lieutenant Olin to Company B and the command of troops, which turned out not to hinder Olin's prospects at all. Blakely's brother was editor of the *Rochester City Post,* clerk of the state senate, and would soon be a state senator and later secretary of state. Bowler wrote Donnelly that he thought Lester promoted Sergeant Hale (of Company E, formerly state senate enrolling clerk) to sergeant major "in obedience to—you know [Ramsey]." Sgt. Maj. Levi Phillips of Company F *was* young for the position but appears to have done the job well; he afterward became a teamster.[50]

As 1st Lt. Lars Aaker noted to Ramsey, the officers, particularly the captains, were quite touchy about their date of rank and thus seniority for promotion. It was "a matter of considerable thought and discussion among our officers what captain will be promoted in case a vacancy occurs in the field officers." When Hoit resigned as captain of Company B, Adjutant General Sanborn backdated Griggs's commission to preserve the rank of the companies, an unusual step. Aaker pointedly noted that, although the other officers thought well of Griggs, they would object to his being promoted ahead of Mattson and all the other captains whose commissions predated his: "They are serious and consider all deaths, resignations—such as Capt Hoyts or any other accident in their favor and I know that a large majority of our officers and men look upon it in that way."[51]

The Third Minnesota was gaining a good reputation, one the officers and men credited to their colonel; they took his measure and were pleased. "We have now a commander Col. Lester who is a soldier and a Gentleman," Mattson assured his wife. "We have seen enough of Col. Lester," observed "M," "to be satisfied that he is every way worth the title. . . . Firm and decided in his commands—though pleasantly spoken—his orders are quickly and cheerfully obeyed—kind and gentlemanly to all, social even to *privates,* he has thus soon won the respect and confidence of every man." Another soldier, "American Boy," reported that "our Colonel is very strict, but we all like him, and cheerfully obey his orders," even his lights-out order, though they did not like it. Several weeks later the same man wrote, "We have been assured by officers of other regiments, that we are stronger, healthier looking troops, and better drilled than one-half the soldiers in Kentucky." In February "Herbert" reported to the *Daily Press,* "Major Thurston, the paymaster, gave us the praise of being the most orderly regiment he had visited." The *Rochester City Post* reported of Lester: "It is as a drill officer, in the field, that he excels. Kind, courteous, patient, and *always* in a pleasant mood, he has won the affection of every man in the regiment. His command is the best drilled and disciplined of the three regiments that Minnesota has in the field." At the same time "Herbert" noted, "Of the Colonel's social character I know nothing; and I know none in the regiment who have even made his acquaintance."[52]

The judgment of the men proved mixed regarding their other field officers. Favorably assessing "Lieut. Col. Smith, who is several years the senior of Col. Lester, goes with us and shares in common with the Col. the confidence of the regiment for his urbane and kindly consideration of the men," they badly missed the mark regarding Major Hadley, whom they termed "a 'no put on airs man,' he never can see how four dollars and a half's worth of 'shiney' braid placed upon the shoulder of a human 'creter,' entitles the wearer of the bauble to a supreme reverence." In his grammatically incorrect common-man pretenses, Hadley was the opposite of their colonel, who observed to Governor Ramsey on 12 March:

"There is every reason to suppose that Maj. Hadley will not remain long with the Regt. and I shall be glad."[53]

The company officers were under their subordinates' inaccurate microscopes as well. Bowler said, "Lieutenant Ingman [of Company F] is a firstrate, kindhearted man, but not much of an officer." When the corporal informed Donnelly that several of the officers "can never pass the examination which they are in daily expectation of," he might well have had Ingman in mind. Some accused Capt. Benjamin Rice of Company H of being pro-Southern since he was a Democrat and his wife had secessionist friends. Defending Rice's patriotism and courage, Lieutenant Colonel Smith observed that "his greatest fault is perhaps a disposition to favor his men a little too much . . . [compared to] most of the other captains." The troops often bought and presented swords to officers they most approved of. When well-liked or respected officers, such as Captain Foster, returned from leave or sickness, their men often crowded around to welcome them.[54]

Company D, the all-Scandinavian unit in the regiment, was different in interesting ways. Early on, it adopted the Swedish-army custom of ending each evening's roll call with an officer reading a blessing followed by the troops singing a doxology. Many of the men showed deference to their officers, though in time the democratizing influences all about them ended this practice. Years later, Pvt. John A. Hokenson, writing the secretary of the Third Minnesota Veteran Volunteers Association, remembered carrying Captain Mattson "over a creek in Kentucky one time to save his new boots from getting wet. Every time I stood guard at his tent I got a cigar and sometimes more." Unlike the other officers' wives, "Mrs. Captain" Mattson was not merely the wife of the commander, she was the leader of the wives and families of the company.[55]

In regards to the soldiers' spiritual needs, Chauncey Hobart, who was in his late forties, was a good chaplain. Private Boxell, among others, thought him a good preacher. At first Lieutenant Colonel Smith marched the regiment to Sabbath services, but later Lester made attendance optional. Hobart visited the hospitalized, buried the dead, and preached at every dress parade until 23 February 1862, when for unexplained reasons he decided to restrict his preaching only on Sundays. In his report of the "Moral Condition" of the regiment, Hobart noted the professedly religious men were not numerous, but the majority behaved morally. Lacking defined duties, he may have reminded Lester too much of Chaplain E. D. Neil of the First Minnesota, whose self-serving absences earned him a dubious reputation. In any event, when Hobart submitted his resignation several weeks later on 5 April, Lester commented to Governor Ramsey that the "services of a chaplain are not required, and . . . are hardly commensurable with the salary. I therefore most respectfully suggest to your Excy [Excellency] that no appointment be made to fill the vacancy."[56]

Despite the ethnic differences and the discrimination rampant in both society at large and within the regiment itself, the men of the Third were coming
together—the foreigners were "their" foreigners—and Colonel Lester was building
an inclusive esprit de corps. In late January Mattson wrote his wife that, after
evening roll call, he had gone to Captain Gurnee's quarters; the company officers
were becoming a cohesive group, accepting Mattson, Aaker, and Hans Eurstrom.
In February, when he learned that the Swedish women were planning a society
to help their Scandinavian Guards, the captain wrote to urge his wife to have
them work with the "American Ladies." His men had received their fair share
of the things the ladies sent, and he wanted to keep the good relations now in
place with Gurnee and others.[57]

Colonel Lester was unable to shift his company stationed in Elizabethtown to
another posting, even though the Ninth Michigan Infantry had its headquarters
and at least one company there as well. The contrast in training between the two
regiments became apparent when Company D of the Ninth conducted skirmisher
drill for the first time on 9 February. Pvt. Henry Rice wrote his parents that the
Michiganders had great fun shooting blank cartridges at each other and then
to "charge anyone and to take it double quick for about twenty yards or more.
. . . [A]s they fire [they] fall down on their faces and then they shoot over their
heads." "E," a soldier in Company C of the Third, noted that "Col. Lester is putting us through the skirmish drill in the most improved style," using Hardee's
(and later Casey's) *Tactics* and an emphasis on aimed rifle fire, use of terrain,
and movement (today known as "fire and maneuver"). Although Col. William
W. Duffield, commander of the Ninth and a veteran of the Mexican War, had
authored a guide for his regiment entitled *Camp, Garrison and Guard Duty,* it
contained nothing on skirmisher drill. At the very least, it certainly was not the
skirmisher drill in Hardee or Casey (or for that matter in Mahan's guidelines
on the subject).[58]

According to a Michigander, February was cold, rainy, and overcast; and
the nights were "blacker than a stack of black cats." Guard duty, drill, camp
life, and cooking all took place in half-frozen mud so deep that the men needed
high-topped boots. "Crooked creek is roaring and tearing down through the
dell," wrote "During the War," a soldier in the Third, "and there is a general
swimming—in mud." Despite the mud, Boxell reported having "excellent fat
mutton in place of beef. . . . [W]e nearly always have soup for dinner" and beans
and pork for breakfast.[59]

"E" reported that three hundred ragged and dirty prisoners, mostly "Mississippi Tigers" taken at the Battle of Mill Springs (19 January 1862), passed through
on northbound trains, a harbinger of changes to come as Buell moved on the
Confederate works at Bowling Green, Kentucky, and Brig. Gen. Ulysses Grant

and Flag Officer Andrew Foote, after taking Fort Henry on the Tennessee River, moved on Fort Donelson. On 16 February Confederate brigadier general Simon Bolivar Buckner surrendered the latter fort. This victory opened the Cumberland River to Union gunboats, which could now move upriver past Nashville. Gen. Albert Sidney Johnston, commanding Confederate forces in the West, soon ordered Bowling Green and the fortifications at Columbus, Kentucky, abandoned. By 23 February, under threat from the Union naval forces, Johnston also pulled back from Nashville to Murfreesboro, allowing Buell's forces, led by Brig. Gen. William "Bull" Nelson's division, to enter the Tennessee capital. The Minnesotans heard the news of Fort Donelson on the twentieth, got paid the next day, and celebrated both events by skipping drill the day after that. Soon rumors began circulating that they were to receive new guns and then go to guard the bridge over Green River. Pvt. Marvin Hathaway of Company I declared: "Heavens! Is this all that the fates have in store for the Third Regiment?"[60]

Before the regiment could be of real use as a fighting force, the men needed working guns. Lester termed the Belgian rifles "wholly worthless—Eight out of ten are now disabled. The men are daily wounding themselves by the *blowing out* of the tubes and nipples." Evidence of this comes from Warren McCarter's testimony in support of Ira Marlett's 1898 pension application, in which he stated that Marlett's right eye was injured "by [the] blowing out [of a] sylender" and that he afterward had to shoot left handed. In addition, "M" reported that every day guns broke, and the Minnesotans could "scarcely find enough in the lot for guard mounting. One of our boys has one marked on the barrel '6 B.C.,' and *he* thinks it means '*six years before Christ.*'" The colonel fruitlessly wrote Governor Ramsey, General Sanborn, and Minnesota's U.S. senators and representative in search of replacements. Brig. Gen. James Ripley, chief of the Ordnance Bureau, informed Sanborn that the government currently had no better weapons available but was working hard to acquire enough proper guns to make good the deficiency.[61]

On 27 January Lester had informed Capt. R. J. Waggener, the assistant adjutant general of the Sixteenth Brigade, that the Third had no more ammunition and that he would not draw more for their Belgian rifles, anticipating that replacement guns would soon arrive. Only a month later Sergeant Major Hale wrote his sister, Lucie, saying, "Now is the winter of our discontent made (hopeful) summer by—the arrival of the paymaster—new clothes and *new guns* a Prussian rifle one of the best arms in the service—you ought to see how glad the boys are—and the happiest man I saw was our much liked Colonel."[62]

Having recently obtained new pants, shoes, gray overshirts, and blankets, along with newly issued Sibley tents, the Minnesotans' cups truly overflowed when they received their new guns. Boxell wrote his wife that the "new guns appear to be good. They shoot a long conical wicked looking ball [a Minié ball] and carry a long ways." Lester informed Ramsey of the occasion: "We have received our new arms and are entirely pleased with them. They are . . . in every respect perfect weapons." Now on dress parade, with blackened shoes, white gloves, dress coats and hats with polished brass, and their Austrian rifles, the Third also carried the new regimental flags that Ramsey had ordered for the state's units. These had first gone to the Second Minnesota, which sent them back to Horstmann Brothers and Company for alteration, before the Adams Express Company delivered them to Lester's command. Boxell wrote his wife that he loved "the blue banner of Minnesota. It has the arms of Minnesota on it. The pioneer plowing and the Indian galloping away on horse-back, and the motto of the State of Minnesota."[63]

On 27 February the troops at Belmont Furnace moved their tents from the meadow campsite to the cinder ground before the regimental headquarters in the company office building. Nearby were several springs with good water, which may have prompted the move. Despite the "snow and sleeting ice," the men drilled in the manual of arms in a large covered space, also performing knapsack battalion drill and squad and company drill as often as possible. Still, they felt ignored and forgotten since the rest of Brig. Gen. Thomas L. Crittenden's division was participating in the Union advance while their regiment remained behind guarding the Louisville & Nashville Railroad. The Minnesotans lacked knowledge of events beyond what they saw along the railroad since, as Sergeant Major Hale wrote his family, "the press in Kentucky (And we get no other publications), has been so completely muzzled that we know not the slightest information of the movement of our nearest neighbors." Buell suppressed the Louisville newspapers from reporting on operations because they were publishing too much information about his plans and movements.[64]

Fortunately, the folks at home still remembered them. When 1st Lt. Edward Baker of Company E returned from Minnesota with a detail of new recruits and the men left sick at Fort Snelling, "American Boy" happily reported that he also brought "innumerable dainties for the boys, in the shape of cakes, preserves, jellies, etc., which goes to show that we are not forgotten by the 'dear ones at home.'" The men had not forgotten their families either, many having allotted pay to them and many others sending additional money home through their company commanders. Captain Gurnee sent home funds given him by nine of his men, while Captain Mattson sent home in his wife's care $1,280 for the families of his unit.[65]

The weather continued cold, rainy, and overcast, bringing disease and death. Pvt. J. W. Goodwin of Company C, a twenty-eight-year-old father of two, died of pneumonia. Meanwhile, Boxell again took sick. Several local families, all Masons, offered to take care of him, but Captain Griggs refused to excuse him from duty unless he went to the hospital. Since Boxell preferred duty with his company to a hospital stay, Dr. Francis Milligan gave him some medicine and sent him along with his company to Colesburg, marching in snow and driving sleet. Roos, who often did daily duty as a nurse, observed that "the doctors are pure scoundrels. . . . They give one day purging pills and the next day pills to stop [the purging]. The certainty is that their [scientific] knowledge stands on weak ground, yet I believe that their greatest knowledge consists in that they can assist one to the other life before a patient's nature can help itself."[66]

Finally, on 4 March the Minnesotans learned that they were not forgotten by the army after all. Lester received orders to "concentrate his entire regiment at Shepardsville and hold it in readiness to march at short notice." The companies at the outposts soon gathered their equipment and headed to Shepherdsville. Most of the men celebrated the change. Some played cards into the night after lights out, while others went to a dance. Battey ecstatically rated drill on 7 March as "1st rate" and had a "likeness taken" of himself for his sister. Boxell and his fellows got a local lady by the name of Levin to make pancakes and a bowl of eggnog for them. At Belmont Furnace several men went outside the lines and bought "a little of the needful," but as "M" observed, Colonel Lester soon smelt "a very large mice" and strengthened the guard, catching several imbibers who were court-martialed and fined a half-month's pay. Some men, including the regimental postmaster and the "orderlies of company H [Almon Strickland] and G [Perry Martin] [were] reduced to the ranks for too free use of the bottle."[67]

After morning formation in heavy rain on 10 March, the companies at Belmont Furnace were ordered to empty their canteens, denying them, as Roos noted, the "strong liquids of which soldiers may not partake, though the officers always got their alcohol." He added that, while packing and breaking camp, the men threw away a lot of clothing and equipment, and "a Negro, who collected them, filled a large sack and must thereby use a discarded chest [to store it all], and this just in our company." The rain ended before the Third started its march at 7:30 A.M., but with no breeze stirring, the heat and high humidity very nearly overcame many of the men on the march. When they made camp for the night in a soaking-wet field just beyond Shepherdsville, "a furious northwest wind" left them thoroughly chilled.[68]

That afternoon Lester read Special Orders no. 63 to the regiment assembled on dress parade. Together with the Ninth Michigan and the Eighth and Twenty-Third Kentucky Infantry Regiments, the Third formed the new independent Twenty-Third Brigade, commanded by Colonel Duffield of the Ninth. When "to the colors" sounded at 7:15 A.M. the next day, with everything packed, the companies formed up on the color line and at 7:30 began their march for Louisville. It was a mud march until the column reached the pike, first a planked road and then macadamized, halting for fifteen minutes every three or four miles. The field musicians played on good stretches of road, and Boxell thought their "loads felt lighter" at those times. The "advance guard . . . [and] the music" led the regiment, its colors in the center, with the ambulances and baggage wagons behind the troops and followed by the rear guard, all making a fine appearance on a straight road. After fifteen miles and crossing several streams, they pitched camp on higher ground.[69]

On Wednesday, 12 March, Colonel Lester conducted his first battalion drill of the full regiment. Company drill and target shooting remained regular exercises. The Eighth and Twenty-Third Kentucky joined as the Minnesotans awaited further orders. Captain Rice of Company H had lived in Kentucky for years and was "an old personal and political enemy" of Col. Sidney Barnes of the Eighth. On Barnes's arrival in camp, Rice greeted him, "saying 'Colonel Barnes, I am happy to see you occupying the position you do.'" Barnes was equally gracious. The regiments camped near enough to Louisville that visitors came out to witness the Third at dress parade and to listen to their bugle band. Normally Drum Major David Hancock and Principal Musician Joseph Mertz had ten fifers, ten drummers, ten buglers, and a bass drummer but only had six of each due to illness; the visitors nevertheless were impressed. Private Boxell was one of many who got a pass to go to Louisville. He visited a family he knew and got some "7 year old bourbon and supper and more bourbon. . . . Mr. Smith got him lager beer and cigars." Pvt. George Brookins was among those who had their likenesses taken by photographers.[70]

A week later the Third Minnesota marched through the city "in column by company," as Musician Frank Redlon remembered, "taking the full width of the streets, with the band nearly taking the shingles from the roofs along the line of march." Boxell reported: "[T]he Colonel [was] riding before, then the music, then company B in two platoons, and the other companies in their order, each in two platoons. . . . As we turned on to fourth street which was too narrow for platoons, we formed into sections. We were greeted by cheers, and the waving of flags and handkerchiefs. . . . We were also saluted by a squadron of cavalry. The reporter for the *Louisville Journal* said we were the finest regiment that ever pass'd through Louisville." The *Louisville Democrat* observed of the Third: "The men are finely armed, and have practiced considerably in target firing. Frontiersmen are proverbial for heroism; and we have no doubt these men will do full credit to the North Star State and their country."[71]

Brookins's photographs were delivered while the Minnesotans waited at the landing. About 12:30 P.M., the left wing (Companies A, C, D, G, and I) boarded the *Undine*, while those of the right wing (Companies B, H, F, K, and E) boarded the *Denmark,* which in peacetime often traveled to Minnesota. The Twenty-Third

Kentucky boarded the *Jacob Strader*, while the Eighth Kentucky boarded the *Nashville* and the *Lady Jackson*. Capt. Thomas Wright of the Eighth noted that "the excellent band of the Third Minnesota [was] playing 'Hail Columbia'" as the boats departed the landing about 9 P.M. Later a "serenade band" played in the *Denmark*'s cabin while Bowler and others wrote letters. He noted to his fiancée, Lizzie, that the companies had raised the money for this band's instruments, which included "five fiddles, 2 clarinets and one guitar."[72]

CHAPTER 3

MASTERING THEIR TRADE

The Twenty-Third Brigade's flotilla of overcrowded boats stopped on Thursday, 20 March, at Hawesville, Kentucky, where George Brookins of Company I finally mailed his photographs home to Vermont. The greetings they received along the Ohio River led Sgt. Maj. William Hale to think that troop movements had become commonplace. Late that day the convoy passed Smith's Landing and entered the mouth of the Cumberland River. Pvt. John Boxell of Company B said that both the Ohio and Cumberland Rivers were running high, muddy, "and full of logs and trees and floating driftwood," causing the convoy to tie up along shore at night because of the danger from snags. Boxell spent the first night trying to sleep in the barbershop and the next two roasting from the heat in a cabin above the boilers. The last night he slept on the dinner table.[1]

On Friday morning Samuel Raymond from Company A died unexpectedly on board the *Undine*. The next morning Capt. Hans Mattson's left wing stopped at Fort Donelson to bury him, and many of the men took time to visit the battlefield and collect souvenirs from the abandoned Confederate camps; the right wing and regimental staff on board the *Denmark* did not disembark. Past Fort Donelson, Pvt. James Battey of Company E thought there were "signs of energy and enterprise," though Hale disagreed, saying he saw "the unmistakable mark of the 'peculiar'" institution. Some people waved to them while others "look as tho they tho't we [should] have staid at home," commented Battey. Arriving in Nashville on Sunday evening, 23 March, the troops slept aboard the boats at the landing near the gunboat USS *Cincinnati,* chained to a nearby pier of the railroad bridge the rebels had burned. The next morning they disembarked among bags, bales, barrels, and boxes of ammunition, clothing, food, and forage to join the "army wagons, horses, mules, and soldiers" crowding the streets. Forming up on the levee, the Minnesotans marched through the city and out along the Murfreesboro Pike; "several persons remarked 'them's regulars,'" recounted Boxell. They established Camp Minnesota at the Ewing place.[2]

Though Sergeant Major Hale thought Nashville once "a rich and beautiful city of some 25 thousand inhabitants," the town was very quiet, nearly half the people having fled. First Lt. Isaac Tichenor of Company F found it worrisome and "gloomy." Few goods were available in the stores and fewer jobs. The *Chicago Times* reported that the citizens to be "bitter, sullen, malignant," and the "better sorts" openly favoring the South. Rumors incited rebelliousness among the remaining citizenry so much that the *Louisville Journal* thought Brig. Gen. Ebenezer Dumont, commander of the city, would need to teach them better manners.[3]

Andrew Johnson, the newly appointed military governor of Tennessee, tightened his rule over the occupied state. When Nashville officials refused to take the loyalty oath, he sent the mayor to the penitentiary and declared the other offices vacant, appointing loyal citizens to those posts. Throughout the occupied South, civilian men seemed more accepting of the occupiers than the women, who as "A" noted to readers back home, "are all secesh, and much more to be feared than the male portion of the South." Calling them "basilisks," Pvt. John Woodbury of Company B claimed that the Minnesotans returned their "melodious greeting[s], such as 'Northern hireling,' 'abolitionist,' [and others], . . . with their sweetest smiles, for honorary titles, we returned a sweet 'Good day, fair lady,' and for lightning glances, we displayed our entire set of ivories, and after a successful siege of four weeks . . . , Nashville ladies and Third Minnesotians were enemies no more." The men of the regiment began learning how to create effective, even good, relations with the women of the South.[4]

Boxell thought that Camp Minnesota, two miles southeast of Nashville, was "the finest camping ground we have ever had. . . . [A] fine spring, with a little grove around it is inside of our camp lines"; the men dammed a space below the spring for bathing. Rows of cedar trees were planted along the company streets, all tall enough to provide good shade. Private Brookins noted that they also did so at the outpost camp along the Mumford Road, proudly adding, "We took pains to keep the ground swept clean." Boxell noted that the "slops and scraps are put in barrels and hauled out of the camp" daily, instead of putting them in a "sink" near the cook tent, and "a little dirt is thrown, everyday, in the sinks, used for privies, to keep down bad smells." On Wednesdays and Saturdays the troops cleaned and aired out their tents and sunned their blankets. Dumont sent "men out examining the regiments," wrote "H.N.G.," who added, "they said our regiment was the healthiest and best regiment in Tennessee."[5]

Settled into its new camp, the troops of the Third resumed drill and practiced "target shooting, and firing by file, by rank, and by company. I am in the front rank," noted Boxell. "The rear rank men's guns point past our heads, and when we all fire at once, our ears ring. We sometimes fire kneeling, and load and fire lying down. . . . We practice skirmishing, and we practice the bayonet exercise a good deal." In another letter he noted, "We have practiced what is called street firing [maneuvers for a secure advance through hostile urban terrain] considerable, to be prepared in case of trouble in Nashville." Within the limits of the possible, Colonel Lester was readying his men for any eventuality.[6]

Rebel colonel John Hunt Morgan had threatened Dumont and his family, requiring that his residence and headquarters be guarded at all times. The Third was assigned this duty, provided guards for Governor Johnson, and also assisted the provost guard. Chaplain Hobart said that they were chosen because their "reputation for honor & honesty is too good—we can be trusted in the city—while some others with whom we are brigaded cannot." The regiment's responsibilities soon expanded to include guarding bridges along the Murfreesboro Pike and the Mumford Road as well as the railroad bridges over Mill Creek. The troops particularly watched for rebel messengers and mailmen.[7]

"The Finest Appearing Regiment"

Soon after their arrival, Governor Johnson reviewed the Third Minnesota at a dress parade. Capt. Jeremiah Donahower of the Second Minnesota, who was in the crowd, later said that he "was not disappointed, their drill in the manual of arms, the march in column by companies, and their execution of several movements exceeding in efficiency my anticipation and then [I] thought them the finest appearing regiment I had seen in the South." According to "A," their brigade commander, Colonel Duffield, attended another dress parade and afterward remarked to Colonel Lester "that he thought he had a good Regiment but that we were far ahead of him." The *Louisville Daily Journal*, having previously commended the Third for its drill, in late April claimed that it was "forced to add still more liberally . . . to the praise formerly bestowed. . . . This regiment [is] the best drilled and most accomplished in the manual of arms . . . that we have seen since the beginning of the war."[8]

After a dress parade on 8 April, Mattson, the senior captain, presented Colonel Lester a Tiffany sword with a belt and sash, a gift from the officers, saying that it was a "token of their esteem of you as a man and a commander. . . . Bright and unsullied as its blade, so is our commander's character, and his military career. . . . Your officers have unbounded confidence in you as a commander." Brookins thought "Col Lesters short speech [in response, citing the work of the officers] a model of the kind & we all think him [Lester] a Col and a man such as are not often to be found." "A" observed, "should Minnesota be honored with another Brigadier General, we earnestly hope Col. L. will be appointed." Officers and men alike, proud of their regiment's reputation, also had great confidence in and respect for their commanding officer.[9]

A key part of building a good regiment was developing solid noncommissioned officers, with good sergeants in the companies. Lester expected his sergeants "to carry a steady hand," Sgt. James Bowler informed his fiancée, Lizzie Caleff, "or down they go." The colonel reportedly kept a book in which he rated the men, with "divers signs and marks," most likely his ratings of their mastery of drill and other skills. Though elected and appointed fourth sergeant in his company over more senior corporals, Bowler still grumbled, "All promotions *now* are made by favor, and without any regard to the wishes of the privates."[10]

Major Hadley, the person most clearly not doing his duty, was "absent somewhere in Kentucky," according to "A." Writing Capt. Oliver Green, General Buell's Nashville adjutant, Lester said that Hadley, whom he wanted discharged, was absent without his permission; worse, the rumor was that he had gotten a furlough from Buell's headquarters. Home in Minnesota, Hadley wrote Green that he was ill and "compelt to report myself unfit for duty." While the *St. Paul Daily Press* defended the Democratic major, the *Chatfield Democrat* reported, in error, that Hadley had been "compelled to resign his commission or be dismissed from the service, he having proved himself to be entirely incompetent for a high private."[11]

Reelected to his state house seat in the 1861 elections, 1st Lt. Lars Aaker of Company D vacillated for several months before resigning his commission. He left for Minnesota on 4 April. The men of his company, meeting in a committee of the whole chaired by Sgt. John Gustafson, "unanimously agreed that we hold him in high esteem as a noble and honorable man, and a true friend," whom they would miss. Pvt. Carl Roos thought Aaker a good man who did his duty as best he could, though "he had limited command ability." He suspected that 1st Sgt. John Vanstrum, one of Mattson's friends, had organized a campaign to convince the lieutenant to resign so he could gain a commission.[12]

The presence of men "unable to do duty" because of chronic sickness or physical incapacity was a problem Lester solved by having them discharged for disability. Some men recovered and rejoined, or attempted to rejoin, the regiment. Others resigned for ill health as a euphemism for alcoholism. Asst. Surg. Francis Milligan, who resigned on 8 April, may well have been, as "A" put it, "the right man in the *wrong* place, for he should have a gold leaf in his shoulder straps instead of two bars," meaning he should have been a surgeon rather than an assistant. Not long afterward, Surg. Levi Butler himself took sick, and a New York doctor cared for the Third Minnesota for a couple of weeks, replaced in turn by a doctor from Cincinnati.[13]

Colonel Lester had little faith in the hospitals, which were only as good as the surgeon in charge. When two seriously ill, bedridden lieutenants of the Third were ordered to the Nashville convalescent barracks, Lester insisted on leaves of absences so they instead could go home and recover, saying their lives would be endangered in a general hospital. In the spring of 1862, reports reached Governor Ramsey of the poor quality of army medical care. He dispatched Dr. J. K. Renner of Saint Paul to "visit the several military hospitals and other places in Kentucky where you learn there are any of the sick" of the Second and Third Regiments to determine the state of their care. Improvement of care in the western armies came slowly, as the reforms initiated in the Army of the Potomac—in field and general hospitals, the ambulance corps, and a transformed medical supply system—filtered out to the rest of the Union forces. Of more immediate effect were people such as "Mother" Mary Ann Bickerdyke of the U.S. Sanitary Commission, who personally forced western army doctors to either improve their care or resign.[14]

Duty in the City

Each morning after guard mount, the new company assigned to Dumont's headquarters marched into Nashville to relieve the current duty company. The general was quartered in a "magnificent residence owned by a man named Cunningham," who Boxell said was "a quartermaster general in the Confederate army." Bordered by a light cast-iron fence, it stood in a neighborhood of "quite splendid and aristocratic" houses. The guards were all armed "with loaded guns and fixed bayonets," two at the front gate, two before the front door, and two in the backyard, with others on the cross streets. Their on-duty appearance, with white gloves, polished brass and shoes, and their "gentlemanly bearing," surprised and impressed the citizens. The troops had orders "not to let any white person pass at all except at the front door & then only such as have business."[15]

Quartered in the empty Episcopal Church of the Advent, located on the second floor of the Odd Fellows Hall, the relief guards stacked their rifles in the aisles. The off-duty troops drilled, practiced street firing, cleaned their dress uniforms, and were sometimes able to spend a few hours in the city. Pvt. Thomas Canfield of Company G thought that the citizenry were "most all secesh and no doubt but what they would try to take it back if possible." The rumors of a rebel victory at Pittsburg Landing (Shiloh) excited the locals, who expected Confederate troops to arrive and liberate them.[16]

Some mornings began with a bit of spirits, as on Tuesday, 8 April, when Capt. Everett Foster marched his Company G into town. Private Canfield said that they stopped at "the lager beer saloon when our capt ordered a hault stack arms we done this in ahurry you better believe for some of the boys mistrusted what was acoming the next order was first section to your beer." Unfortunately, a few hours later Foster got proof that mixing alcohol and guard duty was not a good idea. Servants in a nearby house informed him that a rebel spy "dressed in citizen close [clothes]" was visiting and brought news of the Southern "victory" at Shiloh. The men detained the suspect when he left, but after examining the man's pass and questioning him, Foster, "like a fool, let him go." Not long after they realized that the pass was false. Canfield went with the sergeant to search the town for the man until about 11 P.M., when they gave up the chase.[17]

Rumors abounded in Nashville, starting from the "office of the 'grape vine' telegraph, corner of the square and Cedar street," leading the *Louisville Daily Journal* to opine, "Gen. Dumont [will need] to teach our rebels that they shall not excite the community by circulating falsehoods." Union army rumors of rebel movements also abounded. On Saturday evening, 12 April, fearing an attack after a rumor circulated of 600 rebel cavalry passing through Duffield's lines at Murfreesboro, Dumont ordered the Third to be ready to march at a moment's notice for the city. Every man had "at least 40 rounds in his cartridge box, rations were drawn, the teamsters were ordered to lie within their wagons, and have everything ready to hitch up . . . , the Colonel's horse was ready saddled, and we were ordered to have everything packed" and be ready to fall in at the first bugle call. Shortly, a courier rode in "at a full gallop. . . . In a few minutes Cos F & I had orders to fall in and march to the city." Cpl. James Bowler of Company F thought that they took "the devils . . . by surprise when they heard the quick steady tread of our men . . . up the High street . . . , bayonets glistening in the bright moonlight." Reinforcing Company D, already on duty, each company served two hours on guard and four hours in relief until morning, when Companies D and F returned to camp and Company I took its turn at guard mount.[18]

These attacks, both rumored as at Murfreesboro and real as along Buell's railroad supply lines, were part of the Confederate response to his Union movement toward Chattanooga along the Memphis & Charleston Railroad. Repairs on the Nashville & Decatur Railroad completed, Buell now had the "Michigan Mechanic Fusiliers" working to repair the Nashville & Chattanooga Railroad (which joined the Memphis & Charleston at Stevenson, Alabama) to support his advance; the Michiganders were past Murfreesboro and working to extend the operable line to Wartrace. Wanting strikes at different points along the tracks, Maj. Gen. Edmund Kirby Smith ordered Col. James Starnes's Third Tennessee Cavalry to operate "upon the Nashville and Chattanooga road." Union forces were, as Col. Sidney Barnes of the Eighth Kentucky Infantry wrote his wife, "constantly on the alert and want them to come if they wish." Like many Union soldiers, Barnes sounded disappointed that the only rebel attacks were rumors.[19]

On the cold, rainy, and muddy evening of Easter Sunday, 20 April, Pvt. Carl Carlson of Company D was guarding a bridge on the Nashville & Chattanooga when a local farmer approached his post carrying a torch to light his way home. Thinking the man planned to attack him, Carlson called for the sergeant of the guard and then ran from his post, leaving Sgt. Olof Liljegren to sort things out and calm the confused farmer. On other, warmer days the guards went to their stations with their knapsacks hauled on a wagon, singing as they marched. Other regiments shared responsibility for guarding some of the posts, but others were exclusively the Third's regular duty.[20]

Private Boxell was one of many suffering from the excessive rains. He managed to get Colonel Lester's black cook, Griffin, to bake him "a green apple pie" and thus had a hot dinner. Roos, another sufferer, was pleased because there was "plenty of beer for some days now . . . , three quarts" per day per man. A man from the Fifty-First Ohio of the provost guard entertained them with his "French fiddle," which had a crank to turn, keys for the left hand, and made "delicious music . . . Nellie Gray . . . Pop Goes the Weasel . . . Dixie"; Boxell gave him a dime for his efforts. The Minnesotan also kept an eye on one of the drummer boys, thirteen-year-old George Stringer, who was, he said, about the size of his own son, Billy. Stringer had first "waited on Lieut Meisner of Co H, then was a while with the second regiment, then he came back. . . . [H]e beats the drum well now, and goes with the band all the time."[21]

Pleased with the regiment's showing at dress parade on 16 April, General Dumont invited the men to visit him in Nashville the next day. On Thursday afternoon the Third marched for the capital, all in "dress uniforms, with white gloves newly washed," and formed in from of Dumont's headquarters for his review. Invited to visit the capitol, they marched to and around the building on the "broad stone terrace, and then into the hall that runs through it. Our band played. . . . Col. Lester introduced Governor Johnson," who reviewed them and made a speech. Returning to camp, the men were "somewhat powdered with dust," but as Boxell proudly noted, they had "made a fine appearance."[22]

Several days later Johnson, joined by a throng of citizens, visited the Third's camp for dress parade. He made a lengthy speech in which, according to Sergeant Major Hale, he told the men (and his fellow Tennesseans) that they were "the citizen soldiers of the Union, who have come not to infringe upon one right, but rather to protect us in the enjoyment of all. . . . We care nothing for your negroes, manage them as best suits yourselves, but the Union shall be preserved, and you must obey the laws!" The soldiers responded with deafening applause and shouts of "That's so!" By year's end, however, attitudes had changed, and with the Emancipation Proclamation, the North's goals became both Union and freedom.[23]

Impressive on parade with their clean dress uniforms, blackened shoes, polished brass, and white gloves, their precision drill, appearance, and bearing all prompted observers to regularly ask, "'What Regiment of regulars are those' which is a compliment," as "A" proudly noted. The *Nashville Union* reported that the regiment's passage along Nashville streets had reduced an elderly and "highly respectable citizen of Nashville, whose son was a distinguished officer in the confederate army, . . . [to] tears." Considered "better drilled, cleaner, & more intelligent & orderly" than the other Northern units, according to Brookins, the men took an insult from the Second Minnesota—calling them a "Band Box Regiment"—as a compliment. The growing pride in their drill and training and their confidence in themselves and their officers, especially their colonel, strengthened unit cohesion and built great morale. Recognition from higher authority confirmed their esprit de corps. Bowler (now a sergeant) bragged to Lizzie that Adj. Cyrene Blakely had told him, "Gov Andy Johnson says . . . ours is the best regiment he has seen, and you must recollect he has seen the Potomac regiments, he having been U.S. Senator."[24]

Former Tennessee governor Aaron Brown's widow requested from General Dumont a gentleman-soldier to live with the family and protect them from the soldiery. He asked Lester to find such a man, the colonel tapping Pvt. John Spellman of Company I, one of the older men, for this duty. Amid rumors that the regiment was going to Pittsburg Landing or to Unionist eastern Tennessee, the order soon arrived from Capt. James Fry sending them to Murfreesboro to join the rest of the Twenty-Third Brigade. When Spellman left the residence to return to his company, Mrs. Brown was unhappy, and her "girls shed tears and he bid them good bye." After calling in the companies on guard, pulling in the pickets, and packing their gear, the companies were ready to march when the orders were countermanded. The men repitched their tents and reposted the pickets; Spellman, however, did not return to the Widow Brown's.[25]

When Colonel Lester called on Governor Johnson to bid him goodbye, Boxell reported that the "Governor asked what that meant. We march tomorrow, said Col. Lester." Johnson replied: "That cannot be, I want the 3rd Minnesota Regiment here. They will be worth more than three other regiments." Sergeant Major Hale noted that "no sooner did Col. L. leave then [sic] he telegraphed to Gen Buell at Pittsburg [Landing] a special request that the 3d be left here." Contacting Horace Maynard, Tennessee's lone representative in Washington, D.C., that Buell was taking the Third, as well as the forces at Murfreesboro, and "substantially surrendering the country to the rebels," Johnson implored him to "see the Sec'y of War at once. The effect of removing the troops is visible in the face of every secessionist." He also cabled Buell to retain Twenty-Third Brigade in Middle Tennessee. Buell reassured the governor that no unit would be withdrawn without being replaced and that Middle Tennessee was not being abandoned. Secretary of War Edwin Stanton refused to countermand the general's orders.[26]

As the Third again prepared to march from Nashville, thinking they would not need their overcoats farther south and assuming that they would "be discharged before cold weather comes again," many men sent home clothes they soon regretted not having. The regiment left behind several men, including Surgeon Butler and Pvt. Nils Ringdahl of Company D, who were too sick to make the move. Pvt.

Halver Åkerberg (Ockenberg), a Norwegian in Company D, died in the Nashville hospital, as did Cpl. Amos Lesher of Company K. Lesher was hospitalized on 23 April "with softening of [the] Brain and died of said disease April 24." There were still seven men hospitalized in Belmont and two at Hospital No. 5 in Louisville.[27]

Up at 3 A.M. on Sunday morning, 27 April, the Third began the march at 5 A.M., pausing once an hour. By 11:30 A.M. the men had covered fifteen miles and made camp in a cedar grove. Bowler reported slaveowners visiting the regiment in search of their escaped slaves but "*had* to turn away empty handed, though we had as many as fifteen or twenty with us." That evening Sgt. Bernard McKenna of Company F was reduced to the ranks, for which Bowler blamed "those lazy, blackleg, mock aristocratic Allisons . . . just because he was a poor, hardworking Irishman dray driver instead of gamblers and hotelkeepers like themselves." Transferred to Company C on 1 May, McKenna was promoted corporal on the twenty-sixth; Lester lanced this boil (originating in hometown animosities) most effectively.[28]

Reveille on Monday was at 3 A.M., followed by a breakfast of cold pork, hard bread, and coffee. Boxell reported that the march started at 4 A.M., with "the stars shining. We went 14–15 miles and halted at 10:15 A.M., rested and slept." The men passed cotton fields, forests of tall cedars, black walnuts, hickories, oaks, and poplars; Boxell noted that the waist-high wheat was heading out. Bowler remarked on the "blasting hand of war. . . . [H]omes destroyed and deserted, fields laid waste . . . , [and] helpless women and children left in poverty." The regiment camped six miles from Murfreesboro because the rebels had "burnt some bridges on the turnpike," wrote Brookins, "& we had to take a crossroad & go around them." He added: "Our Col is very careful of his men."[29]

Roos noted "an alarm at 11 o'clock at night," due to the rebel colonel Morgan reportedly being nearby; patrols went out, and the troops "slept with our rifles." On Tuesday, 29 April, the Third began the march again at 4 A.M. and entered Murfreesboro to the music of the Twenty-Third Kentucky's band five hours later. The town was a strategic point worth holding. Eleven macadamized pikes, part of Tennessee's network of good toll roads connecting Nashville and the county seats in Middle Tennessee, all came together at Murfreesboro, and the Nashville & Chattanooga Railroad passed along the western edge of town.[30]

Union forces under Brigadier General Mitchel seized Murfreesboro in late March, and soon afterward the core of the Twenty-Third Brigade arrived to garrison the town and to guard the Nashville & Chattanooga and its various bridges, to control movement on the turnpikes, and to operate against the rebel guerrilla and cavalry bands that threatened Union supply lines. The two railroad bridges and the span carrying the Nashville Pike over Stones River, all destroyed by Johnston's withdrawing forces, were repaired by 1 April. Duffield's Twenty-Third Brigade, Brig. Gen. James Negley's brigade at Franklin, and General Mitchel's forces at Fayetteville all could, as Buell pointed out to Mitchel, concentrate over the pikes and railroad to protect the supply lines for Union forces moving east from Corinth against Chattanooga.[31]

Duffield's troops were also to bring Union influence over the town and surrounding Rutherford County. This post was, for many weeks, the southern-most position at the edge of the Union's battle space. To better control the town, Mitchel appointed Lt. Col. John Parkhurst of the Ninth Michigan to be commander of the "Post of Murfreesboro," with Capt. Oliver Cromwell Rounds, commander of Company B of the Ninth, as provost marshal. Parkhurst improperly continued to command both the town and his regiment.[32]

When the Twenty-Third Brigade arrived in Murfreesboro, Parkhurst encamped his regiment in Joseph Avent's grove. Private Brookins recounted what happened: Avent, a Breckenridge delegate to the 1860 Democratic convention, "remonstrated with Col P.," a Douglas delegate; they were "bitter enemies" from the convention. Parkhurst rejected a $500 bribe but offered to move his regiment if Avent took the oath. When he refused, Parkhurst "pitched his tent in the door yard & put A under arrest & kept guard around the house." The Ninth Michigan's camp was south of Murfree's Spring, running along the west side of Manchester Pike, which crossed Avent's drive just before the Bradyville Pike split off to the southeast. The Eighth Kentucky camped west of the Ninth and south of Murfree's Spring Branch Creek, below the town's elevation by some feet, where the Shelbyville and Manchester Pikes came down into a hollow surrounded by woody groves on the three other sides, these divided by Lytle's Creek; Murfree's Spring Branch Creek flowed along the south edge of town from Murfree's Spring into Lytle's Creek just before the Franklin Pike bridge. Capt. John Hewitt's battery of Kentucky Light Artillery camped east of the Shelbyville Pike and south of Sand Spring. When the Twenty-Third Kentucky arrived, they camped south of Lytle's Creek.[33]

Passing through town, the Third Minnesota made camp in a large clearing, presumably east of the Twenty-Third Kentucky, with Lytle's Creek on its north side. Pvt. John Boxell said that the "camp is level and smooth with a sod of white clover and blue grass. There is a grove nearly all round it." Trees edged Lytle's Creek, the men obtaining their drinking water from springs in the creek's bank. The regiment practiced skirmishing in "a level open woods" to the south, while southwest a few rods was a grove of cedars where the men got boughs for their bedding. To the east lay a large clover field, which was used as the battalion and brigade drill field. Pvt. Marvin Hathaway observed: "This [camp] is out in the woods by itself. The railroad runs within about a quarter of a mile, and the roar of the cars is about the only sound, except those of a martial character, which breaks in upon our camp."[34]

CHAPTER 4

FORGED IN MURFREESBORO

About 2,900 people, almost half of them enslaved blacks, lived in Murfreesboro in 1860. The town grew up around the brick courthouse in the town square. Surrounding it were stores and offices, the Planter's Bank, the town market, the slave market, and the City and Lytle Hotels. By 1859 there was a municipal gasworks, but the war interrupted construction of the city waterworks. A print shop and thirty-five mills and manufactories clustered in the southwest corner of town along the railroad and Lytle's Creek, employing 136 men and producing hats and caps, cotton goods, small arms, carriages, cedar buckets, bricks, and whiskey. The mercantile warehouses, some rather large brick buildings, stood near the junction of Murfree's Spring Branch Creek and Lytle's Creek, an area prone to flooding after heavy rain. The residential areas to the east and north featured many large, impressive homes.[1]

Soon after the attack on Fort Sumter, the Planter's Bank closed, while the carriage shops began making ambulances, wagons, and harnesses and the small-arms producer made revolvers, all for the Confederate army. Other shops produced accoutrements, saddles, and similar equipment. By July the mail no longer went north, goods no longer moved south into Tennessee, and store shelves became barren. Despite the shortages, in December 1861 the local women proudly established a military hospital in the Baptist Union College Building on the east edge of town.

"Truly a Stiff Neck People"

Lieutenant Colonel Parkhurst described Murfreesboro as "one of the worst rebel places in Tennessee—there is scarcely a Union man here." One of those few Unionists claimed that many citizens helped Confederate officers wearing civilian clothes and guerrillas evade the pickets and enter town and even the regimental camps to acquire information. (Escaped slaves also entered the camps, often gaining their freedom.) The "rules of war" were rudimentary, and few precedents guided the occupying commander and his provost marshal in applying martial law. Capt. Oliver Rounds, like most other provost marshals, began arbitrary searches, seizures, and arrests; took hostages; required passes, permits, and oaths; and imposed fines, curfews, and inconsistent and ever-changing rules to create a "police state" of spies and informers. Some dooryards were camped in and others not, some houses guarded and others raided, and while the citizens did not like it, they took every advantage they could of the loopholes and weaknesses of Union policy. Since occupation forces were responsible for public order and safety, marshals tried to use the existing municipal organization whenever possible to conduct business and avoid overloading the troops.[2]

Societal norms and expectations allowed women greater latitude in conduct. They could behave in ways that got men sent to Fort Mackinac, Michigan, or the Tennessee penitentiary. Kate Carney, the teenaged daughter of LeGrand Carney, a prosperous planter and dry-goods merchant whose store stood prominently on the square, complained in her diary for 15 June: "I can't bear to see men so willing to knuckle to such low down scoundrels, after being insulted & trampled upon, as they have been. Men of Rutherford County have lost their courage—perhaps to the women," who talked back, shunned, and otherwise insulted Union soldiers. She failed to grasp the workings of social expectations even after her father, arrested on "what charges no one knows," was imprisoned in the penitentiary in Nashville, a graphic illustration of the differing standards. Carney was one of the merchants and professional men Captain Rounds had demanded take the loyalty oath in order to continue doing business. Thirty of the thirty-seven identified residents refused, thus bringing remaining business activity to a standstill. Murfreesboro became more intransigent under occupation. Alice Ready, the teenaged daughter of former U.S. Representative Charles Ready, noted in her diary on 19 April: "The people are so firm now. The Federals are using every effort to force us to compliance. They will find us truly a stiff neck people."[3]

Captain Mattson wrote his wife that, at its dress parade on Tuesday, 29 April, the Third "attracted the usual attention—the officers and men of these other Rgmts were here looking at us and they are all astonished at our perfection." The next day, in pouring rain, Colonel Duffield held a general inspection of men and equipment and announced that there would be three brigade drills per week. That Friday the men had their first "brigade-drill, and the sight of so many troops was enough to make the merest coward wild with joy." Pvt. Marvin Hathaway wrote: "I never was so proud of anything as I was of the conduct of our regiment. While in other battalions the commanding officers seemed called upon by the awkwardness of the men to do some tall swearing once in a while, in ours there was not a word spoke except by way of command. Every movement was executed with the utmost promptness and regularity. Not only is our regiment splendidly drilled, but one of the best behaved and most cleanly in the service." Pvt. Jonathan Woodbury of Company B noted that their position during brigade drill was "on the 'left flank,' being the position of honor No. 2. The Michigan 9th on the right." Their impressive performance may have set ill with Colonel Parkhurst, who said his regiment had "the point of honor in the brigade and division—it shall keep it."[4]

The infantry regiments were busy picketing the eleven roads and the railroad, particularly the bridges, with the cavalry furnishing two mounted men—videttes—for each post; the artillery had no picket duties. Pvt. George Brookins estimated that, with all five regiments in camp, each had "to furnish about 40 or 50 [men] . . . for Picket guards." The sentries at each post were drawn from a single unit to preserve "their interior organization," or unit cohesion. At night one or two companies stood duty as the picket reserve, according to Captain Andrews. The men not on picket or camp guard duty drilled in the schools of the company and the battalion, "in street fighting and had brigade drill," or went on foraging expeditions into the surrounding countryside. Colonel Duffield later claimed that there had never been a brigade drill, though Lieutenant Colonel Parkhurst noted having commanded brigade drill in Colonel Lester's absence on 27 May.[5]

Rumors and reports of rebels multiplied. A telegraph construction crew was attacked near Pulaski, with all the men either killed or captured. Then, Colonel Morgan's cavalry seized a wagon train carrying convalescent soldiers on 2 May, taking the wagons and leaving the paroled men. Intercepted by General Negley near Pulaski, Morgan fled toward Murfreesboro, but with the alert garrison too strong to engage, he passed on toward Lebanon. General Dumont took up the pursuit with elements of Twenty-Third Brigade, leaving Lester commanding the garrison with orders to have "strong guards on the bridges."[6]

On Saturday, 3 May, pickets were out "two miles from camp," according to Sgt. James Bowler, and slaves began coming to his post on the Salem Turnpike to report a large enemy force assembling at Sand Jarret's planation about halfway to Salem. Later, other slaves reported enemy pickets three miles from his own, and Bowler asked 1st Lt. Isaac Tichenor and two mounted scouts to go check. The Minnesotans flushed out the rebels and got chased back to their own lines. The Southerners then cut the Nashville & Chattanooga track and the parallel telegraph lines, burning cotton bales to try and stop a train six miles north of town. The conductor, warned by nearby slaves, saw the obstructions and reversed his train's movement in time. Lester promptly dispatched four companies under Lieutenant Colonel Smith to repair the track and wire. The men returned with one prisoner, six horses, and two mules.[7]

Captain Mattson had Companies C, D, and I in the field throughout the day, and other detachments went out to chase mounted rebels. While Mattson thought the pursuit exhilarating, Carl Roos disagreed and complained of the muggy warm day and their nocturnal mud march in rain back to camp. In town, meanwhile, the provost guard, including Company B, maintained a line of battle before their post at the City Hotel; after dark the guard shifted to the more easily defended courthouse. At one point a large cavalry force came in "on the pike, sounding almost like thunder," but turned out to be Union horsemen. Pvt. John Boxell wrote his wife that he found, prior to their identification, that he was not afraid of a possible battle.[8]

That evening, after the Twenty-Third Kentucky's band serenaded Lester, the regiments slept until the long roll called them out at 10 P.M. Taking position before the brigade headquarters on the Manchester Pike—the main threat appeared to come from Altamont—Lester positioned the artillery so that one section could fire across the brigade front and the rest of the battery could control the road or fire upon the town if needed. Four days later, on Wednesday the seventh, the Ninth Michigan returned from pursuing Morgan, dragging a rebel flag in the dirt as they marched through town. Colonel Duffield, ordered to command all troops in Kentucky, transferred command of the Twenty-Third Brigade to Lester the following day, and the Ninth escorted him to the depot on Friday. Called out on successive nights, the brigade had standing orders that each man be prepared "with 40–60 rounds and hard crackers in the haversack," ready for the long roll. The continual alarms interrupted sleep, but the men still dressed, armed, and formed up in minutes, even the sick, who were "all bound to go." Sgt. Olof Liljergren of Company D voiced frustration at being called out repeatedly only to, as Pvt. Edward Bailey of Company E wrote, "lay on our arms all night hoping they would come." One evening, as the brigade formed in line of battle, Colonel Lester rode over to Mattson: "He felt so glad that I was there with my Co. . . . [H]e relied much on us."[9]

The people were bitter, fractious, and armed. Two different searches only a few weeks apart turned up substantial caches of weapons. After Parkhurst and Rounds were fired upon on 10 May, a subsequent search turned up "over two hundred stand of fire-arms . . . heavily loaded, and [with] an abundant supply of ammunition, cartridges &c." Governor Johnson responded by ordering Parkhurst to arrest as many people as it took to "have proper effect upon [this] spirit of insubordination" in the town, naming twelve men to be held "hostages for the good behavior of the Citizens of Murfreesboro."[10]

Picket and guard duty "in the enemy's country" was different. Hathaway put it: "Picketing is not the mere form that it was in Kentucky; it has now an object. Scarcely a day passes but some of our pickets bring in prisoners or captured property." Posted in small detachments among a hostile people in a different physical and social environment, these soldiers often suffered great anxiety. The country was different. Hathaway said the area "seems to have gone to sleep, a peculiarity which possesses most disagreeable features." Traveling miles on turnpikes and meeting no one, seeing no one in the gardens or on verandas, encountering no residents on the streets of villages, meeting only straggling soldiers or pickets on the byways and trails, and knowing that around the next bend locals who appeared to be the best of citizens might kill you—all of this was discomfiting. Historian Reid Mitchell rightly termed it "bizarre."[11]

Expectations and rumors of attacks added to this tension. Pickets at their isolated posts stood watch two hours on duty, remained two hours awake in the guard post, and then spent two hours sleeping. When Private Boxell explained guard duty to his son, he ignored the anxieties to focus on the details: for example, the passes required for movement and their allowing only blacks into their camp. This duty was equitably distributed among the men in the Third Minnesota, but apparently not so in the Ninth Michigan. Sgt. Henry Cooley of that regiment noted in his diary that on 16 May he was the "sergeant of the picket on the Salem pike. Had a very good time. Have not been on guard before since last winter." His statement that he "had a very good time" suggests a lack of seriousness and discipline in the Ninth.[12]

Private Boxell again managed to find families, mostly Masons, who provided him meals and some homelike company, often despite their having family members taken prisoner of war by Union forces. He particularly visited a Miss McIlvaine, a wealthy, educated Unionist lady, one of the few in Murfreesboro. Men in other units, including Absalom Harrison of the Fourth Kentucky Cavalry, a brother Mason, also developed friendships across the sectional rift. While these contacts may have provided them useful intelligence, such as who the three of four Union families in town were, at the same time, the soldiers also gave their hosts invaluable information.[13]

Lester as "Acting Brigadier"

When Colonel Duffield transferred command to Lester on 8 May, he neglected to inform him that the brigade was attached to and reported to General Mitchel's division. Only after the general pointedly asked for his reports did Lester learn of this essential command relationship. Both the colonel, who queried Capt. Oliver Green, and Mitchel, who telegraphed General Buell, were frustrated by this failure to properly transfer command. Duffield's command style—in the Ninth Michigan and in the Twenty-Third Brigade and, the correspondence suggests, in his Kentucky command—was marked by a lack of attention to detail; poor communications, especially with subordinates; and routinely seeking guidance for even small matters from superiors.[14]

The Minnesotans were pleased for Lester since his promotion to "acting general" commanding the brigade meant that he might become a brigadier. Yet they thought, as Hathaway stated, "the regiment has met with serious misfortune" in losing him. Lieutenant Colonel Smith, returned from sick leave and now in command, was unable to lead them through the simplest battalion drills and had, as Hathaway put it, "as few qualifications for a military leader as any other common farmer." When Smith resigned for ill health on 23 May, declaring that his liver disease made him "utterly incapacitated for service," Mattson, as senior captain, became acting regimental commander.[15]

The nightly alerts, the sniping at foraging parties and repair crews, and the attacks on pickets were symptomatic of the dangers inherent in occupying an enemy town in the contested region between the main armies. Lester found his ability to respond to threats impaired because two of his regiments, the Third Minnesota and the Twenty-Third Kentucky, were across Lytle's Creek and had to march through Murfreesboro to reach his headquarters. He therefore ordered these regiments to move their camps nearer to the Ninth Michigan's location to "more efficiently . . . protect the town from sudden attack." There was no room for them on the west side of the Manchester Pike near headquarters, so they took over the site of the brigade teams and the mule corral to the east of the road; the teams and mules relocated to the south of the Michiganders. Because the Twenty-Third was out on a scout at the time, the Minnesotans moved the Kentuckians' gear and tents as well as their own, putting shovels and brooms to work as well and soon had the reminders of mules cleaned up and hauled away. After a week or so, Boxell pronounced the new quarters "very clean and nice," meeting the Third's fastidious standards. His Company B was on the right side of the regimental camp nearest the town and to Murfree's Spring, just across the road. The brigade now straddled the Manchester Pike, with the Third and Twenty-Third Regiments closer to the Woodbury Pike, giving Lester the improved response time he desired and concentrating his forces near the two main avenues of expected enemy advance, the Bradyville Pike from the southeast and the Woodbury Pike from the east.[16]

Sergeant Major Hale said that trees shaded the new camp and there was a large, open, level square for drill and dress parades. To the north of their camp was Martha Murfree's house and large fenced-in garden, which had run wild, though the cooks were able to get some goods from it. The regimental bakers finally finished constructing an "oven capable of baking 500 loaves" and then, Hathaway complained, "just as we had got prepared to *live,* orders came for our regiment to seize knapsacks and take the cars" for Columbia—the Maury County seat, which was to host a Unionist meeting that weekend—because the regiments stationed there were too much reduced by providing guards for the wagon trains hauling supplies to Buell's troops in Alabama. Alerted on Friday, the Third departed Murfreesboro at 3:30 A.M. on Saturday, 17 May, with rations for two days, cooking gear, and blankets, riding on open platform cars "amid a shower of dust and cinders," as "S.B." reported. Shifting to the Nashville & Decatur Railroad in Nashville, the Minnesotans arrived in Columbia at noon.[17]

Brookins observed that, "at the prospect of our being ordered off, the sick, lame, & blind [began] to scratch around, declaring they are not going to be left behind"—but they were, along with the teamsters and the camp guards, all commanded by 1st Lt. Lewis Hardy of Company C. Lester, who remained in Murfreesboro commanding the brigade (to Parkhurst's annoyance), put the remaining men from all the regiments on alert. Boxell wrote his wife that, after walking about Murfreesboro, he "went to sleep with my loaded gun by my side and slept untroubled, except by my diarrhea. . . . The guard was strengthened, and extra pickets thrown out, and we were all ordered to Sleep on our arms" because of rumors of rebel cavalry in the vicinity.[18]

Newly appointed assistant surgeon Albert C. Wedge joined the regiment on 12 May, just in time to join the expedition to Columbia. He informed Governor Ramsey that, despite being cared for by a contract surgeon during Dr. Butler's absence on sick leave, the regiment was in good health. Replacing Dr. Francis Milligan, Wedge's appointment, arranged by Secretary of the State Senate A. D. Weber, was done with unusual speed. Unlike newly appointed chaplain Benjamin Crary, the doctor chose to travel by train from La Crosse, Wisconsin; Crary went by steamboat to Saint Louis and became lost in the bowels of the army. Wedge later remembered that the change from his civilian practice to being a regimental surgeon "was sudden and of such magnitude that it almost made me dizzy." As he experienced it, a surgeon's duties were, firstly, to "keep the men under his charge healthy and fighting trim. Secondly, when he falls a victim of wounds or disease then we rush to relieve his sufferings and save his life. The first require his attention to the personal habits of the men, cleanliness, the location of camp, food supply, cooking and prompt attention to the first symptoms of disease so that long sickness may be avoided."[19]

Making camp on a hill outside Columbia, some men attended the "Old School Presbyterian" Church and noted that there were no prayers for the nation nor any mention of war. The following day, Monday, the Third moved to the camp of the absent Eleventh Michigan Infantry to protect a battery from an anticipated attack. Being inside the Eleventh's tents was welcome during the next day's rain, but it was little better than the earlier site, which Hathaway said was "one complete bed of soft mud." Fortunately, the Third boarded open freight cars at noon on Wednesday, 21 May, and by 7 P.M. was back in Murfreesboro.[20]

Hathaway thought Columbia charming. He noted its cleanliness compared to Murfreesboro or Nashville, and, with the Union meeting, concluded that "cleanliness [w]as one evidence of union sentiment," Columbia certainly being "less 'secesh' than any place that I have seen in dixie." Sergeant Bowler reported that "a crowd of ladies showered the cars with bouquets as we passed" through Franklin on the way to Nashville, concluding, wrongly, that Unionist sentiment was rising rapidly in Middle Tennessee.[21]

Boxell, who spent more time sick than well, suffered a relapse of his bilious diarrhea on the twenty-third, for which Dr. Wedge gave him quinine. Remaining very sick, he soon was given an opium pill, then suffered further as it began raining and his tent flooded. His friend Pvt. Charles Wood went to see Mrs. Baird, a rebel friend of the Mason, who sent him a chicken, which was used for soup, and flowers. On Saturday Boxell thought he was getting better. Columbia might have appeared clean and healthy, but the Eleventh Michigan's mud camp was most certainly not as sanitary as the Third's camp. Many of the Minnesotans took sick after their return, both officers and men, so that Capt. John Preston of Company F commanded the regiment for a time. Fortunately, as "During the War" wrote, "it is all a Sunday in town [with few people out on the streets]," since too few men were well enough to be useful in case of trouble. He claimed that cheer dominated the camp, but they had not seen a paymaster in months, leaving most men out of money.[22]

Dr. Wedge sent several men to the army general hospital run by Surg. William Eames of the Twenty-First Ohio in the Union College Building, where the women of Murfreesboro had previously established their hospital. Eames said at first all he had was "the old bunks the rebels had used & the empty filthy rooms they had vacated." But after hard work cleaning the building from top to bottom and getting the "bunks arranged," he had "some twenty men as nurses 12 for guards 3 for cooks . . . five colored persons 3 males & 2 females to do some of the drudgery & one very respectable white woman to help generally." All the black workers were escaped slaves.[23]

Unfortunately, bad feelings developed between Surgeons Eames and Butler. The latter began sending his sick to the new army hospital in the Soule Female Academy Building, on the Lebanon Pike just north of the square, run by Eames's friend and former hospital steward named Rob, who, Eames said, did not "like some things about the sick care of the 3rd Min Reg. Thinks the Doctors [of that regiment] are interfering too much." As relations soured further, Butler, whom Eames termed "a malicious fellow," withdrew all of the Third's patients from the general hospitals on 7 July.[24]

Unlike the general hospitals in the West, which received their supplemental supplies from the U.S. Sanitary Commission, regimental hospitals mostly depended upon local groups. After a couple of months with the Third, Chaplain Crary wrote Lieutenant Governor Donnelly that while some regiments "piteously begged for" hospital stores from families and local ladies-aid societies for soldiers, the Third had not done so (usually the chaplain did the begging for supplies) and had not received any for some time. He bluntly declared: "The kinds of eatables are almost useless. . . . Boxes of slippers and dressing gowns are humbugs mostly."[25]

Regiments lost men to sickness, to discharges for disability, and to detached duty at higher headquarters. Among the last was 2nd Lt. Cyrene Blakely, who was detailed as brigade adjutant. Both officers and men went to serve in various support functions—ordnance, commissary, quartermaster, pioneer (engineer), and transport departments—and often were retained for months or in some cases years. Why 2nd Lt. John Devereaux of Company G led a supply train overland to Pittsburg Landing is unknown, but he did, calling it a "hard and tedious trip." Since January 2nd Lt. James Howlett of Company A had served in the Quartermasters Department in Louisville, finally rejoining the regiment only to serve as Lester's brigade quartermaster. Pvt. Francis Jerry, formerly serving in the commissary depot at Lebanon, Kentucky, and Pvt. Edgar Holcomb, both of Company G, went from Pittsburg Landing to Corinth, Mississippi, serving in the Army of the Ohio's Commissary Department. In May 1862 several men remained on detached service in Louisville or Nashville, while a couple were with Buell's headquarters in Alabama.[26]

In contrast, other men were under arrest awaiting a general or regimental court-martial or were serving their sentences. Pvt. James Fisk of Company B was charged with being absent in violation of orders and of having ignored the guards' orders when he passed through the lines while camped at Columbia. Formal charges and specifications had been prepared and approved, with a general court-martial scheduled, when orders arrived from Secretary of War Stanton discharging Fisk so he could be mustered in as a captain and assistant quartermaster. Congress had appropriated $25,000 to protect emigrants moving west to Oregon, and Fisk, appointed "Superintendent of the Emigration of the Route Between Fort Abercrombie and Fort Walla-Walla," was to organize and lead a group of about fifty men to escort the emigrant wagon trains through the Black Hills and across the Great Plains. The extant correspondence does not explain why he was selected, being a post he had not sought, but his family had extensive connections and political clout. Fisk was ordered to Washington to nevertheless deal with his pending court-martial.[27]

Fisk was only one of several men misbehaving following Lester becoming brigade commander, "During the War" observing that "since which change the Regiment has retrograded 50 per cent in discipline and its former enviable reputation." Most of the "retrograde" actions were minor; only Fisk faced a general court-martial. The Third Minnesota was not angelic, but—within the limits of the surviving documentation—the regiment apparently had a smaller number of men under arrest at any given time and had fewer problems generally than the Ninth Michigan, or many other regiments for that matter. At the same time, not all was sweetness and fraternization among the Minnesotans. Private Bailey of Company E told his father, "We fare little better than doges, the commissioned officers fare like kings and in the end it all comes out of the poor private, but I can stand it but I know what my rights are and I intend to have the[m], in the army or anywhere else." Strangely, in a republican army, the gaps in status between officers, noncommissioned officers, and enlisted men were gaping chasms, even when the officers came out of the noncommissioned ranks. Despite his tough talk, there is no evidence that Bailey was ever punished for anything.[28]

The printers of the *Murfreesboro Union Volunteer,* all enlisted men of the Ninth Michigan, said that Lester was "a worthy successor of our late popular commanding officer" and praised him for his "3d regiment, which he had brought to a high state of soldierly perfection. He is a young man, and seems to feel that he has a reputation to make; hence his movements all exhibit that caution and completeness which mark the perfect soldier. Adjutant Blakely of the same Regiment is also an active, enterprising and popular officer." The paper printed resolutions from the officers of the Ninth praising both Colonel Duffield and Lester. In contrast, Parkhurst wrote his sister that Lester "is not quite the man for the command." On 24 May he further declared that "he is not competent of the command but will probably get along well." It must have galled Parkhurst to have Lester resident in his camp, but Duffield had located both the telegraph office and his headquarters with the Ninth. Whatever the reasons, the lieutenant colonel was looking for ways to undermine Lester. This poison did not, despite contrary claims, spread to his men, according to surviving letters and diaries. Parkhurst's writings reveal an irascible and insecure martinet whose problems became worse when, after the death of his wife, he placed his very young daughters in the care of his sisters and returned to duty with the Ninth in early summer of 1861. Involved for a time with a woman named Josephine, who he came to think had not returned his affections, he then took up with another Josephine, "Jo" Reeves, a Murfreesboro lady who had been mourning her rebel beau.[29]

Picketing was dangerous, scouting expeditions searching for guerrillas and rebel camps even more hazardous, but foraging parties that irritated the citizenry quite considerably made the Union troops vulnerable to being surrounded, surprised, and destroyed. When possible, several companies from the garrison went out on scouting and foraging expeditions, taking animals, corn, and foodstuffs and, as Hathaway noted, having "considerable fun searching rebel houses for arms." William King recounted the rebel side. His neighbor and relative, a Colonel King, refused to take the oath of allegiance and "suffered from much foraging," the Murfreesboro garrison each week loading six to eight wagons with his corn and taking hogs, chickens, and turkeys. Small patrols daily raided along the roads radiating out from Murfreesboro and regularly returned with wagonloads of corn.[30]

The Union garrison also engaged in counterguerrilla activities aimed at returning the rebels to being loyal Union citizens. A key part of this effort was Union meetings. Sergeant Major Hale thought that "there has been a very great change of opinion among the citizens of the town, so that when 4 weeks ago no man dare say one word in favor the Union—now a *call* for a *Union Meeting* on the 24th is largely signed." He thought this a result of a "loss of hope & disgust" for the Confederate cause as well as fear of Union action. When Governor Johnson came to speak at a "Union League" rally held on the steps of Murfreesboro's courthouse, Hathaway thought it "one of those grand union meetings which are springing up spontaneously throughout the state." After two local Unionists, William Spence and Edmund Cooper, spoke, Johnson orated for three hours, urging "the deluded and erring Union men, who had by force or choice joined the rebel armies, to return to their allegiance." Hale's estimate of Murfreesboro's loyalty is as questionable as the spontaneity Hathaway perceived. Pvt. Thomas Canfield of Company G wrote that two companies were present to keep order, one each from the Third and the Ninth, and the crowd did not cheer much: "they darent say nothing if they did they would have been marched off" to the jail. Local leaders did note, however, who seemed receptive to the Union message. Historian Stephen Ash has observed that Southern patriots responded to occupation first by shock and then, like fiery Kate Carney, who refused to play music for two Federal officers who called on her family, the women resiliently "flaunt[ed] contempt for their conquerors."[31]

According to the *Philadelphia Inquirer,* after Johnson's rally and a concert by the Third's band, Spence entertained their correspondent, who reported that at about 11 P.M. the Unionist received word from Lester that some six hundred rebel cavalry were supposedly within six miles of town to capture Johnson, the colonel having surrounded the house the governor was staying in with three companies of infantry. Visiting the Third's camp the next morning, Johnson asked Lester why he had not been warned. The colonel, "with all the coolness of an old grenadier," told him, "I knew they could not capture you, Governor, and I wanted to use you as a bait."[32]

The men from the Third who went to the Presbyterian services that day were summoned back to camp to escort Johnson to his train just as the minister entered the pulpit. As "highly as we all esteemed the Governor," the correspondent "S.B." wrote, "we were not pleased with the idea of a street parade, especially during the hours of worship." The regiment formed up and followed the Ninth

Michigan through town. Carney complained that as her family came home from church, they "met their band in full blast, escorting Andy Johnson to the depot (that craven hearted villain.)" That afternoon her mother brought in a Confederate soldier who had escaped from the town jail and fed him before he left to rejoin Col. James Starnes's cavalry. This support of the Confederacy by local citizens was, Ash has concluded, done as an "extension of the community" and reflected—along with the ebb and flow of guerrilla warfare—the state of civilian morale. As Union soldiers began to appreciate this, they began to consider rebel citizens as legitimate targets of military operations.[33]

Soon after Johnson departed Murfreesboro, Roos noted, soldiers arrested a citizen "thought to be of Morgan's party" who had hidden away "flags, 2 loaded rifles and a cartridge box and more." Three secessionists who snuck into the Ninth's camp to kidnap an escaped slave were caught without passes and detained so that "the Negro came away out of it with a whole skin." The next day "a Negro came into the Michigan camp who had gotten several buckshot in his back from his master"; it is not clear if this was the same man. Some soldiers were sympathetic to local blacks, who crowded "so thick around our camp that it makes it so dark . . . it is most impossible to see," as Private Canfield described to his sister. Others were less so, and few (if any) thought them equal to whites. Canfield noted that many black women dressed "better here than most of the ladies in Minn they dress full as good as their mistresses." The soldiers came to understand that blacks were excellent sources of intelligence, ones often over-looked by their rebel masters.[34]

On Tuesday, 27 May, General Buell accepted Major Hadley's resignation, effective 1 May. Leaving without permission shortly before the Third departed Shepherdsville, Hadley had gone home to Minnesota for his health, also claiming that his wife was "at the point of death." He requested of Captain Fry either an extension of his furlough to 1 June or that "the Genne in Command to accept of my resignation" [sic] effective 21 May. He concluded a letter seeking Ramsey's support, "pleas excuse hast," supporting the *Pioneer*'s claim of his near illiteracy. The *Daily Press* defended Hadley, claiming that the volunteer-officer examining board had not rejected him, though none of the officers of the Third had gone before any board. Saying that he himself was as good a Republican as any man, "Our Army Correspondent" urged the governor to dismiss Hadley or accept his resignation since "the universal sentiment of both officers and men is against him, . . . he having shown himself void of any good sense, and wholly unfit for any position requiring either natural ability or education."[35]

Everyone expected that Mattson would be the first captain promoted. When Lieutenant Colonel Smith resigned because of ill health, Mattson should have moved to the lieutenant colonelcy and Capt. Chauncey Griggs of Company B, who was next in seniority, to the majority. For unrecorded reasons, however, Ramsey chose Griggs as the lieutenant colonel and Mattson as the major. Griggs had no real experience at battalion drill, however, so various excuses were found to allow Mattson to teach him without any public embarrassment.[36]

On 4 June Capt. Clinton Gurnee took Company E outside the lines for skirmisher practice, apparently without informing anyone else. Their first few shots attracted the attention of a returning cavalry squadron, which prepared to fire upon them until the Minnesotans' blue pants suggested that they were Union soldiers, not "graybacks." In town, headquarters responded to the shots by going on alert: the artillery limbered up, scouts started out, couriers stood by their horses—even the sick loaded their weapons—and everyone awaited orders. News that it was just a mistake brought Gurnee before Lester for a reprimand, having not obtained permission from his superiors and putting his men in danger.[37]

Though Murfreesboro was no longer on the periphery of the Union battle space in Tennessee, the region remained infested by guerrillas and partisan raiders. The repairs completed on the Nashville & Chattanooga Railroad made the town an increasingly enticing rebel target. Normal picket and guard duty required about 200 men, another 100–150 troops were in the provost guard, and each unit maintained its own camp guard. With regiments absent at times for various reasons, the remaining infantry units had to provide all of the guard forces. When the Ninth Michigan left on Negley's expedition to Chattanooga on 28 May, the Third Minnesota became responsible for security, meaning each man was on picket duty every third day. Discipline began to slip under the strain, as pickets began "drawing pigs, chickens, &c." When Lester ordered that sergeants command each picket post, *they* then faced such duty assignments every other day. The colonel wrote Ramsey with justifiable pride, saying his "regiment performs its duty with zeal and cheerfulness."[38]

Post commanders, including Lester, desperately needed information and received both rumors and reports from spies, slaves, scouts, patrols, and informants. As Hale noted, such intelligence had major rebel forces operating near McMinnville to the east and Manchester to the southeast. Reports from Negley's expedition strengthened Brigadier General Dumont's belief that an attack in Middle Tennessee was likely. Consequently, Lester extended his pickets farther out the Manchester and Woodbury Pikes and his cavalry patrols covered more territory than usual, all on alert for enemy activity. One cavalry scout stopped for breakfast on Saturday, 7 June, but in doing so relaxed their guard too much after setting too few pickets. As a result only a dozen or so of the seventy men returned from this patrol, most brought in by locals who reported a large Confederate infantry force nearby. Lester removed the sick from the hospitals in town to their unit hospitals and assembled his available forces in line of battle blocking the Manchester Pike, with Capt. John Hewitt training two of his howitzers and a Parrot rifle on the town to discourage any "adventurous" residents.[39]

Middle Tennessee was the only western campaigning region with adequate spring forage to sustain cavalry mounts, and many rebel units moved into the region, increasing both the actual threat level and the flow of rumors to Union garrisons. Based on Lester's reports of activity, Dumont dispatched the Seventy-Fourth Ohio to reinforce Murfreesboro, sending also the Sixty-Ninth Ohio on Sunday. Happily, the paymaster came with the Seventy-Fourth, and the men of the Third lay on their arms with wallets filled with two months' pay. Roos noted that the reinforcing units received "mess and supplies from the battalion," while Hathaway reported the Ohioans very impressed by the Third's drill, unable to "see how we can do that 'secure arms' all together." Of course, no rebel attack took place, and General Mitchel, in northern Alabama, thus thought Lester had overreacted.[40]

Chaplain Crary finally arrived on 9 June, having gone first to Saint Louis, where authorities had no idea where the Third was, then to Corinth, where he met J. P. Owens, the Minnesota agent to care for the state's hospitalized soldiers. From Pittsburg Landing, the two men descended the Tennessee River and ascended the Cumberland River to Nashville, then traveled by train to Murfreesboro. Immediately taking up his duties, Crary buried two men. Owens reported their arrival to Governor Ramsey, noting that, despite many in the Third having suffered from the measles, only twenty-three men had die as of the tenth.[41]

Numerous reports, including one from a spy in Chattanooga, "an intelligent Frenchman," led Generals Buell, Mitchel, and Dumont to believe that the rebels were assembling forces to attack in Middle Tennessee. Edmund Cooper, a prominent Shelbyville Unionist who had spoken at the Murfreesboro Union rally, wrote Governor Johnson of rumors that both Colonels Starnes and Morgan had "crossed the Mountains at the head of Hickory Creek" and were "loitering about McMinnville and Winchester." Mitchel telegraphed Maj. Gen. Henry Halleck, commanding Union forces in the West, "I learned that a heavy force was threatening Murfreesboro and the adjacent posts. I am thus compelled to withdraw General Negley and send him to reinforce Colonel Lester."[42]

As Negley began his return march toward McMinnville, Dumont took an expedition there to deal with the reported rebel concentrations and to fulfill Buell's directive that "the [rail]road to McMinnville [be] put in order." Thinking his troop dispositions were insufficient "for an active defensive position" to hold his lines of supply, Buell began shifting his forces. On Tuesday, 10 June, Mattson wrote that the Third was to leave on an expedition into "eastern Tenn, after a rebel [cavalry] force which had been threatening us for a long time. . . . I doubt whether we can find the rebels—they run too fast for us [infantrymen]."[43]

Dumont's expedition departed Murfreesboro about 6 A.M. on the eleventh, with the Third in the advance, followed by Hewitt's Battery (augmented to twelve guns), the Sixty-Ninth and Seventy-Fourth Ohio, and the Eleventh Michigan, all under Lester's command; cavalry formed the column's rear guard. Mattson, newly promoted to major, commanded the regiment in Griggs's absence. According to Agent Owens, Dumont left behind the Ninth with their camp guard, the pickets, and the sick, too few men to hold the town; Col. Stanley Matthews, Provost Marshal at Nashville, sent units from other posts to secure Murfreesboro in their absence.[44]

Two hundred men of the Third arrived in Woodbury about 5 P.M. and "wash[ed] the dust from our faces (which was pretty thick) and receive[d] some nutriment." Chaplain Crary said the Minnesotans "stood the march better than either of the other Regts"; only the colonel and two men from the Sixty-Ninth Ohio arrived together. About 11 P.M., as the men prepared to resume the march, teamster Albert Stewart of Company H accidentally shot himself—his pistol dropped out of his pocket—the ball passing through his right lung and lodging under the skin of his back. Not expected to survive, he was left behind in "a comfortable room and with a good man." Crary noted that a total lunar eclipse, lasting an hour, began as the march started. The road taken by the column wound along the ridges, the stream banks being too steep. Hathaway reported that "one caisson went over the side and fell a hundred feet"; fortunately, the horses and drivers only suffered scratches. Water was scarce along the way, the men were exhausted, and some soon began straggling and dropping off alongside the road to sleep. According to Crary, blacks continually welcomed the troops "and gave much valuable information. . . . [O]ur officers regard them as reliable friends."[45]

The Minnesotans entered McMinnville on Thursday, "with our colors flying and the regiment in good order, with but very few lagging behind from exhaustion," while "T" noted, "the Ohio and Michigan boys were scattered along the road for miles." The other regiments, according to "American Boy," termed them "perfect horses on a tramp. . . . Allowed to go their own gait the cavalry would have to trot to keep up." Col. Lewis Campbell of the Sixty-Ninth Ohio referred to the Third as "the flying infantry." The Union soldiers foraged "'confiscated' chickens, turkies, geese, and garden vegetables of every description," though they tried not to "disturb the property of loyal people." Strangely, no one ordered them to remove the spindles and looms from a cotton factory employing about one hundred women making cloth for the Confederates.[46]

About suppertime on Friday, 13 June, Dumont ordered Lester to take the Third, nominally riding in wagons; the Second Battalion of the Seventh Pennsylvania

Cavalry; and a section of artillery across the Cumberland Mountains to Pikeville in the Sequatchie Valley. Lt. Col. William Sipes of the Seventh said the passage was considered " impassable for wagons," while a local told Hathaway, "you can never get these cannon over" the mountains; horses reputedly had not made the journey in years. "Walk[ing] and push[ing] the wagons up hill and hold[ing] them back going down hill," both wagons and mules "were in danger of turning over or falling down the ravine." Finally reaching the plateau after midnight, the column frightened an isolated family with their noise. After exhausting their well, the Federals pushed on.[47]

Looking down into the ravines, Roos said that they appeared to be "clad with a yard of luxurious green grass, but . . . it was found to be the tops of large growth, thickly foliaged trees." The men began their descent about 10 A.M. on Sunday. Sergeant Major Hale said the road *was awful*, at times fearful, winding round the edges" of the bluff, just wide enough for a team, but everyone made the "terrible rough passage" and arrived in the Sequatchie Valley five miles from Pikesville. Shortly thereafter, the cavalry skirmished with a battalion from the Eighth Texas Cavalry (Terry's Texas Rangers), and closer to Pikesville the force met the Eighth Texas and Second Georgia Cavalry in line of battle; the rebels gave way after a couple of volleys.[48]

Many of the people in Pikesville were Unionists eager to take the oath, with "T" reporting that "some thirty of the citizens joined our cavalry." Roos noted that, for the first time, Lester issued the men whiskey as they rested until about 4 P.M. before beginning their return march. It was, said Sergeant Bowler, a hot, tedious trudge, and "huge rattlesnakes defied us at every step, scorpions darted . . . up the trees, and lizards crawled about in sickening profusion. Bugs, worms, beetles, spiders, &c." Mattson observed that many men stopped to "cut off their blisters," then marched on. Some fell out to rest for a time in the shade; one man fell asleep in the wrong place and, when a cavalryman fired his carbine, the ball passed through his ankle, missing all the bones.[49]

"Our army steals everything from a thousand dollar horse to a pewter platter, or a broken saucer," Crary disgustedly wrote Governor Ramsey. Whatever the retreating rebels left, the Union cavalry took, usually from the poorest people, who could ill afford the loss of a goose or the day's milk. The chaplain had remained in McMinnville with Dumont, who used him as an officer courier. Hearing rumors that the Pikesville force was under attack, the general decided to march to its relief. He first considered leaving Crary in command of the sick, the lame, and a small guard force but then decided to bring the sick and lame along. Some miles into their march, a messenger from Lester met the relief force with the news that the colonel's command was all right and would be returning.

Dumont's column returned to McMinnville early Monday, leaving "knapsacks, haversacks, canteens, &c. . . . scattered promiscuously along the road."[50]

Lester's force returned to McMinnville about 4 P.M. on Monday, 16 June, and rested. Their departure on Wednesday was delayed to raise a large liberty pole with a flag nailed to it. General Dumont and others made speeches, after which, "H.N.G." said, "we gave three cheers for the old flag and started for Murfreesboro." Entering Woodbury about 6 A.M., Dumont's force remained there until 6 P.M., when they resumed the march through the first rain showers to fall in the region in three weeks. The Third entered their camp east of Murfree's Spring about 4 A.M. on Thursday, the Ohio units settling in nearby.[51]

Resuming brigade command Thursday morning, Lester received Parkhurst's report on the Ninth Michigan's "march to Chattanooga . . . [and his] removal of camp," from Avent's dooryard to the front yard of Major Maney's Oaklands Plantation north of town on 17 June, "to procure water and for other sanitary reasons." With the camp of the Seventh Pennsylvania's squadron and the brigade teams stretching back into the northeastern side of town, Roos commented that the flow of water in Murfree's Spring was quite reduced and unhealthy.[52]

Wanting to concentrate his force, Lester ordered the Third to move again, this time to "in front of the Academy," while Hewitt's battery moved to the regiment's north. He directed Parkhurst to "condense [his] lines to allow Cavalry co [Fourth Kentucky] to come in between 3rd Minn [and] 9th Mich." so as to protection them too. When the lieutenant colonel refused to do so, Lester charged him with disobedience. According to his diary, Parkhurst told the colonel that "the charge was false & he threatened to put me in irons. I told him he was not firm enough to so do. He put me in arrest." Some of the Michigan officers were indignant at this, but Parkhurst remained under arrest until he apologized. Since he did not condense his regimental lines, the lieutenant colonel should have gone to Nashville in arrest for a general court-martial, but Lester chose not to press charges, perhaps because having an insubordinate but competent unit commander was better than one unfit for command.[53]

The new campsite on the college grounds was in "a fine shady grove but the land was rather flat & low," according to Brookins. The space was adequate, and there was a spring of good water, also used by the hospital, that still had sufficient flow. The drought and the passage of men, horses, and teams had packed the ground hard. When, on Tuesday afternoon, 24 June, there was "a terrible thunderstorm," most of the new camp flooded a foot or more deep; Hathaway reported that some tents were accessible only by boat. The rains continued so that all the camps flooded, the water studded with disgusting debris and polluting all of the springs, including that near the Maney mansion. Lester, displeased, searched in the pouring rain for a new brigade campsite that was defensible, not prone to flooding, and with an adequate supply of clean water. He eventually found a site with an excellent spring west of Murfreesboro.[54]

Divided Camps and False Fights

For some years the exact location of this last camp of the Third Minnesota has remained uncertain. Biographers of Nathan Bedford Forrest, historical accounts, and official reports all placed it east of Stone's River and far enough north of the Murfree House that it was not visible by a regiment assembled in line of battle or in Murfree's dooryard. Period topographic maps of the area and the National Park Service's map of "historic conditions" prior to the Battle of Stone's River (31 December 1862–2 January 1863) show forests and fields in that area, indicating that this accepted view is wrong: the spaces just do not work. Existing letters and diaries from the Third and after-action reports indicate, with a high degree of probability, that the actual campsite was west of both Stone's River and the Nashville & Chattanooga's tracks.

Captain Andrews wrote that the site was in "a moderately high and rocky grove" 400 yards west of the Murfree house and across a ravine. Other officers reported that "it was on the Murfree Farm a little to the right of the of the Nashville Pike," with Hewitt's battery nearby. "One Who Was Present" noted in a letter to a Saint Paul newspaper that a cornfield was 300 yards to the left of the camp, a fordable river 250 yards away, and an open wood half a mile away. Bowler said that on 13 July the regiment "wheeled into column, and at double-quick filed up out of the wooded valley," crossed a ford, and marched into the open field before Murfree's house. Only one location, west of Stone's River bounded by the Nashville and Franklin Pikes, fits all of these criteria.[55]

There was space available for the Ninth Michigan, the Pennsylvania cavalry, and the wagon teams, yet Lester did not order the rest of the brigade to move. Historians and contemporary general officers all assumed that a united brigade, camped around the Maney mansion (where Brigadier General Crittenden planned to assemble the full brigade), would have withstood an attack but that this division of forces ensured their defeat in detail. Deferring an analysis of combat ability until later, three key questions remain: Was there a single, defensible, campsite large enough for the brigade that had adequate clean water? How defensible were the actual campsites the brigade used? Why did Lester not order the brigade concentrated at the site he selected west of Stone's River?

On 12 July, guided by Colonel Duffield and Lieutenant Colonel Parkhurst, General Crittenden examined several sites and determined that he would have the Third Minnesota move to the vale below the Maney house, understanding that the spring there was more than adequate. This area had flooded during the recent rains, as had the surrounding camps of the Ninth, the cavalry, and the teams, and the spring still was quite polluted from these sites. Lester's choice was better, with good springs providing plentiful clean water, but the Ninth would have to move too. As Forrest later demonstrated, there were no natural defenses for the camps in the Maney area, while Lester's site had natural defenses that allowed the Third's camp guard to resist two attacks by three to six times their number. Considering defensibility, cleanliness, adequacy of water, and space, Lester's choice was the best place, giving more emphasis to the question of why did he not order the brigade concentrated. The colonel had previously made every effort to concentrate his units, the most recent effort triggering the insubordinate refusal by Parkhurst. Perhaps the answer is found in the maxim to never issue an order one knows, or has reason to believe, a subordinate will not obey.

The camps remained separated. The men of the Third fought the lice, drilled, did target practice, regularly stood guard and picket duty, and went on foraging and scouting expeditions. At the end of June, Lester was called away (there is no record of why or where to), leaving in command Parkhurst, who conducted a brigade inspection and review. On 1 July the brigade received Special Order no. 89, detaching the Twenty-Third Kentucky to another brigade and attaching the Twenty-First Kentucky Infantry and the Fifth Kentucky Cavalry. In addition, units in Murfreesboro were to be ready to march at a moment's notice, while the full brigade was to concentrate in Murfreesboro preparatory to moving to McMinnville. Parkhurst did not acknowledge receipt of this order and did not pass it on to the regiments. He may have failed even to enter it in the brigade order book or to mention it when transferring command back to Lester. On 8 July Captain Fry agitatedly queried, "have you received Special Order No. 89? . . . I sent it by mail and telegraph." Lester soon found the order, acknowledged it, sent out the appropriate instructions to subordinate units, and began preparing to move his brigade.[56]

Parkhurst, obsessed with status and his regiment's position of honor, clearly regarded Lester and the Third as threats. According to several modern authors, Lester reciprocated. The tension infected the men of the two regiments, who were often "glaring at each other" and fought "a civil war all their own on the square and streets of the town." There is *no* evidence in the extant letters and diaries from the Third Minnesota or the Ninth Michigan of any strain between the colonels (except Parkhurst's vitriolic comments) or of any fighting between the men. Indeed, the only recorded fight involving the troops was on 28 June, when Privates Roos and Sven Olson witnessed a "little affair in a saloon" between a rebel and a soldier of the Ninth. The Michigander knocked the rebel unconscious, then kicked him "in his bashful parts." The soldier then drug his opponent by the hair across the street to the provost guard for making inflammatory statements. Roos and Olson were his witnesses.[57]

Agent Owens remarked that the men of the Third received praise for their "gentlemanly and soldierly bearing" as well as for their excellence in drill and their expertise in marksmanship. Given the notations in his own diary and in the regimental records of poor discipline, courts-martial, and the arrest of one officer (charges not specified), Parkhurst had much to be concerned about in his own command. There is no evidence that the men of the Third viewed those of the Ninth with envy or jealousy or that they worried about "place of honor" or preference.[58]

When Buell considered transferring Colonel Matthews and the Fifty-First Ohio (acting as provost guards) from Nashville, Captain Green advised using the Third Minnesota or the Ninth Michigan as the successor guard unit, with either Colonel Lester or Col. John Miller of the Twenty-Ninth Indiana as provost marshal—not Duffield or Parkhurst. Planning to move the Twenty-Third Brigade farther forward, however, Buell selected Miller and his regiment. Correspondence between Buell, Green, Dumont, Matthews, Miller, and Chief of Staff Fry make clear that they possessed great confidence in Lester and his regiment. Similarly, the citizens of Murfreesboro, Unionist and rebel alike, thought well of the colonel, whom "historian" John Spence said was "somewhat the manner of a gentleman," adding that Lester could "be set down as a man a little over common order."[59]

National Salutes, Forrest's Movements, and the Return of Duffield

Throughout the occupied South, including Murfreesboro, and at every Federal post and camp, Union forces celebrated the Fourth of July. Captain Hewitt opened the morning with a "national salute" of thirty-four guns (one for each state). Speeches followed, and each unit had its own celebratory activities. Private Boxell and his fellow hospital patients enjoyed soup and blackberry pies along with other treats from local women. Private Hathaway and his relief were on picket duty and necessarily missed the camp festivities, but they "had a very pleasant time of it," with a good dinner obtained locally, and "argued the point of 'Union and Disunion' with the handsome widow of a 'secesh' officer." The locals were most displeased and observed the day in silence.[60]

Reports of roving enemy forces became common. General Negley complained that more rebel bands were becoming active in the region. Col. Sidney Barnes (in Wartrace) reported enemy troops near the Elk River bridge, and his scouts told of rebel cavalry gathering at Pelham and Altamont to attack the Nashville & Chattanooga Railroad. On 7 July Roos noted the attack on a picket post at Pierce's Mill by dismounted men in citizen clothes; one man was killed and another mortally wounded. Cavalry patrols roamed well beyond the picket lines. One group was attacked, with one man killed and two injured, the survivors making it back to camp. Captain Rounds responded by taking forty men as hostages and also imprisoned twelve men suspected of participating in the attacks. Rumors among the citizens inflated these to four hundred hostages guarded by two hundred soldiers, with the twelve prisoners to be shot.[61]

One of Governor Johnson's supporters, seeking Union protection for his cotton factory near McMinnville, informed Johnson that "Gov. Harris & the Hon. A. Ewing are at Beersheba Springs. . . . Southern cavalry are near in force." Diarist Lucy French also noted rumors of "a large cavalry force at Altamont" preparing to attack the railroad. But such tales had substance. Confederate general Braxton Bragg was planning for a joint attack with Maj. Gen. E. Kirby Smith's East Tennessee army on the Union logistics base at Louisville. In response, General Buell ordered guards on all bridges south from Murfreesboro, many with stockades, and directed Lester to provide forty-man guard detachments to ride every train going south of town. The colonel was also to report the location of every unit and every bridge guard.[62]

Miller, the Nashville provost marshal, cabled Lester of a report placing one of Maj. Gen. William Hardee's brigades in or near McMinnville, adding that his Twenty-Third Brigade would have to provide reinforcements for the Lebanon garrison if needed. Intelligence flowing into Buell's field headquarters in Huntsville, Alabama, and his Nashville rear-area base left him "but little room to doubt that a heavy cavalry force is being thrown across from Chattanooga to operate in Middle Tennessee and Kentucky. . . . I am throwing a strong brigade [the Twenty-Third], with a battery and regiment of cavalry, into McMinnville, a very important point." Colonel Starnes's cavalry was active, and Colonel Forrest and his new brigade had arrived in Altamont, where he met Confederate Tennessee governor Isham Harris on 10 July. Colonel Morgan, already operating in Kentucky, had his telegrapher tap a Union line and send a false report from Colonel Matthews that Forrest had attacked and routed the forces at Murfreesboro. Captain Green later telegraphed Fry: "I am reliably informed that a heavy movement is taking place upon Murfreesboro, via McMinnville from Chattanooga. Over two thousand cavalry, under Genl Forrest, has already crossed the river at Chattanooga when my informant left today week [sic]."[63]

The threats to Union forces were still only rumors when Colonel Duffield, ordered back to his regiment despite his protests, met the commander of the new Post of Murfreesboro, General Crittenden, formerly of the Eighth Indiana, in Nashville. They arrived together at the Murfreesboro depot on Friday, 11 July, where Lieutenant Colonel Parkhurst and the Ninth Michigan met them. Protocol dictated that Colonel Lester and his brigade staff be present as well. Earlier that day, he had provided Fry the reports the captain had requested and wrapped up brigade business in preparation for the change of command.[64]

Army regulations specified that a commander being relieved "turn over to his successor all orders in force at the time, and all the public property and funds pertaining to his command or duty, and shall receive therefore duplicate receipts, showing the condition of each article." According to an aide-de-camp, 1st Lt. William W. Williams, Crittenden and Lester had a long conversation about the state of the units, disposition of forces, the lay of the land, and the opinions of the citizenry, among other things, and that Crittenden assumed command between 9 and 10 A.M. on Saturday. Crittenden, Duffield, and Lester "consulted fully and freely," and with Maj. James Seibert, commanding the Seventh Pennsylvania Cavalry squadron, and possibly Captain Hewitt, inspected the various camps and visited all the picket posts. The general ordered Seibert to double the strength of his pickets on the Lebanon and McMinnville Pikes and and decided, consulting Duffield, to unite the various camps, with the Third moving to the vale by the Maney Springs but deferring this movement until Monday. Officially assuming command at a dress parade of the Ninth Michigan, held in the town square, Crittenden addressed the citizens. Kate Carney claimed that he said the rebels "had not a right to the air we breathed," while postwar accounts say he told those gathered that they only thought they had had a hard time of occupation to date, but on Monday he would begin "an iron rule." About 9 P.M., their work done, Lester returned to his camp, but Parkhurst and "Genl Duffield . . . went downtown in [the] evening & spent the time with great pleasure till 2 o'c A.M." with Crittenden.[65]

Meanwhile, Forrest's command late on Saturday reached Woodbury, where the men watered their horses and enjoyed a good meal. Learning of Round's taking of men and boys the previous day and hearing the rumor that the twelve prisoners would be shot, Forrest promised to do his best to free them, moving his brigade down the pike toward Murfreesboro. About midnight a vidette alerted Seibert "that several men were seen in the night between our Pickets and the town on the Bradyville Pike." Responding aggressively per standing brigade orders, the major "immediately mounted twelve men and went to the point named but after examining the fields and several houses and barns between the Pickets on the Bradyville and Woodbury Pikes and discovering no signs of the enemy . . . returned with the men to camp." By 2 A.M., the key Union officers were abed, Crittenden in his rooms in Lytle Hotel on the square, and Duffield and Lester in their tents in their respective camps. The going and coming of the cavalry ought to have awoken some light sleepers in the Ninth Michigan (or in the Seventh Pennsylvania Cavalry), but with no comments of such activities in any surviving diaries or other accounts, it appears that the men of the Ninth and the partying commanders all slept well. Only the pickets, camp guards, and provost guards were awake and, hopefully, alert.[66]

CHAPTER 5

THE REGIMENT BROKEN

O n Sunday, 13 July 1862, Sgt. Lewis Hancock, commanding the picket detail from Company G on the Woodbury Pike, was the first of the Minnesotans to have his world upended. His post, in a clearing in the cedar woods near the Keogh Place and Double Springs, was about two miles from Murfreesboro. Three men were with him as a reserve, and three others were posted about five hundred feet beyond, one guard on duty for two hours at a time while the other two slept close at hand to awaken "instantly at the least demonstration or noise." About 4:30 A.M., with considerable fog, they heard horsemen coming from town, advancing openly down the road. Pvt. Madison Barber, the duty picket, assumed that they were a Union patrol leaving since it was about the time the cavalry usually departed. Unfortunately for him and the others, it was a small group of Confederates who had moved through the woods and cornfields, avoiding Major Seibert's midnight patrol, to enter the road undetected. Hancock had to call on Barber three times before he challenged the riders.[1]

The twelve or fifteen rebels, mostly armed with double-barreled shotguns (though two had navy revolvers), were within ten yards of Hancock when Barber finally challenged them. They fired on the sergeant when he reached for his rifle. Hancock thought that he had surrendered to guerrillas until he saw his advance pickets surrendering to another squad of rebels. The Southerners marched their prisoners toward town to fool the inner pickets into allowing a "returning scouting party" to approach. After this, the captured pickets began their march to Woodbury and encountered Forrest's main body, moving rapidly west. The fate of only one other picket, who escaped, is known; presumably, most of the others were taken prisoner.[2]

According to Brigadier General Crittenden's and Colonel Duffield's battle reports, all the pickets on duty from dusk to dawn were infantry, the cavalry having withdrawn into town under Colonel Lester's unreported verbal orders. Yet Major Seibert was rousted out in the night by a mounted courier, and the rebels

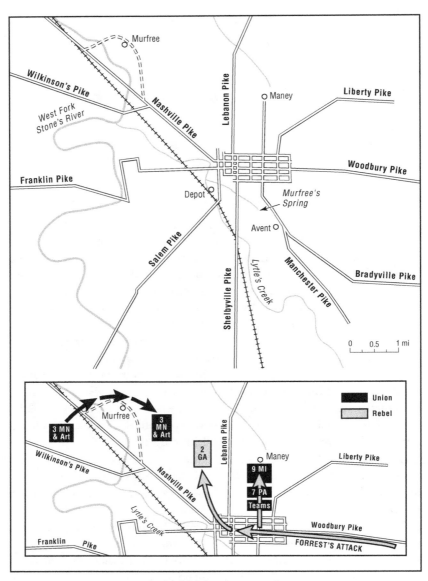

Attacked at Murfreesboro, 13 July 1862.
Map by Erin Greb Cartography.

reported capturing "videttes," or mounted pickets—meaning there actually were cavalry at some, if not all, posts. The companies of the Seventh Pennsylvania Cavalry were being issued new weapons around this time, and one source (but only one) suggests that the men of the squadron in Murfreesboro had turned in their old muskets but had not yet received replacements, which would explain their not fighting. But Seibert's report of the midnight patrol suggests that they possessed some arms, if only pistols and sabers. (Buell's staff later questioned Duffield's misstatements of fact.)[3]

The shots fired at Hancock alerted the men of the Third Minnesota, several miles to the west, who were forming up to go on duty as camp guards. Pvt. Carl Roos was up early and looking for breakfast when he heard the firing and began waking the men of Company D. Assistant Surgeon Wedge, Surgeon Butler, and Chaplain Crary, all sharing a tent, awoke to the sounds of gunshots and yelling as the men began dressing and falling into line. By the time the trio dressed and left their tent, "the long roll was being beaten." In contrast, Pvt. Charles Bennett of Company G, Ninth Michigan, awoke about 4:15 A.M. and "heard two guns in the direction of our pickets on the Woodbury Road," to which no one responded; he recalled thinking it was of no importance at the time, although firing by pickets was the standard alert signal for danger or an attack.[4]

While the Third assembled and Captain Hewitt's battery limbered up, Forrest's horsemen thundered down the pike into Murfreesboro, dividing into three separate columns. This thunder of hooves on the nearby turnpike finally roused Bennett, who claimed that he then began rousting out his fellow Michiganders. One column, mostly Col. John Wharton's Eighth Texas Cavalry, "Terry's Texas Rangers," turned north up the approach to the Maney house, overrunning the brigade teams and the Seventh Pennsylvania without a shot fired in opposition, though the picket ropes hobbling the horses delayed them slightly. A second column (Forrest and the First Georgia Cavalry) headed straight for the square to take the courthouse and jail, liberating the prisoners. The third column (Col. William Lawton's Second Georgia Cavalry, with attached Tennessee and Kentucky battalions) moved north up the Lebanon Pike to take a blocking position within range of Hewitt's guns to prevent the Ninth from retreating and to intercept any relief by the Minnesotans. The provost guard (including a platoon from the Third's Company B) took cover in the upper floors of the courthouse and resisted bravely, so the building was set afire; the blaze was extinguished upon the defenders surrendering. Citizens, several having taken the oath of allegiance, eagerly helped Forrest's men locate the officers living in Lytle's Hotel and in the houses near the square. The women were especially eager to help capture Provost Marshal Rounds, the "tyrant and usurper," who was found hiding under the bed in his wife's room; he rode out of town a captive on the back of a cavalryman's mule in his "summer underwear." A company of Texans took General Crittenden prisoner, awakening him with a knock on his door.[5]

Lieutenant Colonel Parkhurst ordered Maj. William Wilkinson to roust out each company of the Ninth Michigan and have the long roll beat. According to Private Bennett, the regiment began forming in the company streets as the enemy cavalry came up the drive, and Duffield ordered the men to form a square to receive their charge, the doctrinally proper response. (The colonel later claimed that his regiment was "formed and ready to receive them.") Unfortunately, according to Bennet, the men only knew how to form a square from either line of battle or column of march and were thus "in a huddle" of confusion when the Texans struck them. Falling back behind the rail fences before the Maney house, the infantry defended their position with vigor.[6]

"Forward, Guide Center!" The Third Engages the Enemy

Colonel Lester coolly lit a cigar and mounted his horse as the Third Minnesota (less Companies B and C) formed on its color line. He could move in support of the rest of the brigade either down the Nashville Pike (bordered with woods) and through Murfreesboro (occupied by rebels) or across country through some heavily wooded areas (the Georgia cavalry's position). Either route required that the artillery limber up, becoming unusable and difficult to defend. The infantry would have to move slowly, surrounding and screening the artillery, with skirmishers out, yet still vulnerable to attack. The colonel chose the latter route after a "German cavalryman" rode into camp on a foam-covered horse and, according to Surgeon Wedge, informed Lester that the Ninth Michigan was surrounded and that "a hard fight [was] going on."[7]

Lester ordered the regiment forward "by platoons, right wheel," according to Pvt. George Peaslee of Company H. Sgt. James Bowler of Company F recalled that they forded Stone's River "at the double-quick, [and] filed up out of the wooded valley" past Hewitt's artillery camp "into the open field" before the Murfree house. There the regiment halted on a high ridge in the center, Capt. Christopher Andrews of Company I noted, with the "line extending along the crest" and anchored in an old peach orchard. Lester positioned two guns at either end of the infantry, with the Parrot rifle positioned on the right to "have complete range for nearly a mile" toward town. Wedge added that the Minnesotans saw the enemy milling about in "a wooded tract of about thirty or forty acres" approximately three hundred feet to their front.[8]

Private Peaslee remembered that Lester now ordered, "Forward, guide center! . . . and we marched across the field towards town and within a mile." Marvin Hathaway recalled the colonel saying, "'Keep your line well dressed boys, it is the best marching you have ever done." With the second platoon of the skirmisher companies (E and F) held back as a reserve, the first platoons went forward a quarter of a mile to the edge of the timber. "Here we got a view of the rebels," wrote Pvt. Louis Littlefield of Company E. Taking cover at the edge of the woods, the skirmishers began "loading and firing as often as we could get sight of a white head—they wore white hats— . . . and were so near them that we could hear every command."[9]

Sergeant Bowler wrote that "the enemy's bullets [were] flying at us and the shot and shell from the artillery screaming over our heads at the rebels, knocking down bark and limbs from the trees. One ball passed through my coat and one hit Eugene [Stone]'s ankle cutting away his stocking and bruising the flesh a little. He fought like a hero." After some confused milling about, at 7 A.M. the Second Georgia Cavalry finally charged the Minnesotans' line under punishing fire from the howitzers and the infantrymen, the skirmishers having fallen back ahead of the attack. Private Roos of Company D reported: "A Georgia regiment got then the honor to engage us. . . . [H]ad buckshot in their rifles . . . [that] came around me like a hail storm, but did no other damage than to tear parts of my blouse as the greater part of their shots went over our heads."[10]

According to Bowler, Lester was in his proper place in the field, just left of the center of the regiment, and ordered them to fire by rank "with the same circumlocation [sic] and detail which we had become accustomed to at battalion drill." He added that he heard the colonel, who became somewhat excited, say "to one of his staff —'How like h—ll they act.'" Sutler A. B. Cornell wrote: "During the most desperate charges, Col. Lester manifested the utmost coolness, giving his orders with no more excitement than as though he were on dress parade. Lt. Col. [Chauncey] Griggs transmitted the orders along the line with perfect self-possession. Acting Adjutant [Edward] Baker rode as carelessly as though no bullets were whistling through the air. The Captains encouraged the men, who, though never in action before, presented an unbroken phalanx to the enemy, which their utmost efforts could not disperse."[11]

The Georgians' charge broke short of the line under the intense volume of fire, though on the regiment's left flank, according to Pvt. George Brookins of Company I, "5 tried to ride between the cannons & the battalion but 3 of them were shot before getting through." The two survivors were captured. Falling back, the rebels "skulked about the woods," shooting wildly, and wounding only Pvt. Albert Lewis of Company H, who was shot in the face. An artillerist had his arm shot off when a cannon discharged as he rammed home the round. Colonel Lawton of the Second Georgia summarized the action: "The enemy sharpshooters were quite effective," and his attack failed "under the heavy fire of cannon and small arms."[12]

Forrest Attacks the Third's Camp

By this time, the Texans had the Michiganders pinned before the Maney house, and Forrest rode out to find Lawton's Georgians licking their wounds. Rather than directly assaulting the Third Minnesota again, Forrest ordered an attack by about two hundred men on its camp, probably hoping to get the regiment to move to defend its equipment. This force moved north around the Third's left flank, across Stone's River, and through a cornfield to attack the camp, defended by only about thirty men—the camp guard (still on duty after twenty-four hours), the teamsters, and the sick. Unfortunately, the infantry and Hewitt's battery could not provide support to the camp defenders as they were both out of rifle range and out of sight, their only avenue of approach subject to ambush.[13]

The first and second strikes on the camp were repulsed with severe casualties. Forrest, vituperatively disgusted, personally led a third assault. Cpl. Charles H. Green of Company I, who commanded the defense, died of wounds received in the effort. Twenty-one-year-old Pvt. Walter Doyle of Company C was wounded in the right arm above the elbow, leaving him partially paralyzed (and unable to work as a laborer after his discharge in January 1863). Pvt. David Hooper of Company I, one of the convalescent sick, continued to load and fire his rifle until he was surrounded by the enemy, then fixed his bayonet and held his ground until wounded in an arm and could not resist further. Another sick man, thirty-year-old Valentine Woodburn of Company C, was shot in his bed; one of the black servants, "a negro camp-follower," apparently fired a pistol shot that nearly hit Forrest, who promptly shot his assailant dead. The rebel commander then ordered burned "the commissary's, hospital, quartermaster's and officers' tents" before withdrawing his men. During this fighting, Peter LeClair of Company B captured one man and brought him, his horse, and his arms to Lester's line of battle; James Buchanan of Company I also captured a man with his arms.[14]

According to Private Littlefield, Lester initially detached Company E as skirmishers in the direction of the camp, then ordered them to fall back to the main line. Several officers were quite beside themselves when the colonel made no further attempt to assist the camp's defenders, and some remained so for years. Captain Andrews "begged of the Col. to let him take our company [I] and go to defend our camp, but he [Lester] would not let him but sat on his horse and saw the camp burn." First Lt. Damon Greenleaf, Captain Hoit, and Lieutenant Colonel Griggs all requested permission to take a company to protect the camp, but Lester refused, explaining to Griggs that "he would not divide his forces under the circumstances."[15]

Lester sent Cornell, the sutler, dressed in a captured rebel's clothing, to the camp of the Ninth Michigan, who returned with both information on Forrest's forces and a demand from Lieutenant Colonel Parkhurst for assistance. When the firing from town ceased, Lester again "sent a scout through the cornfield to try and get news from our friends," but the man was unable to pass around the strong rebel force on the Lebanon Pike. A messenger came from the Ninth bearing another demand from Parkhurst; Lester first thought him to be a spy before being convinced otherwise. Shortly after noon, another soldier from the Ninth came in, reporting that his regiment had surrendered. Lester's refusal to move to aid the Michiganders upset several officers and men, particularly Griggs, who urged the colonel "to go to the aid of the Ninth Michigan. . . . There was no good reason why we should not have done so." Surgeon Wedge observed in 1910, "We began to feel by this time that our very popular Colonel might be very good on dress parade but was not much of a fighter." Griggs claimed that "had he [Lester] acted promptly there is no doubt we should have punished Forrest severely."[16]

These negative assessments reflect a serious failure to understand tactics. The camp, not essential to the regiment's fighting capabilities, was not worth risking a company. Any relief force would have to descend to the Stone's River ford and move through the woods, all while under enemy observation and subject to attack without the possibility of support from the artillery, whose guns could not brought to bear responsibly on unseen targets. In addition, Cornell's combat reconnaissance informed Lester that the Ninth's situation was already hopeless (thus voiding Griggs's assertion). In his after-action report, the colonel noted that his best approach to the Ninth was across fields and woods against a blocking force "too strong to attempt to push through with any prospect of success." Lester's decisions were consistently those of an experienced tactical commander.[17]

After Forrest withdrew from the burning camp, Lester sent men in to put out the fires. About 8 A.M., "K" reported, "a train of cars loaded with provisions, came in [bound for Tullahoma]." Cpl. Benjamin Densmore of Company E wrote that the men "drew rations for the day, and in fact for the three days following [from the train]," and Andrews's troops returned to camp and got "blackberries, coffee, and hard bread for lunch" from their kitchen tent. Lawton, whose Georgians had skulked about in the woods, unwilling to face Hewitt's guns, promptly sent parties to tear up the track behind the train toward Nashville, but the Union artillery repeatedly drove them off. The Georgians also made a quick but fruitless charge from the woods upon the Third's left wing. The train returned to Nashville after noon. Lieutenant Baker noted that Hewitt "fired at everything in sight and out of sight, on the town, on the now burning government storehouses, and even on a small detachment of our own cavalry," which he presumed were rebels. This detachment also returned to Nashville, where Col. John Miller, the provost marshal, informed Asst. Adj. Gen. James Fry, Buell's acting chief of staff, that

"Lester was confident that he could hold out until re-enforced." Miller dispatched the First Tennessee and five companies from the Fifth Indiana and Sixty-Ninth Ohio, together with a section of artillery, toward Murfreesboro, noting that they would "go carefully & I think reach Lester in time." Reports received by Fry in Nashville and Buell in Athens, Alabama, had Lester holding out at 3 P.M., with more reinforcements on the way.[18]

The Duplicitous Flag of Truce

After noon, Lester shifted the regiment west into the fenced grounds of the Murfee house, with the artillery in front. The position was quite defensible, an attacker having to advance uphill. He also had the surgeons remove their hospital from the house to the reverse slope behind the building, out of the line of fire, where they continued treating the wounded, mostly from Forrest's command. As the Minnesotans, according to "American Boy" (Private Littlefield of Company E) "rested on our arms" before the Murfree house in midafternoon, they "espied a flag of truce coming from town." Lester sent acting regimental adjutant Baker out to meet the flag, carried by 1st Lt. Henry Duffield, the adjutant and brother of Colonel Duffield, escorted by Forrest's own adjutant and guards. Duffield's message was "solely to this effect. Col. Duffield, was mortally wounded and a prisoner with his regiment, desired an interview with Col. Lester at the house of Col. Manning [Maney], where he then was." Baker returned, delivering the message—a direct order despite the polite phrasing—to Lester. In his after-action report, General Crittenden erroneously claimed, "When all was lost except his own command Colonel Lester went under a flag of truce to see Colonel Duffield," implying that Lester asked for the flag. Paul Scott, historian of the Eighth Texas Cavalry, and others solidified this charge in the literature.[19]

Colonel Duffield, wounded early in the engagement, was evacuated to a bedroom in the Maney house, where he remained for several weeks, furthering an existing friendship between him, Parkhurst, and the Maney family. Forrest immediately paroled the wounded men, including the colonel, who thus could write his postbattle report on 23 July, wherein he claimed that, being wounded and "fainting from pain and loss of blood, I was carried from the field, and was therefore not a witness of what subsequently occurred." In reality, he instigated and orchestrated the ensuing meeting with Lester.[20]

Giving Griggs command of the Third, Lester and Baker were taken through town rather than across country. Forrest took the opportunity to maneuver his men to make them appear more numerous, supporting Duffield's subsequent statement to Lester that the rebels numbered at least two thousand men. Entering the house, Major Wilkinson and Lieutenant Colonel Parkhurst of the Ninth and several senior rebel officers greeted Lester and Baker and invited them to join in a drink of whiskey. Saying that he was sick with jaundice and appreciated their courtesy, Baker later stressed that the whiskey was good (meaning untainted), adding that he "mention[ed] thus particularly the quality of the whiskey to refute the rumor that Col. Lester was entrapped and drugged."[21]

Lester met with Colonel Duffield, who was accompanied by Crittenden, Forrest, and presumably Lieutenant Duffield. No direct record of who said what survives, thus what may have happened in this meeting is deduced from later comments and actions. After about a half hour's meeting, Lester came downstairs from his "interview with the colonel commanding," where he refused another drink, "remarking that he 'had but an hour to accomplish what he [Duffield? Forrest?] wished.'" The reference to "colonel commanding" makes clear that Lester was acting under Duffield's orders.[22]

Lester and Lieutenant Duffield, the brigade adjutant, hastily mounted and rode back to the Third Minnesota, leaving Baker, Lester's own adjutant and executive officer, to follow at his best speed on his poor horse. Arriving at the Murfree house, the colonel quickly briefed Lieutenant Colonel Griggs and then very publicly convened his company commanders in a "council of war" on the front porch; many of the troops were near enough to hear all or parts of the discussion. It was, said Corporal Densmore, "quiet and deliberate," and the men understood Lester to say both Colonel Duffield and General Crittenden had advised him to surrender. Baker stated that "Col. Lester urged for a surrender, *earnestly joined by Adj. Duffield* [emphasis mine]," while Captain Andrews noted that Lieutenant Duffield, an active, even agitated, participant in all the discussions and votes, strongly "expressed himself in favor of our being surrendered."[23]

The colonel's argument for surrender began with Colonel Duffield's claims that the Federals were hopelessly outnumbered and that Forrest had cut the rail line northwest of town. Sergeant Bowler heard Captain Hewitt say that he had only an hour's worth of ammunition remaining, but Chaplain Crary noted that Hewitt earlier told him that he had plenty of rounds left. Official reports suggest that the artillery commander might have left some reserve stocks of powder and shells in his camp; in the December 1862 "Statement of Facts," the offices of the Third claimed each of the three howitzers had over 105 rounds remaining, although the Parrot had only 27 rounds left. Another participant claimed that the infantrymen were short of ammunition too, though the "Statement" claimed that the men, after pulling back to the Murfree yard, each drew "fifty to one hundred rounds apiece." Some officers also remarked that rations were short, though Corporal Densmore reported that the men took several days' rations from the train before it departed and had visited their unburnt company kitchens for additional food.[24]

After some discussion, the company commanders voted to continue fighting. At this point 2nd Lt. Isaac Taylor, commanding Company H, and several other officers who favored resistance ran to their companies and sought votes from the men, who all chose to fight. While they were gone, several of the fence-sitting officers were talked into giving up, so that when Taylor returned, Colonel Lester announced that the officers present had voted six to three for surrender. Bowler noted that Lester and Duffield worked hard to get this result. In this council an outsider to the regiment, the brigade adjutant Lieutenant Duffield, played a prominent, if not dominant, and quite improper role.[25]

After the vote, according to Pvt. Simon Reynolds of Company B, Lieutenant Colonel Griggs asked that he be allowed to take command of the regiment and was refused (what he thought he could do is not clear), then Captain Hoit asked permission to "call for volunteers to maintain their position." Denied that privilege, Hoit "drew his sword and severed [sic] it across a rock, declaring that he would never surrender it." The captain's men then proposed to retreat to Nashville and were promptly surrounded and kept in place, though Reynolds did not say by whom. Thunderstruck at the order to stack arms and surrender, many of the men instead broke their guns or removed parts of the locks, throwing them and their ammunition into the bushes, where they also hid their revolvers and knives. (These they reclaimed before going to Nashville.)[26]

The more charitably inclined, like "K," granted "that Lester thought he was doing the best thing he could for us when he surrendered," but most blamed him for surrendering when they wanted to fight. Surgeon Butler was one of the few who from the start accused the colonel of cowardice. Lester had earlier reprimanded him for (unspecified) unprofessional conduct, and "K" suggested that the doctor had attempted to leave the field and had to be forcibly brought back to perform his duties.[27] Some noted Lester's transformation from a cool, collected, and effective combat commander to a dismayed, defeated commander hurriedly seeking surrender, but none linked it to the meeting with Colonel Duffield. Now, so long removed from the event and in the absence of evidence, particularly anything from or by Colonel Lester himself, we can only speculate.

Several observers noted as "K" did, that "it was with the greatest difficulty that he [Lester] kept from crying as he looked around upon his men." But something the troops never knew might have helped them understand their colonel's behavior. Writing that "Genl. Duffield sends a dispatch to the command [Lester's] to surrender to Coln. Forrest unconditionally," Murfreesboro historian John Spence (who apparently was at the Maney house meeting) reflects local knowledge. It appears that no one, neither contemporaries nor modern historians, have read Colonel Forrest's after-action report (or taken it seriously). Writing to Confederate adjutant general Samuel Cooper, Forrest succinctly stated: "After some parley *Colonel Duffield surrendered the infantry and artillery* [emphasis added]." It is reasonable to assume that Forrest knew who surrendered which units to whom and when, and the only artillery and the only infantry not already surrendered to the rebels were under Lester's command.[28]

It is therefore given that Colonel Duffield had already surrendered his whole brigade, including the Third Minnesota and Hewitt's battery. The only thing needed to complete the surrender of Union forces was to inform Lester and order him to lay down his arms. This could be done by a written order carried under a flag of truce, either by Forrest's adjutant or by Lieutenant Duffield. This was not what happened. Instead, Lester was ordered to come in for a conference and returned to his unit with, for lack of a better term, a "minder" (Duffield, the brigade's adjutant), who ensured that he complied with his orders, which went far beyond merely laying down his arms. The instructions to use a council of war to obtain a surrender vote, and the presence of his brother as monitor, suggests that Colonel Duffield had some larger goal than ensuring the surrender of Lester's forces. Remember that General Crittenden came from a family prominent on both sides and had, as had both Duffield and Parkhurst, expectations of a glittering postwar political future. Surrender, no matter if came from honest defeat or from incompetence, would cloud if not destroy that future. By contrast, neither Lester, Governor Ramsey, nor the state of Minnesota have national prominence or consequence. If it was Lester's unenviable situation to stage a surrender and take the consequent odium, then the reports of his being agitated, losing his composure, and being near tears makes sense, as does the statement in his after-action report that "the matter of surrender . . . [was] derived from Colonel Duffield." This was, probably, Lester's best attempt to indicate that he acted under Duffield's orders.[29]

Surrendered

The rebel officers entering camp to supervise the surrender were as amazed at their good fortune as the men of the Third were dismayed at their misfortune. Gathering their canteens, haversacks, and knapsacks, the Minnesotans began their march to Readyville at about 5 P.M. Pvt. John Boxell of Company B went down from his room in the Union College hospital to the road to see his friends off, but only just managed to avoid having to leave too—the rebels claimed that they were fired upon from the hospital and sent many of the patients on the march, over Surg. William Eames's vigorous objections.[30]

Surgeons Butler and Wedge, who were not taken prisoner (doctors were expected to treat the wounded without regard to uniform color), gathered up the wounded—mostly rebel cavalrymen—in ambulances and relocated them to a vacant building nearby, spending the following few days operating. Boxell visited the hospital and said it "looked like a butcher shop." Wedge commented that the women brought "delicacies. . . . [T]hey did treat us very kindly, much better than we had any right to expect." Many families took in wounded men as well.[31]

Two men were killed and eight wounded while fighting to protect the camp. Only one man from the Third was wounded in line of battle, in addition to the unfortunate artillerist who lost an arm. Forrest reported twenty-five killed and forty to sixty wounded. Lawton's report included no casualty data, and the reports from the Kentucky and Tennessee battalions, if ever written, did not survive. The Minnesotans' letters and diaries and Surgeon Wedge's account all agree that the doctors were busy with the wounded until the surrender, then they were occupied treating the wounded for at least two days in the makeshift hospital in town. Their accounts of the engagement suggest that both the force attacking the camp and the Georgians who charged the line of battle suffered heavy casualties.[32]

For some weeks, the Union army had built up a supply depot in Murfreesboro, with uniforms and rations valued at $30,000 in the first newspaper accounts. Very quickly this valuation escalated, with biographer Andrew Lytle claiming that Forrest carried off about $300,000 worth of supplies and burnt some $200,000 more, including 150,000 rations. Capt. William Sipes of the Seventh Pennsylvania Cavalry later reported that 30,000 uniforms were lost. Given the lack of interest shown in this depot prior to Duffield's instructions to draw upon it once the brigade was moved to McMinnville, the $500,000 total is too high, though the $30,000 valuation seems too low. In any case, the rebels destroyed anything they could not take with them. Captain Hewitt's four guns, ammunition, equipment, and animals "became Captain White's battery" and remained in the same brigade as the Second Georgia Cavalry for the rest of the war.[33]

The forty-man train-guard detachment from Company C spent the night of 12 July in Shelbyville, eight miles west of Wartrace on a branch line of the Nashville & Chattanooga Railroad, then returned only as far as that town, where they could hear cannonading to the north. In the afternoon they returned toward Murfreesboro, the "locomotive preceded by details of men on double quick." The twenty men of the "old guard" joined them at the Nashville & Chattanooga bridge over Lytle's Creek, and after hearing news of the surrender, the detachment began their return to Wartrace. For unknown reasons, seven men, including Sgt. John Reeves and Pvt. Nathaniel Parker, remained behind and were captured by a squad of rebel cavalry, who then built fires on the span before taking their prisoners back to Murfreesboro. The guard detachment later returned to extinguish the flames, saving the bridge.[34]

The prisoners marched about fifteen miles on Sunday evening, then resumed their march on Monday, most riding in wagons, though any who could find a horse to ride did so. Sergeant Major Hale, riding Adjutant Blakely's horse, complained of not having anything to eat and of having to use his canteen as a pillow and his overcoat for a blanket. The prisoners covered a total of thirty-two miles, going several miles past McMinnville, before stopping for the night. Many men commented that the men of Terry's Texas Rangers shared their food with them, and many let the tired men ride their horses as a change from the wagons. Roos noted that his captors gave him some cornbread and buttermilk and "had shown me much good will." One guard let Thomas Canfield of Company G ride his horse while the rebel slept on his gun in the wagon. Twice the officer of the guard, thinking Canfield to be one of his men, "road [sic] up to me and ordered me to the rear to guard there but I rather declined telling him that I had a prisoner in the waggon," pointing to his guard fast asleep.[35]

While Canfield chose not to try an escape, thinking that the countryside was infested with rebels, several men did find liberty while on the march, others later at McMinnville before being paroled. Capts. William Mills (Company C) and Hans Eustrom (of Company D), and Lieutenants Greenleaf (of Company I), James Hodges (of Company K), and Taylor (of Company H) all escaped between Woodbury and McMinnville. Wearing "citizen clothes," Eustrom and Taylor got to Nashville, while Mills entered Federal lines at Tullahoma. Taylor claimed that some twelve or fifteen other men also escaped.[36]

McMinnville diarist Lucy French watched the captured men come from the west about dark. First a couple, then a couple more, the cavalry and the Michiganders, then "a company of men . . . with Gen. Crittenden and his staff as prisoners." All night, small detachments of guards and prisoners came into town, one "small detachment bringing in some officers as prisoners. The great body of the train did not commence to come in until after dark." The men were "wearied down."[37]

Many of the men made the mistake of putting their packs on the wagons before falling asleep, some thinking that they had been ordered to do so. Both the wagons and the packs disappeared overnight, leaving most of the Federals with only the clothes on their backs when they were paroled. After paroling the noncommissioned officers and enlisted men of the Ninth Michigan and the Seventh Pennsylvania Cavalry, Forrest processed the Kentucky artillerists and then finally the Minnesotans, which Pvt. James Battey of Company E said began at about 4 P.M. He added that Forrest had "ordered the citizens [of McMinnville] to have supper ready for us." The officers, except for Lieutenants Howlett, Olin (Company B), and Joseph Putnam (Company K), who were sick, were all separated off and sent, guarded by Wharton's Texans, to Knoxville and then to prisoner-of-war camps in the South. Sergeant Bowler wrote to his fiancée, Lizzie: "The officers who voted to surrender tried to avoid their men who openly accused them of shameful cowardice, . . . a meaner sneaking looking set of beings could not be found. . . . Poor Col. Lester! Sunk in one day from the enjoyment of the highest confidence of brave men to the deepest shame and disgrace."[38]

Commanded by Lieutenant Olin, their senior officer present, and a Confederate officer who was mainly there to protect them from guerrillas and citizens, the paroled men of the Third marched first to McMinnville. After eating, the Minnesotans marched back toward Murfreesboro in the rain, but "all order and discipline were at an end," wrote Marvin Hathaway, as each straggling soldier found his own food and drink and slept where and when he pleased. Sergeant Major Hale rested in a dry corncrib in Readyville, then "hired a covered buggy to carry two of us in to town, arriving in good trim about noon." The Northerners continued to straggle in to rebel Murfreesboro until Friday afternoon. Roos, hospitalized on arrival on Thursday afternoon because of blistering on his feet, ate supper at a table, claiming that it was the first time he had done so since leaving Fort Snelling.[39]

When Union cavalry finally arrived in Murfreesboro on Friday, the rebel officer left the parolees. By noon Brig. Gen. "Bull" Nelson had arrived and, Private Brookins wrote, had "taken possession of the town & is putting them through at a great rate. He is a perfect old Devil." On Saturday Nelson ordered the citizens to bring any U.S. property in their possession to the courthouse. Surgeon Eames noted that they "skedaddle[d] to the Court House with their traps. Stacks & piles of guns—cartridge boxes pistols—cutlasses officers trunks—mess kits etc. were piled with the greatest eagerness." Unfortunately, most of the Union soldiers never recovered their personal belongings.[40]

On his way into Murfreesboro, General Nelson stopped briefly at the depot in Smyrna to berate a group of men of the Third Minnesota, who had marched there Friday morning, for not having, according to Private Roos, "arrested our officers and fought on our own." Later, these men took the train from Smyrna to Nashville, where they were joined by Captain Eustrom and others who had escaped during the march to McMinnville. Arriving in their new campsite about 4 P.M., they met Major Mattson, returned from sick leave in Minnesota, who became their commanding officer. Many of the men, including Roos, took time to wash their uniforms after having sweated in 95-degree heat on forced marches.[41]

Boxell and the other hospitalized men who could walk were ordered to Nashville. As a result he could not stay with his friends, Mrs. Baird and her sister, Alice Ready, who "were in mortal dread of all kind of insult robbery and ravishment." Hiring a black man to carry his knapsack part of the way to the train stop near the Third's camp, Boxell arrived in Nashville with his fellows after dark on Saturday.[42]

Those men who had been on furlough and those who had escaped before being paroled were all kept in Nashville, assigned to other duties or units. The Company C train guards were first attached to the remaining battalion of the Ninth Michigan at Tullahoma. The sick were sent to various hospitals: Boxell went to Convalescent Hospital no. 12, where several of his paroled comrades visited him. Those men, many in sore need of new clothing, which was unavailable in Nashville, camped "near to the Penitentiary," honor-bound not to take up arms against the Confederacy, and were thus not able to help garrison the city.[43]

On Sunday, 20 July, the officer-prisoners arrived in Knoxville, staying at "a first class hotel kept by a Union man. . . . [H]ere their swords were demanded." The next day they took a train south, bound for their new home in a disused cotton factory in Madison, Georgia. With broken windows, filthy rooms, and unused boilers in the basement, Captain Andrews thought it "too dirty for a respectable hog-pen." Greeted with the cry "Fresh fish! Fresh fish!" they were assigned the east half of the second floor; Brig. Gen. Benjamin Prentiss and his officers, all captured in early April at Shiloh, occupied the western half. Obtaining shovels and brooms, the Murfreesboro captives set to making their large room acceptably clean. A few days later they received straw bedding and wood to build bunks.[44]

Lacking duties or structure to life in prison, they tried to keep busy through athletics, checkers, chess, and singing in the evenings. Captain Andrews, who bunked with Lieutenant Baker, spent much time writing his well-regarded *Hints to Company Officers on Their Military Duties,* which would enjoy brisk sales in 1863 and 1864; Maj. Gen. Frederick Steele would later compliment Andrews on the book, which embodied Colonel Lester's training and expectations. General Prentiss and his officers planned and implemented an escape attempt but were captured. Both Parkhurst and Crittenden refused to take part in the escapade, and there is no record of any Minnesotans being punished for this failed effort. Andrews noted that Lester maintained good relations with the other officers, though it was doubtful that he would have found Parkhurst's and Crittenden's company congenial.[45]

The Paroled Prisoners of War

Unlike the officers, the paroled enlisted men were returned to their own army's care. Captured just before the new prisoner-of-war cartel became effective, the troops anticipated being discharged but were instead retained in service, being ordered to the prisoner- of-war holding camp at Jefferson Barracks on the southern edge of Saint Louis. Led by Major Mattson, the men arose about 1 A.M. on Thursday, 24 July, and marched to the Nashville depot, where they waited until nearly sunrise to depart; Pvt. Peter LeClair deserted in the interim. Lacking water, the men traveled while lying "like swine" on the floor of boxcars to Louisville, arriving at 11 A.M. on Friday. Marching the three miles to the landing, they boarded the *Forest Queen,* slept on its roof in transit, and enjoyed their first fresh water and food at Evansville, Indiana, on 26 July. Roos noted that they also got plenty of whiskey, and the Norwegians overindulged. During this stop, forty-year-old Pvt. Steward Bliss of Company B deserted, only to enlist in the Twenty-Seventh Michigan Infantry. Pvt. Alonzo Briggs of Company F also deserted before the boat departed Evansville. Rounding Cairo on the evening of the twenty-seventh the *Forest Queen* entered the Mississippi River northbound for Saint Louis. The paroled men of the Third Minnesota disembarked at Jefferson Barracks on Monday morning.[46]

Steaming to Missouri, the men wrote letters home to the newspapers and to their families—many of which were printed. Most, like "American Boy" (Littlefield), proclaimed their eagerness, once exchanged, to go south once the regiment was reorganized "to redeem ourselves from the odium which has been cast upon us for no fault of our own." Devastated, their morale ruined, their esprit de corps and unit cohesion destroyed, and their pride in themselves and trust in their officers drained, the once proud Third Minnesota was a hollow shell. Mattson summarized their plight in a letter to his wife: "It grieves me to see these brave and noble men drove along like a flock of sheep and without arms and poorly clothed. They lost every thing."[47]

CHAPTER 6

RECONSTITUTION AND
THE QUEST FOR REDEMPTION

The Third Minnesota disembarked from the *Forest Queen* at Saint Louis on Monday morning, 28 July 1862. Major Mattson relinquished command to another officer, perhaps 1st Lt. Rollin Olin, and returned to Nashville and command of a convalescent battalion. He wrote his wife that the men were "wild with madness over the surrender and are entirely demoralized." By day's end, authorities at Jefferson Barracks realized that they had no room for the newly arrived parolees and ordered them to go to Benton Barracks. Coming into Saint Louis on the Iron Mountain Railroad the next day, the *St. Louis Republican* observed that the regiment was "a fine-looking body of men, but seem[ed] much dispirited by having been obliged to surrender."[1]

Prisoner-of-War Camp: Benton Barracks

Benton Barracks, three miles northwest of Saint Louis, encompassed about four hundred acres, including the fairgrounds, and had quarters sufficient for several thousand men "built of rough board . . . with cooking and dining rooms & plenty of water from [a] hydrant—brought from the river & 2 or 3 good wells for drinking." Each regiment was housed in a "block" of carefully numbered buildings, all connected by wide covered arcades "in the French style . . . , well ventilated." Sanitation was bad, so diarrhea was common. Female peddlers, "mostly dutch women," sold "principally Pies Cakes Candies & Apples Oranges." Tailor, saddle, shoe, and barber shops, along with "a shooting gallery three degerian [*sic*, daguerreotype] shops Soda Fountains [and] Book Stores," completed the facilities. A railroad siding brought in supplies, while a horse-car line ran into the city.[2]

The regiment was without officers since Lts. James Howlett, Joseph Putnam, and Olin were assigned to duties on the barracks staff; Surgeon Butler and Chaplain Crary were staff officers and could not command them. Consequently, the first sergeants became acting company commanders, the senior sergeants acting first sergeants of the companies, all of whom were to be "obeyed and respect as such until otherwise ordered." Orderly (or 1st) Sgt. Olof Liljegren of Company D, a tall thirty-two-year-old farmer, wrote his father that he was now performing "captains duty," but because no one else in the company could do the job, he was also his own company clerk. Most of the first sergeants commanding were later commissioned, with most becoming good officers.[3]

Chaplain Crary, ignored by the barracks commander, wrote Governor Ramsey that it was "mortifying to me to have rank which is a mere sham." No official definitions or expectations of a chaplain's duties existed, and too many turned out to be self-serving placeholders. Many officers treated them as obstructive civilians, though Colonel Forrest had treated Crary as an officer and thus was not going to parole him; the chaplain managed to escape before the officers left for the prisoner-of-war camp. The Third's men, he reported, "treat[ed him] with the greatest respect and generally yield to my persuasion," no doubt because he was a very good chaplain who served his men spiritually and in every other way he could.[4]

When the Minnesotans arrived at Benton Barracks, prisoners of war were not doing duty as guards or camp police since it might violate their paroles. Shortly afterward, though, the post commander ordered parolees to do duty as camp police and guards. A group of Iowans captured at Shiloh refused to comply and, according to "American Boy" (Private Littlefield), the three men in Company I who joined them in their disobedience were sentenced by a garrison court-martial "*to seven day's hard labor on the public works,* and the [participating] Corporal reduced to the ranks." He added that as many as a hundred men in the entire barracks were "in irons at one time for refusing to break their word, or, to speak plainly, for daring to be men." General Halleck, commanding the western theater, ruled that it was not a violation of parole for the men to do "guard, police, and fatigue duty in their own camps, [since it was] for their own order, cleanliness, and comfort." But many of the men, embarrassed by their "incomplete attire," were not eager to do public duty or even to take advantage of the occasional passes offered them to visit Saint Louis until U.S. Army Adjutant General Lorenzo Thomas finally authorized the issue of new clothes to the parolees.[5]

Chaplain Crary wrote Lieutenant Governor Donnelly that the Minnesotans were "discouraged and demoralized fearfully by the ordeal through which they have passed." Cpl. George Brookins added, "everything goes just as it happens & the Regiment will soon be worthless." Crary saw "no way to prevent the utter ruin of the Regiment, but to secure their return to Fort Snelling for reorganization and recruiting." A few days later the men and their commanding sergeants all signed a petition to Ramsey, asking the "Highly Respected Governor of our state" to use his influence to get them sent home until exchanged. Afterward, their health recovered, they would "fly to arms, eager to retrieve the Murfreesboro disaster . . . and show our country that the Minnesota Third is not unworthy of the proud name she had heretofore borne."[6]

Some men, frustrated at being idle and wanting to rejoin the fight, deserted the Third to join other regiments, including Pvts. Frederick Schilplin and John Pope of Company I, who left and later mustered in to the Eighty-Second Illinois, which joined the Army of the Potomac on 22 October. Their new regiment guarded the approaches to Fredericksburg, Virginia, during the battle there in December, then participated in Maj. Gen. Ambrose Burnside's "Mud March" later that winter. Sometime in April 1863, the army finally caught up with them, and in May, as the Eighty-Second fought in the Battle of Chancellorsville, Schilplin and Pope sat in the provost marshal's guardhouse charged with desertion.[7]

Other men who deserted went home, alone or in groups. Young and impetuous Marvin Hathaway, Company I's newspaper correspondent, took "French leave" on 28 July. Pvt. Robert Terrill of Company G "got mad and swore that he wasent agoing to war any longer," setting off for Minnesota without any money on Tuesday, 5 August. The next day the men were paid for May and June, financing more desertions. Musician Cyrus Redlon of Company A said that he, Sgt. Ezra Champlin of Company G, and "the bugler" left for home, wearing civilian clothes over their uniforms, on a "furlough obtained from the company cook." They passed through Chicago, despite the imposition of martial law to prevent men leaving prior to draft day, and arrived home, surprised to see so many of their comrades there ahead of them. Others deserted for love. Pvt. James McGrath of Company E deserted on 8 August and married the widowed Mrs. Welch, who ran a Saint Louis boarding house. In March 1863 he was thought to be working as a deckhand on a steamboat; the military police never caught him.[8]

Pvt. Carl Roos helped Frederick Miller of Company D desert. They obtained passes to go into Saint Louis, Roos carrying a sack of clothing to send home by express. Miller bought civilian clothes and a ticket to Red Wing on a departing steamboat. Roos remained in the city until late in the evening "in order to not alert in the Company any suspicions about his failure to appear." Pvt. Eugene Stone of Company F and other men just talked and wrote home about their frustrations, their plans to desert, and their hopes to return to Minnesota. By the time the "General Muster of paroled prisoners" was finished on 18 August, Cpl. Benjamin Densmore thought that at least 140 men had gone home.[9]

Discipline decayed. According to Private Roos, Pvt. Carl Sundell of Company D spent two days in a "a 'temple of bacchus' kept by 'ladies of the evening'" and lost all his money. Others got in trouble too. First Sgt. David Morgan of Company F wrote the provost marshal in Saint Louis on 17 August asking that Pvt. John Wilson, "confined in McDowell's College for disorderly conduct," be released into his custody upon his promise to keep him out of the city and out of trouble. First Sgt. Ephriam Pierce wrote regarding Pvt. Anton Imholt of Company C, seeking the release of the soldier, "arrested for Disorderly Conduct by the Provost Guard . . . , [i]f his conduct or his crime is not too serious a character."[10]

Men were, as usual, detached for service at Benton Barracks and other facilities in the area. Detailed as a nurse in the Marine Hospital, Pvt. Donald Gary of Company H remained there until May 1863. Several others were still on detached service in Louisville, Corinth, and Nashville. Pvt. Hadley Green of Company A was discharged because of "wounds received in the Battle of Nashville" in October 1862. Capt. William Mill's Company C was first attached to the Ninth Michigan Battalion, then to the provost-guard unit in Nashville, and later became Company L of the Second Minnesota before the Battle of Perryville (8 October 1862). First Lt. Cyrene Blakely's recruiting party that departed Murfreesboro on 11 July arrived in Minnesota a few days after the regiment's surrender.[11]

Surgeons Eames and Wedge cared for the sick and the wounded who remained in several Murfreesboro hospitals. Their black workers were gone, and no soldiers were assigned to duty, so the able patients did nursing duty until they were sent to Nashville, where they joined Pvt. John Boxell, now recovering from typhoid fever in Convalescent Hospital No. 12. He had discussed with Colonel Miller, commanding in Nashville, the process of discharge for promotion as an officer, then wrote Governor Ramsey to seek "a place in one of the new Minnesota regiments," a move Mattson endorsed, declaring "friend Boxell . . . a true patriot, a good soldier." The major suggested that the candidate go home to do some recruiting, but Boxell instead was assigned to help clean a new hospital building in the Tennessee capital.[12]

Major Mattson commanded a convalescent battalion posted on the outskirts of Nashville, his days spent "smoking cigars and talking with Colonel Ray . . . and the other officers." He lived in town and daily rode out to the barracks. The lone Swede, he felt "like an outsider among everyone" and vented his spleen on "the rich, stingy Americans who think that soldiers are dancing on roses and earning money," wishing for them the opportunity to serve in the army. Nashville was frequently cut off from the North at this time, with no mail and no supplies, as General Buell pursued General Bragg into eastern Kentucky. In Louisville, Bragg's goal, 1st Lt. James Hodges of Company K, who had escaped from Forrest at McMinnville, expected to help defend the city and supply depot, yet sharing with Mattson a strong desire to rejoin the regiment.[13]

On 9 August Adj. Gen. Oscar Malmros sent Secretary of War Stanton a copy of the petition from the Third's men at Benton Barracks: "The regiment is thoroughly drilled, well seasoned, anxious to redeem its honor, and worth two or three new regiments. Can it not be exchanged at once and put into the field?

Answer." Rumors circulated that the Minnesotans might go home to recruit or that they might soon be exchanged. While a few men were discharged for medical disability, nothing else seemed to happen. Governor Ramsey finally returned from his visitation to the western regiments and, beginning on 10 August, met frequently with Malmros and Donnelly on "military matters," particularly regarding the Third Regiment. Worried about the men, Ramsey telegraphed Capt. Oliver Green, Buell's assistant adjutant general in Nashville: "Please send Maj Mattson to St. Louis to take charge of the paroled men of 3d Regt. They are straying off. Ans[wer]." Instead, Mattson served on the general court-martial board and a military commission trying political prisoners that met for two hours daily in the state capitol.[14]

Ramsey's other pressing concern was manpower, particularly recruiting for the existing and new regiments and the pending draft. Simply filling up existing regiments—requiring 1,512 men—was very slow. Lieutenant Blakely, having posted his recruiters to advantage and offering recruits "the same bounty and advance pay as volunteers in new rents," was justifiably pessimistic about how successful they would be for the Third: The regiment was still being held in (technically) a prisoner-of-war camp; competition from the new regiments, especially the Sixth Minnesota, was very strong; and, most importantly, the state of the harvest and the need for agricultural workers. Thomas Steward, for example, refused to enlist in Company G of the First Mounted Rangers "until the crops were all saved and the plowing done." Ramsey and Malmros had difficulty explaining to the Lincoln administration the problems of recruiting in an agrarian frontier state.[15]

To meet the Union's manpower needs, Congress had passed an act drafting 300,000 men from the militia into national service. Draft regulations favored filling up existing units, offering a four-dollar premium to men joining old regiments and counting them against Minnesota's draft quota (2,681 men). Nationally, Stanton declared martial law and ordered that "any person liable to draft, who shall absent himself from his county or State before such draft is made, will be arrested by any Provost Marshal." No man of militia age could leave the United States until after his state's drafting day. Stanton also noted, "The writ of *habeas corpus* is hereby suspended in respect to all persons so arrested and detained." In Minnesota the dispersed nature of the population complicated militia enrollment. Adjutant General Malmros designated the county sheriffs as provost marshals under Stanton's order, adding: "Passes to go out of the State can be obtained on application to the Attorney General. . . . In doubtful cases a bond will be required." Meanwhile, Lieutenant Governor Donnelly informed the War Department that the state could not begin drafting men until 1 September. Governor Ramsey designated Fort Snelling (again) as the draft rendezvous for men to report for mustering in.[16]

The "Indian Uprising" in Minnesota

Events now began in Minnesota that would bring the Third home. Four Dakota teenagers killed settlers near Acton on Sunday, 17 August, then returned home to the Lower Agency (also called the Redwood Agency) to inform their parents and the leaders of the Mdewakanton band. Certain of their fate (the band would not turn the perpetrators over to the state for trial, though the state would punish the whole band until they did), knowing of Union defeats and the departure of Minnesota men for the army, and mistakenly thinking that the new regiments had left the state, the traditionalists who opposed accommodating the onrushing white culture thought this an opportune time to beat back the encroaching settlers. Thus, they began the "Indian Uprising" with an attack on the Lower Agency on 18 August, then raided New Ulm, Fort Ridgely, Fort Abercrombie, and small towns and isolated farmsteads all through the western region of the state. People fled east, some not stopping until the Appalachians; the region would remain depopulated for a decade.[17]

This news reached both the newspapers and Governor Ramsey in Saint Paul on 19 August, the atrocities multiplied with each retelling. The governor, fearing that the survival of the state was at stake, appointed Henry Hastings Sibley, his fur-trading Democratic political rival, as a militia colonel and commander of the "Indian Expedition." Though wholly lacking in military experience, Sibley proved the ideal choice. He knew the Dakota people, their culture, and their language and was known and respected by Minnesotans. The partially formed Sixth and Seventh Regiments became the core of his force, while quickly formed militia "companies" began patrolling their neighborhoods. Under Minnesota Special Order no. 20, Col. Benjamin Smith, commanding Fort Snelling, seized the steamer *Antelope* "to be used in the transportation of troops and munitions of war." Other orders allowed the seizure (with receipt) of wagons, draft animals, forage, and other property for military use; Ramsey's own wagon and team were among the first taken. Acting on his own initiative, Capt. Anderson Nelson ended recruiting for the Third and allowed Smith to appoint Lieutenant Blakely as the post adjutant at Fort Snelling on 21 August.[18]

Colonel Sibley quickly discovered the rawness of his new command: green officers and untrained men with almost no guns or ammunition, few wagons and animals, no forage, and few rations. He realized that he had "to attend to most of the work" himself. Ramsey, meanwhile, cabled General Halleck, Secretary Stanton, and President Lincoln to request the Third Minnesota, ammunition, supplies, and more troops. He also sought permission to delay the draft in his state by a month or more. Lincoln finally overrode the War Department's objections, telling Ramsey to "attend to the Indians. . . . Necessity know [*sic*] no law." The draft would happen when it could.[19]

On Friday, 22 August, Halleck informed the governor that he had ordered the Third sent from Benton Barracks "against the Indians on the frontier of Minnesota." The next day Brig. Gen. John Schofield, the district commander, ordered the Third to "repair without delay to Fort Ridgely.... The Quartermaster in St. Louis will furnish the necessary transportation.... The Regiment will be supplied with arms, ammunition and camp equipage before leaving St. Louis."[20]

The Minnesotans learned of their marching orders on Sunday morning, 24 August, but equipping them properly delayed their departure until that Thursday. Roos was pleased that they received "Austrian muskets, complete" with accoutrements. Though the men did not know it until November, they were exchanged under the new cartel, as were Lieutenants Howlett, Olin, and Putnam (for a Georgian lieutenant colonel). Capt. Emil Burger of the Second Company of Minnesota Sharpshooters, also a prisoner of war, commanded the regiment. Late Wednesday the men embarked on the *Pembina,* departing for Minnesota the next morning. On 30 August, thinking that Lieutenant Howlett had resigned his commission, the sergeants commanding companies wrote Ramsey "respectfully recommend[ing] that Private [*sic*] Benj. Densmore of E company be appointed to Quarter Master to fill the vacancy."[21]

As the *Pembina* passed Winona on Tuesday, 2 September, newspapers announced the regiment's arrival in the state. Red Wing greeted the men on Wednesday with the "thundering notes of welcome" from a cannon. The members of Companies D and E from Goodhue County went ashore, where many left without permission and went home. Carl Roos, meanwhile, "found it not as it should be, because the settlers had not treated my wife as they had promised." Many small settlements had promised to care for the soldiers' families while the men were with the army, but many, including the people of Vasa, failed in their obligations. Although the *Hasting Independent* had reported the troops coming home to "fight the merciless savages," few people were there to greet them.[22]

Eagerly awaiting their arrival, Colonel Sibley wrote Malmros that "in all probability, *this corps* must meet the main attack and that the Third Regiment being disciplined is indispensable as a nucleus and an example to the entirely raw officers and men comprising the large majority of the 6th and 7th Regiments." That Sibley continued to regard the Third as a disciplined force speaks volumes about the rawness of his other units. Adjutant General Malmros appointed Maj. Abraham Welch of the Fourth Minnesota, still recuperating from wounds received at First Bull Run in 1861 and subsequent imprisonment by the rebels, as the new temporary commander of the Third. Many of those who had ventured home on "French leave" began reporting to Fort Snelling to return to the regiment.[23]

Major Welch arrived in Saint Paul early on Thursday, 4 September, as longshoremen unloaded the "ammunition from St. Louis . . . , 55,000 cartridges,

75,000 caps," and artillery rounds, from the *Canada*. Even before the major reported for duty, Malmros directed him to take his battalion to the frontier to protect settlers and operate against the Dakotas in conjunction with "such other forces, as he may find there, over whom he is to assume command." Later that morning the Third arrived on the *Pembina*, disembarked, and "marched up Third street in splendid order." The men then boarded the *Pomeroy*, a smaller boat, for the trip upriver to Fort Snelling, where they made camp on the prairie. Late that afternoon Governor Ramsey visited them. After a dress parade (Pvt. Thomas Hodgson of the Eighth Minnesota thought the Third's manual of arms "almost perfect"), Ramsey spoke to the men. Exonerating them of blame in the Murfreesboro surrender, sympathizing "with them in their disgrace," and understanding that they wanted to go home, he called on them to "go manfully to the front, . . . [to] protect the people from further outrages [and] . . . to bring to condign punishment the savages who had so wantonly butchered our pioneer people." He also told them not to take their baggage because they would return before the onset of cold weather. The next day the troops boarded a steamer (perhaps the *Antelope*) at the fort's landing and headed up the Minnesota River.[24]

In addition to the men who disembarked at various river towns without permission, sick men were left here and there. Among them was Sergeant Major Hale, who was "being doctored . . . *by electricity*" and was unable to take the field. Returning to Red Wing on 6 September, Roos found no one who wanted to go up to Fort Snelling with him, so paying his own fare of $1.50, he boarded a late-evening steamboat for Saint Paul. At the fort he joined about a hundred men who had reported in. Most of them, including Roos, formed into a detachment bound for Fort Abercrombie in the Red River valley. Some remained at Fort Snelling, drilling recruits or working in various departments. Colonel Smith detailed teamster Levi Phillips of Company F, the first sergeant major of the regiment, as acting sergeant major of the post.[25]

From here the story of the Third Minnesota follows five different paths. First, the main body under Major Welch moved through central Minnesota, burying the dead and searching for Indians, on its way to join Colonel Sibley at Fort Ridgely. Second, Roos and his fellows were sent north under Captain Burger to the relief of Fort Abercrombie. Between these two groups, the Third fought two major engagements against the Indians, one at Wood Lake on 23 September, and another at Fort Abercrombie on 26 September. Third, men continued to filter into Fort Snelling and served there until rejoining the full regiment at Camp Release; at this point these three threads become one as the united force, at this time under 1st Lt. Joseph Swan of Company I, rode to Lake Shetek, burying bodies along the way, before returning east through New Ulm, where they foraged intensely upon the residents, who thought them worse than the Dakotas for it. Fourth, several men served in various capacities while on detached service in Kentucky and Tennessee, including Captain Mill's Company C and Major Mattson. Fifth, a number of captive officers remained in the prisoner-of-war camp at Madison, Georgia, awaiting exchange. The last two threads eventually tie back in with the main storyline of the Third Minnesota in November at Fort Snelling.

Major Welch's Command

Welch and his 270 men finally departed Fort Snelling about 4 P.M. on Friday, 5 September, for Carver, the normal head of navigation on the Minnesota River. From there they marched overland to Glencoe, arriving on Saturday. Fourth Sergeant Bowler, commanding Company F in the absence of the more senior sergeants, wrote his fiancée, Lizzie Caleff, that all the citizens had abandoned the town except for the "fighting men and one heroic woman . . . , though not an Indian had been seen there." Welch informed Governor Ramsey that, because the "teams were not furnished me by Burbank & Co according to requisition . . . , I was compelled to press them into service at Carver and Hutchison which caused some delay."[26]

Having to organize local-defense efforts and to give the people some confidence that they could protect their communities further delayed the column. "All the able bodied men [were] ready to abandon" Hutchinson, but Welch forbade it, telling them that he would do all he could to make the town secure and protect them and sending a detachment to guard a gristmill while civilians ground flour. Passing through Center City and Cedar Mills on Monday, Welch's men came to Forest City on Tuesday, 9 September. On the way the column passed the battlefield near Acton, where Capt. Richard Strout's Company B of the Ninth Minnesota had fought, stopping to bury several of Strout's men, "whom we found fearfully mutilated."[27]

The mutilations disturbed the men greatly. Such behavior was contrary to their own Christian principles and seemed proof to them that the Indians were indeed barbarians. The traditionalist Dakotas viewed things quite differently, believing that they would again encounter and fight their enemies in the afterlife. Lacking eyes, arms, and other body parts, their enemies would thus be hampered in that coming combat. For this reason, the Indians also tried to remove their own wounded and dead to prevent them being handicapped for the battles in the next life. After seeing several mutilated corpses—men, women, and children without distinction (the Dakotas also had no concept of a "noncombatant" or that women and children were sacrosanct)—and having heard reports of the rape and sexual abuse of captive white women, the soldiers developed the notion that they had to crush these "savages."[28]

Turning back south to march to Fort Ridgely, at Center City they met a courier from Colonel Sibley, bearing an order for the Third to quickly join him at Fort

The Third Minnesota in the Indian Campaign, 5 September–15 November 1862.
Map by Erin Greb Cartography.

Ridgely, having received "reliable information" that all the roving bands of hostile Indians had united near the Upper Agency. Welch led the column from Center City at sunrise on 12 September. Sgt. Lewis Hancock wrote that "the pace was rapid; there was no turning aside or deviating from the direct course except for lakes or ponds of open water. No time was given for the removal of shoes or socks; the streams and swamps were waded"; the troops did stop to bury one man murdered by Indians. Taking five-minute breaks every hour and a half hour at noon, the troops marched until dark, when "no camp was made; we just dropped to the ground and slept till sunrise. . . . We were within six miles of the Fort." Everyone expected much of them as they entered Fort Ridgely. Pvt. Thomas Watts of Company C of the raw Sixth Minnesota said, "we were glad to see them. They had previously smelled more powder than we had, and that fact was supposed to have a stabilizing effect on such as us." Sibley wrote Governor Ramsey, "Their presence here will inspire much confidence among the new material of the other regiments, and render the whole command much more reliable & effective."[29]

Writing Malmros on Saturday morning, 13 September, about the arrival of the Third, Sibley noted that several of his scarce horses had died for lack of feed, and "the men are suffering much during the present cold weather for lack of blankets, and clothing of a proper kind." He was especially short on food and ammunition, and although his supply depot at Fort Snelling finally had some of the supplies he needed, his quartermaster was unable to find enough wagons and animals to either move them forward or to support foraging from the nearby farms.[30]

Rain continued to fall, "saturat[ing] everything" and turning the roads into mud. The prairie proved little better for wagons, the conditions delaying Sibley's advance until 19 September. Breaking camp, the Third and Sibley's three artillery pieces (two six-pound guns and a mountain howitzer) led the advance across the Minnesota River at Redwood Ferry, crossing and going into camp about three miles upstream from the Lower Agency ruins. Sergeant Hancock of Company G said that the Third was "always in the advance, it did all the scouting," though Sibley had twenty-seven mounted militia who "now and then saw a few Indians." The seventy-five teams were "sprinkled along in the column," according to Pvt. Thomas Scantlebury (Company H, Seventh Minnesota), and each regiment marched in column of companies, two men abreast, with "two lines of skirmishers thrown out on each side."[31]

The men of the Third complained bitterly that the new regiments took too much gear with them, needed two or three hours to get moving in the morning, and had to stop to make camp at about 4 P.M. each day. Naturally, the veterans chose to forget that when they were fresh to the service, they too had marched neither far nor fast, even on turnpikes, and with too much baggage. Corporal Brookins of Company I wrote that the new units "threw up earthworks every night."[32] Like the press and politicians, the men of the expedition saw only slow movement, little food, and inadequate clothing—in short, the deficiencies. Maj. Gen. John Pope, exiled west after his defeat at Second Bull Run (29–31 August 1862) to serve as commander of the new Department of the Northwest and deal with the Indians, under political pressures himself, also demanded a faster pace from Sibley, who replied:

> celerity of movement cannot well take place when my troops are entirely unsupplied with sufficient rations and are necessitated to dig potatoes from the Indian fields to supply the want of breadstuffs. . . . [T]here has never been a time when this expedition has not been in actual want of indispensable articles. Either bread or bullets have in their turn been scantily dealt out, and to-day I find myself with half of the command having been two days without bread; the hard bread dealt out to them, although small in quantity, being in part moldy and unfit for use. If a provision train does not reach me within three or four days my command will be without a ration of any kind.[33]

Sibley had gathered everything he could before leaving, and he should have received the balance of his supplies on the march. Stocks at his logistics bases, Fort Snelling and Saint Paul, were sufficient for recruits in depot but not for an expedition in the field. Worse, and true of logistics since time immemorial, the troops closest to a base were supplied first and best. Hungry and exhausted men who were still learning formation marching will not move rapidly as a group. Realizing that sending untrained troops into any kind of action would assuredly get many of them killed, Sibley took time daily to allow some training. Still the veterans of the Third complained, and it was only in reminiscences in their later years that some finally admitted that the colonel might have been more right than they had allowed at the time.

After days of slow marching, the expedition camped at Lone Tree Lake—misidentified by a guide as Wood Lake—within a few miles of the Upper Agency, on Monday, 22 September. Sibley selected a defensible crescent-shaped ridge southeast of the lake offering good visibility. The troops built breastworks, dug trenches and rifle pits, and placed pickets out half a mile until dark. (There is no record of the Third's old soldiers building field fortifications.) During the night, Scantlebury noted that they heard dogs barking to the north, "and the ducks on the lake were very uneasy." The reason was that the Indians were quietly moving into position for an attack on the Minnesotans.[34]

After breakfast, several of the Third's cooks decided to supplement their scant rations with potatoes from the agency gardens before anyone else pillaged them. Company G's team led the foragers and their wagons, some driven by their civilian owners, in this "wholly unauthorized" movement down the military road to the bridge over the creek draining from Lone Tree Lake. The road continued from the bridge northeast up to the crest of a ridge, then descended gradually to the Upper Agency on the bluffs. Anticipating that Sibley and his troops would, as usual, follow the road when they resumed their march, Little Crow, the leader of the Dakota forces, had his warriors take up positions in the ravines on either side of the bridge and in the tall prairie grass on either side of the road on the reverse side of the crest, ready to ambush the column.[35]

As the foragers crested the ridge, they veered off the wagon track, possibly cutting the curve in the road, and began heading directly into one group of ambushers. The dog accompanying the soldiers began barking. Fearing being run over by the vehicles and unable to move surreptitiously to avoid them, the Indians rose up and began shooting at the party. Pvt. William McGee and the other guards sprang out of the wagons and returned the fire. Several men were wounded, Pvt. DeGrove Kimball of Company G mortally so. Beating back this initial attack, the teams rapidly returned to camp, the guards covering their retreat.[36]

Hearing the firing, Major Welch shouted, "all who want to fight fall in"; the men of the Third streaming into formation. Within minutes they were advancing at the double quick to rescue their comrades. Crossing the bridge, the left wing deployed as skirmishers, the rest of the troops in line of battle. Passing the returning wagons, the regiment advanced steadily for a mile to the north, up the slope, pushing the Dakotas back. After crossing the crest of the ridge, the Indians rallied. From his position in camp, Sibley could see the mounted Dakotas, who now appeared on either side of the Third and began moving to cut off its retreat, and dispatched one of his staff officers. The man hastily rode up and spoke to Major Welch, then turned his horse while "shouting 'Get back to camp the best way you can' and sped away as though he had just escaped 'out from the mouth of hell,'" as Pvt. Ezra Champlin remembered it. Welch ordered his bugler to sound "rally on the Center" ("Rally on the Battalion" was the proper call) to recall skirmishers. According to a postwar account, the bugler, who was from another regiment and had accompanied the Third for fun, had very little experience and blew either the wrong call or mere blasts on his horn.[37]

The reserve fell back in disorder, while the skirmishers retreated with more deliberation, "dealing death to the red skins as they pressed upon us," according to Sergeant Bowler. The Third retreated downslope along an oxbow peninsula, forded the creek, and then climbed the steep clay bank. There, the Indians, firing from the ravine and from behind, wounded many men, including Major Welch, who was carried to safety. Indian Agent Thomas Galbraith's Renville Rangers, a company of mixed-bloods from the Lower Agency, moved up to support the Third. His men took position on top of the bank to provide covering fire as the soldiers crossed the stream and fell back to a knoll nearer camp to make a

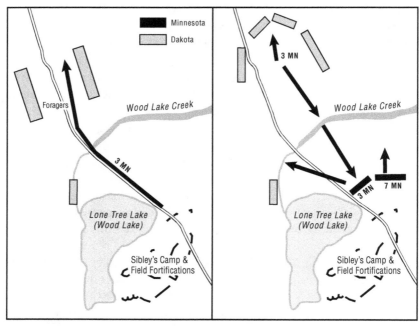

The Battle of Wood Lake, 23 September 1862. (*Left*) Foragers trigger ambush; (*right*) action against the Dakotas. *Map by Erin Greb Cartography.*

stand. The artillery was firing the entire time at the Indians across the lake and in the ravine near the bridge. Lieutenant Olin, serving as Sibley's adjutant, now joined them as their commander and realized that the crew manning the nearest gun was under fire. Gathering some fifty men from the Third, he "made a wild charge into the midst of the savages, completely routing them in our front. This charge was so sudden and unexpected by them that we came nearly to a hand to hand encounter." The reinforced Seventh charged from the Third's right to the north while the Third charged west, driving the Dakotas out of the ravines and up the slope toward the Upper Agency. Cpl. George Brookins observed the Indians retreat "out of that tall grass. They did not stop to fire but kept going at a 2, 40 gait. . . . We followed them about 1/2 mile till they got out of our reach."[38]

Sergeant Bowler noted: "Our friendly Indians fought like tigers. Other Day got three scalps and three ponies. He shot his own nephew, and wouldn't scalp him. Our boys bayonetted all the wounded, but the 7th took one prisoner [who was interrogated]." In an interview in 1894, Jerome Big Eagle (or Wamditanka), a reluctant warrior, said that the Dakotas removed all their wounded from the field of battle but none of their dead, whom the whites scalped. Missionary

Stephen Riggs, the interpreter and chaplain for the expedition, wrote his wife of his shame at such conduct, noting that the men "scalped most of the Indians and manifested very much savageism in reference to them."[39]

Only 4 of the 270 men of the Third present at Wood Lake were killed and 24 wounded, in addition to both Pvt. Richard McElroy, a paroled prisoner of war from Company I, Second Minnesota, who fought and died with Company I, and Major Welch (Fourth Minnesota), who was wounded. Because the Indians made every effort to remove their dead and wounded from the field and later oral accounts and testimony, such as Big Eagle's, do not provide any specific information, no tabulation of Little Crow's losses is possible, only that the Dakotas suffered some killed and more wounded.[40]

First Lt. Adrian Ebell, Sibley's commissary of subsistence, wrote that both Private McElroy and Pvt. Anthony C. Collins of Company A were killed, their heads cut off and scalped, and their bodies mutilated. On 24 September Riggs wrote again, saying such mutilations "exasperated our people so that they treated the dead Indians with great indignity. . . . [T]hey were all scalped, but by whom could not be found out." The missionary spoke against such actions as un-Christian while burying a fourth soldier—who died of his wounds—and "this morning Col. Sibley has issued an order against the repetition of such barbarities. What makes it worse is that many of the officers are as bad as the men in this regard." Convention, myth, and fragmentary evidence assign much of the mutilation of Dakota corpses to a few men of the Third, but Riggs's reference to the behavior of the officers (in the Sixth and Seventh Regiments) reinforces Sibley's broader condemnation.[41]

The men of the Third were sufficiently enraged, particularly the sergeants commanding the companies—Champlin remembered Sergeant Bowler, leading Company F, "roaring like a madman 'Remember Murfreesboro, fight boys, remember Murfreesboro!'"—to be lax in limiting how their soldiers treated the enemy dead. A year later, recommending men for honors, Captain Andrews specifically noted that the two who were "killed [in battle] were scalped. The fact that prisoners were put to torture by the Indians and the dead treated with barbarity seems to distinguish the valor of the wounded who returned to the field or who remained fighting."[42]

The intensity of the Third's combat derived from at least three separate causes. First, smarting from the indignity and disgrace of surrender in Tennessee, the men were looking to "redeem in the field their wounded honor," reflected in Bowler's war cry. Second, having buried too many instances of that "wanton butchery [of] our pioneer people without regard to age or sex," they feared what had happened to the comrades they left behind on the field during their retreat. Last, the governor had charged them to "protect the people from further outrages [and] . . . to bring to condign punishment the savages." The men of the Third were convinced that the "bad" Indians were indeed barbaric savages against whom the normal rules of warfare did not necessarily apply.[43]

Though armed with Austrian rifled muskets, the men of the Third thought the Dakotas better armed then they. In contrast, the state adjutant general commented in his 1862 report that the Indians had such poor arms, mostly double-barreled shotguns, that very often the balls striking the soldiers were "so nearly spent in force as to render them comparatively harmless," suggesting the use of insufficient powder charges. Archeological evidence suggests that the Indians were short on ammunition and delivered aimed fire at the retreating Third and the artillerists.[44]

Late on Tuesday, 23 September, Sibley wrote his report of the battle, the "decisive battle" he had sought to break the Dakotas. (Interestingly, Little Crow also had sought a decisive battle and thought Wood Lake the place for it, while Sibley wanted to fight on the open prairie.) Ignoring the Third's role in triggering the engagement, the colonel carefully reported the actions of each commander and unit involved, pointedly noted his need for bread and ammunition, especially for the artillery, and praised the surgeons for their "cool expertise." Volunteer surgeon Joseph Hippolyte Seigneuret, a medical graduate of the University of Paris, treated many of the men, but because he was a foreigner and lacked a commission, the other surgeons paid him little respect. The Third suffered the brunt of the casualties, both in dead, who were buried on the field, and in wounded, most of whom were cared for in camp or at Fort Ridgely. The most seriously wounded who could travel, such as 1st Sgt. William Morse of Company I, were evacuated to Fort Snelling. Morse was later sent home to Saint Cloud on a furlough to recuperate. (On 11 October he sought an extension of the furlough from Drs. Butler and Thomas Potts, the Fort Snelling surgeon, writing Butler that "as soon as I can sit on a horse I shall join the Regt.")[45]

While some men looked for souvenirs, others dug potatoes in the Upper Agency gardens since rations were short. Reverend Riggs caught some soldiers throwing books out of a missionary's home and rescued many volumes, reprimanding the men for their actions. "They were as bad as Indians" and resented his interference, Riggs wrote his wife, but after he got them to understand his work as a missionary to the Indians, "they made up good friends." Some troops found his missing mission bell and brought it into camp, ringing it often. On Thursday, 25 September, the expedition moved ten miles west across the Yellow Medicine River to camp at Hazelwood.[46]

The following morning Bowler wrote that "a flag of truce came into camp announcing that the hostile Indians had taken the young women" and anyone who could drive a team from Hazelwood, having fled west toward Big Stone Lake and leaving children and older women with the peaceful Upper Agency band at their Camp Red Iron. Forming up, Sibley's force marched over and established Camp Release nearby. In the afternoon the colonel took two companies of the Sixth Minnesota, "with music and flying colors," and entered the Dakota camp. There the Minnesotans received the captives and escorted them to Camp Release. Brookins wrote, "We found about 25 white women and children & a lot of Half breed prisoners & nearly all of the plunder." Bowler observed, "The women many of them—have been treated awfully."[47]

Guards were posted to prevent the friendly Dakotas, who had little food and depended on rations from Sibley (whose commissary was bare), from running away. The colonel wrote his wife that "unless soon supplied from below, the command will have to subsist on potatoes alone, of which fortunately there is no lack." A week later he observed, "We are pretty near a starving condition in camp, subsisting principally on potatoes." Pvt. John Wood, Company F of the Sixth Minnesota, complained that they were "all out of flour, bread and sugar so we have nothing to eat but beef and potatoes." Despite the shortages, the men found the energy to hear Riggs preach on Sunday, to drill, and to stand inspections.[48]

Realizing that only mounted forces could corner the Indians and force them to fight, General Pope decided to mount the Third Minnesota, his most experienced unit. He began purchasing 650 animals locally since War Department could or would not provide the necessary animals. On 29 September he ordered one hundred of the regiment's men working in Fort Snelling's Commissary and Quartermaster Departments relieved of duty to report to Lieutenants Swan and Blakely. Drawing what horses, saddles, weapons, and equipment available, eighty-five men finally departed on 2 October.[49]

Occasional alarms triggered the beating of the long roll at Camp Release. When the first of these happened on 30 September, Private Wood of the Sixth was mending his blouse. Donning it, he grabbed his gun and went out with the Third "in a double quick. . . . [T]he alarm proved to be a false one." Discipline in the Sixth was rudimentary, and the men of the Third also became slack, not paying attention to minor details like which regiment the man next in line belonged to. Lieutenant Olin, commanding in place of the wounded Welch, wrote Sibley that, lacking officers, "everything is irregular and unsatisfactory. Discipline cannot be carried out—as it should be." He recommended commissioning the sergeants in command of companies, which the colonel favorably endorsed in forwarding the letter to Ramsey.[50]

Although only a fourth sergeant, Bowler commanded Company F and would gain promotion unless the absent senior sergeants did some "log-rolling for commissions." Writing Donnelly that "now if I can do anything for myself I am going to do it," Bowler asked if the lieutenant governor would "be kind enough to see to that matter for me." First Sgt. Stephen Rhoads of Company G so impressed his men that they wrote to Ramsey asking that he be their captain "in preference to all." Capt. Everett Foster and 1st Lt. John Devereaux were prisoners of war, and the governor had already approved Colonel Lester's recommendation to promote Rhoads to second lieutenant. Sergeant Hancock, who was still awaiting his shoulder straps after, as he saw it, Devereaux cheated him out of them during the formation of the regiment, was quite disappointed.[51]

Many of the men of the Third were unhappy with Sibley because of the short rations, slow pace, and lack of pay, especially after several of the new regiments got their pay and bounties. Of course, lacking proper muster rolls following the loss of regimental records at Murfreesboro and the ignorance of proper procedure on the part of the sergeants commanding, the paymaster could not pay them. Sergeant Bowler, one of the more outspoken critic, asked Donnelly "what possessed Gov. Ramsey to fasten such a dog as Sibley is to the Indian Expedition." The colonel appears to have been ignorant of such criticism, writing his wife, "I believe that officers and men are satisfied that everything has been accomplished, that could be done with the very limited appliances at my disposal." In his reports Sibley regularly complimented the Third for its conduct and bravery, terming it his best unit.[52]

Following instructions, on 28 September Sibley appointed "a Military Commission . . . to try summarily the mulato and Indian or mixed bloods now prisoner." The board consisted of Col. William Crooks of the Sixth, Lt. Col. William Marshall of the Seventh, and Capts. Hiram Grant of Company A and Hiram Bailey of Company C from the Sixth as judges, with Lieutenant Olin, Sibley's adjutant and the commander of the Third, as judge advocate, serving as both prosecutor and defense attorney. By 5 October about thirty prisoners had been tried, "of whom twenty including one negro, have been sentenced to be hung." Fearing that "a hundred or more will soon pay the penalty for their misdeeds" as Little Crow's band broke up and many of his followers came in to surrender, Sibley determined not to hang any until the trials were concluded.[53]

In early October Sibley's force moved to Yellow Medicine, where the troops began winter preparations by making the buildings useable and constructing an oven large enough to "bake a barrel of flour in at once." The winds picked up, blowing "like a hurricane," according to Private Wood, who happily noted the arrival of a supply train with "sugar, flour and hard bread again and we will live once more." It also brought news of Lincoln's preliminary Emancipation Proclamation, which created "quite an excitement in camp" and pleased Sergeant Bowler, a prewar abolitionist. On 8 October Lieutenant Swan's eighty-five mounted men arrived with word that the entire regiment would be mounted.[54]

While newspapermen, politicians, and the men of the Third all focused on Wood Lake and the Minnesota Valley Campaign, the detachment that relieved

Fort Abercrombie experienced equally hard fighting; both campaigns helped in rebuilding the unit cohesion, morale, and esprit de corps of the regiment. When the *Faribault Central Republican* complimented the Third on their fight against the "red devils," the editor mostly referred to Wood Lake but noted, "We trust they may soon be exchanged, their ranks filled, and under proper officers be again sent where they can vindicate their courage and daring against the rebels." He reflected the sentiments of most frontier Minnesotans, who welcomed these rough veterans as their saviors. Though at the time the men thought the actions of Captain Burger's detachment of lesser importance, it was an arduous and more hazardous mission than the men under Sibley experienced.[55]

The Abercrombie Expedition

Fort Abercrombie, a typical frontier post without walls or bastions, lay on the west side of the Red River of the North, the better to guard the ox-cart trails north to Pembina and project U.S. power in the northern fur country. Its garrison was Capt. John Vander Horck's Company D of the Fifth Minnesota. When the captain learned of Indian attacks near the fort on 23 August, he sent to Saint Paul for reinforcements and began building barriers between Abercrombie's buildings. On 3 September Governor Ramsey responded by ordering the dispatch of a relief expedition under Capt. Emil Burger.[56]

The core of Burger's force was the sixty-odd men of the Third Minnesota, commanded by Sgt. Abraham Dearborn of Company G; Sgt. Frederick Pell of G was Burger's adjutant. Companies D of the Seventh and G of the Ninth, both newly recruited, and a howitzer commanded by Lt. Robert McHenry rounded out the detachment. Dearborn's men rejected the Belgian rifles that were first offered them because they too often lacked "locks or tubes [nipples for percussion caps]," according to Pvt. William E. Hale of Company G; as for those that had them, "the tubes would fly out the first time they were fired." Unhappy with such action, Burger inspected the guns, agreed with his men, and "promised to see that we were better armed." To their surprise, the next day "several wagon loads of all sorts of guns—double and single barreled shot guns, squirrel rifles, and long Kentucky rifles" were delivered from the gun stores of Saint Paul under a requisition by the governor. Choosing their weapons, the men carried their "own lead, powder horn and bullet moulds."[57]

The expedition began their wagon march, departing Fort Snelling on 11 September in a heavy rain that turned the roads into mud. In Minneapolis they crossed the Mississippi River on the Nicollet Island suspension bridge and marched up the east bank through Osseo and Monticello. Five days later they arrived at the Sauk River crossing at Saint Cloud, where the men "reorganized as a sharpshooter corps under the name of the 'Minnesota Rifles.'" One man, ill from alcohol, was sent back to Fort Snelling, where he died. From Saint Cloud to the fort at Sauk Center, the land was flatter and wooded, with many small lakes, and the ground was quite saturated from the fall rains. Many of the deserted houses were burned out. The column passed refugees fleeing south with only the clothes on their backs. Entering each woods, the Rifles led the way as skirmishers in case of Indian attack.[58]

After Sauk Center, they were on the prairie. Guard duty here was different as the Indians used the tall grass for cover and the soldiers had to work in pairs, "lying prone, behind a hillock" over which they could just see, and listened intently. At Wyman Station Burger's men camped with a company from the Tenth Minnesota and a squadron of cavalry, awaiting their supply train and reinforcements, Company G of the Ninth and Captain Freeman's company of mounted men. At an abandoned Indian camp, the scouts found a wagon, oxen, livestock, and plundered family items. Camping by the Pomme de Terre River, Dakotas taunted them from a distance.[59]

Indians were far out on their flanks as the Minnesotans forded the Otter Tail River. All the people at a nearby "exchange [house] for the post stage" were killed, except one badly injured woman who had escaped and crawled seventeen miles toward Fort Abercrombie. Someone had buried the dead whites but not the muti-lated dead Indians. A heavy overnight rain brought dense morning fog on Tuesday, 23 September, during which a dozen ox teams wandered off, forcing the cavalry to ride out to retrieve them. The Dakotas set the prairie afire as the expedition approached the Red River of the North, but the flames fizzled out in the damp grass before reaching the ammunition wagon. Twenty or thirty Dakotas in blue pants came out of the woods along the river—the cavalry had been unable to prevent their crossing—and the infantry went in pursuit at the double quick but failed to catch up with them. After crossing the river themselves, the troops marched another six miles to Fort Abercrombie, where they enjoyed a "well appointed" meal.[60]

Built on a steep-banked ox-bow peninsula and protected from assault on three sides, Abercrombie was vulnerable to sniper fire from the woods and brush across the river, which made drawing water and tending the horses hazardous. The garrison was unwilling to enter the threatening woods, so on the twenty-fourth, the Rifles went in, returning with several badly mutilated Dakota corpses. Alerted that evening, the force spent an hour under arms in the company street by their tents, but no Indians came; five Swedes dressed but would not come out of their tent until Sergeant Dearborn drove them out. Following an early breakfast, the men had just resumed work on the fortifications when Dakotas attacked out of the woods, killing a teamster and a horse; a bullet splintered the handle of Roos's shovel. The troops took cover in the buildings and gathered their arms.[61]

Roos was posted in a log blockhouse overlooking the river. A bullet entered through a rifle slit, passed between his arm and side, and buried itself in the opposite wall. Others of the Minnesota Rifles were, according to Roos, "real daredevils—running up onto the fortifications when they fired their shots." Private Hale observed that the men with Kentucky rifles were shooting the Indians out of the treetops into which they had climbed to fire down into the fort. The Dakotas finally withdrew, taking their dead and wounded with them; the Rifles again went out to clear the woods of any remaining Indians and then set about clearing the underbrush to deny cover. The cavalry found a large bell and plundered loot in an abandoned Indian camp nearby. Failing to search carefully before burning the camp, an undetected barrel of gunpowder exploded in the flames. Another company found whiskey in a different camp and brought it back to the fort to share. The unexpected whiskey ration made the men happy that evening.[62]

The next day the cavalry began preparations to depart for Fort Snelling for mustering in to U.S. service. Captain Burger only wanted ten cavalrymen and ten riflemen to accompany the civilian wagon train, but the cavalry all intended to go. The Minnesota Rifles collectively had no intention of spending the winter "three hundred miles from civilization" and without pay. The civilians wanted them along as further protection and offered to provide food if Captain Burger refused to issue rations for any who joined the trek. At dawn on Monday, 29 September, before this mini-mutiny became too serious, the Dakotas launched a vigorous attack cut short due to the lack of cover. The Indians quickly withdrew, "with howling and alarm, which was quite different than a victory song," taking their casualties with them. That afternoon, on the way out to a brick-making yard, the Rifles found sheep scattered in the woods by wolves and carcasses abandoned at their approach, which provided food for the first day of their southeasterly march.[63]

Departing Fort Abercrombie at 5 A.M. on Tuesday, the wagon train crossed the Otter Tail River at Breckenridge, where the troops buried a man murdered and scalped at the burned stage station. The ferry was damaged, and one horse fell onto its back in the water, nearly drowning. The Dakotas followed the column from a distance as far as Lake Chippewa. Fearing an attack, each night the "wagons and teams were corralled, women and children were placed in the inside, rifle pits were dug, and pickets stationed at a considerable distance out." Welcomed in Saint Cloud on Sunday, 5 October, some of the men got a bit exuberant and broke a door window in a saloon. They camped three miles north of Saint Anthony on Wednesday, though several men went on to Fort Snelling, wishing to see friends who were departing the next day to join Sibley's expedition. The wagon train and the balance of Dearborn's detachment entered Fort Snelling on the morning of Thursday, 9 October.[64]

That same day Lieutenant Swan and his mounted detachment arrived at Camp Release, accompanied by Chaplain Crary. Lieutenant Olin wrote Colonel Smith, noting that some of the men complained of the injustice of their position—those who reported in late "had been better treated than those who have . . . borne the hardships of the campaign." He thought the troops had reason to "feel themselves aggrieved," having trusted Ramsey's "short war," leave-your-baggage-behind claims. Many wanted to go home and help their families, who were not prepared for their long absence, let alone the coming winter. Still in the field with the weather turning colder and the winds picking up, they lacked underclothing, many wore threadbare uniforms, and—without winter gear—were freezing; only "through the kindness of the officers of the 7th Regt" could Olin get them overcoats. At Swan's request, Sibley sent Acting Quartermaster Sergeant Densmore to Fort Snelling to obtain as much winter clothing as he could and ordered him to personally report back with the supplies to ensure that he did not get assigned to the post's staff. Both Swan and Sibley attributed some of the supply problem to Lieutenant Howlett's failure to care for his men. He was on duty as Snelling's quartermaster and was thought to have taken a post on General Pope's staff. All of Sibley's field officers endorsed a request to Governor Ramsey to commission Densmore in his place.[65]

Despite their grumblings, Smith's endorsement to Olin's letter summarized the Third Minnesota well: "There is [sic] no better men if properly officered." Chaplain Riggs had a different measure of the regiment. "Although they appear well on drill and fight well in the field," he wrote his wife, "in camp they are an unruly set of fellows" due to having no officers. He thought them lacking in religion as well. Chaplain Crary's first sermon, wherein he reminded the men "of those we had left at home" and condemned their "profanity and vulgarity," undoubtedly pleased Riggs.[66]

A band of Dakotas came near to Camp Release on the evening of Saturday, 11 October; they were captured and imprisoned in the log jail. On Sunday Colonel Marshall led an expedition west in pursuit of Little Crow's fleeing warriors. He took Companies D of the Sixth and B of the Seventh, a mountain howitzer, and a detachment from the Third (fifty mounted men, fifty on foot) under Lieutenant Swan. Another column went out on Wednesday, led by Capt. Orlando Merriman, with Company B of the Sixth, ten of Lt. George McLeod's mounted scouts, and twenty-five mounted men from Company A of the Third under Sgt. Jonathan Fox. Capturing a few Indians, they quickly returned to Camp Release. Marshall's men stayed in the field.[67]

During their first night out, Marshall's men had neither food nor feed for their horses. On the second day their supply train caught up with them, bringing rations for six days, forage for two (all that Sibley could find), tents, and ammunition. By the third day they ran out of crackers and had no wood for fires. After a cold, frosty night, they captured a Dakota camp, the warriors surrendering when the soldiers did not kill the women and children. The Indians had flour, and taking two sacks, the troops made flour-and-water pancakes. After this feast, Marshall left a guard on the captives and set out after another band ten miles away, capturing and bringing them back. That night the men dined on an Indian's ox.[68]

Crossing the Lac qui Parle River, the detachment entered Dakota Territory near mile post twenty-six on the edge of the Coteau des Prairie, a flat highland that rises to nine hundred feet and stretches some two hundred miles, then marched northwest, paralleling the Coteau. As they encountered Indians, they took the men prisoner and sent the women and children to Camp Release without an escort. Learning that "27 lodges [were] near Two wood or Chou-on-pa Lake" three days earlier, Marshall took the mounted men and the howitzer in pursuit, leaving the infantry and his supplies to come on as fast as they could. Surprising a camp of ten lodges, the Minnesotans captured thirteen warriors and families, then moved on and captured the other twenty-one men of this party.[69]

Back at Camp Release, the troops built fireplaces in their cabins in preparation for winter. On Friday, 17 October, another supply train came in, though without mail. Lieutenant Blakely led another mounted detachment of the Third into camp, each man leading an extra horse. Companies A, C, and K were mounted, and the lieutenant took command of the regiment. A few days later a company of the Eleventh Minnesota came in with more horses for the Third. Though still sick, Sergeant Major Hale accompanied them, riding in a wagon, and complained thereafter that the food was monotonous, consisting of a steady diet of potatoes and beef; when the salt ran out, the cooks tried making biscuits that he described as "most ruinous to all digestive powers save those of an ostrich."[70]

In most states, enlisting meant giving up one's right as a citizen to vote, but after considerable debate the Minnesota legislature passed a law on 27 September allowing its soldiers to vote and providing commissioners to accept those ballots in the field. Sergeant Bowler cast his soldier's vote on 20 October, most likely in support of his friend and neighbor Ignatius Donnelly, who was a candidate for Congress. Most of the men supported Republican candidates, though there were some Democrats in the ranks.[71]

No voting commissioners visited Colonel Marshall's command; it was still heading west, moving to within thirty-five miles of the James River in what is now North Dakota. Returning to Minnesota, they endured days of hard marching and flying dust. On their last day out, the weather shifted suddenly, the morning turned "freezing cold" with high winds, and the troops marched over twenty miles. Cpl. George Brookins wrote his brother that he "suffered more with the cold that day then I did any day last winter in Ky. We have no under clothes. . . . We could not walk fast enough to keep comfortable. It was so cold that we did not stop at all in the whole distance but kept walking till night. Water froze all day long." The detachment entered Camp Release about noon on 21 October, with

389 men prisoner and only 100 women and children, most of the others having been sent ahead. The entire expedition suffered from the cold and especially the winds. Tents were blown down, cook fires went out, dirt flew everywhere, and the animals were starving and "nearly worn out by incessant labor."[72]

With no reason to keep the troops out on the prairie, Sibley determined to move back to the Lower Agency, which the men welcomed with cheers and the firing of the twenty-four-pound cannon. Bowler wrote Lizzie of his hopes, shared by many of the others, for a furlough and a "piece of good bread with butter on it, a good cup of tea in a clean cup and saucer on a clean tablecloth, with kind friends and pleasant faces to meet my gaze." He added that he felt out of place in a building, and "to shake hands with, or to speak to, one of the feminine gender would be very much like an elephant walking on eggs." The men posted at the agency, meanwhile, had become quite comfortable, having acquired furniture, dishes, and the appurtenances of home, expecting to be there until the "trial & execution of the savages was accomplished."[73]

On the eve of departure, the men continuously rang Rigg's large bell and enjoyed the warmer weather until a "cold northwester" came up, blowing down tents, and the temperature plummeted. Despite the weather and "a strong line of sentinels entirely around my camp," Sibley noted that he had "the greatest difficulty in keeping the men from the Indian women. . . . [S]ome way or other, a few of the soldiers manage to get among the *gals,*—and the latter, I notice, take care not to give any alarm."[74]

Sergeant Dearborn's Fort Abercrombie detachment settled in at Fort Snelling on Thursday, 9 October. Roos had time to write his friend Carlson, who was managing his family's finances, authorizing him to pay his wife twenty dollars in cash, not "town orders," the citizens of Vasa having failed again to help the soldiers' families. Swept up into the routine of post activity, the new arrivals stood guard, the night of the tenth they reported being "unusually cold." The next day Roos washed his lice-ridden clothing for the first time since 29 September, and on Sunday the Scandinavians listened to the Reverend Lindquist's sermon.[75]

Dearborn's detachment, "transformed into cavalry" with two horses per man, left Fort Snelling in the late afternoon of 17 October, crossing the Minnesota River to Mendota (on Sibley's ferry), they moved down the west side of the river through Shakopee and Belle Plaine before recrossing to enter Saint Peter on the evening of 20 October. Each night was colder than the previous one, and Roos, at sixty, felt his age and every mile his pony had traveled as they entered Fort Ridgely before noon on 22 October. The next day the group passed through the lower reservation, a region Roos thought quite beautiful. At the Lower Agency, Softus Rasmussen, a forty-one-year-old Dane whom the Swedes had treated very badly, switched to the Norwegian tent and invited Roos to join him.[76]

The Regiment Reunited

Sibley moved his command and his prisoners to the Lower Agency, in doing so also reuniting the Third Minnesota. Captain Mills and Company C had arrived in Saint Paul on the *McClellan* on 16 October and reported to Fort Snelling. After a few days there, the company moved west to join Sibley's force. By 27 October only the exchanged officer-prisoners, who were now furloughed; the men on detached service, such as Major Mattson; and a few recalcitrant takers of "French leave" were absent. Lieutenant Olin and the military tribunal at Camp Release continued their hearings, convicting most of the accused, whom Roos described as "tall and well-built men, many half-breeds among them." Roos added that most of the soldiers spent their off-duty time "plundering . . . the Indian shanties and decorating themselves with the finery left behind."[77]

Colonel Sibley sent Lieutenant Blakely to Saint Paul to obtain the books and forms necessary for mustering and paying the regiment, including the "possession of the Books of the Regiment understood to have been recovered." Company B's record of events for August 1862 at Benton Barracks includes the following tantalizing note: "Paroled prisoners . . . arrived at Benton Barracks. . . . Company books and papers mostly saved." If these were the books Blakely sought, he did not obtain them, returning only with blank books and forms.[78]

Both men and horses rested for several days before the regiment received orders to "march toward the Indians" who were reported to have massacred settlers near Lake Shetek and to be moving west toward the Coteau des Prairie. This punitive expedition, 450 mounted men and twenty-four wagons commanded by Lieutenant Swan, departed in bitter cold weather on Thursday, 30 October. After marching twenty-five miles up the Redwood River toward the German farming settlements around Lake Shetek, the main body turned south, while a small group continued up the Redwood to Lyons Trading Post before turning for the lake. The Dakotas had fired the prairie, and the wind blew dirt and soot into the troops' faces, making their march more miserable.[79]

At Lake Shetek the regiment first camped between three lakes and a creek, where the troops could harvest hay and corn for their animals. Slaughtering some of the loose livestock, the men nicely supplemented their hard crackers. In one plundered house they found the absent family's bible opened "on a manure hill," and Roos recorded that at nearly every dwelling they "found the house's dog lying killed" and became very familiar "with the Indian's method of slaughter, which was precisely as wild animals do." After several days they shifted camp to another creek and buried more settlers. Company F of the newly raised Twenty-Fifth Wisconsin joined them at this time, and also set about burying the dead. Two companies of the Third were sent in pursuit of the perpetrators. The troops rode two days past the Pipestone Quarry, going thirty miles into Dakota Territory, before turning back because their horses were giving out, unable to subsist on frost-killed prairie grasses. Brookins noted that the men returned with a fair amount of pipestone and were busily "carving pipes and rings."[80]

Having buried all the bodies they found, on Friday, 7 November, the Third marched to New Ulm, making camp on the edge of town about 2 P.M. That once-thriving community was now mostly burned, littered with decaying animal carcasses from the Dakota attacks in August, and was inhabited only by the "lowest class . . . such as whiskey sellers & gamblers." Garrisoned by Companies F of the Eighth Minnesota and I of the Twenty-Fifth Wisconsin, the post was commanded by the Twenty-Fifth's major. Chaplain Crary had ridden ahead of the regiment, and at his urgings the saloons were closed. After their hard, gruesome duty on quarter rations, the men thought this an injustice.[81]

The soldiers lacked money, and no one was willing to provide feed for their horses, so they broke into the storage buildings and took what feed they needed. Having cared for their horses and pitched their tents, the men liberated poultry for supper and then sought refreshments. The owner of the Dakota House was the first to open for the soldiers, selling whiskey at ten cents a shot. When he realized that they could not or would not pay, he tried to close up, but the men, according to Roos, "helped themselves, and since the space did not allow everyone to participate, keg after keg was carried out, along with whisky, until the saloon's inventories of the wet variety were completely plundered and the doors and windows destroyed. A store and several other houses were then [plundered] for food and other small knick-knacks." Intoxicated men rode their horses through town, fired shots, and paid no attention to either Lieutenant Swan or Chaplain Crary. The next morning one of the soldiers thanked the citizens for "the kind treatment that they had received" and hoped that they could return to enjoy more of New Ulm's hospitality.[82]

General Pope initially planned to keep the Third on the frontier over the winter and ordered its battalions to take station at Fort Ridgely, Hutchinson, and Saint Peter. After crossing the Minnesota River, one battalion headed west for Fort Ridgely, while the other two went east, arriving in Saint Peter that afternoon. A small squad, an "advance guard," rode ahead, hoping to repeat the fun of New Ulm. But Capt. A. K. Skarr, the provost marshal and a no-nonsense veteran of First Bull Run, was ready for them; there were no incidents. At Saint Peter they and their horses rested, but the men had to "steal corn from fields at great distances" to feed the animals. Roos got his seven-year-old "devil to ride on" mare shoed and then swapped her for a "smaller, pretty animal, a pleasure and joy to ride on." Lieutenant Liljegren celebrated his commissioning by buying beer for Company D. When Quartermaster Densmore arrived with wagons loaded with clothing, he was surprised to find the troops there rather than at the Lower Agency.[83]

The battalion sent to Fort Ridgely arrived there on Saturday and began to settle in to the barracks. On Wednesday, 12 November, they were ordered to march for Saint Peter to join the regiment, turn in their horses, and prepare for a foot march to Fort Snelling. General Pope had decided to send the Third south as soon as possible. The battalion left that afternoon, covered eight miles in bitter cold and a stiff north wind, and made a "comfortable camp" in a deep ravine. The men made the thirty-seven miles to Saint Peter the next day. Here, they learned that they would keep their horses for the journey to Fort Snelling. The whole regiment set out on Friday, 14 November, for Henderson, where the men had to sleep under the stars, their blankets becoming covered with snow, because the townsfolk would not let them take quarters in public buildings. At Carver the citizens welcomed them more warmly, and Roos happily slept in a saloon. During their last day out, a foot of snow fell, and Captain Mills treated them to beer at one stop.[84]

The Regiment at Fort Snelling

The veterans' entry into Fort Snelling shocked the recruits there. Pvt. Thomas Stewart, a newcomer to the Minnesota Mounted Rangers, admitted that his ideas of discipline and troop movement "suffered quite a tumble" as the "rather lawless" small groups of the Third, whooping and hollering and "togged out in full Indian . . . headgear," arrived. Assigned quarters in the stable area, the men cared for the animals one last time, then at least some, according to Roos, "were treated by our friends . . . to whiskey," which did not improve their respect for authority. Only Company C had its payroll in proper order and got paid on Thursday, 20 November, then departed on leave, while the rest of the companies had to report to Maj. James Phinney's office in Saint Paul the next morning. Companies B and K, first in line, received their pay. Company E was also paid, though the record is silent as to when and by whom. At that point the "money suddenly gave out," as the paymaster found that he had only $500 and $1,000 bills on hand, and no bank in the city would exchange them for smaller bills.[85]

The six unpaid companies were now without quarters, rations, or money. Expecting them to leave on furlough, the fort quartermaster had reassigned their quarters and terminated their rations. The authorities told the men that they would be paid when they rendezvoused at Winona before heading south. Hungry, homeless, and broke, they had no means to get home and responded to this insult by raising "the red flag," according to Roos, and "marched through the streets [with] screams and threats, . . . went into and out of stores, took lashes and horsewhips and demanded free drinks from the saloons" congregated along Third Street, threatening to attack Pope's and Phinney's offices in the International Hotel located there. When the general called out the Seventh Minnesota, the soldiers refused to intervene and arrest the men of the Third. Lieutenant Colonel

Griggs finally came out and talked to the men, promising them their pay and leave if they would only go back to Fort Snelling and be patient for a few more days. Because there was no room that night at the fort, most of the troops found places to stay in Saint Paul. Roos spent time discouraging the martial aspirations of his thirteen-year-old son, Emil, a broom-maker's helper, who was eager to join the regiment as a drummer boy. Within a few days, Pope gave each man a "general furlough for an indefinite length of time," and the paid-off soldiers went home to parties, dances, and other festivities. Some twenty men and Lt. Edwin Hillman of Company C did not get the news and reported at Winona after their fifteen-day furloughs, only to be sent back home.[86]

The *Pioneer and Democrat* was sympathetic to the soldiers' plight, but the other capital city newspapers were hostile. The *Daily Press*, Ramsey's paper, denounced their "rioting and other disorderly conduct," while the *Daily Union* accused the Third of treating the residents worse than rebels in an occupied city. Saying that "they reconnoitered the grocery and whiskey shops in force, and *foraged upon them* extensively," the paper concluded, "We have heard of the insubordination of the Third Regiment before, but we had a practical illustration of it yesterday." When Sergeant Densmore's twelve-year-old brother, Orin, wrote that "the St. Paullites hate the Third and the Third hates St. Paul," he may well have been correct.[87]

By Sunday, the unpaid men were again enjoying quarters and rations at Fort Snelling; Roos complained of the heat from the stove in his room. The men had no duties to keep them busy, so many roamed the streets of the two cities, some getting into smaller or larger mischiefs. The newspapers reported both fact and, especially, rumor of every misbehavior; everything was the soldiers' fault, particularly any offense against the Indians encamped nearby.[88]

Private Stewart of the First Mounted Rangers, said that the Dakotas were "threatened repeatedly with attack by citizens of the cities" and "were rather shy of civilians as they went through camp, for they did not know but that the civilians came there for the purpose of shooting them." To protect these families, Colonel Marshall moved their camp from the prairie west of Fort Snelling down to the river flats below the bluffs, where they were out of the wind and within the post's picket lines. The Indians had no fear of the soldiers, and Private Wood of the Sixth Minnesota noted that "there was some fine looking indian girls among them or rather half bread [sic] they was more or less white." Historian Stephen Osman has noted that the "St. Paul newspapers . . . [made] veiled references to unexpected pregnancies among Dakota girls and an increase in sexually transmitted diseases in the Fort Snelling garrison."[89]

The papers excitedly reported on all real or rumored crimes committed against the captive Dakotas, usually placing the blame on soldiers. In the instance of the shooting of a Dakota woman by soldiers doing target practice, the *Daily Union* claimed that she was first "seized by a number of soldiers and brutally outraged." The *Minnesota State News* commented: "We have no sympathy with the semi-savage, brutally revengeful feeling, which seems to be exhibited towards the helpless prisoners held at Fort Snelling. . . . Yet within the last ten days, a squaw has been shot, and an Indian man has had his throat cut. The *Pioneer* relates with a species of brutal exultation that the latter was interred 'in an orifice in the earth face downward.'" On 4 December the *Weekly Pioneer and Democrat* reported that Colonel Marshall "informs us that the reports of Indians having been killed at Fort Snelling by soldiers are entirely destitute of truth." In the only known such incident, a woman had indeed been "subject to an infamous outrage," having "strayed some distance from the Fort" beyond the picket lines, thus an act most likely committed by civilians rather than soldiers. Truth was irrelevant; the Third was and remains blamed for both the imagined and the lone real incident.[90]

Lt. Joseph Putnam of Company K was finally relieved of duty at Benton Barracks and arrived at Fort Snelling, where Colonel Smith detailed him as post adjutant on 14 October. Major Mattson remained on the court-martial board in Nashville until late November, despite pleading by Ramsey to have him return to Minnesota to command the regiment. Only after the governor and Malmros wrote Adjutant General of the Army Thomas that they wanted Mattson to help reorganize the Third was he finally ordered home, arriving in early December. (Captain Rice, on detached service with the general court-martial board since April 1862, remained there until February 1863.) In September Ramsey had first asked Stanton what he could do to provide at least temporary officers for the Third. Adjutant General Thomas finally replied on 15 October that Stanton had authorized the appointment of officers, but that "when original officers are exchanged one set will then be mustered out." Having already determined to commission the sergeants commanding the companies before all others, the governor announced their appointments, with most taking the oath between 1 and 11 November; 1st Sergeant Morse was delayed in doing so until 1 December.[91]

The officers held as prisoners of war were exchanged on 24 October, but most did not arrive in Minnesota until just before the pay riot. Captain Andrews wrote that they had ridden cattle cars from their prison in Madison, Georgia, to Salisbury, North Carolina, then boarded railroad coaches and arrived in Richmond, Virginia, on 12 October for incarceration in Libby Prison. Upon exchange, the officers went under flag of truce on the U.S. steamer *John A. Warner* to Fortress Monroe, then by sea to Annapolis, Maryland. In Washington, D.C., they received their pay and a furlough. Lieutenant Colonel Parkhurst wrote that he and Brigadier Generals Crittenden and Prentiss visited the War Department on 16 October and then "called upon President Lincoln. . . . [H]e is quite ugly & inferior looking." Most of the officers traveled together to New York before going their separate ways: Colonel Lester went to Geneseo in western New York; while Lieutenant Colonel Griggs and Captain Andrews visited family in New England. Lieutenant Devereaux returned to Minnesota on 23 October, the *Daily Press* observing that his "experience of Southern hospitality has not increased his affection for rebels."[92]

Most of the exchanged officers reported for duty in Saint Paul by 23 November. The enlisted men made their feelings clear. Like Sergeant Major Hale, they "were glad enough to meet most" of them, but they would not serve under officers who had voted for surrender, thus giving them "a terribly cool & insulting reception." The *Winona Daily Republican* reported that Lester said he intended "to demand an investigation" to clear both his name and the regiment's so both could "emerge triumphantly from the disgrace which certain interested parties have skillfully and persistently attempted to heap upon" them. "S" wrote the editor of the *Pioneer and Democrat* to say that the men would read what Lester had to say, but until then they would act on "what we know of his connection," concluding that Lester should resign.[93]

Reorganizing the Regiment

Governor Ramsey telegraphed Adjutant General Thomas on Friday morning, 5 December, asking that the army accept the resignations offered by Lester and the captains. That afternoon he received a copy of War Department Special Orders no. 371, dated 1 December, announcing the dismissal, by verbal order of the president, of Colonel Lester, and Capts. Mark Clay, Clinton Gurnee, John Preston, William Webster, and—to everyone's surprise—William Mills. Lts. Adolphus Elliot of Company A and Isaac Tichenor and Samuel Ingman of Company F were also dismissed (though since they had no vote, the grounds for dismissal remain unknown). Captain Hewitt of the Kentucky battery, who also had voted for surrender, was not dismissed, thus raising questions about motives and process.[94]

Soon after returning to Saint Paul, Griggs, Andrews, and Hoit jointly wrote General Pope, recapitulating what they termed as Lester's failure to support the Ninth Michigan "to advance on the enemy" or to protect the supply depot from destruction (revealing their continuing failure to learn to think tactically). Hearing rumors of this letter, Captain Gurnee denounced the secret missive and requested from Stanton a "court of inquiry into the conduct of officers of regt at Murfreesboro." Joined by other paroled officers, Andrews's group sent "A Statement of Facts Concerning the Surrender" to Malmros and Ramsey, wherein the signers claimed that the Third Minnesota did nothing but stand about, repeating the official interpretation and flatly contradicting their own experiences. Someone also began a whisper campaign among the enlisted men against Major Mattson, who had been absent from the regiment on sick leave at the time and was still on duty in Nashville. The resulting lack of support prevented his being promoted to lieutenant colonel to the benefit of Andrews.[95]

The army ignored Gurnee's request for a court of inquiry as well as a joint request from Company F's officers. There is no record of Lester requesting a court; if he did, it was also ignored. In August 1866 Sen. David Nelson wrote Stanton asking that the order of dismissal be revoked so that the December 1862 resignations could be accepted. The secretary of war refused. In 1891 Captain Clay managed to obtain a copy of the charges against him, then wrote Sen. William Washburn, who endorsed his request, asking for a copy of the charges against all of the officers. Redfield Proctor, secretary of war by that time, refused to provide this, citing the "dangers of releasing evidence which could be used against parties." He added that Clay's knowing who had signed the Griggs letter "might operate to their prejudice." Proctor apparently thought that the official history could not stand any serious examination.[96]

Most people assumed that Griggs would become the new colonel, Mattson the lieutenant colonel, and until his surprising dismissal, that Mills would become major in a reorganized Third Minnesota. "Citizens of Goodhue County" sought a colonelcy for Mattson, while other groups wanted him promoted lieutenant colonel. Ramsey endorsed one such recommendation: "Mjr Mattson is recognized as a deserving officer." When the officers met at the American House in Saint Paul, with Griggs in the chair, they passed a unanimous resolution, "Maj Mattson to remain with us as Major of the Regt." Mattson, in turn, graciously moved that, because of "his opposition to the surrender," Andrews be named the lieutenant colonel. The motion passed unanimously. Mattson, though thought deserving, was not "Yankee"—otherwise this travesty of protocol would not have happened. Governor Ramsey duly commissioned Griggs as colonel and Andrews as lieutenant colonel while Mattson remained the major.[97]

The dismissed officers thus were replaced. The resulting promotions opened the second lieutenancies to the newly commissioned first sergeants. Writing his father in Sweden, Liljegren told him of their lack of pay, the likelihood of their going south, and, almost as an afterthought, his being commissioned an officer—in class-conscious Sweden the Liljegrens could not have dreamed of such a thing. Second Lt. Francis McDonald had commanded Company H from Benton Barracks until it assembled at Fort Snelling to go south; Captain Rice remained on duty with the general court-martial board in Nashville, 2nd Lt. David Misener was still visiting family in the East, and 1st Lt. Isaac Taylor had gone "home to await the current of events." After reorganization, however, McDonald became supernumerary, and although he was considered deserving of a better position, none could be found; he was honorably dismissed from the army. There is no record of his being paid for his service.[98]

Not everyone was happy with the promotions. The *Rochester City Post* reflected the unhappiness in Company K over the appointment of Hiram Gates (of Saint Paul) as its lieutenant. Though the *Post* thought several of the company's sergeants qualified for promotion, every colonel viewed them as inadequately prepared for commissioning, largely because Captains Clay and Hodges were usually absent on detached service and unable to properly train them. In Company F, where all the officers were dismissed, 2nd Lieutenant Bowler, formerly fourth sergeant, now became captain. Otto Dreher, formerly Company A's first sergeant, became the first lieutenant, while Sergeant Morse of Company I became the second lieutenant. First Sergeant Morgan and the other sergeants of the company were all passed over, leading to serious disciplinary problems.[99]

The whole regiment was last paid on 17 June, and the *Pioneer and Democrat* rightly observed that many of the soldiers' families were nearly destitute. Ramsey was a good war governor who did his best to take care of his troops. He worked to move Washington and Saint Louis to get the men paid, telegraphing the entire state congressional delegation repeatedly, as well as Secretary Stanton, General Halleck, and the U.S. Army paymaster for funds, but all to no avail. Though Capt. Thomas Saunders, the U.S. disbursing officer in Saint Paul, had sufficient small bills on hand, he could not make those available to Major Phinney to pay the Third without authorization, which did not come. In the end the money had to be sent from Washington, and the six companies did not receive their pay until just before they departed Winona for the South.[100]

Before leaving on furlough, the sixty-three men of Company G received their pay, less 10 percent, and gave the bankers power of attorney to collect their funds. Company I made similar arrangements, and each man received four months' pay by express. The other companies made no such arrangements, and an officer or first sergeant had to remain behind in Minnesota to collect their pay, which proved to be a futile effort. The *Daily Union* criticized the government for making the soldiers "lose largely to get partial payment" and noted that the proprietor of the Minnesota House in Saint Paul, who had taken in the homeless and unpaid soldiers for the night, was finally paid.[101]

On Thursday, 4 December, some two hundred men of the Third enjoyed a "sumptuous complimentary dinner" served by the women of Minneapolis. Lacking money, Roos languished at Fort Snelling until Major Mattson found him, loaned him five dollars, and took him to Red Wing in his own carriage. On 13 December Roos celebrated the Lucia Festival with "Old Man Mattson." Another evening, the soldiers of Company D enjoyed "a drunken party . . . at the school house." They properly waked Pvt. Halfer Eklud on 5 January 1863 "with a robust party," and on Twelfth Night at Mistress Williard's, they "had much enjoyment of dancing and games." There were festivities at Stillwater, Rochester, and Mankato, while Lake City hosted a New Year's Ball for the soldiers; often the whole regiment was invited to these events.[102]

A few men spent their entire furlough at Fort Snelling. Watching recruits drill or "rats as large as half grown kittens" leap out of newly opened flour barrels to attack the cooks quickly diminished in interest. Skating down the river to Mendota or Saint Paul to visit friends or saloons was more reliably popular. Pvt. Chauncey Gibbs of Company G was accused of picking Charles Hackett's pocket and was pursued to Red Wing, where he was arrested and returned in manacles to Saint Paul; the justice of the peace ruled that the charges were not substantiated. Even visiting Minneapolis could be hazardous. One soldier, Pvt. Warren Lincoln of Company A, defended a citizen attacked by "Irishmen" and was beaten for his trouble; he later died of his injuries. This began a running series of fights between soldiers and Irishmen.[103]

Assured that the remaining six companies would be paid, General Pope ordered the regiment to assemble on 10 January 1863 and go south. Colonel Griggs ordered that Companies A, B, D, F, H, and I, Surgeon Butler, and the noncommissioned-officer staff report at Fort Snelling, while Companies C, E, G, and K, Surgeon Wedge, and Major Mattson report to Lieutenant Colonel Andrews at Winona. Lieutenant Howlett, the regimental quartermaster, made all the arrangements for transport, quarters, and subsistence. The men traveled without arms, accoutrements, or equipment, all of which had already been turned over to the officials at Fort Snelling.[104]

A few companies came together to march to their rendezvous point, but most men arrived singly or in small groups. Some communities recognized their leaving with a dinner or some celebration, but most of the troops departed unnoticed. The editor of the *Goodhue County Republican* did compliment the men of Company E for their behavior while on leave, offering "three cheers and a tiger for the glorious Third, and may success attend them ever."[105]

Andrews left Saint Paul by stagecoach late on Thursday, 8 January; traveled the 125 miles by road in twenty-four hours; and arrived in Winona ahead of the men, who were to arrive on Saturday. The rain and thawing weather made the river ice too weak for normal winter use. The officers and soldiers took quarters in the courthouse and in vacant stores as they arrived in town. Many of the small groups stopped along the way to visit friends or to enjoy a meal. Company D first assembled in Red Wing and attended a party given by Tanner Melander, remaining until Monday evening, when they began their trek, traveling in "snow and sleet," fog and rain.[106]

The men at Fort Snelling went overland by wagon. To ease the passage of the troops over the mud roads and to alleviate the strain on civilian communities along their route, this contingent traveled in three groups: Companies B and D left on Thursday, 15 January; then H and I on Friday; and finally A and F on Saturday. The weather was miserable, just cold enough for sleet and icing at night but warm enough during the day for the roads to become muddy. Companies H and I thanked the citizens of Hastings for their hospitality, saying that they hoped "to prove ourselves not unworthy of such kindness." The women of Red Wing provided "a good supper and breakfast" for Companies A and F, according to Captain Bowler, and all the men again remembered that town's generosity and support; Bowler also noted the failure of Lake City to provide any food or place for rest. Companies B and D arrived in Winona on Monday, 19 January.[107]

While in Winona, Lieutenant Hoit of Company B wrote Surgeon Potts at Fort Snelling to seek a pension for the unfortunate Joseph Eigle, who "was ruptured at Louisville, Ky while loading Freight for the Government on board the Steam Boat *Denmark* March 19, 1862. . . . [H]e was accidentally shot in the left thigh at Nashville Tenn on or about the 15th April 1862. He was also shot in the left hand in an engagement with Indians at Wood Lake, Sept 23, 1862, and is now unfit for any service in the employ of the Government." The unfortunate Eigle remained hospitalized at the fort.[108]

As the regiment gathered and waited in Winona, the weather continued warm enough for rain and melting of the snow and ice. The men enjoyed fine snowball games, met the local women, and enjoyed good parties. Companies A and F arrived Wednesday morning, just in time to attend a fine and extensive luncheon provided and served by the women of the city. On Thursday Lieutenant Colonel Andrews ordered the first detachment to leave for La Crosse, while Colonel Griggs finally departed Saint Paul. Something (now unknown) happened that day that caused the editor of the *Winona Republican* to waspishly observe on Friday that "some of them [the Third's soldiers] would improve their character and reputation if they acted with more propriety . . . instead of securing contempt and curses, which they did here."[109]

After passing through Centerville and La Crescent, each detachment crossed the Mississippi River to La Crosse through a region of sloughs and islands where the channel narrowed. Riding wagons (that cost the government seventy-five cents per man) in snow and sleet on "roads streamed like brooks," the men arrived thoroughly soaked and took quarters in the courthouse; Roos and others paid fifty cents, a very high price, for rooms in an inn. About 3 P.M. on Saturday, 24 January, the entire regiment marched to the depot and boarded cars for Chicago.[110]

Fort Snelling in the summer of 1862.
Courtesy of Stephen E. Osman.

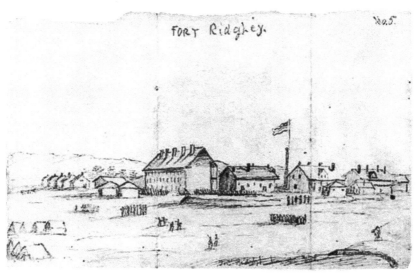

Fort Ridgely in September 1862.
Courtesy of Wilfrid J. Whitefield Papers, Minnesota Historical Society, Saint Paul.

Gov. Alexander Ramsey, 1863.
*Courtesy of Prints and Photographs Division,
Library of Congress, LC-BH832-791.*

Adj. Gen. John Sanborn.
Courtesy of Wayne Jorgenson.

Col. Henry C. Lester.
*Courtesy of Winona County Old Settlers
Association Collection, Winona, Minn.*

Col. Chauncey W. Griggs.
Courtesy of Roger D. Hunt Collection,
USAMI Collections, U.S. Army Heritage and
Education Center, Carlisle, Pa., CWP107.36.

Brig. Gen. Christopher C. Andrews.
Courtesy of J. David Johnson.

Pvt. Carl Roos.
From Vasa Illustrata, *155B.*
Courtesy of Stephen E. Osman.

Maj. James Hoit.
Courtesy of Stephen E. Osman.

Col. Hans Mattson.
From Vasa Illustrata, *154A. Courtesy of Stephen E. Osman.*

Five sergeants of Company F.
Sgt. (Capt.) James Bowler (*second from left*), and 1st Sgt. David Morgan (*right*).
Courtesy of Unique Images Collection, Minnesota Historical Society, Saint Paul, E425.12/p8 (4388).

Capt. Cyrene Blakely.
Courtesy of Wayne Jorgenson.

1st Lt. Rollin Olin.
Courtesy of Stephen E. Osman.

Surg. Albert Wedge.
Courtesy of Wayne Jorgenson.

Asst. Surg. Nahum Bixby.
Courtesy of Wayne Jorgenson.

Capt. Joseph Swan.
Courtesy of Wayne Jorgenson.

1st Lt. Hiram Gates.
Courtesy of Joel E. Whitney Collection
Minnesota Historical Society, Saint Paul,
por/15712/r2 (87923).

Maj. William D. Hale.
Courtesy of J. David Johnson.

1st Lt. Ezra Champlin.
Courtesy of J. David Johnson.

Capt. Lewis Hancock.
Courtesy of J. David Johnson.

CHAPTER 7

THE REGIMENT RESTORED

Several hours after the soldiers of the Third Minnesota boarded, their train left La Crosse on Saturday evening, 24 January 1863, and arrived in Chicago about 4 P.M. the next day. Onlookers remarked that "they look hard—rough set of fellows." The *Chicago Times* elaborated that they had "all the appearance of veteran soldiers . . . and all doubtless are educated more or less by the peculiar kind of warfare in which they have engaged." The railroad provided the officers and noncommissioned staff officers "a splendid dinner at the Briggs House." The men, left to their own devices, found the tavern keepers eager for their business. Colonel Griggs had posted guards at "the saloons to keep the men in line," but, the *Times* complained, a group "repaired to the bar-room of one of our hotels, smashed the furniture, and threw the bottles and glasses about freely"—New Ulm reprised, but with better glassware. Griggs personally paid for the breakage, and no arrests were made. Cpl. John Berrisford, Company B's baker, took this opportunity to desert. He later enlisted as "John Ford" in the Twentieth Battery of New York Artillery, and his postwar biography proudly notes service in both units without mentioning the desertion.[1]

That evening the Third departed on a different railroad; crossed the flat, rain-flooded southern Illinois prairies; and arrived in Cairo at 11 P.M. After sleeping on the cars until morning, the men discovered that they had arrived opposite a "little city square." Pvt. Carl Roos of Company D wrote that the men then "rushed into the saloon of a German," who dispensed a lot of beer and wurst only to learn that he was not to be paid; his saloon survived the visit. Cairo, located at the very southern tip of Illinois where the Ohio River flows into the Mississippi, is below the level of the two bordering rivers. Surrounded by levees fifteen to twenty feet high, it was "a real mud hole," low lying and bad smelling, with ruined buildings on stilts and streets of deep mud. Lieutenant Colonel Andrews informed Governor Ramsey that the regiment's new post was a pit of disease. Their predecessor unit, the 128th Illinois, whose barracks the Third inherited, was "reduced to nothing scarcely, by sickness, deaths, and desertions."[2]

Griggs and Andrews, incensed at being assigned to "guard . . . saloons in this mud hole," telegraphed Ramsey and Sen. Henry Rice seeking transfer "to [Maj. Gen. William S.] Rosecrans department, if we were not destined for Vicksburg." Lent one hundred Austrian rifles, sufficient for guard mount, the officers sought Springfield rifles for their men. After a few days the Third was reassigned to garrison a fort overlooking the levee where the transports and gunboats tied up. Here, the men stuffed the barracks walls with stolen straw to block the breezes but nevertheless froze. Meanwhile, the noncommissioned-officer staff hired a contraband to cook for them at two dollars per week and had him steal the straw they needed. Officers lived better, the field-grade officers and adjutant sharing two rooms, a kitchen, and a cook (in "an old not haunted building"). Company officers lived well too; Capt. James Bowler of Company F and two others shared a room, a kitchen, and a cook; enjoyed good soft bread, fresh meat, and coffee, and had all of their food served on dishes. Bowler claimed that everyone was "in the finest of spirits," a judgment Roos certainly did not share. In addition to stealing hay for their beds and scrounging coal for their stoves, the men had to kill "a whole army of big rats . . . , large, luxurious and fleshy like 3 week old suckling pigs." Doing fatigue duty by carrying water for the cooks was a punishment for missing one of four daily roll calls. The carters had to either wade through mud knee deep or, in a cold snap, slip and slide on the icy sheets that passed for streets.[3]

Dressed in their newly issued uniforms but still lacking firearms, the regiment "presented a fine military appearance" when inspected on 31 January. The *Pioneer and Democrat* informed their friends that the men looked "healthy, cheerful, [and] vigorous, . . . the best of order and discipline prevails" among them. The reporter added, "the band has been organized and increased, and new bugles and drums drawn for it," and formed into something of an after-hours "serenade band" of "five fiddles, two clarinets, and one guitar."[4]

The men of Company A, supported by the regimental officers, requested that Capt. William Webster be reinstated as commander of their unit, claiming that he only reluctantly supported surrender. When Webster was restored (in rank and seniority), 1st Sgt. Jed Fuller of Company F, who had been named their new captain but was not yet commissioned, became their second lieutenant. Quartermaster Sgt. Benjamin Densmore was confirmed in his position at this time, while Cpl. Judson Shaw of Company C, a dentist from Maine, became commissary sergeant and Nahum Bixby, who was discharged for disability in May and had reenlisted in September, became hospital steward. The company first sergeants were appointed, and all the men temporarily assigned to Company

C after the surrender returned to their original companies, as did Pvt. Walter Doyle (to Company B) and the others wounded at Murfreesboro who were at Fort Snelling awaiting discharge for disability.[5]

On Monday morning, 2 February, the new draftee Thirty-Fourth Wisconsin arrived by train, but instead of relieving the Third, it boarded transports for Columbus, Kentucky. The Minnesotans' complaints that they did not wish to spend the war in Cairo's mud changed to happiness when orders were read at dress parade also sending them to Columbus. The men began a frenzy of packing and preparations for their departure. Tuesday morning at 7 A.M., the first five companies departed on the cold, windy three-hour voyage to Columbus. The other companies followed later in the day; Chaplain Crary remained behind to see to the sick. Their new camp was on a field of mud inside Fort Halleck, perched on the bluffs overlooking the city and the river.[6]

Columbus mud was different in kind from Cairo's goo. It routinely stalled unloaded six-mule teams, while water carriers scaling the precipitous two-hundred-foot bluff thought it exceptionally greasy. After the mud defeated all efforts to move a large cannon down to the landing, including the use of seventeen pairs of oxen hitched together, the men of the Third received the task; "the gun carriage went to pieces in the mud, . . . [so they] had to pull [it by] the tow carriage," according to Roos. The Columbus streets were so bad that they almost made the men long for Cairo's thoroughfares.[7]

One Friday the Mississippi iced over, and by Sunday a raw south wind pushed the river ice into "great masses . . . preventing boat traffic." A week later the weather was nice and warm, and the men played ball. Griggs conducted an evening school for officers. Mud or ice, he insisted on clean camps policed every day after reveille and on drill for the men. Griggs and Andrews begged, pleaded, and complained to get the regiment issued guns, preferably Springfields. Finally, on 17 February the Minnesotans received several hundred English Enfield rifles and enough supplemental Austrian rifles so that they could conduct battalion drill, though few men had a complete set of accoutrements. In a very short time Captain Bowler was convinced that only a company of the Sixteenth U.S. Infantry were better than his regiment, even claiming, "we can beat them, I know." Lester's influence remained omnipresent but not admitted, manifested in Griggs's orders and Bowler's pride. Chaplain Crary soon wrote Governor Ramsey, "there is no regiment here [in Columbus] so orderly, quiet, and diligent."[8]

Major Mattson commanded daily operations since Andrews was on duty with the district general-court-martial board. He led a detachment to arrest "some harborers of guerrillas." Pressing a Mr. Phillips as guide, Mattson posted guards to protect the man's property and left Pvt. Warren McCarter of Company K in charge. When the detachment returned, McCarter was absent and so was ten pounds of tobacco, valued at ten dollars. Sentenced by a general court-martial to two months in Alton Military Prison, McCarter languished in the Columbus guardhouse into August because his sentence was not published (a requirement often overlooked).[9]

Confederate activity increased as Major General Rosecrans, commander of the Department (and Army) of the Cumberland, abandoned his outposts to concentrate his forces for the coming summer offensive. Fort Heiman, garrisoned by the Fifth Iowa Cavalry (known as the "Curtis Horse"), which included several Minnesota companies, and Fort Henry across the Tennessee River were both abandoned, creating a power vacuum in western Tennessee and Kentucky. On the night of 20 February, a Confederate captain named Cushman escaped from Columbus's prison; guards Marion Freeman and Thomas Douglas of Company C, both privates, were charged two weeks later with neglect of duty for "allowing rebel prisoners to escape." About a week later one man recognized a "civilian" as one of Brigadier General Forrest's officers and had him arrested as a spy.[10]

Brig. Gen. Alexander Asboth, commanding the Columbus District, had his own spies out. They reported that thousands of rebel troops under Maj. Gens. Gideon Pillow and Joseph Wheeler were near the mouth of the Duck River in Tennessee. Asboth began efforts to retake the abandoned forts to protect Major General Grant's supply lines as he campaigned against Vicksburg, Mississippi. He ordered the Third Minnesota and the Fortieth Iowa to be ready "at a moments notice to march with three days cooked rations in haversacks & 100 rounds cartridges." The Third now had sufficient accoutrements only because the general gave them all of the Twenty-Fifth Wisconsin's gear. Not receiving permission to operate in Rosecrans's department, Asboth canceled the alert. The men relaxed, played ball, and patronized Sutler Daniel Rohrer's store; a few skipped dress parade to play cards and were punished with guard duty.[11]

Soon afterward, Maj. Gen. Stephen Hurlbut, commanding in Memphis, authorized Asboth to "act without regard to departments, these places being cut off from their proper subordination." Immediately requesting gunboat support from Capt. Alexander Pennock, Rear Adm. David Porter's flag captain commanding the navy's northern river posts and squadrons, Asboth again ordered troops, including the Third, to be ready to march with three days' rations. Pennock promptly assigned the vessels for the mission, informing the general that the transports would arrive on 12 March to board the troops.[12]

Awakened at 4 A.M. on Thursday, 12 March, by the beating of the long roll, the Minnesotans boarded the steamer *Bostona,* along with an Indiana battery, a company from the Sixteenth U.S. Infantry, and Asboth and his staff. The 111th Illinois, the Twenty-Fifth Wisconsin (their accoutrements restored from the Third, which had received all of its Enfields and accoutrements), and a squadron of cavalry were on the *J. D. Perry.* The infantry all carried three days' cooked rations and left their baggage and camp and garrison equipment behind. The gunboats USS *Tuscumbia,* USS *Lexington,* USS *Brilliant,* and USS *Fairplay* joined them at Cairo as the boats turned into the Ohio River. Stopping at Paducah for provisions, the flotilla entered the Tennessee River on Friday and arrived off Fort Heiman Saturday evening. A large slough lay between the fort and the landing; men and supplies normally moved across it by flatboats.[13]

Lacking flatboats, the soldiers disembarked about five miles upstream at Paris Landing and marched overland to enter the Heiman entrenchments on its landward side. Before the Curtis Horse had abandoned the post, they had burned the barracks, but the stables and several shanties remained intact; according to Tennessee author John Eisterhold, the cavalrymen had dared not go very far from the fort, even in large numbers, for fear of attack. Asboth ordered the Third and the 111th, a squadron of cavalry, and a section of artillery to garrison Heiman, designating Colonel Griggs as post commander. For unknown reasons, the Third camped between the fort and the slough, downhill from a large pile of manure. The men drew their drinking and cooking water from the slough and were disgusted when, as the rains ended and the water level dropped, they found it contained pig carcasses, horse cadavers, and other debris, making for what Roos called "a tasty soup . . . [an] ambrosia of a drink."[14]

After enduring "eternal pork" since the cooks could not requisition beef, the men, overjoyed when they received a tub of salt beef from the commissary by mistake, refused to help return it. Cooks often supplemented rations by either trading issued rations or paying cash, drawn in lieu of rations, for fresh fruits, vegetables, and other delicacies. The flour, cattle, and pigs taken in raids were either retained and cooked by the confiscating unit or held for issue by the commissary. Many cooks were incompetent at their duty, unfortunately, and too often rations became spoiled and uneatable, the men falling ill to a range of alimentary diseases as a consequence.[15]

Spies and "secret service" men were regularly used to identify suspicious people and places, which thereafter received regular visitations. The Third's first "scout" or expedition against Confederate or guerrilla forces began on 21 March. Riding a gunboat upriver to the Big Sandy, the men seized salt, whiskey, cotton, tobacco, and eggs and also brought back "14 Negro women and children who came into camp and sought protection"; the hospital patients got quite drunk on the whiskey. An early objective for them was to seize enough mules and horses to mount a company. Within a month or so, the Third (and probably the 111th) had enough mules to mount all the infantrymen in a large expedition. Riding the *Robb* and other lightly armored "tinclad" gunboats, which carried twenty-four-pound Dahlgren brass howitzers, or transports armed with army field pieces, the Third exercised extensive operational reach with the advantage of naval-gunfire support. Moving mounted infantry many miles before putting them ashore increased the element of surprise, even though the steep, vegetation-covered river banks limited the number of usable landing points. The regiment abandoned its previous practice of patrolling roads and towns for the advantages brought by useable intelligence, night operations, mobility, and firepower, in the process building an impressive record in antiguerrilla operations. Unfortunately, most Union forces operating in thoroughly rebel territory, including the Third, employed harsh tactics (such as taking of hostages and retributive burning) that only reinforced civilian support of guerrillas.[16]

Many of the scouting operations were routine, going unmentioned in either the monthly regimental record of events or in the letters and diaries of the men. Most of those that were documented involved interesting events or important prisoners taken. A few were of considerable importance for the development of the Third Minnesota. On Saturday, 27 March, a very large scout, 150 men each from the Third and the 111th along with a section (two guns) of artillery, went out on the *Silver Lake* and the *Robb*. Lt. Cmdr. LeRoy Fitch and the "timberclad" USS *Lexington* escorted them. Colonel Griggs commanded the landing force, which included sailors from the *Lexington* led by their executive officer. Moving upriver, Griggs put troops ashore at places "reported to be infested by guerrillas," tied up at night to avoid grounding or hitting snags, and arrived at Boyd's Landing in time to seize chickens for breakfast. The troops then proceeded inland twenty-four miles to a cotton factory producing fabric for the Confederate army. After blocking the road with cordwood to impede an attack by a nearby rebel cavalry regiment, the sailors "remov[ed] the running gear" and took it, the yarn, and a mule team onboard the *Lexington;* the factory building and the housing for the workers were unharmed. At one plantation, a known rendezvous for guerrillas, the raiders seized horses, 225 bales of cotton, and two rebel cavalrymen, who received "transportation free of charge to Paducah." With five feet of water over the Colbert Shoals, Fitch sent his gunboats upriver to shell a rebel camp at Tuscumbia Landing near Florence, Alabama. Returning downriver with the scouting force, they stopped at a farm owned by a zealous enforcer of the Confederate conscription act and "brought away about 1,000 pounds of bacon, all the corn they could carry; also three mules and a wagon"; Griggs kept the bacon for the garrison since the cooks were short of meat. On another scout Capt. James Hoit of Company B nearly got "gobbled up" but, warned by a slave of approaching rebels, was able to seize enough horses and mules "to advance backward on the double quick till he arrived in sight of Fort Heiman."[17]

The first scout Mattson led reestablished him as an officer and combat commander in the men's eyes. Rebel artillery fired on the *Lexington, Emma Duncan*, and "two cannon boats" at the mouth of Duck River on 24 April. The next day the major took Companies C, E, F, and K out on the *Lexington* and *Emma D,* putting ashore at Paris Landing and proceeding inland to the nearby town. Dividing his force, one group scoured the Paris area before returning to the fort with prisoners and loot. Another moved north as far as Murray, Kentucky, before returning with their prisoners and items. Mattson and Capt. James Hodges's Company K had a "hard ride" but brought back a notorious rebel lieutenant and other captives along with the obligatory forage.[18]

Densmore concluded that Mattson had "the faculty to both command troops and to accomplish his mission," while Crary informed Lieutenant Governor Donnelly that the major "has gained the entire confidence of the men," who now thought that he deserved promotion at the first opportunity. The troops attributed the great success of this expedition—numerous prisoners, including notable men, along with food, animals, property, and freed slaves—to Mattson's leadership. The major himself felt the change in them from a wary "prejudice . . . to the old love and confidence. . . . I am well satisfied and know that I have come to the turn in the road—I think I am a good officer."[19]

Second Lt. Olof Liljegren led Company D out to Big Sandy on 17 May to deal with guerrillas harassing the post's cavalry squadron. About 11:30 P.M. the men surrounded a farm where they thought the rebels were staying. It was so dark in the woods that Roos and the others could not "see the comrade in front." The Minnesotans were approaching their quarry, guided by the light from a bivouac fire, when someone made noise crossing a fence and spooked their prey. At one point four of Liljegren's men tried to flee, but he "caught two of them and led them, one in each hand, back to their places as if he had naughty, small boys to deal with, for Liljregren is a large and strong man." The other two met Capt. John Vanstrum at Big Sandy and had him thinking that "his whole company [was] destroyed." In fact, the company captured one rebel and his horse, the captive admitting to being one of Forrest's troopers.[20]

On 18 May, when Capt. Edward Baker of Company E led a joint scout of men from the Third, the 111th Illinois, and the Kentucky cavalry, he noted that they purposely neglected to take provisions or forage, planning instead on "forcing an entertainment for 70 men and horses" on select local hosts. He admitted a certain ambivalence, but the Kentucky lieutenant was overflowing with confidence. This scout depended in part upon Pvt. Perry Martin's ability to impersonate a rebel sympathizer. Martin had gone out two days before in civilian clothes; when the main body "found" him, they chased him awhile, shooting wildly, and then took him "prisoner." At least one "good Union man" warned Martin that his revolver was showing through a rip in his coat, but several others offered to help him escape; their kindnesses were suitably rewarded.[21]

The second of Mattson's noteworthy scouts began on 26 May, when he led Companies B, D, G, and H and some cavalrymen out, taking steamers upriver. Landing on the west side of the Tennessee, the force "scoured the country thoroughly" through five counties and part of a sixth, capturing four officers, including the "notorious Col. Dawson," two guerrilla chiefs, other soldiers and guerrillas, horses and mules, and "a large rebel mail." They also confirmed the existence of a major rebel recruiting station across the river. The major lost three couriers bearing orders between detachments, a Kentuckian, and Pvts. John Hancock and Francis Jerry of Company G, who were severely wounded and captured. Principal Musician Joseph Mertz, though seriously ill, was commended for his "meritorious conduct," while Mattson emphasized that "the conduct of Corp. Jesse Barrick . . . is particularly worthy of mention." Barrick had tracked guerrillas Major Algee and Captain Gizzel into the brush, found them as they were finishing lunch, and took them prisoner; in 1917 a review board judged Barrick deserving of the Medal of Honor for this "most distinguished gallantry in action."[22]

Scouts were exciting changes from routine: no drill, no fatigue parties, and no rations. The men lived off the local citizenry while out. Cpl. James Boardman's account of Mattson's second scout bears this out: "dinner at Williams . . . get supper with old Brush . . . breakfast at Mr. Banhooks, dinner at Prett's . . . supper at Lipes." The larcenous ransacked smokehouses, while the curious searched bedrooms and dressers. Sergeant Major Hale was one man who noted the consequences of their actions. He asked "a negress what she & her little ones would do for meat [Griggs having taken it all; she replied] . . . 'I don't know Massa be right hard on us poor black ones but it right and we must get along till you all come an free us.'" Pvt. Thomas Canfield of Company G told a woman that it was hard for him to see a white woman doing fieldwork; she only turned her head and sighed sorrowfully.[23]

Much of this particular scout was conducted in rain resulting from a hurricane, the earliest offseason storm on record. After crossing western Florida and sinking the bark USS *Amanda,* the storm tracked northwest across Alabama, degenerating into a tropical depression along the Tennessee River before crossing the Ohio River. Boardman noted the rains on 29 and 30 May, but being assigned to forage in Paris, the weather would not have affected him as it did the men in the brush.[24]

Since Fort Heiman was the only safe Union port on the Tennessee River, it saw a lot of traffic. The *Lexington* arrived on 12 April in time for its officers to attend Crary's 10 A.M. Sunday service. The next day the *Covington, Queen City,* and *Argosy* arrived at the landing. On Tuesday the army's "marine brigade" arrived on six steamboats and two gunboats, with all their horses, equipment, and artillery. Ten smaller steamers and two more gunboats stopped on Thursday. Cavalry from the Army of the Cumberland frequently visited Fort Henry, especially the Minnesotans in the Curtis Horse, bringing in horses and mules confiscated from civilians. These visitors often crossed over to Fort Heiman to visit or draw new clothing. After one squadron received new uniforms, Roos saw their abandoned pants, a huge pile of them, glistening in the morning sun—and moving due to hordes of lice. When the marine brigade departed, they took all of the best horses they had confiscated, leaving behind their worn-out nags; the civilian owners arrived at the fort too late to claim their property.[25]

Men who were not out or preparing to leave on scouts drilled and performed garrison duties—and a few got into trouble. With Colonel Griggs commanding the post and Lieutenant Colonel Andrews still on duty with the Columbus court-martial board, Major Mattson commanded the regiment and was rebuilding it to high standards, helping the men meet his expectations and using both firmness and mercy in the administration of justice to "punish the guilty [and] . . . reward the good and able." Many of the miscreants came from Company C, where the dismissal of Captain Mills had come as a devastating shock, and from Company F, where the loss of all the officers and the passing over of the senior sergeants in the commissioning of new ones bred discontent.[26]

On Thursday, 30 March, Pvts. Orrin Case, Handley Richardson, and Harry Lowater used passes forged by Lowater and Pvt. Ira Marlett (all from Company C) to cross the picket lines. Going to the farm of W. F. Sparks, they asked for water, were told to take what they needed, went to the henhouse and grabbed some eggs, and then filled their haversacks with meat from the smokehouse along with flour and sugar. When Mrs. Sparks and her daughters challenged them, one man threatened them with a revolver. Caught, the men were all charged with conduct prejudicial and forgery, Case and Richardson also with theft. Captain Hoit found them all guilty. Fined a month's pay, Lowater and Richardson had half their hair cut off, served two weeks on bread and water, and then two additional weeks of labor while wearing "rogue" on their backs. Case was fined half a month's pay, but Mattson remitted his two weeks of hard labor while wearing "thief" on his back because of Case's "previous good character and conduct." Marlett received two weeks of hard labor and a public reprimand.[27]

On 1 April several men in Company F accused Captain Bowler of giving Pvt. Peter Landschott worthless bills to circulate, offering to share the proceeds. That same day, saying Bowler was "a personal enemy of myself and knowing that as along as this feeling exists . . . I cannot thus do justice to Co F," 1st Sgt. David Morgan resigned his position. Mattson forwarded the charges to Griggs, who ordered Bowler and the witnesses to Columbus for a general court-martial. In Columbus Bowler stayed in a nice private room, while the men probably stayed in the Soldiers' Home. Landschott testified that the accuser (whose name is unreadable in the transcript) told him that "he would have revenge against the Captain. . . . [T]he Captain had not used him right, and he would do all he could to bring him down." Cpl. Johnson Truax testified that the accusers were Morgan and Sgt. William Allison, who were mad that Bowler (formerly fourth sergeant) was promoted over them. Lieutenant Colonel Andrews testified to Bowler's character and ability. After the trial ended, the men returned to Fort Heiman and Bowler resumed command while awaiting the verdict. Both Pvts. Joseph Pulford of Company C and Joseph Sibley of Company G were also tried by general courts-martial in Columbus. Convicted of larceny, having stolen a "gold breast pin, a set of gold earrings, [and] another gold breast pin from citizen Miggles," Pulford was sentenced to two months of hard labor at Alton Military Prison. Charged with theft of a black felt hat and a clarinet, the total value being enough to merit a general court, Sibley was fined a month's pay.[28]

A general muster of the regiment on 3 May provided a snapshot of the men present, accounted for, and absent without leave. Daniel Gray of Company H remained on duty at the Marine Hospital in Saint Louis. Marvin Hathaway of Company I, formerly doing duty in the district print shop with Louis Littlefield of Company E, was now sick in Indiana. Both Simor Mayers of Company B and William Alvey, a telegrapher, of Company H were also on duty at district headquarters. Littlefield corresponded with the *Goodhue County Republican* and with soldiers in the First, Second, Fourth, and Fifth Minnesota Regiments, indicating that the private soldiers had their own inter-regimental connections. Changes in personnel, who was on detached service, deserted, returned, got discharged, and the intake of new recruits meant that the regiment was always changing, though around a solid core. From that core came the new officers, including 1st Sgt. Jonathan Churchill of Company B. Churchill was to be promoted second lieutenant in that company and immediately began serving in that role and so referred to by the men, though he was not yet mustered in to his new rank. Although it is unclear if he assumed the uniform and insignia of his new rank early or not, or whether he joined an officers' mess or remained with the company sergeants, the little evidence available suggests that this would not have been unusual behavior. Once the commander had assurances that the governor would issue the new officer a commission, that man often began assuming his new duties and roles right away.[29]

Roos noted that "each third man of everyone 'fit for duty'" was on either picket or extra duty. Because the locals were "nearly all rebels," according to Pvt. George Brookins of Company I, the men knew from experience the importance of being alert and doing guard duty well. Mattson dropped the hammer of justice on Pvt. Ezra Sargent of Company G when he refused to do picket duty and struck a superior officer; he was charged and found guilty of violating the 9th Article of War and received a week at hard labor. Captain Bowler at one time reported, "Detachments are out pressing Negroes and teams to work on the fortifications and foraging for supplies."[30]

Fort Heiman attracted escaped slaves in large numbers. Chaplain Crary ran the post's camp for contrabands (some of whom had fled their owners and spent days traveling), feeding the families and organizing work details. After Grant ordered all of his units to support the forming of colored regiments and to work to reduce antiblack prejudice, Crary's camp became a preserve of recruiters. Some of the ex-slaves were requisitioned to labor on the entrenchments. Refugees of all kinds were "suffering terribly for provisions, clothing[,] & hundreds of them flocked to the shore & begged to be taken aboard [one] of the boats and taken to free states," according to Private Brookins. Many of them paused at Fort Heiman for these or some other reasons. Rumor at one point had General Forrest's cavalry a day's ride away—an encounter many of the contraband hoped to avoid but that the soldiers eagerly anticipated. In addition to runaways, Confederate spies were drawn to the fort as so many moths to a candle. Sgt. Nathaniel Parker of Company C reported that 2nd Lt. William Grummons caught one spy "outside the lines with a full description of the place and the number of the troops."[31]

Mattson sent a detachment of soldiers and a wagon master under Corporal Boardman to Columbus in April for unspecified reasons. Boardman recorded their journey occurring between 14 and 21 April, noting the steamboats they rode and their lodgings, particularly the Soldiers' Home in Cairo. There, after a man was shot down in the street, "two lady nurses" visited their room and inquired if they needed assistance. Boardman did not mention the detachment's mission, only that it was successful. The regimental records are also silent in this regard, but given the presence of a wagon master, the detachment probably collected the regiment's baggage, camp and garrison equipment, and the wagons and teams and brought them forward to Fort Heiman.[32]

By early May, according to "American Boy" (Private Littlefield), having shifted their camp onto the bluff above the manure pile, the Minnesotans now had "splendid water, a nice spring brook within a few rods of our camp." Though Colonel Griggs had banned all women from camp on 16 April, he did not specify laundresses, who may have remained; certainly many ex-slaves were working within the lines. The Third was practicing the same camp cleanliness and discipline that Lester had enjoined upon them and remained healthy, especially compared to the 111th Illinois, which was "half sick, and lose from one to two [men] every day, by death, while our boys are as tough as bricks." The commander of the 111th issued a general order that cleanliness was important and the men should hereafter use the sinks (latrines), referencing an order from Asboth to the same purpose, a clear contrast to the Third Minnesota's camp.[33]

Chaplain Crary submitted his resignation for medical reasons on 8 May, a request supported by Assistant Surgeon Wedge. General Asboth reluctantly endorsed the request but still appointed Crary as the assistant superintendent of contrabands, assigning Sgt. John Seibel of Company H, a forty-three-year-old farmer who spent twelve years in the army of Hesse-Cassel, as his assistant and drillmaster. Seibel was one of the first men commissioned into a black regiment—as a first lieutenant in the Second Tennessee Heavy Artillery (African Descent). Crary and Seibel took 185 contrabands from Fort Heiman on board the *Navada* to the camp of instruction for black regiments at Island No 10. Quartermaster Sergeant Densmore was detailed to serve as Crary's clerk, while Commissary Sergeant Shaw and Sgt. Abraham Dearborn of Company G were detailed to serve as cadre with the contraband regiment forming at Columbus; all three men soon became officers in the Second Tennessee Heavy. Although recommended for a commission in that regiment, supernumerary 2nd Lt. Francis McDonald instead had his commission in the Third revoked on 8 June; mustered out retroactively to November 1862, he returned to Minnesota.[34]

Taking advantage of the confusion caused when Captain Webster's returning detachment fired to clear their guns, "2 prisoners escaped from the guard house" on Wednesday evening, 13 May. The guard beat the long roll, and everyone turned out in line of battle, staying there for an hour until things were sorted out. After fourteen men from the Third were arrested outside the lines without passes on 16 May, an upset Griggs ordered the post provost marshal, Capt. Benjamin Rice, to send out the provost guard to arrest all officers and soldiers lacking passes.[35]

Active service was hard on equipment, supplies, and clothing. On 20 May Capt. Everett Foster of Company G drew "two Enfield rifle muskets, complete, 2 sets infantry accoutrements complete, 1000 elongated ball cartridges cal. .577, [and] 1 packing box" from the regimental quartermaster. Two days later most of his men received "flannel sack coats" and quite a few needed boots. Despite the wear and tear on men and materiel, and the inability to drill as an entire battalion, the regiment received excellent ratings from the XVI Corps inspector general following a dress parade and a grand review. Bowler noted to his wife that the inspector had ordered them a set of colors—which for some reason Griggs had never requisitioned—one that the Third apparently never received.[36]

Transitioning from Guerrilla Fighting to Siege Warfare

Deciding that he needed more troops to protect his forces besieging Vicksburg from attack by Gen. Joseph Johnston's army in eastern Mississippi, General Grant ordered General Hurlbut, commanding XVI Corps, to "reduce the garrison at Columbus and the District, . . . [Brig.] Gen. [Nathan] Kimball to command the reinforcements for Vicksburg." Telegraphing Asboth on 29 May, Hurlbut ordered him to send the Third Minnesota, the Twenty-Fifth and Twenty-Seventh Wisconsin, and the Fortieth Iowa to Vicksburg. Each man carrying with him five days' rations and one hundred rounds of ammunition, the units took only two ambulances, six wagons, and "no tents except shelter tents," per orders to "reduce baggage to the minimum." Fort Heiman was again abandoned. Upon receiving Asboth's orders, Griggs ordered the 111th Illinois to move to Paducah and the Third to prepare to embark as soon as the steamboats arrived. The post quartermaster began receiving the tents and equipment the units were not taking with them. The 111th boarded the *Armada* on 31 May and, accompanied by a boat full of contrabands, departed north. The *General Anderson* arrived soon after to take the Third. With Mattson's four companies still out on a scout, the regiment remained in camp, where the men scavenged the clothing and equipment abandoned by the Illinoisans.[37]

On 30 May, having avoided all the rigors of the antiguerrilla campaign, the deserters from the Third, having spent the winter at home and, as Roos put it, "had it well while we . . . here had the devil's time of it," now rejoined the regiment. Roos complained that "they [were] fit and flourishing, but we, on the contrary, [were] sickly and emaciated." He was quite annoyed with those from Company D whom he termed "exploiters."[38]

Just after midnight on 3 June, Companies B, G, and H arrived at Fort Heiman. At 6 A.M. the next morning, the regiment struck tents and boarded the boats. Cmdr. Seth L. Phelps reported that the Third abandoned Heiman "in a stampede." Company G abandoned cook gear, a bass drum and sticks, a bugle, and two axes, for which Captain Foster later requisitioned replacements. Captain Vanstrum and his detachment from Company D were still out, but their comrades packed their things on the boat as a messenger went out with instructions for them to meet the regiment at Columbus.[39]

At Fort Heiman, as "D" reported to the *Pioneer and Democrat,* "hundreds of citizens have come in voluntarily and taken the oath, besides several who were forced to do so." By returning horses to their owners if they took the oath, Griggs's headquarters was "thoroughly posted in reference to the presence of rebels . . . , and we are enabled thereby to capture many noted persons of this stamp in a range of eighty miles." Having learned that, as "Gill" of the Curtis Horse put it, "guerrillas cannot exist unless aided by the people of the country through which they pass," the garrison had protected and encouraged Unionists in their foraging while punishing secessionists for their treason.[40]

Mattson had succeeded in reforging the regiment. In a letter to Lieutenant Governor Donnelly, Chaplain Crary said: "The men are the best soldiers by far that I have seen in the service. They go out with the cavalry scouting, and can travel about as fast. . . . We have broken up guerrilla bands, have caught many of the worst of them . . . , [and] have subdued the rebellion in our territory." "Gill" judged the Third rightly just before the regiment left Fort Heiman: "I hazard nothing in saying the Minn. 3d is a No. one regiment. . . . I wish uncle Sam had many such men. You can always look for a good account from the 3d regiment."[41]

At 11 A.M., with seven companies on the *Bow [Ron?] Accord* and parts of three others (D, F, and H) and two hundred or so contraband on the *Arizona,* the boats departed, arriving in Paducah in late afternoon. Several men expressed packages home, including boxes of scavenged clothes. The men on the *Arizona* shifted to the *Izetta,* where the officers secured staterooms. Bowler, and presumably other officers too, "laid in an ample stock of the necessaries of life crackers, cheese, ham, &c., to last me through to Vicksburg." Leaving Sgt. Lewis Hancock of Company G in the hospital, the regiment continued to Cairo, where Musician Mertz was promoted to drum major and transferred to the noncommissioned-officer staff.[42]

Private Littlefield reported that "the 'bully Third' . . . , a tougher, rougher, merrier set of boys it would be hard to find anywhere," arrived in Columbus on 4 June, got paid for March and April, and went ashore without permission. Some men dined at the Soldiers' Home, while others, including Boardman, attended the theater. There, one actor joked, why was the Third "like a gambler who had bad luck?" Littlefield replied, "No one could tell. [Answer:] Because they are always ready to try it again." During the night before their departure from Columbus, Pvt. John Wilson of Company F fell overboard, with all his personal effects, and drowned. Roos described Wilson as a pleasant middle-aged man who was a good friend despite the "language limitations." (Wilson, aged twenty-two, got into trouble in Saint Louis in August 1862, according to the service records.) Captain Webster of Company A and Surgeon Butler became sick and were left behind. Captain Vanstrum and Company D had not arrived in Columbus when the brigade departed south.[43]

Brookins noted that the old rebel fortifications on Island No. 10, which they passed at midmorning on Friday, 5 June, were disappointingly small. To Roos's disgust, some of the "Vasa Boys" stole oiled blankets from "recovering artillery soldiers" released from Columbus hospitals, justifying it by their own lack of raincoats. At Memphis the flotilla fueled and departed without anyone going ashore, though the officers wrote General Asboth to recommend that Sergeant Densmore be commissioned in a black regiment. Chaplain Crary also sent along a copy of Major General Pope's order meritoriously promoting Densmore, a promotion rescinded due only to a lack of vacancies in his company. The boats arrived at Helena, Arkansas, about 11 P.M. on Saturday, "welcomed . . . with music," though Roos did not mention by whom or why. South of Helena, river travel was safe only in daylight, so the brigade did not depart until Sunday at daybreak. Their transports waited off the mouth of the White River for a gunboat to escort them to

Vicksburg, since even during the day, guerrillas fired on most of the passing boats.[44]

On Monday, 8 June, the boats were off Young's Point, opposite the mouth of the Yazoo River, where Admiral Porter based the "mass of transport boats as well as gunboats" composing his fleet. Two days earlier, in an attempt to relieve pressure on the besieged Vicksburg garrison, Confederates under Maj. Gen. Richard Taylor had attacked both Young's Point and the post at Milliken's Bend, where two recently raised regiments of black troops "gave the rebels a terrible cleaning out—drove them 14 miles," as Brookins put it. Proceeding up the Yazoo past the remains of a rebel pontoon bridge and another clot of transports and gunboats, the brigade reached Haynes' Bluff in the evening. The massive fortifications there formed part of Grant's outer line, protecting the actual siege forces from attack by Johnston's army. Going farther upstream, the brigade disembarked at Sartaria, forty miles from the mouth of the river, and marched rapidly out to Mechanicsburg, a few miles to the southeast. Sgt. Philip Roesch of the Twenty-Fifth Wisconsin noted that their route was through fields of head-high corn that blocked the breezes; consequently, many men suffered sunstroke. Moving inland a mile on the bluff, the men drew and pitched their shelter tents, and a few received new rifles. They could "hear the mortars & cannons plainly . . . , a big gun every few minutes," day and night. A barrage on the night of 12 June lasted more than three hours; Captain Bowler observed that the "light artillery sounded like firecrackers going off while the heavy siege guns and mortars chimed in at the rate of about five in a minute with a roar that shook the earth."[45]

All of their supplies came up the ravines carving the bluff face, which were so steeply angled that most men had to use the bushes growing along them for handholds. The water was bad—everyone suffered diarrhea—and the sun beat down unmercifully, leaving many suffering from sunstroke. Rain on 10 June turned the camp into a gluey, "tenacious red clay" mess. Each regiment provided two hundred men for daily picket duty; still more did daily fatigue duty. The pickets claimed that they could see Vicksburg, and they certainly had a grand view of shells arcing skyward in the nightly bombardments. Captain Vanstrum and his portion of Company D finally arrived on 11 June. The next day Chaplain Crary arrived with the men from Company B assigned to assist him in administering the contraband camp. After drill and inspection, the regiment moved camp to a damp but mowed cornfield that fronted on a well-traveled road. That night the men laid on their arms "to support a battery in case we were attacked." The only enemy to appear, however, were "fourteen head of young cattle. . . . Colonel Gregg [sic] promptly detailed two men from each company to 'serve them up' for rations." Lieutenant Colonel Andrews had regular charge of the division's fatigue parties, digging trenches and rifle pits and felling trees for abatis and obstructions to block and channel the movements of an attacker.

Mattson claimed that the men were "quiet, orderly, cheerful, and obedient . . . , ready to go where ever duty calls them" (though Roos's diary questions cheerful). Clearly, the men understood their new mission, leading Roos to think mythically that they, "the warriors[,] might with the sun's [first] gleam, get to invite their iron maidens to death's dance."[46]

Some men went down to the Yazoo to fish, while a very few went bathing in the river. On his first swim Roos saw a log that turned out to have "life and appeared to have the desire to better my acquaintanceship"; he swam for shore and then ran. Other soldiers lost limbs to the alligators in the river and surrounding bayous. Cpl. James Lindall of Company D and a few men killed a five-foot-long alligator (but apparently did not eat it). In pouring rain and "pitch darkness" on Monday, 15 June, the Third marched down the gorge to its new camp, two miles closer to Vicksburg, on "swampy and muddy ground" to work to extend the fortifications further, pleasing General Sherman, who thought the work "well adapted to the end in view." The healthy men remained on picket and guard duty, the walking sick (including Roos) were on fatigue duty.[47]

While on outpost duty here, the men hungrily defended their lines from marauding pigs and ferocious grazing cattle, harvested green corn and blackberries, and replaced much of the army's worst rations with fresh food. Once relieved and moved into a reserve position, they took their liberated cotton, slaves, mules, and cattle with them. Scouts daily brought in prisoners as well, Parker estimating some two hundred horses and thirty prisoners on 18 June alone; Roos helped build a stable for ten of the new horses. Despite drills, inspections, and policing of the camp, the Minnesotans had time for picking berries and relaxing, many even planting bushes to shade their tents. Andrews and Mattson received permission to visit the "army & works before Vicksburg," where they talked with General Grant and dined with Brig. Gen. John Sanborn.[48]

Sergeant Baker reported that "the Adjutant General" of the U.S. Army, Lorenzo Thomas, who was in the Vicksburg area to promote the raising of black troops in the West, inspected their brigade at dress parade on 23 June. Boardman said that this parade dissolved in heavy rain as the officers, fearing that their uniforms would get wet, sought shelter. The men of the Third were already busy about "the colored business," both as trainers of new soldiers and as commissioned officers in black regiments. Pvt. Henry Collins, a printer and musician in Company E, was detached to serve as first sergeant in the Fourth Louisiana Infantry (African Descent). Finally discharged from the Third and commissioned in the Second Tennessee Heavy as a lieutenant, Densmore was sent to Fort Pillow to recruit for his new unit. After returning to Minnesota, Chaplain Crary visited Densmore's father to tell him that his son had impressed General Asboth (as had Crary himself) for "systematizing the contraband department" and had gained additional notice for his ability to supervise the work of black laborers on the fortifications.[49]

Faced with a growing sick list, General Kimball's divisional medical director ordered the building of a large hospital, and "the most stringent sanitary orders . . . [were] rigidly enforced" by the medical officers. The director blamed the poor health of the troops on the swampy and "very miasmatic locality" for endemic malaria; the "inferior quality of the water," which was very hard, "with lime and magnesia with a large quantity of vegetable matter in solution" that contributed to diarrhea; and the "extremely filthy conditions in which some of our camps had been left" by previous units, whose men showed a "general indifference to proper camp hygiene, using the nearest bush." As part of his hygienic efforts, Kimball ordered that the officers and men in his division eat by company messes, with the officers supervising the cooks and maintaining cleanliness. To enforce this directive, one medical officer did nothing but inspect the policing of the camps and their cooking facilities. The frequent rains, high temperatures (from very warm to blistering, energy-sapping hot), and high humidity left the men enervated. Brookins complained, "It requires all the energy a person can summon to do even what little duty we have to do in camp." The Third fared better than its fellow regiments in terms of illness and disease; only Pvt. John Ripley of Company C died during this period, of "Congestive Fever on the Brain."[50]

Fortunately, by the end of June, the Minnesotans were only engaged in picket and fatigue duty and foraging, bringing in lamb, beef, pork, chickens, potatoes, onions, and fruit obtained from Confederate supporters. Grant's miners, meanwhile, planted charges under two rebel redoubts, which were blown up on 1 July, causing "three 'darkies' [to be] blown over to our lines," according to Bowler. Rumors had the rebels building flatboats to escape across the Mississippi into Louisiana. When "a death-like silence" developed after 6 P.M. on Friday, 3 July, Bowler was not alone in thinking that it was the pause before a major attack, writing, "we expect to hear some heavy work before night." The next morning the batteries at Young's Point fired "a national salute," and at 9 A.M. "the rebs replaced their flag with a white one." Regiments were quickly "out in line hurrahing," and the Third's band joined others in playing patriotic airs like "Hail Columbia, Dixie, and Yankee Doodle." The Fourth Minnesota was the first regiment to enter the fallen fortress city at noon, and its flag soon flew over the city's courthouse. Pvt. Philander Folsom of Company K wrote, "by the Report of the cannons . . . , Grant was celebrating pretty well before Vicksburg." The Third and many other units "held Divine services all day," with a prayer meeting in the evening.[51]

On Sunday, 5 July, General Sherman's order sending Kimball's provisional division east to picket Oak Ridge was read at morning inspection. The regiments were to be ready "in 10 min[utes] with 100 rounds per man and 5 days rations," leaving tents and equipment behind. Within the hour, the Third marched, in a dry heat that turned roads to dust—"at least 3 inches deep just like flour"—and raised huge clouds that settled on the sweating men. Reaching their new campsite at 3 P.M., the men occupied the "leaf huts and bed places" of the departed troops and fed their lice too. Officially guarding a fork in the road from Black River to Vicksburg, the Minnesotans spent their time "slaying cattle, pigs, sheep, &c, and having a good time." The officers of Companies D, H, I, and F, on the left flank, took quarters in a church, slept on the seats, and used the pulpit for a dining table. Griggs found "a fine residence" on the right flank for him, Andrews, and Mattson to use. Parker claimed that he had "found good water, corn, and fruit" among the rifle pits and likely had two of the three.[52]

Sergeant Major Hale visited Vicksburg and thought that the rebels looked tired and thin, as did the paroled men passing through their lines, adding that "many evinced a strong desire to be exchanged & go at it again." (He completely missed the parallel to the feelings the men of the Third had held a year earlier.) Whether Hale was merely visiting or was on guard duty at Grant's headquarters is unclear. The different corps, divisions, and regiments shared this honorable duty, which Sergeant Parker and a detail from the Third performed on 15 July. Discipline began slipping in Kimball's division, and blaming the officers for the laxity, he ordered hourly roll calls, daily instruction "on guard and outpost duties" (a frightening weakness), the reading of the Articles of War to each company every Sunday morning, and passes to be required to leave the unit for any reason, even to go visiting or fishing. He also insisted that officers' reports "be done right and on time." Captain Bowler served on the division's general-court-martial board, which had over one hundred cases on its docket, while Major Mattson went to Snyder's Bluff to join the busy general-court-martial tribunal there.[53]

Personnel changes continued, sometimes consequential for the whole unit, sometimes only for the individual. Marvin Hathaway of Company I witnessed an amputation in Memphis and visited an embalmer who worked on enlisted men for half price before rejoining the Third on 16 July. First Lt. Cyrene Blakely of Company K was ordered to Minnesota to serve on General Sibley's staff, while 2nd Lt. Joseph Putnam of Company K, Sibley's aide-de-camp, learned the signals business on his own, passed the relevant tests, and was commissioned into the new Signal Corps, becoming a signals officer in the Department of the Cumberland. Musician Myron Putnam of Company E was discharged at Fort Snelling on a surgeon's certificate of disability on 9 July, having "done no duty for nine months" due to the "chronic ulceration of the left leg" not healing. On 7 June Adjutant General Thomas requested the enlistment papers for Pvt. John Conrad of Company C, aged eighteen, who had required parental permission to enlist; all must have been in order because Conrad remained with the regiment until June 1865. Lucien Allen of Company C was promoted to second principal musician on the noncommissioned-officer staff on 1 July. Both Privates Freeman and Douglas remained in the guardhouse at Columbus, without charges filed against them, while Privates McCarter and Pulford remained held there long after their sentences ended because their verdicts had not been published. Pvt. Steward Bliss, who deserted from Benton Barracks in August 1862 and joined the Twenty-Seventh Michigan Infantry, returned to the Third Minnesota; all the higher commanders, including Grant, approved Captain Hoit's request that Bliss "be restored without a court-martial." Pvts. John Pope and Frederick Schilplin of Company I, who also deserted at Benton Barracks and joined the Eighty-Second Illinois Infantry, were placed in the guardhouse at Georgetown, in the District of Columbia, and charged with desertion. Colonel Griggs wrote Provost Marshal General James Fry asking that they be "released . . . and sent forward" to the Third, personally vouching for their "prompt report to me without being in charge of an officer or under guard" since they were "good and faithful soldiers" in whom he had confidence. Finally ordered to rejoin their regiment, the phrase "under guard" crossed out, Pope and Schilplin gathered their gear and travel orders and set out without the normal officer or noncommissioned-officer escort to find the Third.[54]

Chaplain Crary's resignation was finally accepted by General Grant in late June, and Colonel Griggs wrote to Ramsey (now the former governor and the U.S. senator–elect) praising Crary's service, "in this I am joined by all officers and men," noting the "great value" of a chaplain's service. He recommended the appointment of the "Rev. Mr. [Simon] Putnam of Afton. . . . The self-sacrificing patriotism of Mr. Putnam needs no better guarantee then his service for nearly a year as a Private in the ranks of this Regiment" (in Company E; Musician Myron Putnam was his son).[55]

Colonel Griggs himself resigned to deal with personal affairs. On Wednesday, 15 July, Lieutenant Colonel Andrews went to Snyder's Bluff to walk Griggs's resignation through channels. The brigade, division, and corps commanders all approved it. He then took a boat to Vicksburg, where "Gen Grant's adjutant accepted [it] without asking." Andrews returned to the regiment the next morning. After both officers addressed the men at dress parade, Griggs transferred command to Andrews and departed for home. The new commander moved quickly, examining the regimental papers in the adjutant's office and acting to recognize the deserving men. He ordered company commanders to report on those who had "distinguished themselves in action while in service in this regiment" for valor or exemplary action, with details of their conduct. Four days later he wrote Adjutant General Thomas, recommending several men for the new Medal of Honor for their actions at Murfreesboro, including Densmore, Pvts.

Heman Pettibone and Frederick Miller, and Cpl. Charles Green of the camp guard. He singled out Pvt. Peter LeClair, who "captured one of the enemy and brought him with his horse and arms to our regiment then in line of battle"; Pvt. James Buchanan, who "captured one of the enemy with his arms"; and Pvt. David Hooper, a convalescent who "continued to load and fire till closely surrounded by the enemy, refused to yield a prisoner to him, and fixed his bayonet and held his ground till he was rendered incapable of resistance by a wound in his arm." Andrews also recommended Cpl. Jesse Barrick for the medal for his actions while on a scout from Fort Heiman in May.[56]

With 148 men on the sick list, Andrews ordered the men to avoid eating unripe fruit or badly cooked food and emphasized the importance of clean quarters and a dry pallet, all intended to improve the unit's health overall. Private Roos and many other men suffered from "small red blisters . . . , which caused much scratching"; others merely wished for cooler weather. Whether it was cleanliness or Andrews's dietary advice, something was working. The Twenty-Seventh Wisconsin had one or two deaths a day for the two weeks previous; in contrast, the Third had only one total.[57]

On 20 July General Grant advised Maj. Gen. Cadwallader Washburn, now commanding XVI Corps at Vicksburg, that Kimball's division would be going "up river as soon as coal arrives for the boats," writing Maj. Gen. John Schofield, commander of the Department of Missouri, that the "division [was] to operate in [Maj. Gen. Sterling] Price's rear." He told Hurlbut, still in command in Memphis, that Kimball's were "the only troops I have not exhausted and worn down [by] . . . long and fatiguing marches through the dust and heat." At dress parade on Tuesday, 21 July, the Third Minnesota was ordered to be ready, and at 7 P.M. the regiment began the march for Snyder's Bluff, arriving at 10 P.M. While the men waited for the boats, Andrews kept them busy cleaning themselves, their clothes, and their equipment. The very sick, to be left behind, were moved by wagons from the camp at Oak Ridge. Paid up, the troops broke camp to board, but the boats did not arrive—transports were scarce. Grant finally pressed the marine brigade's boats into service to move the division, showing how important he thought this movement was, one brigade at a time to Helena. At 9 A.M. on 24 July, the Third boarded the *Aristocrat* with the rest of Col. Milton Montgomery's brigade. They were to report upon arrival to either General Kimball or, in his absence, the post commander. A few men remained behind to guard the equipment they could not get aboard.[58]

CHAPTER 8

The Arkansas Expedition
and Little Rock

The Arkansas Expedition had two principal objectives. One was to destroy "the rebel [Sterling Price's] army as an organized force" to protect Unionist Missouri from invasion. The other was to gain control of Arkansas. The state would serve as the base for a future expedition into East Texas to interdict the movement of people and goods from there into the eastern Confederacy and to establish a base for dealing with French imperialism in Mexico. Major General Halleck, now the U.S. Army chief of staff in Washington, thought Arkansas would provide a safe logistical base for the Texas venture, while holding the Arkansas River would secure the Union's supply line into the Indian Territory (modern Oklahoma). To President Lincoln, taking Arkansas, and particularly the state capital, Little Rock, offered an opportunity to experiment with policies aimed at restoring or reconstructing the nation.[1]

After his March 1862 victory at Pea Ridge in northwestern Arkansas, Brig. Gen. Samuel Curtis marched for Little Rock, but Confederate resistance deflected him eastward, and he instead occupied the Mississippi River port of Helena. Brig. Gen. James Blunt operated in Northwest Arkansas after his victory at Prairie Grove in December 1862, but he made no move for the capital. Now, in the summer of 1863, Maj. Gen. Frederick Steele was to take Little Rock and hold the Arkansas River. But disease had decimated Steele's forces assembling at Helena, causing General Grant to send Brigadier General Kimball's Provisional Division, his freshest division, to Arkansas. Colonel Montgomery's brigade (which included the Third Minnesota) disembarked at Helena on the afternoon of 26 July. A sickly place with a high water table, poor drainage, susceptibility to flooding, and surrounded by both malarial swamps and soldiers with poor sanitary habits, the port town was the anteroom to the sickest, most disease-ridden state in the nation, according to the 1860 census. Sent to camp below the levee two miles from town, the Minnesotans immediately began improving their site, located in a grove of trees on a rise close to the river, with shade-giving bushes. Only about fifty men were sick.[2]

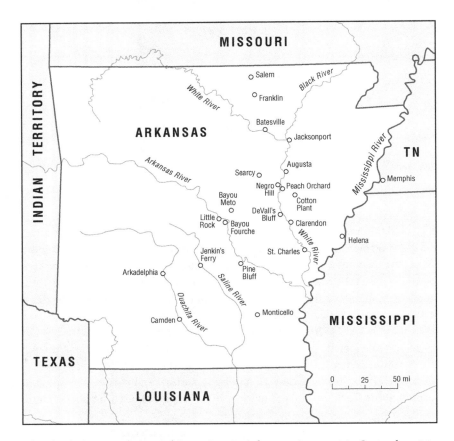

The Third Minnesota's Area of Operations in Arkansas, August 1863–September 1865.
Map by Erin Greb Cartography.

The men cleaned and repaired their gear, gathered supplies, and drilled, spending much time on picket and guard duty and foraging. Each company provided twenty men, two sergeants, and an officer to the regimental forage party. On one foray Capt. James Bowler "gobbled about 100 negroes and as many mules." Owners had abandoned many of the plantations and farms.[3]

On Friday, 7 August, Col. William McLean, commanding the division in Kimball's absence, reviewed the Third on dress parade and praised it as the "best regiment he has seen in the volunteer service," according to Lieutenant Colonel Andrews. General Steele and his staff conducted a grand review of the division on 12 September and seemed pleased with the Minnesotans' "fine military appearance." The XVI Corps inspector general declared that the Third was one of the four best regiments in the corps. Sergeant Major Hale proudly noted the compliments from general officers, saying that the regiment had "fully regained the high position we held" before the surrender at Murfreesboro.[4]

To reduce his need for animal feed and forage, Steele limited the number of wagons allotted each regiment; units with over four hundred men, including the Third, were allowed five wagons, two ambulances, and a dispensary wagon as well as two hospital tents. Andrews gave up one wagon but gained two ambulances. Surg. Albert Wedge fully stocked his dispensary wagon. Every company was to have "5 spades and picks and axes," and brigade commanders were to make sure personally that all wagons were in good condition and ready for use. To reduce personal baggage, officers were forbidden to bring boxes and trunks. All surplus garrison and camp equipment and personal baggage, clearly marked, was stored in warehouses in Helena. Each man was to have 40 rounds of ammunition in his cartridge box, with 120 rounds per man carried in the wagons. Andrews requisitioned 60 rounds per man to make up a shortage.[5]

Convalescents and those with minor illnesses went to brigade and division camps and hospitals, tended by soldiers who were mostly "too feeble to march" but capable of providing minimal nursing, all supervised by a few overworked hospital stewards and surgeons. They were to move to DeVall's Bluff once the expedition reached the White River town. Convalescents capable of standing guard duty were to protect supply boats. Hospital boats took the seriously ill men to general hospitals, first in Memphis, and then farther north. Steele's medical director, following the new best practices, established an ambulance corps; 1st Lt. Isaac Taylor commanded the wagons of the Second Division (as the Provisional Division was redesignated) at Helena, utilizing convalescent soldiers. This turned out to be a very useful innovation.[6]

Pvt. Carl Roos, feeling his years, began negotiating with Capt. John Vanstrum and Major Mattson for transfer to the Invalid Corps. Stubborn, despite his age and illness, Roos refused to go even to the convalescent camp and made the march, often delirious, while riding in a wagon. In the report for July, 360 men were present for duty in the Third, while six officers and 120 men were sick, many of them remaining in Helena, including 2nd Lt. Olof Liljegren, Pvt. Henry Lowater, and undercook Alfred Parks (undercooks were black men enlisted as cooks in volunteer white units).[7]

Before departing Helena, Colonel Andrews sought information on Pvts. John Pope and Frederick Schilplin who, though he did not know it, were already on their way west to rejoin the regiment. Another letter went to the provost marshal at Columbus, Kentucky, trying to get Pvts. Warren McCarter and Joseph Pulford released from jail, though without any apparent success. On 30 August, to Andrews's surprise, all four men arrived in camp. Pope and Schilplin returned to duty without a trial.[8]

On 1 August Andrews, Mattson, and Capt. Everett Foster had mustered in to their new ranks as colonel, lieutenant colonel, and major; 1st Lt. John Devereaux, relieved of duty as brigade adjutant, became captain of Company G. Quartermaster James Howlett was "on special service in the Department of the Northwest" to settle accounts from his time as Fort Snelling's post quartermaster. In his last official act as company commander, Foster filed yet another ordnance report for guns lost at Murfreesboro and drew equipment, including haversacks, bugles, shelter tents, and hat insignia. He reported in inventory for his company forty-six Enfield rifled muskets and three thousand cartridges, with five hundred rounds expended in target practice.[9]

Although the Arkansas River was "the natural line of operations *during the season of high water* [emphasis mine]," one man described it as "a glorified drainage ditch . . . [but] one of the changeablest river[s] . . . , rising one day and falling the next"; it was considered too variable to be depended upon below Little Rock. Steele therefore planned to march up the White River to DeVall's Bluff, then cross to Little Rock along the Memphis & Little Rock Railroad, shifting from the east to the west side of the White at Clarendon. Brig. Gen. John Davidson, commanding the cavalry division, reported that the river was at its highest level "since 1844, 4 miles wide in spots," but narrowed before Clarendon. Knowing Steele's plans, Lt. Cmdr. George Bache of the USS *Cricket*, judging the riverbanks at Clarendon unsuitable for a pontoon bridge, ordered two navy coal barges brought up to serve as ferries.[10]

The March to Little Rock

The expedition's advance guard began the march late on Tuesday, 11 August. The Third Minnesota, the rear guard for its brigade and division, left camp about 7 P.M. on Thursday. With 422 men, it was one of the largest regiments in Steele's command. Each man carried four days' rations in his haversack and a full cartridge box. Before departing, Andrews addressed his troops, emphasizing the need to preserve "honor and health," and reminded them that they were to prevent "straggling, marauding, and setting buildings on fire for the sake of discipline"—and as part of Lincoln's desire to win the hearts and minds of Arkansans.[11]

Crossing the flat alluvial delta lands in oppressive heat, too many men abandoned blankets, knapsacks, and clothing—all items they would dearly miss very shortly. Thousands of feet turned dirt roads into dust clouds that covered the soldiers. Water, particularly drinkable water, was scarce, and Steele, lacking barrels (he had ordered six hundred and received none), was unable to bring water from Helena. Miasmatic swamps, overrun by ants, mosquitos, scorpions, snakes, spiders, ticks, and more mosquitos, lined the river side of their road. On the plantations and farms on the other side, stripped bare of food by preceding units despite orders, the soldiers saw another aspect of the "peculiar institution": mulatto slaves and slave children who appeared white.[12]

Closer to Clarendon, the soldiers saw "only white females and old men" but few crops. Abandoned cattle and pigs were plentiful in the woods, serving as replacements for the army's "fat pork," which made so many men sick. The correspondent for the *Chicago Times* claimed that the available water, drawn from stagnant sloughs and bayous covered with a "green-yellow grease," made that from the Chicago River a "nectar" in comparison. The countryside was more wooded near the town, and there were more small farms, run without slaves, that along with their owners appeared to be slovenly and lacking enterprise.[13]

During a "halt on the march," Pvt. George Gregg of Company G repeatedly attacked Cpl. James G. Canfield without cause. When 2nd Lt. Stephen Rhoads separated them, Gregg threatened "to whip said Canfield if he had to whip the commissioned officers first." Refusing to go on guard duty and told that he would be charged if he persisted, Gregg replied, "'court martial and be God damned and kiss my ass' or words to that effect." Found guilty of "conduct Prejudicial" to good order and discipline for attacking Rhoads and of violating the 6th, 9th, and 21st Articles of War for attacking Canfield, Gregg was sentenced to confinement at hard labor for the rest of his term of enlistment, to forfeit all pay due, and to be dishonorably discharged.[14]

The regiment straggled into camp at Clarendon for seven hours' rest, settling in to the mostly burned-out town to recover health and strength. One Iowan called Clarendon "the very home and head-quarters of ague in bulk and quantity." Mattson noted that many regiments had fewer than one hundred men doing duty. The Third, in contrast, had only forty men on the sick list and even detailed men to help the Eleventh Ohio Battery, which had only twenty-five effectives. The divisional quartermaster took more men from the regiment, Roos included, to guard his temporary warehouses; Roos received sugar, green tea, and pepper as a reward. The sutlers and some itinerant peddlers set up shop to sell tobacco (at two dollars per pound) and whiskey (at one dollar a pint), while some soldiers played a steamboat's calliope. As Steele's sick list grew, General Grant encouraged Major General Hurlbut, commanding at Memphis, to ignore department boundaries and provide whatever the expedition needed. Hurlbut sent another brigade, asking that Steele treat it well.[15]

Foraging was a primary activity for the Union troops. Captain Bowler took one hundred soldiers and twenty-five teams out twenty miles to untouched areas, where his men depopulated poultry yards, emptied corncribs, cleared out smokehouses, and took fruit and garden produce. Sending the teams back with a strong escort, Bowler and a small detachment scouted and stirred up the locals; men took their guns and hid while the women were frantic in fear. They encountered only three guerrillas, who fired at them and fled. Late returning to camp, the captain learned that they had been presumed "grabbed."[16]

On Thursday morning, 20 August, after a grand review, the first troops began crossing the White River on the navy's coal-barge ferries and a pontoon bridge. After the cavalry and the artillery were on the other side, the infantry began crossing. On Sunday the Third finally crossed the White, riding a barge, then marched five miles west, crossing Oak Bayou on another pontoon bridge and watching several teamsters drive their teams and wagons into the water; one wagon damaged an "India Rubber" pontoon. Fortunately, all of the Third's wagons made it intact, and the regiment arrived at its campsite, a small, filthy rebel field fortification.[17]

This leg of the march to DeVall's Bluff led through heavily timbered areas laced with sloughs and bayous, punctuated by prairie outcrops, and quite lacking in drinkable water. Farm and plantation wells were incapable of meeting the needs of even a company. Mosquitos attacked in hordes, and the nights were cool. Lacking the tents and blankets that they discarded along their route, the men were sleepless and miserable. Their sick list began growing. Two days out of Clarendon, Company D had less than twenty men able to march, with only a sergeant to lead them. Surgeons rode up and down the columns, dispensing brandy to alleviate sunstroke. The sick men from Helena and Clarendon passed the marching column on transports, arriving a day early at DeVall's Bluff; "many crawled out on the shore, where some died unattended and were to be seen on the bank the next day, unburied."[18]

As the expedition entered DeVall's Bluff, so many surgeons and hospital stewards were sick that the entire medical system collapsed in disarray. Friends cared for the more fortunate men, while the others had "to do the best they can for themselves or go untended." Too many just laid down and died. Surgeon Wedge was alone caring for his men and did well; the Third had fewer men die and fewer hospitalized than most (if not all) the other regiments. As the grave details buried the dead in the woods—"laid out in full uniforms on sawboards, their parade beds," as Roos termed it—Steele reacted in fury, demanding better care from the doctors. Hastily erecting hospital tents, the medical staffs moved to build a major hospital complex to meet the need, with fatigue parties demolishing abandoned buildings and operating the nearby sawmill to provide the lumber necessary. A major storm on Thursday, 27 August, blew down the hospital tents. The Second Division established another ambulance corps for DeVall's Bluff (the unit at Helena continued in operation there for several more months). Men detailed to serve as nurses could not bring up rations for the sick, and Steele again reacted angrily, this time at the failures of the supply systems. Every man needed fruits and vegetables, but only poor beets, Irish potatoes, and horrid onions were available; even the army's desiccated variety was not to be had. Scurvy beset both the sick and the "healthy."[19]

DeVall's Bluff turned out to be an ideal location for Steele's forward supply depot. Built on a plateau opening surrounded by an oak forest on the edge of the bluff at a bend in the White River, bounded by a ravine on one side and a "real wilderness" on the other side, a small garrison could easily defend it. The riverbank was firm, and boats could pull close to shore to unload goods, either into warehouses or for transshipment via wagons and rail cars. With few swamps and bayous nearby and springs that yielded drinkable water in adequate quantity, it proved a healthy enough place.[20]

Cpl. Philander Folsom of Company K wrote his sister that the cavalry regularly skirmished with the rebels and took numerous prisoners. Among those were unexchanged men who still carried their paroles from Vicksburg. This wholesale violation of paroles, repeated at many times and places, was a key factor in Grant's later termination of the prisoner-of-war exchange cartel. Some infantrymen, lacking an enemy to fight, sought whiskey and wine at $1.50 a pint, a high price for bad liquor. Others turned to religious services and camp meetings, an early manifestation of the religious revival that took hold in the Army of Arkansas in the coming months.[21]

Like many officers, Major Mattson had promised his wife that he would resign and come home—in July. Now, in late August, he was in deepest Arkansas, writing his unhappy spouse: "I shall come home this fall if God is willing and if the government will accept my resignation" (which he never submitted). Mattson was wise enough to tell Cherstie that he dreamed of her (amid his lack of food and bedding), but Mrs. Mattson, like many other soldiers' wives, was not altogether happy with her soldier-husband.[22]

Colonel Andrews appreciated the value of mobility, from the Third's experiences using mules against the Dakotas and while operating from Fort Heiman against guerrillas, and requested that the Third be mounted, "with all the privileges [that is, pay] of cavalry." Grant had the authority to mount any regiment in his department, and Captain Bowler claimed that Hurlbut had ordered Steele to mount the unit. Infantry mules did not bring the "privileges of cavalry," however, so Andrews refused the animals and kept the Third walking.[23]

Steele's force began the march from DeVall's Bluff on 29 August, following the line of the railroad through Brownsville. Still the largest and healthiest of his units, the Third too left behind its sick and convalescents. All, that is, except for the oldest and very stubborn man in the regiment, Carl Roos, who insisted that he had "not entered the warrior's path" to go to a hospital and, disobeying direct orders again, rode on in a wagon. He said that looking in either direction from town, a line of covered wagons, animals, and soldiers stretched as far across the prairie as he could see. It was an impressive sight. On the march on Tuesday, 1 September, many men were overcome by the heat. Reaching Brownsville, the troops drew water from a "muddy and stagnant bayou" and foraged, ignoring Steele's clear orders; more men became sick.[24]

On Sunday, 6 September, the Third led their brigade for ten uneventful miles, then skirmished with rebels for two miles, taking several pickets prisoner. Wanting to flank General Price's defensive works before Huntersville, the terminal of the railroad across from Little Rock, Steele sent the regiment to find an undefended ford across Bayou Meto. Cavalry skirmishing delayed their movement on Monday. Tuesday night the regiment camped on a large plantation; Sergeant Major Hale claimed that the corn here was twenty feet tall. The soldiers devoured everything (the army being on half rations) and took fencing for firewood. Sporadic skirmishing with the enemy continued to slow their progress. On 9 September the advance guard drove the rebels across the Arkansas River but had to wait for a pontoon train to come up.[25]

Col. Adolph Engelmann, commanding the Second Division, ordered the Third Minnesota and the Eleventh Ohio Battery, in which many Minnesotans were serving temporarily, to lead the advance. Moving out at 3 A.M. on Thursday, two days' cooked rations in their haversacks, the regiment took position behind a low levee along the river's edge, with the battery to their left. Andrews positioned his best sharpshooters in front of the artillery to protect the gun crews. Rebel pickets and artillery, visible across the river, did not attack the engineers until they had completed the pontoon bridge, then "pop went a rebel cannon right at it—that started the music." Excited, Mattson later reported that he could not stop the men from getting "up in the highest points and watch[ing] for the shells and shout and cheer."[26]

Shelled out of their first positions, the rebel defenders moved deeper into the woods; shelled out again, they took yet another position, only to be again shelled out. After two infantry regiments crossed the river and secured the bridgehead under the Third's covering fire, the cavalry rode over to pursue the retreating rebels. The infantry returned across the bridge and, with the artillery, marched up the east side toward Little Rock. Entering "strong rebel fortifications" so recently abandoned by Price's men that they left "small arms, cooking utensils & food" in their hurry, the Minnesotans appreciated the warm, rebel-baked "corn dodgers (cornbread)."[27]

Provost Guards in Little Rock

Hastily withdrawing from the now indefensible city, the Confederates only partially damaged their pontoon bridge across the Arkansas River at Huntersville and failed to prevent General Davidson's cavalry from entering the capital late on Thursday. The next morning, 11 September, Steele ordered Andrews to report with his regiment to Davidson. Crossing the bridge, the Third Minnesota marched in column by companies to the state house, becoming the first Union infantry regiment to enter Little Rock. (Years later this was the event the regiment's veterans chose for their memorial painting in the new Minnesota State Capitol.) Andrews became commander of the city and Post of Little Rock, and the Third was designated part of the provost guard, along with the Forty-Third Illinois (Engelmann's German regiment, which included a Scandinavian company) and the Seventh Missouri Cavalry. The regiment took quarters in the capitol itself, each company taking a "large room, some have carpets and beautiful furniture," for its quarters. Andrews selected the supreme court's chambers as his post headquarters and, being sick, laid on the floor and began doing business—the first item being to appoint Captain Bowler as his adjutant. Mattson chose the Law Library, "an elegant room with about 2,000 law books," for regimental headquarters. Company officers shared the smaller rooms.[28]

Little Rock was a pretty town, sitting on a rocky point sixty feet above high water. Laid out in a grid pattern, the city had gas light, impressive mansions, business blocks, and good hotels, theaters, and churches. Saint Johns' College, which was used by the Confederates as a military hospital complex, now served Union forces in the same capacity. There were other, less savory, businesses catering to a variety of vices. The state penitentiary became the military prison, with Capt. James Hodges of Company K as superintendent. Buildings at the U.S. arsenal, near the college, housed the Forty-Third Illinois and another hospital dedicated for enlisted men; the rebels had removed all the arsenal machinery to Arkadelphia before abandoning the city.[29]

Selected for the provost guard "because of its efficiency and good discipline," the Third stood out despite its recent losses to disease. Still one of the largest of Steele's regiments, hardier and healthier than the others, it had the appearance and attitude of a rough-and-ready unit prepared to march against Indians, guerrillas, or rebels with equal relished and effect. On parade, the Third was a "bandbox regiment," with white gloves, ordered ranks, and crisp responses to minimal commands. Impressionistically, because we lack adequate data, the Third had few men in arrest (and those mostly on minor charges), reflecting well on Mattson's efforts.[30]

Steele now held the core of the Arkansas River valley, and the Confederates retreated into southwestern Arkansas, basing their state government at Washington, an unremarkable small town. As the occupation forces settled in, rebel forces began to reorganize for resistance. Cavalry operated against Union outposts, including Pine Bluff, outside the Third's area of provost operations. Guerrilla attacks on pickets rarely affected the Minnesotans' daily work, but espionage and disaffection in and around the capital were of interest.

Union priorities shifted from conquest to the pacification of occupied areas as well as the expansion of Union influence and control into no-man's land as rapidly as possible. The Third was now the primary instrument implementing Lincoln's ideas of reconstruction in Little Rock, policies more conciliatory than Steele himself preferred. With their successful experiences at charming the locals, particularly the women, in Nashville and Murfreesboro, the Minnesotans were a very good choice for the face and fist of Union occupation. They again gained from resident civilians first a grudging and then a more willing acceptance of themselves, then of their authority, and finally of the Union. The Third deserves part of the credit for the success in establishing civil government far more quickly than Lincoln envisioned.[31]

Rainfall in the upper reaches of the White River diminished while the expedition was busy seizing Little Rock. Water levels below DeVall's Bluff fell, and few of the available steamboats and fewer gunboats could safely navigate the shallower river. By 17 September the army was on quarter rations, and despite orders to the contrary, every regiment foraged for food, each commander fondly hoping the resulting complaints would be vague as to the units involved. Andrews took the opportunity to instruct the garrison to be "temperate in their diet" and to keep themselves and their camps clean while directing company commanders further to inspect their kitchens daily—all reflecting standard practices in the Third. The timing was hardly felicitous for dietary advice.[32]

Even on reduced rations, Steele and Andrews ensured that needy citizens who took the oath of loyalty received help from army stocks. If the troops were on full rations, so were the locals. Alleviating food shortages, guarding the Sisters of Mercy's convent (they ran a hospital and received rations), escorting women to their country homes, and being good neighbors otherwise composed the core of policy. In addition to maintaining law and order and dispensing the charity for the poor and homeless, the provost guard was responsible for public services, including sanitation. The troops enforced the provost marshal's regulations on theaters, the circus, saloons, gambling houses, and other places of entertainment while also keeping order on Markham Street, where "for two or three squares, every third house [was] a negro brothel." Andrews called on the men to be honorable and lawful, both in executing their duties and when off duty. Though instructed to march their posts without pausing to talk, sentries were to be polite to passing citizens just as patrols were to be courteous. Their conduct reassured the initially fearful residents, and civilian diarists suggest that the Union soldiers behaved better than their rebel counterparts.[33]

Transferred from Montgomery's to Col. Oliver Wood's brigade before leaving Helena, the regiment now transferred again, this time to the Third Brigade in Brig. Gen. Samuel Rice's Third Division, joining the Twelfth Michigan Infantry and the Eighteenth, Fifty-Fourth, Sixty-First, and 106th Illinois Infantry. The only unit from the Third Division in Little Rock, the Third Minnesota represented it at a grand review on 18 September. Steele complimented the regiment upon its "'esprit de corps' and general appearance." Writing the *St. Paul Pioneer and Democrat*, "O" claimed that their bugle corps had "charmed him . . . , being if not artistic at least original," and, in an echo of Nashville, added that the Third was "gaining many lukewarm to our side."[34]

As Little Rock residents realized that they were safe under Union occupation, that news spread, and those who had fled or who had sent their children away now began returning and bringing the children home, quite outnumbering those who left for Confederate-held areas. Many took the oath of loyalty—some sources report as many as two hundred per week—and men who either had avoided Confederate military service altogether or had deserted the rebel army began joining Steele's new home guard. Many also were doing "good service as scouts," capturing several bushwhackers. Captain Bowler grumbled: "If these things were transpiring in the Army of the Potomac uncle Abe would have to sneeze over it and make a proclamation, and the NY papers would have big headings to magnify it to the world. But, being in the west, and especially in Ark., it is hardly noticed." He also mentioned that twenty ex-rebels had joined the Third and that other regiments had added recruits too.[35]

General Hurlbut had dispatched locomotives and railcars from Memphis to replace the equipment damaged by the rebels. Soldier-mechanics also repaired what equipment, cars, and track they could. As soon as the trains began running, the rebels commenced destroying track and attacking the trains, forcing Steele to station troops to patrol the line, guard its bridges, and effect repairs. The army railroad operators plated some of the "platform cars . . . with boiler iron, making them bullet proof," and troops riding the trains carried loaded guns. By late September the trains were running dependably between Huntersville and DeVall's Bluff, bringing in civilian as well as military travelers and goods.[36]

Business activity revived and shops reopened in Little Rock, while local farmers began bringing produce in to town, and the army went to full rations. The theaters and circus were all doing a thriving business, and the churches were full of soldiers. Pvt. James Lockney of the Twenty-Eighth Wisconsin noted that the Presbyterian minister's sermons were "guarded and non-committal," but the music was good. Sergeant Major Hale attended a Catholic Mass on the morning of 15 September and the Presbyterian service in the afternoon. Mattson lodged across the street from the Roman Catholic church and enjoyed its music. The citizens seemed to accept the soldiers, even when the chaplain of the Thirty-Sixth Iowa usurped the Methodist pulpit. Capt. Thomas Stevens of the Twenty-Eighth reported that at Episcopal services on 18 October, the women "responded audibly to the prayer for 'the President of the United States.'" Comments in soldier letters and diaries regarding the different faiths and their attending different worship services suggests less bigotry in the ranks than historiography might indicate, raising larger questions about day-to-day relations between individuals and small groups of different faiths.[37]

Into the early spring of 1864, provost-marshal spies kept a close watch on local gatherings, and the guard broke up those that seemed disloyal, as the Third's letters report. The spontaneous meeting of pro-Unionist citizens on Monday, 19 October, came as a surprise to the informants; the guard monitored the organized meetings that followed, and individual soldiers began to attend them when off duty. Pro-Union societies formed in several other towns—Unionist sentiment was more common in central Arkansas, though not as strong as in northwestern Arkansas. The Little Rock committee, assuring Lincoln of the loyalty of the state, sought Steele's assistance in restoring loyal government by holding an election to fill the vacant seat in the U.S. House of Representatives. The two main factions of Unionist sentiment each had a newspaper and an army supporter. Isaac Murphy and Col. William Fishback of the Third Arkansas Infantry (U.S.) were supported by General Davison and were the more radical. They published the *Unconditional Union*. Dr. Cincinatus V. Mader, a prewar newspaper publisher and rebel army surgeon, and A. C. Rogers, a Pine Bluff plantation owner, published the conservative *National Democrat* with the support of Col. Francis Manter of the Thirty-Second Missouri, Steele's chief of staff. Though the general personally preferred the Mader-Rogers faction (he had many friends in that group, having served in Arkansas before the war), surprising in view of his private opposition to Lincoln's conciliatory policies, he had Andrews provide each journal access to paper and presses, allow the employment of soldier-printers, and pay them to print official orders and notices.[38]

The Unionist movement grew rapidly, holding regular Saturday meetings, and related groups met on other evenings. The strength and fervor of the movement surprised secessionists. By late November, the factions agreed to send delegates to a constitutional convention at the state capitol in January 1864. Lincoln's plan for Arkansas as a laboratory for reconstruction did not envision this, as it was coming *up from the people* and had developed so quickly. As a result, there was some exchange of sharply worded telegrams as the Arkansans, Steele, Stanton, and Lincoln came to agreement about timing (the locals won the arguments about the date of the election) and process.[39]

As observers and guardians of this gestation, the men of the Third Minnesota were at least partially responsible for it. Implementing Lincoln's conciliatory policies their way had made the Union more appealing. Grant, Sherman, and most U.S. generals favored a "hard war" approach and supported Davidson in his harsh criticism of what he viewed to be Steele's too-conciliatory policy. Davidson soon came to treat his fellow general as an enemy, criticizing him for every failure in Arkansas. Many senior officers accepted his claims, and though most realized in time how unfair most of the criticisms were, none admitted their error; this precipitous movement toward reconstruction horrified them. The Confederates also loathed these same policies. A rebel colonel complimented Steele for his "forbearance, justice, and urbanity," while other Confederate authorities encouraged partisan leaders to control their men to improve the "image" of the Southern cause. Pvt. Charles Musser of the Twenty-Ninth Iowa noted that, as a result, both rebel citizens and soldiers were deserting the Confederacy. First Lt. Otto Dreher of Company F, in Minnesota to recruit, reported that ex-slaves were joining the new black regiments, that several white Union regiments also were forming in Arkansans, and that "the ladies of Little Rock have generally repudiated secession, and are for the Union to the backbone." By now, the men of the Third knew the value of gaining feminine loyalty.[40]

Where or why Pvt. Charles Thomas of Company I acquired a government mule is unclear, but he had, and in late September he sold it, "a poor lazy one," to "Thornton Beal (ACAD [a citizen of African descent])" for twenty-five dollars. After several days Beal noticed a very faint "U.S." brand and attempted to make things right. Thomas instead offered him a bill of sale. Convicted of conduct prejudicial by a field-officer court, Thomas served a month of hard labor and lost a month's pay. It is unclear if Beal got his money back. On 1 October Pvt. Thomas Doig of Company E refused to do duty, called his sergeants "damned SOBs," refused to give his name, and then ran away; there is no record of the proceedings of his trial or a verdict. Two weeks later Pvt. Joseph Sibley of Company G, after a roll call, refused to take his place and march for dress parade, violating the 21st (absent without leave) and 44th (missing parade) Articles of War. He claimed that he had no blouse to wear and that 1st Sgt. Ezra Champlin had told him not to go "unless he was properly dressed." Sibley plead to the specifications but argued that he was not guilty of the charges; a regimental court-martial found him guilty and sentenced him to four days' hard labor. Two months later he was still in the Military Prison in Little Rock.[41]

In need of alcohol, Lieutenant Rhoads of Company G tried to buy some from the commissary but lacked the necessary permit from a superior officer. On 16 October, after the post adjutant's clerk, Pvt. Henry Curtis of Company F, refused to make a permit and forge the colonel's signature, Rhoads forged the permit himself, adding both Andrews's and Adjutant Bowler's signatures. The gallon of whisky he purchased became very expensive after a general court-martial found him guilty of conduct unbecoming an officer and a gentleman, of forgery, and of making a false representation, ordering that he be dishonorably dismissed from the service on 16 November. Discipline in Company G began to improve immediately thereafter.[42]

Company K remained a problem due to the ongoing absence of Captain Hodges and only one officer, 1st. Lt. Hiram Gates, on duty with the company. On the evening of 2 December, Colonel Andrews discovered Pvts. Grover Lansing and Warren McCarter sitting down while guarding Steele's headquarters. A regimental court-martial found them guilty, but when Andrews (who filed the initial charges) reviewed the findings, he disapproved the sentence because Congress had terminated both regimental and garrison courts-martial for the duration of the war, replacing them with field-officer courts (in the act of 17 July 1862).[43]

Rebel cavalry attacks on outposts and guerrilla attacks on pickets did little but inconvenience the Union occupiers. Espionage proved a greater hindrance, and throughout Union-held Arkansas, spies gathered information on troop strength and morale, camps, fortifications, and the identities of local collaborators. Anyone could enter Union lines, but leaving meant first taking the oath of loyalty, which most people, on principle, would not swear if they expected to violate it. Military tribunals tried spies under War Department General Orders no. 30, which called for the death sentence for those found guilty.[44]

On Wednesday, 30 December, pickets on the Stagecoach Road west of Little Rock stopped David O. Dodd as he was leaving the lines without a pass (being a seventeen-year-old, he had not been required to take the oath). Dodd had passed through the lines the day before, surrendering his pass as he exited, but after staying with relatives for the night had gotten lost and reentered the lines. Now he had a problem. Dodd showed his birth certificate, contained in a notebook, to the officer of the guard, who noticed a page filled with the dots and dashes of Morse telegraphic code, which he could read. The young man had detailed notes of fortifications, unit strength, and other sensitive information. Arrested, tried, and convicted of espionage, Dodd was sentenced to death by hanging. Steele approved the sentence. On Friday, 8 January 1864, Dodd, showing great composure, rode on his coffin to the gallows on the parade grounds at Saint Johns' Hospital. Several infantry regiments, including the Third, formed three sides of the square and witnessed his execution. Most of the men were quite satisfied that justice was done, age not being an issue for them. But Confederates soon turned Dodd into a boy martyr for their cause. Steele responded quickly and creatively, reinterpreting General Orders no. 30 by terming spies and guerrillas as "political citizens." This allowed military courts to sentence those convicted to hard labor or to death, with the sentence commuted to hard labor, for the duration of the war. The general thus neatly avoided creating more martyrs while keeping miscreants from making more mischief. The choir of his critics disliked this policy change as well.[45]

In 1862 the army's medical department was more poorly administered than its justice system, making the hospitals worse than the prisons. By the end of 1863, even in the Trans-Mississippi theater, the medical system, its personnel, and its hospitals were dramatically improving. The U.S. and the Western (in the Trans-Mississippi theater) Sanitary Commissions had successfully pressured the army and Congress to allow a second assistant surgeon (a first lieutenant) in each regiment; the Third gained Asst. Surg. Moses Greeley. Defining the functions of the regimental and the general hospitals necessitated improving the competency of the surgeons. Creating ambulance corps was a part of this process. Two Third Minnesota diarists provide windows into these changes. Sgt. James Boardman of Company B took ill and remained at Helena until he traveled on the hospital steamer *R. C. Wood,* first to a Memphis general hospital, then to Hospital No. 1 at Jefferson Barracks. His diary suggests that the hospitals in Saint Louis were up to the new standards by the time of his arrival. He described an inspection by the department commander, Major General Schofield, and his staff, an indication of how important medical care had become to the military. In Little Rock the army opened an officers' hospital in the Woodruff mansion in town, enlisted hospitals in the arsenal buildings and at Saint Johns' College, and a separate hospital for black soldiers and undercooks.[46]

The Little Rock hospitals opened as the reforms were being implemented, all witnessed by Carl Roos and recorded in his diary. Sick and often delirious from the start of the march to Little Rock, Roos was first treated in the regimental hospital. When Saint Johns' College hospital opened, he moved into Ward Seven, where he and several lice-ridden German cavalrymen were left by the attendants in rude bunks in a large, drafty room with windows twelve feet high and two inadequate fireplaces. Roos was so ill that he could not get warm during the chilly, early October nights, even when wearing his pants and his overcoat. By the end of the month, though, every man had his own bed—an iron frame—with sheets, pillow and pillowcase, wool blankets, and "a thick cotton quilt or half blanket with a white bottom and dark blue flowers," the bedding regularly laundered. New features included laundry facilities for the men, regularly emptied "night chairs" that replaced the chamber pots, and a kitchen and dining room that were "equipped with all of the latest features for saving time and work." Hospital rations improved or declined along with the supply of army rations, but the cooks tried to supplement the bland issue pork and beef hospital rations with ham, chicken, rice puddings, tea, and coffee. Roos was even "prescribed Lager beer as medicine."[47]

Northern governors and legislators had pressured the army to move sick men out of the "sickly" miasmatic, malarial South—and particularly out of Arkansas. Boardman was one of those sent north. At Saint Louis the Western Sanitary

Commission and local citizens provided patients with a range of reading material and food stuffs, including butter, eggs, and ham. Once convalescent, Boardman went to work blacking heating stoves and received passes to go into Saint Louis, where he bought fruit, read *Leslies' Illustrated,* and generally amused himself. On Christmas Day 1864 the commission provided patients a fine dinner and an oyster supper.[48]

Roos resumed his negotiations to transfer into the Invalid Corps, now renamed the Veteran Reserve Corps, once he began feeling better in late October. The surgeons judged him to be suffering from fatigue, exposure, malaria, and age and associated debilitation. Lieutenant Colonel Mattson learned that if Roos took a discharge for disability now, he would receive a half pension of four dollars per month, so he arranged for his discharge papers to remain undated so that Roos could draw full pay until he departed for Minnesota. When Mattson led a recruiting detachment home, the old soldier accompanied them, all arriving at Fort Snelling on 16 December. Mattson more than likely found ways to have the army pay Roos's travel expenses and provide him rations.[49]

Veteran Volunteers

Despite the best efforts of the recruiting parties, supported by bonuses and having the "encouragement" of the draft behind them, enlistments in the army were woefully inadequate. To solve the crisis, Congress began enlisting black men into the U.S. Colored Troops (USCT), creating an opportunity for white men to gain commissions in these units. To retain experienced volunteer soldiers once their initial terms of service expired, Congress offered those veterans who reenlisted for the duration of the war a $402 bonus and a thirty-day furlough at home (plus travel time). The best solution was for all or most of a volunteer unit to reenlist, thus preserving their collective experience and their organization. If three-quarters of a company, regiment, or battery reenlisted, the "veteran volunteers" received the bonus, the furlough, and a distinguishing sleeve mark as members of a "Veteran Volunteer" unit.[50]

By 23 December three-quarters of Company K had reenlisted, claiming the distinction of the first company in the VII Corps to do so. By year's end, all fifty-three men had signed up, and Captain Hodges and the other men on detached service returned to join the company to go home on their furlough. Captain Bowler expected, correctly, that Company F also would "veteranize." Colonel Andrews made a concerted effort to sway all of the men in his regiment to reenlist, addressing them on 5 January 1864. He urged them to renew their commitment on grounds of patriotism (they were "worth more to their country than the new men"), personal satisfaction ("they would not be contented to be in civil life and leave others to strike the finishing blows"), and personal gain (the bounty). He argued "that for the honor of the state and good of the service they should keep the 3d regt in existence as long as the war lasts."[51]

Mattson promised several men who wanted furloughs with family in eastern states that they would obtain one. Andrews targeted some men, including Peter Shippman from his old company, for special attention. Not all were convinced. Cpl. Thomas Canfield of Company G wrote his sister that "being a veteran all of ones days don't hardly pay I think that I am as big a veteran now as I care about being." He later reenlisted, partly from peer pressure and partly out of patriotism. By 7 January 352 men had reenlisted, and General Steele proudly informed Gov. Stephen Miller that the Third was a veteran regiment. Andrews telegraphed Senator Ramsey with the same news.[52]

Historians have discussed various possible motives soldiers had for reenlisting. Gerald Linderman has offered the psychological argument that the promise of a furlough worked for the fatalistic. Earl Hess and James McPherson favor the ideological motives of Union and freedom. Reid Mitchell and others support loyalty to and pride in the "primary group" (the regiment) along with peer pressure. James Robertson argues that economic incentives—the certainty of army pay and bonuses versus possible or probable unemployment at home—were paramount. Colonel Andrews appealed to each of these motives, and the men themselves cited one or more in explaining their decisions, but available evidence does not favor any one over another for the majority of those who reenlisted.[53]

Company K departed Little Rock on 12 January 1864, crossing the river in small boats since ice had closed the pontoon bridge. Ice also delayed the steamboats on the White River, and the men waited in Memphis because every available boat was in service taking Sherman's XVI Corps on a "secret mission" to the Red River. The troops eventually made their way to Cairo, boarding a train that stopped in Chicago, where the men presented Captain Hodges a fine sword. Resuming the trip, they were snowed in west of Madison before finally arriving in La Crosse on Saturday, 6 February. Leaving in stagecoaches on Wednesday, the men went home; only Captain Hodges and Lieutenant Gates, from Saint Paul, went to Fort Snelling to report.[54]

The regiment got a "treat . . . on account of being veterans" on 26 January and learned that policies had changed. After two Ohio regiments departed together, leaving their brigade so shorthanded that it was ineffective, Steele established a board to determine the units entitled to leave and when they could go home. Companies A, D, and F were authorized the furlough and began preparations to depart. The remaining six companies would go later—much later as it turned out. The men who did not reenlist were assigned to other companies. Andrews arranged for five men from New England in Company F to be detailed to escort a prisoner to Washington and then take their veteran furlough. Troops on detached service were recalled, all those going on furlough were paid, and the authorized companies departed on 7 February. This group had no trouble getting to Cairo, where undercook Willis Cowan of Company F (even undercooks received furloughs) deserted. Changing trains in Chicago on the fifteenth, they became snowbound between Tomah and La Crosse for three days. Coming up the Mississippi River on sleighs, the men stopped on Saturday in Red Wing, where Company D scattered for home. Company F dispersed in Hastings on Sunday, while Company A finally arrived in Saint Paul on Tuesday, 22 February.[55]

Captain Bowler did not accompany his men home as planned. On Wednesday, 20 January, he and Colonel Andrews spent the afternoon at the newly opened racetrack. General Steele loved horseracing, and some two thousand citizens and soldiers attended. This was Andrews's first time at a race. That evening another officer accompanied them to the circus. Just after they sat down, the bleachers collapsed, and Bowler's leg broke at the ankle. He and two men who reenlisted late in Company F departed Little Rock on 22 February.[56]

Visiting family and friends, doing work at home, sleeping, attending parties, and performing a little recruiting kept the men busy. Among their new recruits were William Sears, a blacksmith (his son, Richard, later founded Sears, Roebuck, and Company), who joined Company K and his father-in-law, forty-four-year-old Joshua Burton, who joined Company C. Charles V. Moon, a seventeen-year-old "accepted new recruit . . . presented" by G. Nelson Moon, presumably his father, who received a fifteen-dollar recruiter's bounty for joining Company K. When the unit returned south in early March, it boasted 48 new members, bringing Company K to 101 men. Mattson's recruiting party did well too, and Companies A, D, and F also brought in recruits, though not as many as Hodges's men did.[57]

In late March the three companies rendezvoused at Fort Snelling, where they and Mattson's detachment began the journey south, going in smaller groups overland in wagons to Winona and La Crosse, quartering in the courthouse until everyone reported. One man in Company F, twenty-one-year-old Pvt. George Baker, a fair-complexioned teamster with blue eyes and light hair, had made a friend. Her husband, Mr. Charles Carr (aged forty-five) of Rosemount, Minnesota, accused Baker of committing adultery with his wife (Cordelia, age thirty-one). On 26 March Dakota County District Attorney J. R. Slatter asked General Sibley to telegraph an order to Winona to have Baker held pending arrest by the sheriff. No such a telegram survives, however, and in any case, Baker was appointed regimental orderly soon after his return to Little Rock.[58]

On the night of Tuesday, 29 March, David Morgan, a former first sergeant, and several other men from Company F got drunk; returned to the courthouse in La Crosse for their rifles, saying they were going to avenge an insult; and ignored 2nd Lt. George Jameson's order to put down their weapons. Cursing,

Morgan and Pvt. John King used their gun butts to knock out door panels while trying to open a latched but unlocked door. Once back on the street, Morgan threw down his rifle, which discharged; a field-officer court later found Morgan guilty of conduct prejudicial and fined him a month's pay. The next morning the detachment took the train south to Cairo, where the post commander detained them because guerrillas were active. Released on 5 April, the men boarded the *Hilman* bound for Memphis and camped at Fort Pickens while waiting for another boat; they arrived in Little Rock on Wednesday, 13 April.[59]

Displaced into log huts on the statehouse grounds when the constitutional convention met in January, the six companies that had remained in Little Rock performed mostly routine duty: drill, drill, police patrol, drill. Colonel Andrews soon added some variety by ordering the garrison to spend one hour per day, except on Sundays, at target practice. He went with the Third to Honyer's plantation to watch them shoot on 11 March. But target practice did not offset the boredom, and several men turned to alcohol. Capt. Edwin Hillman of Company C resigned to avoid a court-martial, leaving Major Foster with only one officer in each of the present companies. While the sergeants stepped into the breach, this proved insufficient, and discipline slipped. On 29 March Pvt. Henry Glass of Company G was "so Drunk as to render him unfit for duty as a soldier"; swearing, he refused to obey his company commander. Pvts. Henry Coil of Company C and Michael Stahler of Company E were both charged with violation of the 45th Article of War on 8 April; each becoming "so drunk that he was unfit to perform the duty of a Patrol Guard . . . and failed to go out with his relief." The inspector general complained about the Articles of War not being read as required at dress parade.[60]

Elections for the new Unionist state government and for ratifying a new state constitution began on 13 March. Soldiers guarded the polling places while Arkansan soldiers "electioneered . . . for different candidates" and voted. This led to complaints that troops were influencing the election, something Andrews denied: "I have never seen a fairer election." The provost guards protected the polling places in Little Rock. By 18 March sufficient returns were in that Steele, writing Lincoln, estimated that some ten thousand men had voted, most supporting the new constitution.[61]

Effects in Arkansas of the Red River Campaign

In the spring of 1864, Lincoln and Halleck determined to proceed with the Red River Campaign, sending Maj. Gen. Nathaniel Banks's army and Rear Adm. David Porter's gunboats and transports up the Red River to Shreveport while General Steele moved from Little Rock via Arkadelphia to Shreveport, where the unified force would then march into eastern Texas. Steele thought it an absurd idea and said so. His logistics system was too fragile and incapable of building up the stocks of supplies he would need to support his force between Little Rock and Shreveport. Confederate and Union foraging parties had stripped western Arkansas bare of food and animal forage. The winter rains, giving way to spring rains, ensured the roads would be quagmires into which wagons and mules alike would sink. He feared that Price would seize the opportunity to disrupt the formation of a Unionist government in Arkansas and might even move into Missouri. Despite his objections and opinions, he began preparations for the march, designating those units that were going and those that would remain to protect his logistics base. The Third Minnesota was to stay in Little Rock, but the Sixty-First Illinois replaced the Forty-Third Illinois, which marched with Steele.[62]

Union forces marched south from the Little Rock fortifications on 23 March. The provost guard's duties now expanded to include picket duty and some of the scouting and foraging previously done by the departed units. Brigadier General Kimball, commanding the VII Corps base, turned to newly promoted (9 January 1864) Brig. Gen. Christopher Andrews, who took on additional responsibilities while retaining his command at Little Rock. Steele specifically mandated continuing the conciliatory policies in his absence. When Brig. Gen. Dandridge McRae, who had too many officers and too few enlisted men, increased his rebel recruiting activity near Augusta on the White River, Kimball had Andrews lead an expedition to disrupt his efforts. All six companies of the Third departed Little Rock for DeVall's Bluff on 30 March, where a company of the Eighth Missouri Cavalry awaited them.[63]

CHAPTER 9

FIGHTING GUERRILLAS AND
DISEASE AT PINE BLUFF

L ed by Maj. Everett Foster, the battalion of the Third Minnesota, numbering 186 men (a quarter of them new recruits), joined forty-five horsemen from the Eighth Missouri Cavalry aboard the *Dove* on Thursday, 31 March 1864. Escorted upriver by the USS *Covington*, Brigadier General Andrews instructed them to take prisoner anyone 'lurking about the shores whom we suspected would carry intelligence" to the enemy. By doing so, the expedition gained knowledge of enemy dispositions and acquired a guide who led them "through darkness, rain, and mud" to an empty enemy campsite on the Cache River.[1]

Reboarding the *Dove*, the force arrived at Augusta about 5 A.M. on 1 April. Ashore, Andrews threw a picket line around the town and questioned "citizens and colored men" before the men moved out on the Jacksonport Road in search of McRae's recruiting camp. A mile out of town, the column encountered enemy pickets; cavalry drove the rebels two miles down the road before they scattered. A few miles farther on, the Union force met a group of enemy horsemen, among them McRae and his staff, and nearly captured them.[2]

Near Fitzhugh's plantation the infantry found an abandoned wagonload of hams, on which they lunched when stopping about twelve miles out of Augusta. As the men prepared to march back to town, McRae's cavalry charged on them from out of the woods. Instead of fixing bayonets and forming a square, they received the enemy horsemen in line of battle, volley fire dismounting and killing many of the rebels. Cheering, the troops then "charged on them . . . [and] drove them back into the woods."[3]

Attacked at Fitzhugh's Woods shortly after beginning their return march by 450 or more dismounted rebels, the infantry battalion and the cavalry, dismounted, deployed as skirmishers, the men cautioned to take advantage of every shelter. By their excellent marksmanship, they repulsed the enemy, then fixed bayonets and counterattacked. Adj. Ezra Champlin was cited in reports for his heroism as he rode the Union line among "a shower of bullets, directing &

encouraging the men." Andrews's horse was shot out from under him. Extending his flank to protect his line of retreat, the general gained a water source and made McRae think he was retreating. The rebel commander ordered another attack, and the Third "poured forth a fire more damaging and deadly" than before, repulsing the Confederates.[4]

After a short rest, the Union column resumed its march to Augusta and the *Dove,* vulnerable to attack as they crossed a narrow causeway over a swamp. The rebel cavalry refused all orders to attack, however, as their will to fight was gone. Approaching town, the infantry dressed ranks and marched in with flags flying, singing "'Down with the Traitor!'" With them were thirteen captured rebels, several horses, and some freedmen. Second Lt. Olof Liljegren noted that he no longer heard complaints "about being a soldier. We are having a lively time. It sounds as if the rebels are all around us."[5]

Andrews's force left behind eight men killed in the second engagement (seven of them from the Third), including Sgt. Corydon Bevans of Company E. According to Col. Hans Mattson's later account, Bevans refused to be carried off the field, urging the men "to take their place against the enemy which they did nobly." Pvt. Henry Farnsworth's body was lost in the chaos of the fighting. Seventeen wounded men also remained behind (sixteen from the Third), including Pvt. Orrin Case of Company C, whose wound "rendered him almost helpless and entirely unfit to perform manual labor"; he did return to duty thereafter as a clerk. Chaplain Simon Putnam wrote that, before leaving, the Minnesotans broke the guns of their wounded comrades against trees to render them useless to the rebels. Sgt. Thomas Canfield of Company G wrote his sister, "We have heard but little from our wounded and left for dead up White River." Most of those men slowly returned to Little Rock, remaining there when the Third moved to Pine Bluff.[6]

Although one of McRae's men, W. W. Garner, wrote his wife that the outnumbered rebels had defeated the Third after a two-hour fight, the truth was that the outnumbered Minnesotans badly beat McRae's force, which suffered twenty to twenty-five men killed and sixty to seventy wounded. Col. Willis M. Ponder of the Twelfth Missouri Infantry (C.S.), McRae's second in command, told Capt. George Knight of Company E, who was on occupation duty in 1865, that the Third was "the hardest lot of men . . . that he ever ran against." Thirty years later General McRae told Minnesota historian Return Holcombe that he had at least six hundred mounted men, mostly experienced and armed with Enfield rifles, carbines, or shotguns, and had intended to capture the entire Union force north of Augusta. Clearly, both McRae and Ponder thought Andrews, who accomplished most of his objectives, had the better of the engagement.[7]

Returning to Little Rock on 3 April, the Third received a detachment of recruits, who were assigned to companies. Among them were Philander Skillman, who joined his brother, Franklin, in Company G, and Gottfried Hauser, a forty-three-year-old Swiss gardener who claimed to be a veteran of European service, though "proof [was] not yet in hand," and was assigned to Company F. Mattson assigned one or two sergeants from each company whose sole duty was to conduct "a school for the instruction of the new recruits."[8]

Several prisoners came south with the recruits and stood trial soon after arrival. A general court-martial on 9 April found Pvt. Philip Miller, whom Capt. John Preston had improperly enrolled in Company F in 1861, guilty of desertion and sentenced him to serve twenty-six months in the army (the time he was away from the regiment) and to "do his duty." Brigadier General Kimball rejected this verdict, noting that the only evidence of guilt was verbal testimony, there being no muster-in roll, and this was insufficient for conviction. Major General Steele agreed, discharging Miller and sending him home.[9]

Finally confirmed by the Senate and mustered in to his new rank, Andrews was serenaded by the Third's band on 14 April. Addressing the regiment, he said that "it was more honor to be Col of the 3d than to be any common Brig Gen." The officers of the regiment then joined Andrews in his quarters to celebrate his promotion. He received his first command as a general officer when General Kimball ordered him to take the provost guards and again disrupt McRae's continued recruiting in the Augusta region. On Monday, 18 April, detachments from the Third Minnesota and the Sixty-First Illinois took railcars to DeVall's Bluff to join the Eighth Missouri Cavalry. There, the Third boarded the *Commercial* and the Sixty-First the *James Raymond*. Proceeding upriver on Tuesday, they met a company of Kansas cavalry at Cotton Plant, then landed at Augusta, where Colonel Ponder of the Twelfth Missouri (C.S.) was captured. The Union force of nine hundred infantry and two hundred cavalry then moved against a Confederate cavalry camp, which they found abandoned. Interrogating captured rebels, Andrews learned of a threat to a First Nebraska Cavalry detachment stationed at Jacksonport, farther up the White River at the mouth of the Black River. After dispatching a warning message to the Nebraskans and sending to DeVall's Bluff for reinforcements, he marched to join the Nebraskans, hoping to capture McRae's command between the jaws of the two Union forces.[10]

Missing McRae, Andrews sent Mattson and the Third out foraging before reboarding the boats. The colonel wrote his wife of this march, saying that the men "had to cross four bayous and build rafts to cross on . . . , [riding] about 35 miles with the cavalry" in rain and without "a bit to eat" or any sleep for "two days through mud water and swamps." The whole force returned to DeVall's Bluff on 24 April with eight prisoners, including Colonel Ponder, one of Major General Price's dispatch bearers with his papers, "75 able-bodied colored recruits, 60 head of serviceable horses and mules, and $2,000 worth of contraband cotton."[11]

Though the Third was to remain overnight at DeVall's Bluff while the Sixty-First Illinois boarded waiting railcars to return to Little Rock, several men, mostly from Companies G and K also boarded the train. Missing their morning roll calls and thus absent without leave, they were soon tried in Major Foster's field-officer court for violating the 21st Article of War, found guilty, and fined half a month's pay. Most of the men explained, as did Musician George Godfrey of Company B, that when the regiment arrived at DeVall's Bluff, they assumed that they were to immediately return to Little Rock. Godfrey admitted hearing that the regiment was to go on the next train, but he was sick and felt that he could not remain in camp. Not finding his commanding officer, Godfrey "left with several others" for Little Rock. Pvt. Alfred Parks of Company B offered the common excuse "that he had no intention of committing any evil and regrets very much his thoughtlessness in disregarding the Article of War named." Foster found Francis Hamlin, who had joined the regiment on 8 April, guilty but thought that, "being a recruit and probably induced to go with others," his sentence should be remitted; Col. Powell Clayton, commanding the Post of Pine Bluff, agreed.[12]

Pvt. William McGee of Company G provided a different reason from the others. He and the other provost guards on duty from the Third, he claimed, had verbal permission from Asst. Provost Marshal Willet DeKay (captain of Company E) "that they might, if they desired to, go with the Regiment . . . with the express understanding that they were to report back to Capt. DeKay immediately after returning." After diligently searching for and not finding 1st Lt. Lewis Hancock, his company commander, he took the train for Little Rock. Hancock vouched for his story and noted that McGee was soon after promoted corporal "for uniform good conduct." McGee plead guilty and was sentenced to be reduced to the ranks and forfeit half a month's pay, but Colonel Clayton, though accepting the guilty finding, rejected the sentence.[13]

Riding the open cars back to Little Rock on Monday, a warm and pleasant day, the men anticipated several days of rest and routine. That evening at tea with General Kimball, Andrews learned that the Third was to go to Pine Bluff to temporarily reinforce the garrison while he took the Sixty-Second Illinois and a cavalry squadron from that post to escort a very large supply train to General Steele and his forces, then at Camden. The Twelfth Michigan Infantry and the Fifth and Eleventh Ohio Batteries from Little Rock would bolster the escort.[14]

Transferred to Pine Bluff

About 3 A.M. on Tuesday, a courier awakened Colonel Mattson with orders "to march with the Regt immediately to . . . reinforce Genl. Steele." The wagon train, the Twelfth Michigan, and the Ohio batteries left Little Rock at midday, crossing the Arkansas to take the road on the north side of the river. With each man carrying three days' rations and forty rounds of ammunition, the Third departed on the *Leonora* for Pine Bluff on Wednesday, accompanying General Andrews. The Arkansas was running high and fast, the passage was dangerous, but the regiment landed safely at Pine Bluff at dusk. There, Andrews learned that at Marks's Mills on 25 April the rebels had destroyed or captured Steele's entire supply train foraging out from Camden for supplies. Wanting units whose fighting qualities he knew, the general decided to take the Third with him instead of the Sixty-Second Illinois. Shortly after, the wagon train from Little Rock began crossing the river on flat scows.[15]

The 106 wagons already at Pine Bluff moved down the road to Camden very early Thursday morning with neither orders nor a guard, "merely to get out in line" and make room for the 120 Little Rock wagons. The Twelfth Michigan had just crossed the fog-shrouded river when it was sent on a mud march in increasingly heavy rain to catch up with and stop the rogue lead elements. Late that evening the twenty-mile-long train began moving toward Camden, about seventy miles southwest of Pine Bluff. Steele's chief of staff informed General Sherman that, "loaded with scant five days' rations . . . , [it] comprises all the land transportation . . . [and] every horse and mule" available to the Federals in Arkansas.[16]

Sometime on Friday, 28 April, a courier from Steele found Andrews with an order to turn back. Having left Camden on Wednesday, the army was then waiting to cross the flooded Saline River at Jenkins's Ferry (about thirty miles west of Pine Bluff) before rebels could come up in force and destroy it against the river. On Saturday, as the train reentered Pine Bluff, the men faintly heard cannonading to the west, where Steele's forces had finally made the crossing and were heading toward the Little Rock fortifications. Emboldened by their successes against Steele in Arkansas and Banks in Louisiana, the rebels began regularly harassing Union pickets and outposts. On Sunday, 1 May, a wagon train entered Pine Bluff carrying wounded soldiers, including "some negro Soldiers," who, Lieutenant Liljegren observed, "fought in the [unidentified] engagement desperately and showed no mercy to the rebs."[17]

A strategic point for the Union occupation of Arkansas, Pine Bluff was a river port at the junction of several interior roads. Though several buildings were burned or damaged by cannon shot when the rebels tried and failed to retake it in October 1863, the town still boasted all of the urban conveniences: a billiards room; a newspaper and bookstore; saloons; and churches, several of which attracted soldiers. General Andrews sang at the Episcopal church when he was in town. Methodists had a melodeon (a reed organ), but only the women sang. Roman Catholics worshipped in a frame building with a gallery, bell tower, and a melodeon. They sang, treated visiting soldiers politely, and heard good sermons from their Irish priest.[18]

Pine Bluff did not, however, have enough space to accommodate the Third and the Twelfth Michigan. The soldiers had to camp on the Williams farm on the edge of town without tents or baggage; some men from the Third's Company E slept in a corncrib. The Williams carriage, kept in the barn, was vandalized, for which Pvt. David Foss of Company E was blamed; Major Foster's field-officer court found him not guilty. After the regiment was attached to the garrison, the Minnesotans moved to a different camp on a bayou just outside of town. Pvt. James Crosby of Company I noted that "a yellowish scum cover[ed] the water," which sickened the men. Digging a well, the water table proved to be very close to the surface, so it actually tapped the same polluted water source. Mosquitos, flies, poisonous snakes, and a lack of shade combined to make Pine Bluff particularly unhealthy for the regiment. Lacking vegetables, the men soon suffered scurvy; cases of malaria multiplied, as did both diarrhea and dysentery; and typhoid cases soon appeared on the sick list.[19]

On Sunday, 8 May, rebels drove in the pickets on the Lower Monticello Road, while pickets on the Hot Springs Road reported that a scout came in with a captured "Rebel mail and six prisoners." General Andrews feared an attack and, as senior officer present, ordered the clearing of woods and brush on the perimeter of town and the construction of additional fortifications. Escaped slaves did some of the labor, but most of the work parties were composed of soldiers. Reduced by sickness, the Eleventh Ohio Battery needed more men from the Third to fill out its ranks and to help construct a redoubt for its three guns on the north side of town.[20]

After Andrews returned to Little Rock, Clayton ended the overengineering of the fortifications—Andrews had wanted walls 12–15 feet thick at the base; Clayton favored 2–3 feet—and limited the clearing of woods and brush to 1,300–1,600 feet from the works. Built in a zig-zag line to provide crossfire for the batteries and riflemen, the walls made from heavy clay soil provided good protection. The colonel shifted his picket lines and videttes and used wire fencing to hinder attacks at some points to reduce his manpower needs and to speed construction. As each major section was completed, Clayton rewarded the men with an issue of what Pvt. James Lockney of the Twenty-Eighth Wisconsin termed "the "worst and most firey" whiskey.[21]

Structured like guard details, the fatigue parties had two reliefs, one on duty and one resting in whatever shade could be found. Some officers allowed their relief to return to camp on their own account after their day's work was done; others required a roll call and marched the men back to camp. Pvt. William E. Hale of Company G assumed that his relief officers were of the first variety on 13 May when he left for camp and missed roll call. The officers agreed that he had done an honest day's work but *had* absented himself without leave; Major Foster fined

Hale a quarter of a month's pay. Musician Michael Farrell of Company I assumed that his work party was going to the sawmill; after morning roll call he went back to camp to get his laundry, which he then left with a washerwoman in town. But his party was not at the sawmill, and Farrell was deemed late and absent without leave; Foster helped his memory in future by fining him half a month's pay.[22]

Throughout Arkansas, disease reduced the numbers of men available to do duty as the rebels increased their attacks. In response, Steele shifted units to hold key points and to protect supply lines effectively, in the process changing the composition of his brigades. Mattson complained to his wife at being in the same brigade with the Fifty-Seventh U.S. Colored Infantry. Andrews's Second Division was scattered across central Arkansas, while the First and Third Divisions were concentrated, drilled together, and prepared for field service. The Third Minnesota and the four other units from the Second Division at Pine Bluff were from each of Andrews's three brigades. This dispersion did not affect morale, for the inspector general reported good morale in *all* of the infantry regiments. Chaplain Putnam reported that the behavior of the officers and the men was "such as becomes at once the soldier and the man. . . . [T]he best of discipline prevails, and the camp is a model of cleanliness."[23]

Despite ninety-degree heat and frequent rains, Mattson thought that the health of the regiment was "fairly good" on 18 June. On that same day scouting parties reported rebel pickets and rebel forces nearby. Soon the pickets near the Third's camp were driven in, the regiment formed in line of battle, and Company H went across a bridge to assist the guards. Clayton then ordered the construction of a new outer line of defenses, with additional cannon, sited to control all of the approaches to town. Fatigue parties of fifty to seventy-five men from each regiment went to work, while patrols, often a mix of infantry and cavalry, went out twelve to fourteen miles every day. Heavy rains turned the roads into mud and forced the fatigue parties to make fortifications of mud in the mud. In addition, the river began rising so that every swamp, bayou, and low point filled to overflowing.[24]

On Friday, 17 June, the day after this attack, 1st Lt. Hiram Gates of Company K, commanding a guard post on the Sulphur Springs Road, returned to camp several times while on duty, staying for an hour each time. He had done the same at Little Rock in December 1863, receiving only a reprimand, but with the increased threats at Pine Bluff, he was arrested, tried, convicted, and dishonorably dismissed the service. Tightening security further, Clayton even sent two "lost females" (prostitutes) across the river outside the lines; some Wisconsin men tried to sneak them back that night but earned jail time instead.[25]

Five days of rain swelled the Arkansas River, which undercut its banks, dropping part of one unit's camp into the water. The ground became saturated, and the sinks filled and overflowed, making the already polluted water even worse. The rains finally ended on 23 June; the next day dress parades resumed. The Third held the position of honor since Mattson was the senior infantry colonel, and the regiment passed the inspection of arms with praise; the Sixty-Second Illinois, in contrast, was seriously deficient, which Clayton addressed in scathing terms. On Saturday, 25 June, the Twenty-Eighth Wisconsin won a prize from the post commander for being best in field movements, while the Third won the prize for best in manual of arms. On July 10 inspectors complimented the Minnesotans for their cleanliness and the condition of their equipment, also noting that their "camp [was] thoroughly policed, . . . [with] good sinks." The increasing sickness among the men was, at this point, confined mostly to the new recruits.[26]

The river made an oxbow turn at Pine Bluff, forming a peninsula opposite the town, where Clayton worried that rebels could position artillery to fire on his positions. He decided to extend his defensive perimeter across the river and up the peninsula to its narrowest point, where he established a "chain guard." Having finally obtained sufficient equipment, he emplaced a two-hundred-yard pontoon bridge, supported by thirty boats and anchored by nine more, between the two parts of his defenses. Scouting parties pushed out further and more aggressively. One infantry scout, 350 men strong, went upstream on the *Miller* on Saturday, 2 July, to chase guerrillas. The rebels repeatedly cut the telegraphic link to Little Rock and attacked the repair parties sent out. Both sides foraged over the country; Clayton's men needed to bring in fifty wagonloads of animal feed per day. The men of the Third were tasked for these duties despite their swelling sick list.[27]

Scouts from Pine Bluff and the navy's gunboats both reported Confederate movements in the area. Steele's headquarters in Little Rock seemed to discount or ignore the navy's reports; it remains unclear if Clayton had access to them. Regardless, his own scouts reported heavy rebel activity too, with forces under Brig. Gen. James Fagan gathering to the south at Monticello and Price's command moving along the edge of Clayton's area of operations. The colonel feared that his post was not sufficiently secure if Fagan and Price operated jointly against him and thus pushed the construction of additional fortifications.[28]

The Third's campsite exposed the Minnesotans to diseases, a situation made worse when Surgeon Wedge ran out of quinine and later all types of medicines. Pine Bluff was at the end of a tenuous supply line that first resupplied the main body of VII Corps before all other forces. The shortages now suffered in Pine Bluff were due to two fires. In February a steamer loaded with medicines had burned at the dock in Louisville, Kentucky. Then in June, a medical warehouse in Saint Louis had burned. Maj. Gen. E. R. S. Canby, commanding the Military District of the West Mississippi, suspected sabotage in both fires. With the summer dry spell upon them, the White River was low, boat traffic was restricted, and what supplies were available moved slowly in Arkansas. Making this bad situation worse, Asst. Surg. Moses Greeley was on detached duty at the military prison and Asst. Surg. Nahum Bixby was ill, leaving only Surgeon Wedge and Hospital Steward Charles Bolander of Company D, a thirty-four-year-old physician, available to treat the sick.[29]

First Lt. William Grummons of Company C, still unhappy after being passed over in 1861, now complained that Mattson was promoting men into other companies, passing over deserving officers and sergeants. As a case in point, he noted that Mattson wanted Sgt. Bonde Olson of Company D promoted to first lieutenant in Company K, following Gates's dismissal, in preference to several second lieutenants and Company K's sergeants. The colonel was, Grummons asserted, favoring ethnic Swedes, several of whom were already officers. Governor Miller, with personal experience of both regimental command and politics, asked Mattson to clarify the rules he used for promotion. Replying on 27 August, after arrival in Minnesota on furlough, Mattson said that seniority was the primary factor, though if the senior in line was unfit, unqualified for the position, or about to muster out, he could be bypassed; the colonel had discretion "to put the right man in the right place." Miller then required that he certify there was "no man in Co K fit for the Lieutenancy of that Company." Mattson did so, noting that with Hodges gone, "it becomes absolutely necessary that one of the very best men should be put in command of the co. . . . After consulting with the Senior officers of the Regiment in regard to him [Olson] I was advised by them all to ask this promotion for him on account of his eminent qualifications for the position." The senior first sergeant in the regiment, Thomas Hunter of Company K, was not qualified to command a company but was deserving of promotion to second lieutenant in Company F, "there being no person in that Co as much entitled to it as he is." Olson was commissioned on 18 September, Hunter on 2 October. Mattson received the flexibility he wanted while Miller received clear and consistent guidelines.[30]

In July rebel activity increased yet again, and Mattson now commanded the "entire upper wing" of five fortifications on the western edge of Pine Bluff, with three infantry regiments, three batteries of light artillery, and two squadrons of cavalry at his disposal. He claimed that his forces were "longing for Poppa Price and his ragmuffins" to challenge them. When most of Clayton's Fifth Kansas Cavalry departed for Little Rock and discharge from the service, manpower became extremely tight; Mattson thought that the veteran companies awaiting furlough would have to wait a lot longer. By late July guerrillas were operating all along the Arkansas River from Pine Bluff to Fort Smith, harassing trains and patrols on the Memphis & Little Rock Railroad, and attacking shipping on the White River, while rebel cavalry ranged the countryside to attack Union patrols and outposts. To Mattson's surprise, despite these increased threats and the decreased manpower available to counter them, on 3 August he received orders to send the last six companies due veteran furloughs home.[31]

A Summer without Medicines

That same day the colonel ominously observed in a letter to Mrs. Mattson, "it is fearfully sick here this summer. . . . [W]e have had no medicines for three weeks." Reporting monthly to Adj. Gen. Oscar Malmros in Saint Paul, Mattson noted that the sick list ranged between two hundred and three hundred men from August through October. Many years later, speaking to the Military Order of the Loyal Legion, he said that hundreds were ill during this season: Of the nearly eight hundred men, about half of them new recruits that he had "brought to that horrid graveyard, . . . there were not enough fit for duty at the beginning of August to bury our own dead," forcing him to borrow burial details from a newly arrived unit.[32]

Capt. John Devereaux of Company G and 2nd Lt. Thomas Hunter of Company F commanded a ninety-man detachment of recruits, including their first draftees, which left Fort Snelling on 21 July on the *Mollie Mohler,* bound for Cairo and the Third Minnesota. Described by the *Daily Press* as a "fine body of men . . . [who] bore their lot good naturedly," the group had a fine passage to Cairo, then transferred to the *Atlantic,* which hobbled in to Memphis with only one side paddle working. There the detachment shifted to the *Kate Hart.* The USS *Neosho* met the *Hart* at the mouth of the White River and escorted it upstream. Part way upriver, the *Hart* had to take the *Neosho* in tow but abandoned it when the warship ran aground. The *Hart*'s rudder then broke, and the captain had to steer using his paddlewheels up to DeVall's Bluff. Four men were left in Little Rock hospitals as they passed through the capital on their way to Pine Bluff; one of them later died.[33]

Among the drafted men was Lewis Emery, a thirty-year-old veteran of the First Minnesota Infantry, discharged after being wounded at First Bull Run in July 1861. Why he was drafted instead of a nonveteran is unknown. Reporting to Fort Snelling on 6 July, Emery found that many of the draftees were married and many were religious. Some had received a local bonus, whereas others (including Emery) had not; there was no rule of consistency. Assigned to Company G, in which he found several friends serving, he did daily duty as a nurse in the regimental hospital and cared for the newcomers as they quickly took sick; many died. Cpl. George Moore of Company A and Sgt. Thomas Canfield of Company G were among the sergeants whose sole assignment was to train the new men. The Third was successful at attracting volunteers throughout the war and received only a small number of draftees, most of whom came with this group.[34]

With all the newcomers, the Third now had the minimum number of men needed to have three field officers, which meant, Mattson wrote his wife, that he could not resign his commission and return home. In truth, had he submitted his resignation, General Steele would have unhappily accepted it, but the good colonel liked commanding his "own quick regiment" and had no intention of leaving it. Mattson offered her an olive branch of good news in the same letter: he was coming home with the furloughed veterans. In addition to the veterans on furlough, the groups returning to Minnesota included those on sick leave and others discharged for disability. This most debilitated detachment left Pine Bluff on Friday morning, 12 August, on board the *Annie Jacobs* and the *J. H. Miller*. On the eve of their departure, the First Division's inspector general observed that, between "standing Picket Guard one day and working on the fortifications or handling Govt Stores the next . . . , Sick lists are rising to an alarming height and men are dying rapidly." The troops, he observed, did no drill, got little rest, and suffered low morale.[35]

General Andrews welcomed the veterans to DeVall's Bluff with a "nice fresh roasted beef" dinner and helped them on the boat, providing ice and a barrel of ale for their voyage. He observed that "they have suffered a good deal at Pine Bluff"; Cpl. Charles Strand was more emphatic: they "were in such a pathetic condition . . . [that] their own mothers wouldn't have recognized them." Their trek home was uneventful. Arriving at La Crosse, Mattson telegraphed for permission to leave the men from southern Minnesota towns at the river port nearest their home. Lt. Col. John Averill, the superintendent of the volunteer recruiting service, approved and had the necessary paperwork sent from Fort Snelling.[36]

Meanwhile, Clayton, now a brigadier general, was short of cavalry and ordered the remaining companies of the Third to send out mounted patrols. Pvt. Jay Pratt of Company A, a three-year man, wrote on 25 August that the troops going out on a scout drew "horses and carbines and revolvers. . . . I think the whole regt will be mounted"; it soon was. Private Skillman remembered choosing a horse from those left behind by the Fifth Kansas, then selecting bridles, saddles, and other unfamiliar items that he and his fellows mostly had no idea how to assemble, let alone how to put on a horse.[37]

The mounted infantrymen had to master staying on their animal while maneuvering in columns of two or four. The horses were experienced cavalry mounts that knew the maneuvers and bugle calls far better than their riders. The old hands had some idea of what the calls were about and how to properly handle and maneuver the animals from their prior experience riding mules; they doubtless enjoyed watching the inexperienced men learn the necessary skills on the job and under threat. One recruit, on outpost duty on the Monticello

Road, provided such a show. Skillman related that the man had watered his horse and "started back . . . at a mild gallop; but directly . . . the horse broke into a mad race, coming straight in my direction. Then . . . the saddle turned slowly and went under the horse's belly. The recruit evidently got tired of the saddle." The horse, now lacking a rider, dashed into the group of hitched animals and knocked another recruit over a fence. If Company D's duty was typical, then the mounted men were on either picket or patrol duty for ten days at a time.[38]

Rebel and Union pickets could often see each other. Clayton was not about to risk defeat outside his fortifications, and the rebels were unwilling to attack him; instead patrols and small detachments fought each other. Guerrillas were out in force, even attacking and burning the *J. H. Miller,* whose captain was arrested on suspicion of complicity for having refused to allow the black troops on board to retain their weapons. Steele sent two infantry regiments to Pine Bluff as reinforcements; with them, Clayton became more confident. Increasing the patrols guarding the telegraph line, he sent additional patrols downriver looking for rebels attempting to cross, all in obedience to Steele's commands. The Third participated in many such expeditions. With three months' rations in his warehouses, well-placed artillery in extensive fortifications, plentiful ammunition, and an escape route across the pontoon bridge if either portion of his defenses fell, Clayton began reconnaissance-in-force operations—that is, looking for a fight—despite Steele's disapproval.[39]

The Pine Bluff garrison had little free time to enjoy either "The Lady of Lyons" at the theater or its star, an "infamous character noted & well known among . . . many soldiers who know her by sight at least, if not more intimately." Several senior officers, including the bachelor Clayton, frequented the theater. Capt. Edward Reddington of the Twenty-Eighth Wisconsin noted that many of his regiment's officers gambled heavily, as did the general, who on 27 August banned gambling on post. In the Third's records and letters, there are no indications of illegal or immoral conduct that would weaken discipline or increase arrests. By all accounts, the Minnesotans enjoyed the company of women, though only a few men married Southerners, but none while in Pine Bluff.[40]

On Wednesday, 24 August, scouts encountered a large rebel cavalry force, perhaps 15,000 men, going up the Saline River, presumably a part of General Price's command moving to invade Missouri. Most of his army crossed the Arkansas above Little Rock and moved too fast for the VII Corps to do more than harass it in passing. Clayton responded to the apparent increase in rebel activity by requesting the issue of two hundred rounds of ammunition per infantryman. VII Corps ordnance staff also provided one hundred rounds of carbine and fifty rounds of revolver ammunition for each cavalryman and two hundred rounds for each artillery piece, promising more if needed. Clayton's men aggressively scouted his area of operations and foraged heavily, encountering rebels mostly passing through. Guerrilla activity dropped off in September and October as most went with Price into Missouri. In late October, after the Third transferred to DeVall's Bluff, the tired, defeated, and partially disorganized rebel army retreated to its strongholds in southern Arkansas to lick its wounds.[41]

At the end of August, the Third Minnesota in Arkansas, then commanded by Capt. James Hoit, had 324 men in convalescent camp and 44 men, including Dr. Bixby, their only surgeon, in the regimental hospital. Despite monthly reports to Adjutant General Malmros, Governor Miller was unaware of the regiment's massive sick list, but he was quite concerned at the plight of the suffering Sixth Minnesota in Helena. In late July he sent Dr. Levi Butler, the Third's original surgeon, south as the state's agent to investigate and help the Minnesotans there. Although Butler never moved up the Arkansas or White Rivers from Helena, his reports benefited the Third as Miller joined other midwestern governors in demanding that their troops be sent to healthier locations in the northern states, a request granted reluctantly in September.[42]

When Miller finally realized the extend of the Third's plight in early August— the total lack of medicines, the absence of surgeons, and the huge numbers of sick and dying men—he instructed Colonel Mattson to have Bixby request a "temporary supply of the most necessary articles and I will get the Sanitary commission to furnish them." After Dr. J. V. Wren of Saint Cloud declined, the governor appointed Dr. F. B. Etheridge, former surgeon of the Fifth Minnesota, "Surgical Commissioner on behalf of the State" to accompany the state's commissioners to accept ballots from soldiers (for the 1864 general election) and visit Little Rock, Pine Bluff, Helena, and other places where Minnesota troops were known to be suffering. General Sherman had banned civilian movement on the western railroads, but Miller complained to the War Department, which reissued General Orders no. 295, directing military personnel to provide Minnesota's commissioners the assistance they needed to take the soldiers' votes. Etheridge's commission and accompanying paperwork were sufficiently vague so that he could travel with the voting commissioners, bringing with him fifty dollars' worth of quinine for the Third. After Mattson arrived in Saint Paul on furlough and informed Miller more fully of the Third's plight, the governor wrote Asst. Surg. Gen. Robert Wood in Saint Louis asking that the regiment be given "all possible relief," particularly that their surgeons be returned from detached duty.[43]

General Canby, having accepted the anti-Steele views of the general officers in New Orleans, sent inspectors general throughout the units of the VII Corps in late September seeking flaws. Steele and his army were considered inferior because of the logistics issues they encountered during the Red River Campaign, the poor health of their animals, and the high disease and death rates among the troops. Condemning the Thirty-Second Iowa's camp as "filthy" and noting that a quarter or more of each infantry regiment in Pine Bluff was sick, the inspectors noted on 6 October that over half the 494 men in the Third Minnesota, mostly recruits, were ill. But their conclusion did not fault the unit: "The regiment has always sustained a high reputation for its police regulations. The locality at Pine Bluff seems exceptionally unhealthy."[44]

Dr. Etheridge arrived with the quinine on 4 October to find that the army had finally managed to provide medicines to Dr. Bixby, who had recovered enough to help care for the 400 men in camp. There were still 345 men sick, and according to Capt. James Bowler, only 20 men were fit for duty. Most of the deaths in the regiment at this time occurred among the new recruits, particularly the older ones, such as thirty-nine-year-old Pvt. Alpheus Bulen.[45]

The real curative for the Third's troubles came on 9 October, when the regiment was ordered to take post at DeVall's Bluff, a move Steele's adjutant termed "a sanitary measure." Another order sent 15 sick men, part of a larger 150-man group from Pine Bluff, to Northern hospitals via special steamers. Several hundred soldiers, including some from the Third, were soon sent to the large general hospitals in Memphis. Too numerous for the hospital vessels, many were moved on regular transports carrying normal passengers and cargo and thus had no special medical care or food. Miner Monroe, a black undercook in Company H, was one of several men who, too sick to move, remained in the hospitals at Pine Bluff; he died on 12 October, leaving "no effects." Others, including Pvt. Robert Fulton of Company F, were quarantined at their outpost camps; Fulton died of typhoid fever on 19 October at the camp on Pennington's plantation.[46]

The furloughed men, meanwhile, arrived in Minnesota. Some of the ill or debilitated got to see home but did not get to die ashore; former captain Charles Nudd of Company A died of "a congestive chill" as his steamer approached Hastings on 25 August. Chaplain Putnam got home, where he died on 24 October, surrounded by his family. But the largest (and healthiest) group, led by Mattson, arrived at Fort Snelling on 25 August, turning in their guns and accoutrements at the fort. Adjutant General Malmros took "possession of the State Colors of his regiment until called for" by Mattson, who took time to review with Malmros and Governor Miller the regiment's service and requirements, particularly their continuing need for more recruits.[47]

Every county had a quota of recruits, and many townships provided bounties to encourage enlistment and avoid a draft. John Slater, a German farmer, enlisted in the Third for one year and received a one-hundred-dollar bounty, one-third paid on enlistment. Levi Debel, a French Canadian, enlisted on 4 September, got his partial bounty, and then deserted five days later. The Third's recruiting party, assisted by the recovering veterans, did very well, in part because the regiment had an enviable reputation. As 1st Lt. Ephraim Pierce of Company F pointed out, the Third was "well officered, and being mounted," was a desirable unit to join. Among the new recruits were brothers Andrew and Lewis (Lars) Norelius. Andrew, aged thirty-four, was baptized with Hans Mattson at the Swedish Baptist Church in Rock Island, Illinois, in the early 1850s and served as minister to the church in Cambridge, Minnesota. Lars was a twenty-one-year-old farmer. Their brother, Eric, was the pastor of the Swedish Lutheran Church in Vasa, where Mattson was a leader of the church and civic communities. Andrew probably served as an unofficial chaplain, at least for Company D, once he arrived in Arkansas.[48]

The *Hastings Independent* observed that the returning men were well behaved, "all the soldier boys go right to work, showing they know their duty both in the field and at home." But the *St. Paul Daily Press* noted: "Unfortunately, in nearly every veteran regiment that comes home, there are more or less bad men, who get into trouble and bring a stain on their comrades. Peter LeClair, a veteran of the Third, is one of these." LeClair had already experienced every form of army trial and now "was found guilty at Police Court" on 27 August for stealing a four-dollar stereoscope from Martin's Photograph Gallery. Unable to pay the fifteen-dollar fine, he was jailed for three weeks.[49]

The veterans, their health restored, assembled at Fort Snelling, retrieved their arms and colors, and departed south on 3 October on board the *Damsel.* Shifting to the *Belle Memphis,* the troops arrived in Memphis on 7 October. Mattson wrote his wife that he was glad that she had not come south with him because Price remained active in Missouri. After waiting several days, the men boarded the *Tycoon* for the trip up the White River. Stuck on a sandbar for three days and their food running short, Mattson obtained provisions from a passing "govt boat," secured a flatboat, and supervised the transfer of enough cargo to float their vessel free. Boats coming downriver reported being fired upon, so Mattson kept sixty armed men on watch continuously. Once freed, the *Tycoon* joined the small flotilla waiting at Saint Charles for a gunboat escort. Landing at DeVall's Bluff on 17 October, the colonel wrote Mrs. Mattson: "good news—the regt is relieved from Pine Bluff is now at Little Rock and will be here tomorrow—we will build houses here and stay over winter."[50]

The four Minnesota companies at Pine Bluff departed on 16 October on board the *Annie Jacobs,* leaving behind men in hospitals at Pine Bluff and at Little Rock as well as a detachment of healthier men to bring their baggage on another boat. As the *Annie* approached Little Rock, one of the recruits, "Mr. A. V. Hamlin . . . , was lost overboard"; he was a forty-two-year-old farmer from Maine. Most of the men sent north to hospitals survived, but Pvt. Edward Williams of Company K died of chronic diarrhea, and Pvt. Peter Moobeck of Company H died of malarial fever, both while ascending the Mississippi River on the hospital steamer *D. A. January* on 17 October. As the companies of the Third reunited at DeVall's Bluff, each was taken aback. Emery, from Pine Bluff, thought that Mattson's veterans "looked ragged and I hope will be healthy." Mattson wrote Malmros, "it was painful to see these men; their sufferings have been terrible; they resemble more dead men than active soldiers, not one is fit for duty."[51]

CHAPTER 10

RECOVERY AT DeVALL'S BLUFF

DeVall's Bluff was, according to "Miles" of the Seventh Minnesota, who passed through on his way from Memphis to Little Rock in October 1864 just before the Third arrived, a "military post of some consequence. It has extensive fortifications, camps, shanties, pens, puddles, sutler's shops, Ambrotype galleries, etc., arranged with no reference to order or convenience." Paymaster G. M. McConnell was more negative when visiting back in July: "Hay, hard-tack, bacon, coffee . . . quartermaster's, commissary's, sutler's, traders,' and speculators' stores and traps were stacked in apparent inextricable confusion." The place stank of rotting vegetables and dead animals, and the water was bad, making clear for "Miles" "the necessity of the large hospital here, and an explanation of the very extensive grave yard adjacent."[1]

Pitching their tents near the White River, the men of the Third Minnesota slowly began constructing winter-quarters buildings out of logs. Colonel Mattson wrote to his wife, urging her to come south, "I shall build a shanty for you and we shall have a sweet time"; she rejected his blandishments. The Minnesotans soon resumed company and battalion drill and began preparing to discharge the remaining three-year men who had not reenlisted. On 6 November Mattson led their brigade in review before Major General Steele, who inspected the infantry and artillery. Earlier in the day, as the general examined the fortifications, an arriving supply boat, the *Celeste,* struck a snag and sank at the landing.[2]

Many of the men to be discharged were on detached duty. Most of them, including Pvt. Louis Littlefield, who was in the print shop at Cairo, were relieved of duty and sent to join the regiment. Several men in specialized positions, including Pvt. Chauncey Gibbs, an apothecary by trade serving as the clerk for the superintendent of general hospitals in Memphis, were discharged and mustered out at their duty posts. Pvt. Madison Coleman and most of the other hospitalized men were mustered out upon release from the hospital and went directly home. Coleman was accompanied by his brothers, Seldon and Addison, all of whom had served in Company A. Some men complained to Governor Miller that, being discharged at DeVall's Bluff, they had to arrange and pay for their own travel to Minnesota, suggesting that some discharged men returned as individuals rather than as members of an organized unit. Miller received neither an answer nor a change in policy from the army in response to his queries. The mustering out and discharge from service of the 145 three-year men on 14 November reduced the regiment below the minimum strength required to justify three field officers, prompting Mattson to request sufficient recruits to restore the regiment to that level; enough new men arrived to allow the Third to retain all of its field officers.[3]

Men who planned to take jobs working for the army or had found opportunity in Arkansas were happy to be discharged at DeVall's Bluff. The army paid well: Pvt. George Brookins of Company I, described by Surgeon Wedge as "broken down in health," began working as a clerk in the DeVall's Bluff Quartermaster Depot at seventy-five dollars per month plus rations and anticipated getting one hundred dollars per month in due time. Former captain Edward Baker (Company E) leased a plantation from the Treasury Department and operated it with freedmen. Former colonel Chauncey Griggs was among those who returned south to Little Rock "ready and willing to make a pile [of money]."[4]

Pvt. Marvin Hathaway was one of the men mustered out from the convalescent camp at Fort Snelling. In late December he wrote the Saint Paul newspapers denouncing conditions in the convalescent barracks: "there are few places within our lines where the soldier suffers more from want of proper clothing than at Fort Snelling." Pointing out that without the descriptive lists the quartermaster would not issue soldiers clothing, he said the men lacked overcoats and blankets and had to sleep on the floor in filthy conditions. While Governor Miller ordered an investigation, other correspondents weighed in. On claimed, "'MPH' [Hathaway's pen name] does not talk like a veteran," while another made counterclaims. The commander of the convalescent detachment declared that he inspected the quarters daily. Twenty-five soldiers wrote Col. Robert McLaren of the Second Minnesota Cavalry, the post commander, refuting Hathaway's claims. While the truth is indeterminable for lack of evidence, the uproar ensured a higher level of care and concern thereafter, which might have been Hathaway's intention.[5]

Several men who sought discharge instead were charged with desertion. In every case they either failed to get their sick leave properly and officially extended or the regiment had lost track of them and incorrectly listed them as absent without leave. Pvt. John Cochran of Company B, hospitalized at Fort Snelling without a descriptive list, and Pvt. Kelber Wilkerson of Company A, sick at home until he reported to the fort, were both charged as deserters. Cpl. Lewis Kimball, wounded at Fitzhugh's Woods, failed to get his sick leave properly extended and was declared absent without leave. Pvt. Arne Arneson of Company B transferred into the Veteran Reserve Corps after being released from the fort hospital and for a time was listed as a deserter on the Third's rolls.[6]

By this late stage of the war, fewer men were willing to enlist, even with bounties and the threat of the very unpopular draft. The Third had fewer draftees than other regiments and only seven known substitutes. Some draftees never joined the regiment, including Charles Marples, who mustered in on 6 June and never appeared in camp. After serving at Fort Snelling for months, Marples received a furlough in January 1865, after which he went to Winnebago City as a recruiter for a month or so before returning to the fort. Tallef Halverson of Company B appears to be the only substitute who served until the Third returned home. Henry Graham, hired by Thomas Simpson of Winona as his substitute, deserted the day after he mustered in and received his partial bounty. The other substitutes died early in their service.[7]

Draftees and substitutes joined the new volunteers, reporting to the draft rendezvous compound at Fort Snelling, to await shipment to their various units. Most men could not obtain a pass to leave the rendezvous, where they were unhappy with their treatment and food. One draftee wrote the *Minnesota Volksblatt* on 23 October 1864, saying that those confined in "the 'bull-pen' are not only penned up like wild beasts and criminals, but all treated as such, being actually *starved*." A petition soon demanded better food. The *St. Paul Pioneer Press,* the Democratic organ, supported the petitioners, while the Republican paper, the *St. Paul Daily Press,* dismissed the whole thing.[8]

All the pressure from Northern governors to move their sick and wounded men to healthier hospitals north of the Ohio River resulted in the opening of several general hospitals in river towns and railroad cities, usually in repurposed hotels. When the first 160 soldier-patients were sent from the Jefferson Barracks Hospital to the new Swift General Hospital in Prairie du Chien, Wisconsin, at least two members of the Third were in the group. Crossing the Mississippi, these patients took a train to Chicago, riding in decrepit cars with no nurses, no food, and only the floor to sit on. Changing trains in the city, they had to find breakfast for themselves, often eating it on the cold streets, and boarded overcrowded and rickety cars. Arriving in Prairie du Chien, everything changed as they were greeted, given hot water and towels to wash up, and then enjoyed a fine dinner provided by the women of the town. Unfortunately, within the month, Pvt. John Barnes of Company G died of consumption, while Pvt. Frank Brunell of Company B died of chronic diarrhea.[9]

Restored to Duty Again

The veteran volunteers and their new colleagues at DeVall's Bluff completed the construction of winter quarters and began doing picket and guard duty.

Bushwhackers were increasingly active, threatening the Memphis & Little Rock Railroad supply line and causing Major General Canby concern for the security of the supply depot. Ordering a brigade and a battery of light artillery sent from the XIX Corps, and a battery of twenty-pound Parrot rifles and another of six-inch rifles from Morgana, Louisiana, he ordered new fortifications constructed; the healthy men of the regiment went to work building them.[10]

As the Third's effective duty strength increased, the Minnesotans began participating in foraging and scouting expeditions. Their first opportunity came after Brigadier General Andrews, learning of guerrilla activity near West Point, ordered Mattson, still commanding the brigade, to send out a scout in "great secrecy." The colonel specified three companies, one each from the Third, the Sixty-First Illinois, and the Ninth Kansas Cavalry. All guerrillas in Arkansas and most Confederate forces, even infantry, were mounted, and Union infantry needed a strong cavalry force to intercept and pin the enemy in place so the foot soldiers could come to bear. Capt. Otto Dreher of Company F, commanding this scouting party, had only fifty Kansas cavalrymen, normally too few to be effective. Steele was deficient in cavalry units, and most of the animals were weak from hunger and overwork. Still, Brigadier General Davidson, formerly commander of the cavalry division and now chief of cavalry in the Military District of the West Mississippi; his friends on Canby's staff; and Canby's assistant inspector general of cavalry all accused Steele of using "*unnecessarily large* [emphasis mine]" cavalry scout and picket forces, thereby overworking the horses, who then consumed too much precious forage. Most of these criticizing officers had no understanding of just how different the war in Arkansas was. In addition, Steele had removed Davidson from his command for insubordination; he was now seeking payback.[11]

Andrews and his staff issued very detailed orders to Captain Dreher to "capture rebel prisoners to obtain information." The *Elba,* a less-expensive vessel to charter, was not available, so Andrews had to hire the *Commercial;* undoubtedly, rebel spies learned of this. Departing upriver on Wednesday, 16 November, Dreher briefly landed cavalry at Peach Orchard Bluff, then put infantry ashore at Negro Hill to march fifteen miles to West Point. The Minnesotans captured a "Lieutenant Oliphant, a notorious fellow," and ten other rebels. Taking "what chickens and household furniture that we want," the men returned to the landing, boarded the vessel, and went up to Augusta, where thirty-six more prisoners were captured. Returning downriver, rebel artillery fired on the *Commercial* from a canebrake.[12]

Several men from the Forty-Third Indiana captured at Marks's Mills escaped from the rebel prisoner-of-war camp at Tyler, Texas, and entered Union lines near DeVall's Bluff on 23 November. They told Brigadier General Andrews, who interviewed them, that the prisoners in Tyler were sick with scurvy; their diet consisted of cornmeal, beef, a half ration of salt, and very little else; and they lacked medical care. He also learned that Pvt. Marion Freeman of the Third's Company C, a cadre man with the Fifth Arkansas (African Descent), was a prisoner there. (Freeman died at the camp on 3 December.)[13]

Veteran furloughs, the mustering out of so many men (even whole units), and disease all reduced the effective strength of the VII Corps. Andrews could not use the reinforcements from the XIX Corps for anything except scouts and other "military duty"; his own units had to construct the fortifications and perform all of fatigue duty, hard labor that weakened the men. Though malaria receded during the winter, the chilling rains and bursts of severe cold encouraged other diseases and ailments.[14]

In November Major General Price and his tired, defeated rebel soldiers, though still intact as combat forces, along with refugees from Missouri, retreated through western Arkansas. Andrews responded by increasing the strength of his pickets and ordered daily target practice "according to the principals [sic] laid down" by the War Department. Mattson made sure that his regiments did target practice. He also ordered the schooling of officers and noncommissioned officers in army regulations, tactics (small-unit as well as brigade tactics), and "military office business," the sergeants also learning the management of men in quarters; Andrews's Hints to Company Officers was probably a training manual. Brig. Gen. Alexander Shaler retained the orders for target practice after he relieved Andrews in command of the Second Division. Every time Mattson became acting brigade commander, he ordered target practice and schooling, suggesting that the regular commander, Col. William Graves of the Twelfth Michigan Infantry, was not as interested and that some regimental and company leaders found the tasks too bothersome.[15]

On 6 December the regiment "paraded out to see a deserter shot." Mattson later ordered a scout to go out under Capt. Joseph Swan, consisting of Company I from the Third, one company from the Sixty-First Illinois, and one hundred cavalrymen. Going upriver on the Mattie to sweep the region about Augusta, the men returned to report that the people there were "in great need of salt" and that the principal rebel commander in the area, Col. Archibald Dobbins of the First Arkansas Cavalry (C.S.), promised not to attack a boat coming to take cotton, presumably in exchange for salt, though his motive is unclear.[16]

Mattson himself led out 400 infantry from his brigade, with 150 cavalrymen from the Ninth Kansas, taking the Kate Hart and the Sir William Wallace up to Augusta. Foster commanded the infantry. The companies from the Third went ashore again at Negro Hill and marched to West Point, another detachment landed at the mouth of the Little Red River, and Mattson and the rest of the force landed at Greg's Ferry on the Cache River, the infantry securing the ferry to give the cavalry a secure line of retreat. Pvt. Lewis Emery of Company G wrote that they searched every house on the way to West Point and in that town, looking "for firearms, rebs, or anything contraband," and captured three men and their horses, "a few colored individuals, and some other tuck." Back at Negro Hill, the detachment boarded the boats and went up to Augusta, where they seized a "lot of contraband goods on their way from Memphis," including ten barrels of salt, pork, and molasses. Rebels were overrunning the region, foraging cattle and corn from the residents. On the return voyage Mattson learned, too late, that the rebels were working a saltworks near Augusta.[17]

At the end of November, the inspector general was pleased with the Third, though he thought their recruits, an "awkward and not a generally good looking set of men," were slovenly and dirty but "show[ed] a willingness to do right [but] they are ignorant of what is right." A month later, though many of the recruits were sick, he judged them much improved, keeping their rifles, equipment, and clothes clean and in good order. He praised the cleanliness of their camp as well and recommended that other units adopt their practice of carrying away the kitchen slops in barrels rather than dumping garbage in the sinks. The stables and mules were well kept, and he rated the regiment highly on discipline. He noted that in the past month the Third had taken "eighty prisoners, including fourteen commissioned officers"; horses; and large quantities of contraband goods, though they destroyed much of what they found. He concluded that "the picket duty is well done. These troops are well instructed in this."[18]

General Canby finally relieved Steele of command of the VII Corps and the Department of Arkansas, appointing Maj. Gen. Joseph J. Reynolds, formerly XIX Corps commander, in his place. General Andrews solicited contributions from his division officers for a presentation sword for Steele; the officers of the Third elected not to do so, declaring that Steele "has not done right by us," though their reference is unclear. The transfer of command was not the formal affair envisioned in army regulations but an almost accidental meeting in the middle of the White River: Steele and his staff departing downriver, Reynolds traveling upriver. Once in command, Reynolds quickly moved to tighten discipline, particularly by removing drunken officers, and replaced several corps staff officers, including almost all of the provost marshals, including Capt. Willet DeKay of Company E in Little Rock, who promptly resigned his commission effective 9 January 1865. The most important effect of the change in department command was in expectations and attitudes. Reynolds and his staff arrived convinced that the worst units in the army formed the VII Corps and that Arkansas was the swamp into which they sank.[19]

Reynolds issued an unprecedented directive on 24 December 1864 that read: "Tomorrow being Christmas, all fatigue duty except such as may be necessary, will be suspended until Monday morning the 28th inst." In prior years Christmas was officially just one more duty day, but reflecting changes in the larger society, it had become a holiday if not a holy day. Capt. James Bowler and the officers of the 112th U.S. Colored Infantry (USCI) celebrated Christmas together, suggesting its observance was widespread in the VII Corps.[20]

The New Brooms of Change

On Monday, 26 December, General Shaler relieved General Andrews as commander of both the Second Division and the Post of DeVall's Bluff. Several officers from the Third Minnesota, including Bowler and others commissioned into the black regiments, came to say goodbye. The captain wrote home that he had dinner with Colonel and Mrs. Mattson, who finally had acceded to her husband's blandishments at some point in November. Andrews issued a circular letter to his division, complimenting the troops, then departed for his new brigade command, accompanied by his aides-de-camp, 1st Lt. Ezra Champlin and 2nd Lt. Heman Pettibone of the regiment, and his personal staff. For the Third Minnesota, this was a most significant loss—Andrews had been their patron and protector.[21]

Shaler agreed with "Miles" that DeVall's Bluff had just "grown like topsy," and he did not like it. A military road and new streets were laid out that necessitated the removal of buildings and moving the stacks of goods. New construction, including a house for his family, and a more ordered arrangement improved both the appearance and the efficiency of the post and town. He ordered the construction and use of screened sinks and the proper disposal of "refuse matter of any kind," including manure and dead animals, either by burning or by dumping into the river. The Third's camp, in its order and cleanliness, must have stood out to him as a model of what could be. The general also banned the sale of liquor to soldiers, on post or on boats at the landing, and ended the practice of troops working in their off-duty hours for civilians for pay.[22]

Despite his ban on liquor sales, Shaler soon became a silent partner in restaurants and especially saloons owned by Daniel Upham, a speculator who arrived in Little Rock and then shifted to DeVall's Bluff after Shaler became post commander. The general arranged for Upham to get the necessary permits, provided cargo space on guarded transports, and regulated business in his area of responsibility to the benefit of his partners. Likening DeVall's Bluff to gold-rush San Francisco, Upham wrote his brother that he was investing widely because "there is money in anything here. . . . Shaler is good for anything there is here I think." All of Upham's letters went first to the post commander, who read them before sending them on. Corruption and its accompanying societal disorder grew exponentially. Sgt. Thomas Canfield of Company G commented on 5 February that "two or three men . . . [were killed] every night," adding that a "Colored

Gent" killed a soldier who got too "officious with his Lady." Two months later he noted a killing and a stabbing at the bowling alley.[23]

The year 1865 began with the execution of a deserter from the Twenty-Second Ohio who had joined a band of rebel marauders. The brigade, Mattson again in temporary command, formed three sides of a square to witness the firing squad's work. Although rebel activity decreased for a few weeks, scouts still captured guerrillas. Work on the fortifications continued, and Shaler instructed officers commanding fatigue parties to obey the orders of the engineer lieutenants in charge of the works, to ensure that the men worked four full hours each day, and to make sure that "the work is done and done well." The men vastly preferred DeVall's Bluff to Pine Bluff; as Fifer Henry Applegarth of Company G explained to his cousin, at Pine Bluff the band often played the death march twice a day.[24]

In mid-January the Third provided a protective force for the crew constructing a telegraph line from DeVall's Bluff to Saint Charles, where another detachment took over security of the line to Helena. The army had discovered the value of timely information shared widely and was busily connecting its various major commands more fully. Little Rock was already connected by way of Fort Smith and Saint Louis, and this new line added a second link via steamboats from Helena to Memphis. Another detachment helped build a post chapel. Pvt. Andrew Norelius of Company D, formerly a pastor, was one of these men. He may have functioned unofficially as chaplain during the interim from Chaplain Putnam's death until the 11 January arrival of the new chaplain, Methodist minister Anthony Wilford. Many of the more religious men attended services offered by other chaplains, Emery favoring those by the Twelfth Michigan's chaplain. He also attended a bible class with men from the Twelfth, another aspect of the religious revival that swept through the VII Corps.[25]

The men of the Third had received their last pay in July 1864. The deputy paymaster general in Saint Louis replied to Colonel Mattson, who asked when the men might be paid, that would be paid again when Congress provided funds for that purpose. This meant that families back home were not getting the allotment payments that many depended on, and soldiers often asked *them* to send money. Officers had to buy their own food but were not receiving their subsistence allowance, nor were their servants paid, though the local paymaster would issue a "voucher for the use of a private soldier" to pay any soldier-servants. At the same time, though, money was available to pay men discharged for promotion, a considerable inequity. Governor Miller pointedly wrote Secretary of War Stanton regarding the consequences on families and on morale: "This is discreditable to our great government, to the soldier, and distressing to his family." Geenral Reynolds complained to General Halleck, having discovered that most of the units in the VII Corps had received no pay since June and most had received only their first bounty installment. General Canby complained as well and ordered that officers who lacked funds could draw rations for their families and servants. Reynolds noted, however, that this too was producing "much dissatisfaction and suffering," damaging morale.[26]

While the Third had only one officer serving with each company, the others on detached duty at various postings, the 112th USCI had gained its lieutenant colonel (John Gustafson of Company D), four captains, ten lieutenants, and Bowler, as well as most of its cadre men from the Third. Mattson was annoyed at Bowler's long absence, which left his company led by a lonely lieutenant, Thomas Hunter. The colonel wanted his officer returned, along with the other men assigned from the Third. Gustafson responded that Steele had promised Bowler the colonelcy of the Fifth Arkansas (African Descent) and thus should be commissioned in the unit. Reynolds rejected Mattson's request, and Bowler and the men remained detached to serve with the various black regiments. Mattson did have a point, however, for he had 202 officers and men detached, leaving the Third Minnesota with only 494 men and around 12 officers present for duty. The regiment formed a third of his brigade's strength; the other four regiments were husks of their former strength., and the engineers judged the brigade too small to effectively man its section of the defensive works.[27]

Some of the officers on detached duty were serving with higher commands. These included 1st Lts. William Morse of Company F, who was an assistant commissary of musters, and William Akers of Company I, who was the assistant quartermaster for the First Brigade. Enlisted men with certain job skills—for example, printers, mechanics, and telegraphers—good clerks, or those who had gained a reputation for skills or dependability were difficult to pry loose from the Telegraph Corps, the Military Railroad, the Pioneer Corps, and post and higher headquarters. Some men had interesting, if not unusual jobs; for example, Pvt. John White of Company K was a "Detective [in the] Provost Marshal's" Office in Pine Bluff. Mattson regularly assigned older men to duty in the Soldiers' Home—one example being Sgt. John Crummett of Company I, age thirty-four— or in the Sanitary Rooms—such as Private Emery, also thirty-four—or to serve as nurses in the various hospitals. The effective drilling or scout strength of the regiment was further reduced by the men needed to keep the unit functioning: bakers, teamsters, blacksmiths, nurses, clerks, and others.[28]

Crime (and consequential punishment) happened, perhaps due to the lack of pay, from the influence of Shaler's growing corruption, or perhaps because some men were just prone to trouble. Musician William Day of Company E stole stamps worth $3.50 from Lieutenant Colonel Foster's office. Pleading guilty, he commented that he did not think there were that many stamps and showed no understanding of having done wrong. Pvt. Peter LeClair (who had been jailed by civil authorities for theft while on furlough) went absent without leave between 16 and 22 January 1865 and faced a general court-martial. He admitted that after going off duty at the Remount Camp sawmill, he had visited some "girls he had become acquainted with" and stayed overnight. Returning to camp the next day, he got several quarts of whiskey, returned to the women, and remained with them, drunk, for four days until the whiskey gave out. He was sentenced to one month of hard labor in the military prison. Foster sentenced five men charged with unspecified but minor "conduct prejudicial" offenses to "police and fatigue duty" for ten hours a day for three days. In contrast, Pvt. Charles Bradish of Company C was convicted of serious (unspecified) charges by a general court-martial and was sentenced to loss of pay, confinement in a military prison for his term of service, and a dishonorable discharge.[29]

Pvt. Patrick Tammany, a forty-two-year-old draftee in Company G, was marginally fit for service. While on picket duty on 5 February, he threw away his rifle and ran and hid from the approaching relief squad, thinking they were rebels, a violation of the 46th Article of War. He was sentenced to imprisonment for the balance of his term and a dishonorable discharge. Not knowing of his trial, Father John Ireland, former chaplain of the Fifth Minnesota and a curate at the Cathedral of Saint Paul, wrote Colonel Mattson seeking Tammany's discharge from service since he was over the draft age. Mattson and General Reynolds both endorsed the request, but the army adjutant general merely ordered him released to serve the balance of his term.[30]

From a Trickle to a Torrent of Surrenders

Guerrilla activity increased again in late winter, but regular Confederate forces began surrendering. General Reynolds authorized post commanders "to accept the parole of all armed men who may surrender themselves. . . . [N]o paroles need be exacted from unarmed men." The routine of fatigue, picket and guard duty, foraging, and scouting expeditions continued. Though the records are silent on particulars, the hazards of outpost and expeditionary duty remained high. Lewis Hancock was promoted to captain of Company G on 18 April, having convinced Mattson that he was "much improved in his duties as an officer and especially in the management of his company." He had his photograph taken wearing a sack coat (not a uniform coat) with black shoulder straps bearing small gold captain's bars, all intended to reduce his profile as a target for any rebel sharpshooter looking for officers.[31]

On 14 February Mattson wrote to Governor Miller asking that the Third receive "a reasonable share of the drafted men," three hundred or so, to bring the regiment up to minimum strength. So many citizens were now trying to obtain deferments from the draft that there were "problems," particularly in the

Rochester Provost Marshal's Office. Men thronged the office prior to drafting day, appearing before the examining board to seek an "exemption from disability to military service." The Rochester board granted so many exemptions, especially in Faribault, that the state provost marshal ordered that all exempted men from that town be reexamined; The process discovered that over one-third of them were "improperly stricken from the rolls" for medical reasons. On 8 March the *Rochester City Post* headline read, "Excitement in the Provost Marshal's Office . . . Drafting was slowed," the same issue reporting the removal of the examining board (Dr. W. W. Mayo, a Marshal Less, and a Commissioner Cole). Despite outraged calls by veterans for punishment, nothing seems to have happened. Scandal generated excitement in DeVall's Bluff too. Reynolds had relieved Brig. Gen. Eugene Carr, the commander of the Independent Brigade, in disgrace for dissipation. On 9 February, Carr and "a party of officers and ladies [came from Little Rock]. . . . They were drunk on the train and behaved in a very unbecoming manner" as they attempted to board the *Rowena*.[32]

Meanwhile, Private Emery demonstrated propriety and self-confidence. Helping the sanitary agent bring a load of books from Little Rock, he dropped one box at the river's edge, for which the agent roundly cursed and insulted him, with reference to his left hand, crippled at First Bull Run. Emery rebuked the agent civilly, then sought reassignment. While the agent never apologized, he did change his behavior, and Emery remained in a very good billet. He attended the dedication of the new post chapel on 26 March and reported that, to the chaplain's pride, there had been only one instance of cursing during construction, when a man cut his hand. The service ended with a rousing rendition of "Rally Round the Flag, Boys."[33]

Several men sought commissions in the black regiments raised in Little Rock. A board of senior officers reviewed the applicants for commissions in these units as to their "capacity and fitness for the correct and efficient discharge of the duties of an officer," paying some attention to questions of integrity as well as mastery of the military arts. A large number of men from the Third, including Cpl. Andrew Pyburn of Company K, who passed the exam in late March and was commissioned a second lieutenant in Company H of the 113th USCI, were commissioned into the black units. With eighty-two men so commissioned, the Third "may have been" the largest supplier of officers in the Union army for the black regiments. Not all candidates passed the exam, though. Pvt. Eugene Stone, formerly first sergeant of Company F and a friend of Captain Bowler's, went before the board and, to Bowler's surprise, was rejected. The board may have suspected his integrity; some months later Stone took a deceased soldier-neighbor's personal property and did not send it home. Pvt. George Godfrey of Company B and Cpl. Justus Clark of Company C were rejected too.[34]

Recruiting of black soldiers was difficult, and in March the 112th USCI, 113th USCI, and Eleventh USCI were merged to become the 113th USCI (New). The three lieutenant colonels and Captain Bowler vied for the colonelcy, with Bowler settling for being the regiment's major; Lieutenant Colonel Gustafson of the 112th USCI, formerly of Company D of the Third Minnesota, was not chosen and was to be discharged. All three regiments had seen field service and were recognized for bravery. Reynolds later commended Capt. Richard Custard, formerly first sergeant in Company G, and nineteen soldiers from the former 112th for their defense of a "train of cars" on 2 April. He pointedly contrasted their behavior with that of a courier private from the Twelfth Michigan, who displayed cowardice during the same engagement.[35]

On 1 April, writing from Fort Snelling, Private Marples instructed his wife to "sell the sheep as fast as you can"; the market for wool was declining and soon collapsed, and he sensed the shifting fortunes of war. On Saturday, 8 April, cannon roared all day as the VII Corps celebrated the fall of Richmond (the previous Monday). News of Gen. Robert E. Lee's surrender spread more rapidly. In Saint Paul the *Daily Press* headlined it under a triumphant eagle, and in Little Rock Reynolds fired "two hundred guns." That evening Little Rock residents celebrated with "an illumination . . . with bonfires, rockets, music, and bad whiskey." Rumors that General Johnston had surrendered as well soon circulated—the war was ending.[36]

Lieutenant Colonel Gustafson had departed Little Rock on 14 April, carrying two hundred dollars for Mrs. Bowler. The next morning half-hour guns began firing at sunrise; soon thereafter a departmental order announced the assassination of President Lincoln. Everyone, Bowler informed his wife, was "to abstain from all business, except from necessity, officers and soldiers to remain in camp." Mattson said the men of the Third were "wild with grief." Bowler concluded: "This fills the cup of vengeance to overflowing. . . . I shall never forgive the traitors who have brought about this terrible event." Minnesotans guarding rebel prisoners in the military prison agreed; when one of the incarcerated cheered for John Wilkes Booth and threw his hat, a "man by the name of [Pvt. Felix] Stark [of Company A] immediately loaded his gun and shot the rebel dead; several other prisoners were killed after they too expressed joy.[37]

Sergeant Canfield of Company G wrote his sister on 21 April that Lincoln's death had cast "quite a gloom over our late victories. They have been mourning at the Post for the last three or four days." General Shaler ordered no official recognition at DeVall's Bluff, however, not even the lowering of the flag to half-staff. Finally, the townspeople closed their stores and draped them in crepe. Mrs. Mattson started for home after the assassination. Writing to her on 23 April, Colonel Mattson was optimistic for the war's end, reporting that Lt. Gen. E. Kirby

Smith was expected to surrender his army soon. But it proved not to be quick and easy with him. Smith tried to entice his troops to follow him into Mexico and establish a colony, but few were interested; the venture failed.[38]

Previously, Sgt. Edward Phileo's insolent letter to "Uncle Abe" of 1 April might have escaped penal notice. Mattson, thinking he had no option, endorsed it without comment and sent it on after Lincoln's death. General Reynolds censured the colonel, who was instructed to punish Phileo. Replying by endorsement to Reynolds's chief of staff, Mattson apologized for letting the letter go up the chain of command and said that he had reprimanded Phileo, whom he termed "an otherwise good man and sergeant who deeply regrets his action."[39]

The rebels in the Trans-Mississippi needed time to receive confirmation of the eastern surrenders from sources they trusted before they would lay down their arms. Duty, sickness, boredom, crime, and punishment all continued in the Third Minnesota. Thoroughly soaked while working hard, Private Emery took some medicinal ale from the sanitary stores, abashedly telling his disapproving wife that he had not drunk so much as to have "to hold on to the lamp post or anything of the kind." Pvt. William Flora, also of Company G, did get drunk—on guard duty, no less. Lieutenant Colonel Foster found him guilty in a field-officer court of conduct prejudicial, fined him a month's pay, and sentenced him to fourteen days of police duty. Private LeClair was also caught drunk on guard duty, but he was tried by a general court-martial. Found guilty, he forfeited six month's pay, was confined to nine months of hard labor in the military prison, and was to be dishonorably discharged. General Shaler disapproved the fine and discharge while approving the prison term.[40]

When Pvt. Nicholas Gross of Company F refused to "clean mud off his pants" and swore at his sergeants on 16 April, he was arrested and tried on a charge of conduct prejudicial; Foster sentenced him to seven days of police duty and a reprimand. Pvt. Joseph Cayou of Company I broke down a citizen's door and entered his house on 19 April, addressing the women there in an insulting fashion (by suggesting they were prostitutes). He was charged and found guilty of conduct prejudicial, leaving camp without a pass, breaking down a civilian's door, and using bad language by a general court-martial. Sentenced to lose two months' pay and to serve two months at hard labor in the military prison, Cayou remained incarcerated into July, when he was finally mustered out under the War Department order regarding one-year men.[41]

The entrepreneurial Daniel Upham noted that "'Bushwhackers,' 'Gorillas' &c are plenty around here [DeVall's Bluff]," adding that the White River was over flood stage. One man at a home farm, a militarized colony of Union refugees, said that "in many places the river appears to be fifty miles wide. Nothing but water for fifty miles." Couriers carrying dispatches between Reynolds and rebel commanders, particularly Brig. Gen. M. Jeff Thompson, found their task impossible, and both Thompson and Major General Fagan refused to surrender. Despite this, Reynolds assured Fagan that Federal forces would cooperate in "alleviating as far as may be, the sufferings of non-combatants"; would help families moving south out of Union lines to cross rivers; and would facilitate movement of supplies to families in Union areas. Throughout the South, the Union army provided public transportation for refugee families, white and black, to abandoned plantations, where they received seed and assistance in plowing and cabin construction. At the end of April, Lieutenant General Grant ordered Reynolds to release all of his rebel prisoners who took an oath of amnesty and loyalty and instructed him to invite the rebels in the field to "lay down their arms, on these terms, but only parole" soldiers who could receive immediate amnesty under the president's amnesty proclamation. The war was winding down, regiments in the East were being discharged, and military employees were being laid off everywhere: the Little Rock Quartermaster Depot employed 1,036 white and black civilians at the end of March but only 774 at the end of April.[42]

CHAPTER 11

PACIFYING ARKANSAS

The War Department began discharging units following the Grand Review of the Armies in Washington, D.C., on 23–24 May 1865. Units completed muster-out paperwork at their last duty station, then traveled home. Minnesota units went to Fort Snelling, where the men would settle their accounts with the government and receive their final pay before discharge. Soldiers kept their haversacks and other personal-issue equipment and could purchase their Springfield rifle and accoutrements. Governor Miller personally sought the early discharge of all Minnesota units, citing the state's severe labor shortage and especially the "exposure of our lengthy frontier to savage marauders." Many units had been last paid in the summer of 1864, and he requested that the men be paid rapidly to relieve the economic sufferings of their families.[1]

Col. John Averill, the state's chief mustering officer, began preparing to receive the returning units at Fort Snelling. Several smaller formations had come home to a quiet welcome at the Saint Paul Soldiers Home on their way upriver. Thinking this unsatisfactory and desiring something more substantial, a committee of men from each ward, along with a "Committee of Ladies," all met at the state capitol on 1 July and planned a formal welcoming for the units. By September these committees were adept at receiving a returning regiment.[2]

Unfortunately, the freedmen of the South needed protection and assistance, diplomacy to end the French imperial adventure in Mexico needed forceful backing, the hostile activities of Indians on the western frontier needed military attention, and rebel armies in the Trans-Mississippi theater, showing no signs of surrendering (or of fighting), needed watching. Volunteer units initially slated for discharge, including the Third Minnesota, were retained in service. Rumors of the regiment's fate were plentiful. Sgt. Thomas Canfield of Company G summed it up nicely when he wrote his sister, Cordelia, on 10 May: "everything is in such a hubbub down here now since our glorious victories and the sad news of the President's death, that we don't pretend to believe anything we hear."[3]

Scouts reported that General Smith's officers were trying, without success, to get their men to go "to Mexico to establish a colony," and the rebels in Arkansas showed no signs of surrendering when Colonel Mattson wrote his wife on 8 May suggesting that the Third would be among the last units to come home. To help the rebels make up their minds, the regiment sent an expedition up the White River on the *Izetta,* destroying every flatboat the Minnesotans could find to keep the rebels from crossing. For Mattson, the routine of paperwork continued, as did promotions and resignations. The men on detached service began returning after April, then in August the cadre for the black units returned. Lieutenant Colonel Foster resigned on 2 May, and Major Hoit was promoted in his place. The 4 May morning report of Company C noted that its members were all together in a barracks for the first time since the Third came south in 1861. Sergeant Canfield had a fine time on a pass in Little Rock, since a friend had a part interest in a theater.[4]

The regiment shrank as the army discharged one-year men who were married or were seriously ill in hospitals. Volunteers, including George Herber, and draftees who never joined the regiment in the South, including Charles Marples, mustered out on 8 May. Most of the remaining one-year men mustered out in July. On 2 August 1st Lt. Eben North of Company G commanded a detachment of 100 such men to Fort Snelling, having custody of their muster-out rolls. This group arrived at the fort on the Northern Line's *Sucker State* on 9 August, receiving their final pay and discharge the next day. By mid-August only fifteen officers and 281 men remained on duty with the regiment; the rest were still on detached service, on leave, sick, or absent without leave.[5]

Occupation Duty

In a letter of 14 May to his wife, Mattson, in addition to noting the "capture of Jeff Davis," stated that the regiment was ordered to Batesville to establish a post and a district encompassing northeastern Arkansas. Happily, it was also miles away from Brigadier General Shaler, with whom the colonel now had serious, unspecified, disagreements. Major General Reynolds gave Mattson not only his own regiment but also two squadrons from the Ninth Kansas Cavalry. He also gave the colonel an ambitious mission: first, to make the citizens of the district safe by restricting travel to main roads, organizing the men into home guards, and "scour[ing] the country for bushwhackers"; and second, to "encourage agriculture . . . and re-establish commerce," especially by assisting the bigger merchants (like Upham) who had "approval from higher levels," licensing retail shops, and ensuring that the citizenry were not abused.[6]

The Third boarded the *Izetta* on Friday morning, 19 May, arriving the next afternoon in Batesville. Pvt. Lewis Emery of Company G liked the town, saying the houses were well shaded, the water was good, and it was "a pretty place." Mattson was pleased too; among other things, his headquarters mansion was bigger and better furnished than Shaler's. The men quickly "built a fine camp of small houses, covered with shelter tents." The residents seemed welcoming and Unionist, though Mattson's distract encompassed many slaveowning delta planters, diehard rebels, and the poorer, more pro-Union highlanders, who often had menfolk in the Union army and in guerrilla bands resisting pro-Confederate oppressors.[7]

Mattson's General Orders no. 1, printed on an old press the troops found, politely asked all white males over age twelve and all female heads of families to register with his post provost marshal. As his soldiers settled in, first loyalists and then ex-rebels came in to take the oath and promptly formed home-guard companies to protect their communities. The colonel wrote Adjutant General Malmros on 25 May that his greatest problem was starvation, and he was feeding hundreds with army rations. Major General Pope, observing that "the whole country is destitute in that vicinity," ordered Reynolds to send a boatload of rations to Jacksonport. Reynolds had already assigned Mattson a steamboat and given him "unlimited power to draw on commissary stores at DeVall's Bluff." The colonel did not distinguish between rebel and Unionist in dispensing aid and often included "a government mule . . . to carry the load" of commissary goods home. In his 1883 reunion address, Mattson recalled this extreme destitution in northeastern Arkansas and the ignorance of the people, particularly the women, who seemed not "to know how many children they had or their husband's full name . . . , but they were fond of snuff." The more educated women he termed "perfect ladies but awful bitter rebels."[8]

After some negotiations, the rebel general M. Jeff Thompson agreed to surrender his men. Mattson was ordered to shift his headquarters and four companies (selecting B, C, I, and K) to Jacksonport, where Thompson would surrender to Maj. Gen. Grenville Dodge from Saint Louis. Other companies went to Searcy (A and F) and Augusta (E and H), leaving two (D and G) in Batesville. The larger detachment arrived in Jacksonport on 30 May to find the town full of rebel officers who did not appreciate having Mattson and his Minnesotans among them. Both rebel soldiers and local citizens were bitter, and the place was, the colonel said, "low—not near as good as Batesville." He wrote Mrs. Mattson that the people were "awful rebels. I have not seen a woman yet—they shut themselves up and feel so sour and full of treason that I fear they will burst."[9]

The Third served as the "host" unit for the surrender and paroling of the rebels. Several Minnesotans thus witnessed Thompson's speech to his paroled men: "Many of you, have been skulking for the last three years in the swamps . . . , but you rally like brave and gallant men around Uncle Sam's commissary stores, and

I have now come to surrender you, and hope that you will make better citizens than you have soldiers." He told them to give up or get rid of their arms, go home, work hard, take care of their families, and "avoid political discussions. We have talked about the niggers for forty years, and have been outtalked; we have fought for four years for the niggers, and have been d—d badly whipped. . . . [T]he Yankees have won the nigger, and will do what they please with him, and you have no say in the matter."[10]

Confederate outfits were no longer a threat, but the guerrillas, also called "bushwhackers," who had already degenerated to theft, rape, and murder either to settle grudges or simply for the thrills, were now the impediment to peace. Reynolds ordered his commanders not to accept paroles of unarmed men—they might be bushwhackers who had hidden their guns. "Loyal" guerrillas too caused no end of problems for post commanders, who were responsible for the safety of all the citizens in their districts, including paroled rebel soldiers. Mattson reported that a "Capt. Gleason" had taken two ex-rebels from among their families and killed them because of their wartime loyalties and Gleason claimed to be a Unionist. The threat was so severe near Searcy that Col. A. R. Witt (Tenth Arkansas) requested from Capt. Otto Dreher of Company A at Searcy arms and protection for his men.[11]

Several VII Corps staff officers, including Capt. James Hodges of Company K, went out with escorts to reconnoiter the countryside and accept paroles. Hodges went from Little Rock to Clinton and then Yellsville in Marion County, bordering Missouri and west of Mattson's area of responsibility. Several groups were responsible for the bulk of the violence in that area, particularly the "'Independent Feds,' . . . 'Williams' Men,' and 'Chris Venlon's Men.'" People were "robbed of all their stock and possessions . . . , living on leaves gathered as greens and bread made of Slippery Elm bark." As far as Hodges could determine, the former rebels were not at fault, but the bushwhackers who preyed on secessionist and Unionist alike.[12]

Writing his wife on 11 June, Colonel Mattson said, "Our work here goes on well and quiet" as he organized civil government, often lending "pensmen and accountants . . . to help start the new books and accounts." Good relations came from personal interaction between his men and the local citizens, on the streets, at dancing parties (he claimed that he did not dance), horse rides, and Masonic events, wherever and however the community and soldiers came together. Mattson claimed to be "regarded as a sort of Father of all the people . . . around here" and noted, "the citizens, especially the Ladies, are becoming very . . . friendly." The men of the Third were again winning over the women.[13]

Both the good citizens and the "hard cases," on whom "the iron hand of power was freely used," needed help coming to terms with the changes wrought by Union victory, particularly the status of the former slaves. A "very tidy negro woman" reported to Mattson that her husband was killed by their former owner. "A leading physician, a man of fine address and culture," the assailant told the same story she did. He admitted to flogging the man's eight-year-old son for "some mischief," and when the father took the boy and started for town, he pursued them and shot the man. Mattson noted, "He was perfectly astounded when I informed him that he would have to answer to the charge of murder before a military commission at Little Rock, where he was sent at once for trial."[14]

By midsummer, bushwhackers were less of a problem, and the citizens—white and black—were at work in the fields, assisted by occupation authorities in clarifying relationships and rights. As the district quieted, Reynolds expanded Mattson's jurisdiction, and companies moved to new postings. Company I went to Powhatan on the Black River, while Company G went to Salem in Fulton County. Private Emery remained behind in Batesville, caring for a "Mr. Paine," who later died. On Friday, 21 July, Emery set out for Salem, carrying only his knapsack, and arrived Sunday morning. Writing his wife a few days later, he observed that it was not a "very dangerous country when one can travel fifty miles alone without as much as a jack knife to defend himself." He thought Salem belonged "to history, every building being destroyed, and nothing but ruins to mark the spot." Shifted again to Franklin, his company did even less guard duty, the men having time to sleep and to walk about, but Emery complained at the lack of news and reading material—easy, boring duty.[15]

Homesickness and Discontent

Unlike the demobilized eastern armies, the men of the VII Corps saw no end to their service; they wanted to go home too. Celebrating the Fourth of July with speeches and picnics, Mattson enjoyed "an old-fashioned barbecue," which only made the longing worse. Unfortunately, when the Third mustered in as a veteran-volunteer unit, the mustering officer had used a form of the oath that committed the veterans to a full three years of service; now there were questions. Traveling to Little Rock, Mattson had a "very pleasant visit. . . . Genl R[eynolds] complimented me and the Regt very highly." He endorsed the colonel's request for muster out: "This regiment cannot well be spared at the present . . . , [but] their claims for discharge are just." Mattson's meetings with Arkansas's governor, Isaac Murphy, and other civil officers explained Reynolds's reticence. As he reported to his wife afterward, "everybody is so pleased with my management of affairs up in the country that I was highly complimented and lionized everywhere."[16]

Despite all the praise, though, the men were unhappy. Mattson feared that his Minnesotans might "mutiny—lay down arms—refuse to do duty and go home," thus disgracing their honor; he thought that only companies "D-A-H . . . would remain faithful." In Little Rock on 9 August as a witness in a general court-martial, the colonel again talked with Reynolds but concluded that "the prospects for my Regt to go home are not very good," which would lead to trouble. During his absence in Little Rock, "the soldiers had quite a row. . . . [L]ast Thursday [10 August] two companies B & K . . . refused to do duty"; the men regained their senses later in the day, though, and did perform their responsibilities. In Company G, Emery wrote, some men "tried to kick up quite a breeze," but he made it clear that he would do duty "alone with the captain until I could leave honorably." But things quieted down.[17]

Some men did mutiny, while others merely loosened the bonds of discipline. Teamster John King of Company F, "driving a US team containing several officers" while drunk on 14 August, stopped the vehicle, struck Capt. Jed Fuller of Company F; attacked Capt. John Vanstrum of Company D, who dismounted to protect himself; and kicked and struck Asst. Surg. Nahum Bixby. He was charged with drunkenness and violating of the 9th Article of War (striking a superior officer), but General Shaler ordered the charges rephrased since "drunkenness is not a military offense." King remained in the DeVall's Bluff jail pending trial until 19 September, when he was finally freed, mustered out, and sent home, one of the last men discharged. On 16 August Pvt. John Kester of company K went to a Mr. Anderson's farm; took and killed a suckling calf, violating the 54th Article of War; and committed conduct prejudicial. He was convicted by a field-officer court, but the reviewing authority remitted his sentence of a loss of a month's pay because of previous good service.[18]

On 17 August Shaler approved general-courts-martial sentences for Pvts. Orville Golden of Company A and David Petty and James Malloy of Company E. Golden, who violated the 9th Article of War (attacking a superior officer), was sentenced to two months' imprisonment and loss of two months' pay. Petty, guilty of disorderly conduct but not of "disgraceful language to a superior officer," was publicly reprimanded. Malloy was found guilty of conduct prejudicial, lost three months' pay, and was to serve three months at hard labor. On 2 September Captain Dreher requested Golden's release, saying that when he was sober, he was a "quick and orderly man." All three went home with the regiment.[19]

On 18 August Mattson learned that the regiment was to muster out and go home. This cured the homesickness and troubles. He wrote Mrs. Mattson on 21 August that the Sixtieth USCI had arrived in Batesville to relieve them, then began recalling companies from their outposts for movement to DeVall's Bluff and mustering out. General Reynolds relieved all of the Third's men on detached service in the VII Corps and ordered them to rejoin the regiment. The Sixtieth buried two of their own soldiers on 27 August. Mattson noted that the funeral procession was an "imposing sight, good band, finely dressed soldiers, best of order

..., [and] a great crowd of liberated slaves following in the rear. The white people look on in amazement. Never before was a negro buried with such honors."[20]

Orders Home for Discharge

Departing Jacksonport on 28 August, the reunited regiment arrived in DeVall's Bluff the next day. Mattson was, despite suffering from malaria, a happy man. He believed that the Third would be leaving in a week for Minnesota, and on 1 September he was overjoyed at receiving the news that his wife, who was pregnant, had safely delivered their son. Promising to "telegraph from La Crosse" (in 1861 he could not have telegraphed Red Wing from anywhere), Mattson asked her to meet him at Saint Paul's Metropolitan Hotel since he was "obliged to go right up with the Regt to Fort Snelling."[21]

Not knowing of the events in Arkansas, Governor Miller telegraphed the army adjutant general on 29 August seeking the Third's discharge. On 3 September General Reynolds cabled Miller that the Third was mustered out and had movement orders for home: "Col. Hans Mattson and twenty-six (26) field, staff, and line officers and four hundred and fifteen (415) enlisted men of the 3d Minnesota Veteran Infantry Volunteers are hereby placed en route for Ft. Snelling, Minnesota for final payment, they having been duly mustered for discharge. The Quartermasters department will furnish transportation."[22]

A "detachment of Co. G"—consisting of Pvts. William Flora, a thirty-three-year-old Arkansan, and William Logan, a thirty-four-year-old South Carolinian, who both had enlisted at Little Rock in the fall of 1863—and a "detachment of Co. I"—including Sgt. John Spellman, a thirty-three-year-old musician, and eighteen-year-old musician Charles Lombard, who had enlisted as a drummer boy—were discharged at DeVall's Bluff on 2 September.[23]

The Third Minnesota, including several black undercooks, boarded the *Rowena* and departed DeVall's Bluff on Tuesday, 4 September. The regiment stopped overnight in Cairo on 7 September, where the Minnesotans apparently changed to the *Annie Johnston,* a faster boat. Arriving in La Crosse about midnight, 10 September, the men departed early the next morning. Alerted by their informants in Cairo and in La Crosse, the Saint Paul "soldiers reception committee" began preparing "to receive and entertain" the regiment. Captain Moulton of the *Annie* telegraphed the committee from Reed's Landing, upriver from Wabasha: "I have the Third Regiment on board. The Colonel wishes to proceed directly to Fort Snelling and not make any stop at St. Paul. Answer at Red Wing."[24]

The citizens of Red Wing welcomed the regiment with a banquet, at which Capt. Lewis Hancock of Company G presented the flag given them in 1861 by the "loyal ladies of [Louisville]" to the city. Later Sunday morning aboard the

Annie, the officers of the Third voted their thanks "for the very liberal and splendid reception given us by the city of Red Wing on our arrival to-day. . . . [W]e recognize . . . the uniform kindness of the citizens of Red Wing on this and all former occasions of our sojourn there." They also voted thanks to the captain and crew of the *Annie Johnston* for their kindnesses.[25]

Refusing Saint Paul's Hospitality

The women of the Saint Paul committee were busy in their kitchens preparing food, the Great Western Band was preparing to join the firemen in leading the regiment to Mozart Hall, and the various dignitaries were assembling, speeches in hand, to welcome the Third Minnesota home. Adj. Gen. John Peller (Malmros having resigned) asked W. R. Hubbs to inform Mattson "that the ladies had made preparations to receive the regiment and hoped it would stop." After talking with Mattson at the Hastings landing, Hubbs cabled Peller: "Colonel Mattson will not stop with his regiment at St. Paul." The *Daily Press* reported that "this was considered decisive and the ladies who had been busy all day in their laudable efforts . . . were informed." They ceased their labors.[26]

Brigadier General Andrews, home on leave, had no more idea why the regiment rejected the capital city's welcome than did twentieth-century author Walter Trenerry, who termed it an "unexplained incivility." Captain Hancock provided one reason for this calculated action in 1918. Shortly before the regiment returned, "an article appeared in a St. Paul newspaper to the effect that the 8th Minnesota had redeemed the honor and courage that had been lost by another organization, referring to our regiment. This was bitterly resented and [we] declined entertainment by St. Paul on our return." Mattson wrote his wife on Tuesday, 12 September, "we had a reception tendered us at St. Paul last night, but declined to accept, we don't think that St. Paul can treat us well, especially the governor."[27]

In the beginning, when the Third departed the capital in 1861, some men remarked on the lack of enthusiasm and support evidenced during their march through the city. Local newspaper commentary following their surrender at Murfreesboro in July 1862 denigrated the men and their regiment. The way most Saint Paul residents and their newspapers treated them when the men were homeless and unpaid that November rubbed salt into the men's wounded pride. Later, the city paid little notice to the detachments that came home on veteran furlough. The *Hastings Conserver* supported this line of analysis, saying, "in resentment of former neglect they [the men of the Third] refused to stop."[28]

From comments to Mrs. Mattson, and given a certain stiffness in correspondence, it appears that Colonel Mattson was not entirely happy with Governor Miller either. Differences over promotions might partly explain the rift. Mattson did not know that Miller was unaware of the regiment's medical problems in

1864 and did not know of the governor's efforts in 1865 to get the men paid and later discharged. In any event, the *Annie Johnston* carried the Third Minnesota past the darkened Saint Paul wharves and arrived at the Fort Snelling landing early in the morning of Tuesday, 12 September.

By midday, regimental and company staff and clerks were busy with the paperwork involved in discharging the regiment. The state took custody of all the Springfield rifles and accoutrements the men did not purchase and received all the records, flags, and equipment that was not turned over to U.S. Army quartermasters at Fort Snelling. Mattson requested that Governor Miller issue honorary (brevet) commissions to several men. For Captain Vanstrum, he sought a brevet to major; for 1st Lts. Bonde Olson and Andrew Borland, captaincies; and for 1st Sgt. Phillip Quigley of Company G, a first lieutenancy. For the noncommissioned-officer staff and the remaining first sergeants who, had the war continued, would have been commissioned, he sought second lieutenancies. Miller issued no brevet honors to any unit, including the Third, perhaps because the other colonels did not ask.[29]

The Third Minnesota's last dress parade was on Saturday, 16 September, at which Mattson's last general order was read, praising the men—the regiment's "bone and sinew, the true representatives of our noble young state, have ever reflected honor and credit on that state"—for their faithful service, "from the northwestern frontier, against the savage Indian foes, to the deadly swamps of the Yazoo and Arkansas valleys, against the haughty Southern rebels," strangely omitting their service in Kentucky and Tennessee. Paid earlier in the day, once the men were dismissed, they began their journeys home, individually or in small groups of friends.[30]

Mattson wrote his wife on Friday that he would "be the happiest man living in a couple of days when I get through with the cares and responsibilities of the command." The officers were paid off and discharged on Monday morning, 18 September. Later that day the colonel finished the last of his paperwork, cleaned off his borrowed desk, and surrendered the last of his government property. Closing the door of his temporary office at Fort Snelling, Hans Mattson began the journey home to his family and life as a civilian.[31]

The *Hastings Conserver* wrote the epitaph for the Third Minnesota Infantry as it reported the regiment's passage upriver for discharge: "One by one the brave regiments return and quietly melt away into the civil walks of life. The Third has seen much hard service and numbers among its number some of the best fighting blood of the state."[32]

EPILOGUE

The Regiment in Memory

The editor of the *Hastings Conserver* said that the men of the Third Minnesota took up the plow or pen as if they had never left. Veterans were considered stable, solid, diligent citizens, a view also favored by earlier generations of Civil War historians. But during the late twentieth century, Gilded Age specialists favored a competing story structured around the number of homeless, criminal, or mentally unstable veterans and accounts of the veteran, his widow, or his orphan repeatedly raiding the Treasury for pensions—somewhat similar to the portrayal of Vietnam War soldiers and veterans as homeless, drug addicted, ticking time bombs of post-traumatic stress. Developments in combat psychology and medicine and a more objective examination of the historical record allows the construction of more nuanced, realistic portraits of veterans in the post–Civil War world.[1]

Recent scholarship suggests that Civil War veterans shared many common characteristics with veterans of other wars, including those who have fought the modern insurgencies. That is, some soldiers returned home hale and hearty, unaffected by their experiences, and settled down to a remarkable domesticity, while others came back in some way disabled but strove to make as normal a life as they could for themselves and their families. Some returned with demons aplenty that in one way or another consumed them.[2]

The Third Minnesota suffered a small number of combat casualties, with only seventeen killed. Two men shot themselves by accident, a number were injured by disintegrating Belgian rifles, and several more were hurt while loading freight or building fortifications. Most of those who died succumbed to malaria, dysentery or chronic diarrhea, and rheumatism, while many who served with the regiment suffered from bouts with one or more of these illnesses. Sunstroke impaired many. The records suggest that, despite their varied afflictions, the majority of veterans successfully transitioned into civilian life, formed or rejoined families, and were productive and involved citizens. At the end of the war, most were too young—involved with families and careers, with too much potential or too little money and time—to be interested in reminiscing. Col. Hans Mattson organized the first reunion in 1870, attended mostly by the older men. By the mid-1880s, however, in a pattern typical of veterans twenty years after their war, the "boys" of the Third, their families grown, had the time, resources, and renewed interest to attend what had become annual reunions.[3]

The Third Infantry Regiment Association

The Turner Band welcomed the seventy not-so-old veterans to their first reunion on Thursday, 20 October 1870, in the Minneapolis Opera House. After several addresses, the men approved a constitution drafted by Maj. James Bowler's committee on permanent organization and adjourned to the Nicollet Hotel for a fine dinner. The second reunion was in Minneapolis in the fall of 1884. Regular reunions began only in 1886, with the third meeting, hosted by General Andrews, which met in Winthrop Post Hall of the Grand Army of the Republic (GAR) in Saint Paul. Andrews and Cols. Chauncey Griggs and Mattson all spoke, their remarks printed in the reunion pamphlet. This and subsequent publications reported on the meetings, attendees (including supernumerary 2nd Lt. Francis McDonald of Company H and dishonorably dismissed 1st Lt. Hiram Gates of Company K, both in 1887), letters received, and either summarized or reprinted the historical addresses delivered. These provided the basis for putting individual memory into context and for their memorialization.[4]

In 1890, at the seventh reunion, the veterans elected "J. W. Green, a son of Corp. C. H. Green . . . 'who was sabered and shot to death,'" to honorary membership. In 1899, again in Minneapolis, the men voted to confer honorary membership upon the wives and children of the servicemen, ensuring the future of the association. At this meeting "Reuben Griggs, colored, of Kokomo, Ind." presented himself for membership, claiming that he enlisted in Company B in 1861. (There are no records of a "Reuben Griggs" in the regiment.) Since the surviving members of the company did not recognize or remember Griggs, his application was tabled to 1900; the attendees then raised money to help him return home. There is no evidence of any of the black undercooks attending reunions or receiving association mailings.[5]

History and Memorialization

The association never mentioned Charles Lombard's short regimental history from 1869 in its papers or publications and never moved to sponsor the writing of a unit history. When the state government organized the committee to write and publish *Minnesota in the Civil and Indian Wars,* the association selected General Andrews to write the Third Regiment's contribution. Its only efforts at history were the addresses given at the reunions recalling some event or eulogizing a comrade. Instead, the veterans focused their energies on memorializing their service. The association also elected Andrews to represent them on the state commission to place monuments at important battle sites and was involved in planning the paintings and displays of battle flags and war memorabilia for the new Minnesota State Capitol. On 14 June 1905, the senior office present, Major Bowler, lead the veterans, following their last color bearers, as the regiments paraded their flags from the old building to the new one.[6]

At the 1905 reunion, before a smaller crowd, so many having attended the capitol ceremonies, General Andrews reported on the progress of sculpting and placing the battlefield monuments and noted that there were questions regarding which regiments would be honored with paintings in the capitol. Rep. Ezra Champlin (a lieutenant in both Companies G and D) led the association's committee that successfully promoted their case before the capitol commission. The next year the GAR national encampment met in Minneapolis 12–18 August. The association held its reunion early, on 13 August, so its members could attend the opening ceremonies at the encampment. Representative Champlin reported that the committee decided that the painting honoring the Third Minnesota would be of its entry into Little Rock, since only parts of the regiment had fought at Wood Lake or at Fitzhugh's Woods. General Andrews reported on the Minnesota monument at Vicksburg and the wording chosen for the plaque honoring the Third Infantry.[7]

Completed and framed, the Third's was the first painting placed in the capitol in 1910. It depicted neither a battle image (such as the Second Minnesota at Missionary Ridge) nor of a conquering army entering Vicksburg (as did the Fourth Minnesota's painting), instead it was of dirty, weary soldiers entering a captured state capital. Some men, unhappy that it was not a battle scene, agitated in 1917 for a replacement featuring the Battle of Fitzhugh's Woods and General Andrews, who wanted to be portrayed on his favorite "brute" of a horse. Neither Association Secretary Maj. W. D. Hale nor Capitol Commissioner (and former association president) Pvt. W. E. Hale liked the horse—or the idea—and it faded away. Other men sought a medal commemorating service in the Indian campaign, another idea that died for lack of interest.[8]

After taking their first group photograph on the steps of the Minneapolis Court House in 1907, the attendees rode streetcars to the state fairgrounds north of Saint Paul to participate in a joint reunion of all the Civil War units. At their business meeting Champlin reported that the legislative committee to secure a site for a monument at Wood Lake had selected the Third's campsite as its location. They ventured in 1908 to Red Wing, where the veterans were welcomed at the depot by the E. A. Welch GAR Post, named for the regiment's commander at Wood Lake, and the post's drum corps, led by the Third's chief musician, David Hancock. The fine dinner, reminiscent of those served by the mothers and grandmothers of the current women of Red Wing, won the men's hearts yet again.[9]

For several years thereafter, the reunions were held in the homes of the children. Victoria Bowler Law hosted the 1914 meeting, which included families. The association's secretary died suddenly in 1915, and Frank L. Bowler became acting secretary. At that year's reunion, Edgar L. Mattson was elected secretary, the first nonveteran in the association's leadership. A veteran of the Twenty-Third Kentucky, a regiment brigaded with the Third at Murfreesboro, attended the 1917 reunion, and former governor Samuel Van Sant spoke on war preparedness. The Elks Band greeted the veterans at the Red Wing depot in 1918; Law was elected the first nonveteran (and female) president that year. The Great War raging in Europe drew comment in the letters included in the pamphlets and reunions from 1914 through 1919. In Minneapolis in 1919 the veterans welcomed Lts. (J.G.) Edgar and Chester Jaeger, USNR—Colonel Mattson's grandsons—to speak of their "World War" service.[10]

The Third's war was now long past, overshadowed by a more horrible global conflict; fewer veterans attended the reunions, but men who had not previously attended, such as Pvt. Walter Doyle of Company E, began coming and holding office. In 1921 the association met for the first time at the Minnesota Veterans' Home at Minnehaha Park in Minneapolis. J. L. Uptegrove, a veteran's daughter, hosted the men at her home in one of their rare ventures into Saint Paul in 1922. The next year in Minneapolis, Doyle became second vice president, and the children now became the workhorses of the association. B. H. Bowler hosted the 1925 meeting at his home in Excelsior, a streetcar suburb of Minneapolis, where a backyard photograph was taken.[11]

Meeting at the Veterans' Home in 1926, with Vice Pres. Nanny Mattson Jaeger in the chair—the current president, Pvt. George Brewer, having died—the sons and daughters determined to place a memorial window in the Veterans' Home chapel. Five daughters met to plan the design and raise the funds, assured by several fellow descendants of their support. Created by the Minneapolis firm of Weston and Leighton at a cost of $240, the window featured the VII Corps badge, a crescent inverted above a five-pointed star, and was inscribed: "In honor of our fathers who served in the Third Regiment, Minn. Infantry U.S. Volunteers, 1861–1865. Let us in our nation's life a true memorial raise."[12]

Pres. (Pvt.) Heber Hare and Vice Pres. Jennie McIntyre and Effie L. Barwise led the 1927 meeting, highlighted by the successful installation of the window. The 1927 pamphlet included a photograph of Chief Musician Hancock, now 101 years old. Meeting at the Veterans' Home in 1929, the veterans, "having the assurances of the younger element" to handle all arrangements, voted to hold a 1930 reunion at the Andrews Hotel in Minneapolis. Nine old soldiers attended that gathering, five in 1931, and none at the 1932 reunion, where the twelve descendants in attendance dissolved the association.[13]

Regularly gathering to recall their past, their comrades, and their experiences, the veterans had exchanged news of the present too. The annual pamphlet published addresses, letters, and obituaries, while noting attendance, honorary members, and officers. Some addresses and notes referred to events at Murfreesboro, revealing the long hold that action had on some of the men and their conflicted acceptance of the official history of the surrender. The pamphlets and the letters the association secretary received provide much of the existing evidence regarding the postwar lives of the men of the Third Minnesota Infantry.

The Veterans of the Third Minnesota

The men left the field, forge, and account books—many leaving wives and children too—to serve in the Third Minnesota. Most of those who returned home picked up the threads of life with nary a bobble. Many returned with new skills—as clerks, telegraphers, mechanics, or even as leaders and managers—and with a strong self-knowledge fashioned lives and careers very different from their prewar dreams. Some moved about, the single men married and started families, some opened farms and businesses, and many became involved in public affairs, either as civil servants or as politicians.[14]

One small group—Lt. Col. Everett Foster called them "Our Fools"—either took their discharges in Arkansas and sought their fortunes there or returned first to Minnesota and then went back. Only a few remained after the end of Reconstruction, marked by a violent affair called the "Brooks-Baxter War" (1874) that returned Arkansas to an analog of its prewar social and political conditions. Discharged in November 1864, Pvt. George Brookins of Company I became a supervisor in the Huntersville quartermaster depot, returning to Minnesota after being laid off in the summer of 1865. William Allison of Company F, who did well gambling while serving as a court-martial clerk, was also discharged in November and soon opened a "sporting house" in Little Rock, losing heavily; in 1886 Foster said that Allison had yet to recoup his losses. Bernard McKenna of Companies F and C became a first lieutenant in the Fifty-Seventh USCI; discharged for disability, he suffered from vertigo caused by sunstroke while at Vicksburg. He owned a hotel and billiards room in Little Rock despite suffering severe rheumatism and heart troubles.[15]

Shortly before mustering out, Capt. William Akers married a Little Rock "belle," whom Mattson termed "the most bitter rebel of that portion of Arkansas." She came north with the regiment, then the couple went back to manage a plantation near Augusta, where some fifty disguised men "klukluxed" (hunted) Akers out of his home, drove off his black hands, burned their quarters, and "when he fired into their ranks, they overwhelmed him"; his wife saved him. The Reconstruction governor returned Akers to Woodruff County as the sheriff, "the terror of assassins and other evil does." He later held federal clerkships, then became a manufacturer of paints and varnishes in Little Rock.[16]

Capt. Benjamin Rice of Company H resigned in July 1864 and operated a plantation before opening a law firm in Little Rock and being elected U.S. senator from Arkansas (1869–73). He later practiced law in Denver and then in Saint Louis and died in Washington, D.C. Capt. Joseph H. Swan of Company I resigned in December 1864 and practiced law with Rice. Surviving the political turmoil of Reconstruction's end, he remained in Arkansas until his health failed, then returned north, practicing law in Sioux City, Iowa.[17]

Pvt. James Coates of Company I went home to Minnesota, then returned to Arkansas and studied law with Rice and Swan, being admitted to the bar in 1870. He married a daughter of Arkansas lieutenant governor Calvin Bliss, served as U.S. pension agent during the Grant presidency, and in 1880 served one term as county and probate judge in Pulaski County, later becoming commissioner of the U.S. District Court for Little Rock. Coates remained involved in the community until he died in an automobile accident in 1922.[18]

Capt. James L. Hodges of Company K also returned to Arkansas in 1866 and took up a plantation before acquiring a contract to manage the state penitentiary. According to Foster, Hodges made a fortune, then lost it during the violent political convulsions at the end of Reconstruction. Moving to Colorado, he made and lost another fortune. In 1889 Hodges was in the process of recouping his losses by government service.[19]

Lt. Col. Everett Foster was himself a "fool." Resigning in May 1865, he ran a plantation on the Arkansas River and lost everything in 1868, then worked for the Internal Revenue Service. President Grant appointed him surveyor general of Louisiana, and Foster lived in New Orleans until the 1878 yellow fever epidemic drove him north to Dakota Territory. In 1900 he moved to Washington, D.C., and worked for the U.S. Senate until 1917. Attending a GAR convention in Portland, Oregon, Foster became ill and remained in the West, living with one of his children in Watsonville, California.[20]

Sgt. Maj. William D. Hale mustered out from the Fourth U.S. Colored Artillery (formerly the Second Tennessee Heavy Artillery) in February 1866 and moved to Pine Bluff, where he ran a cotton plantation. He then served as a Freedmen's Bureau agent before returning to Minneapolis in the fall of 1867. Becoming involved in the railroads building out from Minneapolis, he partnered with William D. Washburn in the Washburn Milling Company. Later Hale was an officer or director of several flour-milling firms and railroads, and both Pres. Benjamin Harrison and Pres. Theodore Roosevelt appointed him postmaster of the city. A president and then longtime secretary of the Third Infantry Regiment Association, Hale died at sea on board the SS *Mongolia* while traveling to Honolulu, Hawaii, in January 1916; he was buried in Lakewood Cemetery in Minneapolis.[21]

Pvt. Charles Bradish of Company C joined the Eighteenth U.S. Infantry after his release from military prison in December 1865. According to a 1916 letter he wrote, Bradish helped survey the route of the transcontinental railroad in the summer of 1867 and remained in the West as a railroad worker, stage driver, scout, city marshal, and deputy sheriff, also claiming membership in the U.S. Secret Service. Unlike Bradish, Charles Humason of Company K resumed a military career late in life. He came home from the war to his wife in Rochester; worked as a grocery clerk, a farmer, a hotel keeper, town and city clerk, a clerk in the lumber business; and was elected auditor of Olmsted County. In the 1880s he served as the chief clerk in the Adjutant General's Office until he was appointed major and assistant adjutant general in 1891. He then went into private business until Governor Van Sant appointed him Civil War records clerk in the Adjutant General's Office in 1893, a post he held until his death.[22]

Immediately after returning to Red Wing, Pvt. John Pfieffer of Company D left for Sweden to bring over his widowed mother. First working as a stair builder and carpenter, he then went to work for the Red Wing Manufacturing Company. Former Quartermaster Sgt. Benjamin Densmore also returned to Red Wing, after discharge from the Second Tennessee Heavy Artillery (African Descent), and was cofounder of the Red Wing Ironworks. Neither he nor Pfieffer entered public service.[23]

Capt. Edward Baker of Company E owned the Diamond Flour Mill in Red Wing and was a pioneer in the "new process" of milling that used porcelain rollers, developed in Hungary, and the new middlings purifier to produce a finer grade of flour. He served on the city council and was chairman of the Goodhue County Board of Commissioners for many years. Capt. Willett DeKay of Company E also returned home to Red Wing, where he held a variety of public offices, including marshal and health officer. DeKay was the U.S. postmaster for the city for several years before his death in 1891.[24]

Bvt. Capt. Ezra Champlin of Company G returned to become a farmer in Garden City. He was elected a Democratic state representative from Blue Earth County for the 1875 and 1887 sessions. He switched to the Farmers' Alliance Party and was elected again in 1891, serving as Speaker of the House. After returning to his Democratic affiliation, he served as party chair in 1896. Champlin was the regiment's commissioner for the capitol painting.[25]

Capt. John Vanstrum of Company D moved to Saint Vincent in Kittson County in the far northwestern corner of the state, then moved to Hallock, the county seat, and served as sheriff for ten years. From 1891 until his death in 1902, he was county register of deeds. His friend and fellow Swede Capt. Hans Eustrom moved to Hallock in 1879 and served as the county auditor for eight years before becoming a land agent for the Great Northern Railway.[26]

Two bachelors settled farthest from Minnesota. Pvt. John Early of Company C moved to Cuba shortly after the Spanish-American War (1898) and remained there into the 1920s. In 1917 he sent several photographs of Cuban revolutionary cavalry, both mounted and in a wagon, before his jewelry store. Cpl. Philander Chamberlain of Company A served as treasurer of San Mateo County, California, from 1881 to 1917 and claimed in 1917 that he could "dance all night with any of the girls or boys." He died in Redwood City on 30 November 1928.[27]

Benjamin Sanderson of Company B, severely wounded at Fitzhugh's Woods and discharged for disability at Fort Snelling in October 1864, returned home to farm. Marrying in 1866, he and his wife moved to Jasper County, Iowa, taking up 80 unimproved acres. Known for his stock raising, Sanderson increased his holdings to 280 acres, had a reputation as an advanced farmer, and was a township trustee. He died in bed on 14 September 1911. Coming home to a farm in Sibley County, Sgt. James Crosby married and soon became a deacon in the local Baptist church. In 1910 the Crosbys moved to a farm in Grand Junction, Colorado, to be near a son. The couple died on the same day in 1931 at the home of yet another son.[28]

William Sears of Company K returned home to Stewartville, then moved to Spring Valley, where he opened a wagon shop and became a city councilor. His son, Richard W. Sears, founded the mail-order firm of Sears, Roebuck, and Company. Clark Angell of Company A, discharged for disability in Nashville in July 1862, returned home and became a photographer in Litchfield, there joining the Frank Dagger GAR Post no. 35. He photographed most of the members, including Albert Van Spence, an escaped slave who joined the Union army and was a GAR comrade.[29]

Several black undercooks came "home" with the regiment, but the only known story is of Alfred Gales, who upon discharge took a "freedom name"—Alfred Miller. He worked as a laborer in Saint Paul, married, and had two children. In 1890 he applied for a pension, citing rheumatism, weakened vision, and age. Miller died of gastritis in 1892, shortly after gaining a pension, and was buried in the Soldiers' Rest section of Elmhurst Cemetery with other veterans. Changing his name caused difficulties for his widow, Narcissa, in receiving her widow's pension.[30]

Capt. James Bowler of Company F became major of the 113th USCI and served until mustered out in April 1866, refusing a commission as first lieutenant in the regular army because it entailed a significant loss of pay. Returning to civilian life in Nininger, he moved his family to a homestead in Bird Island in 1871 and was elected a state representative from Renville County in 1879. Moving to Minneapolis in 1891, Bowler entered the real-estate and home-loan businesses and served as state commissioner of dairy and food (1899–1901).[31]

Dismissed the service by President Lincoln on 1 December 1862, 1st Lt. Adolphus Elliot of Company A became a successful homeopathic medical doctor. Dying without heirs in 1902, his death ignored by the association, he endowed the Elliot Hospital, a 120-bed, three-operating-room, state of the art facility. The first clinical teaching and charity hospital, it opened at the University of Minnesota in 1911; the building remains a key part of the university's health-sciences complex. The 1911 pamphlet recognized Elliot's generosity.[32]

Rollin Olin, first lieutenant in Company B and captain of U.S. Volunteers on Sibley's staff, was a baseball fanatic who organized the North Stars Base Ball Club in 1863 in Saint Paul. A "fierce pitcher," he represented Minnesota at a baseball convention in Chicago in December 1865. After mustering out in 1866, he was vice president of the state baseball players association and active in the GAR, the Military Order of the Loyal Legion, and in Masonic affairs. Elected mayor of Owatonna in 1871–72, his banking partnership (1868–72) ended in bankruptcy, and he moved to Detroit. After graduating from the Medical Department of the University of Michigan, he had a very successful medical practice in that city from 1877 until his death in 1910.[33]

Cyrene Blakely, first lieutenant in Company K and captain and acting assistant commissary of subsistence, U.S. Volunteers, was the adopted brother of David Blakely, publisher of the *Rochester City Post* and Minnesota's secretary of state during the war. After the war, Cyrene managed the Blakely Printing Company, which in the 1870s he moved to Chicago. There, he established the C. H. Blakely and Company, printers of sheet music—most notably John Philip Sousa's; brother David managed the John Philip Sousa Band. Cyrene also founded the United Typothetae of America, a trade association.[34]

The chaplains all returned to active ministries after their service, and it is impossible to tell if their war experiences changed their career tracks at all. Chauncey Hobart, a veteran of the earlier Black Hawk War (1832), was a pastor and presiding elder for Methodist Episcopal congregations in Wisconsin and Minnesota until his death in Red Wing in 1904. Methodist preacher Benjamin Crary soon moved to Saint Louis to edit the *Central Christian Advocate*. In 1872 he was the presiding elder in Colorado, then moved to San Francisco, where he died in the spring of 1895. Anthony Wilford, another Methodist Episcopal minister and the regiment's last chaplain, in 1880 was living with his family in Zumbro in Wabashaw County, where he presided over a congregation.[35]

Discharged in 1863, Surg. Levi Butler returned to his Minneapolis practice, then Governor Miller sent him south to visit Minnesota units in 1864. Returning home, he ended his practice and formed a succession of lumbering firms (Butler & Walker; Butler, Mills, & Morris; and finally L. Butler & Company), with investments ranging from the northern pineries to saw and planing mills and wholesale yards. The first commander of the first GAR post in Minneapolis, Butler was elected a state senator, serving in 1871–77, before his death in 1878. On discharge in 1865, Surg. Albert Wedge returned to his bride in Albert Lea and formed a partnership with another doctor, together also opening a retail drugstore. When the partnership dissolved, Wedge continued his own practice and the drugstore, except for when he served as a collector of internal revenue for the federal government between 1881 and 1883. He owned and operated a very successful stock farm and served as president of the First National Bank of Albert Lea. Entering politics, he served as a state representative in 1870–71 and as a state senator in 1881. Wedge also served as assistant surgeon general (at the rank of lieutenant colonel) for the Minnesota militia on the staffs of the various governors between 1881 and 1895.[36]

Col. Chauncey Griggs came to Little Rock in 1864, seeking his fortune. Wiser, he soon returned to Saint Paul to serve seven years as an alderman, two terms in the state house of representatives, and three terms in the state senate. A banker and a partner in the wholesale grocery firm of Griggs, Cooper, & Company, he also partnered with James J. Hill in Hill, Griggs, & Company, a fuel and steamboat-transportation firm. Relocating to the West Coast, he formed the Saint Paul and Tacoma Lumber Company becoming a pillar of that industry.[37]

Brig. Gen. Christopher C. Andrews switched to the Republican Party during the war. A few years afterward, President Grant appointed him minister (ambassador) to the Kingdom of Sweden and Norway, serving until 1877. Owner and editor of the *St. Paul Daily Evening News* in 1880–82, he served as U.S. consul general to the empire of Brazil in 1882–84. Appointed chief fire warden of the new Minnesota Forestry Department in 1895, Andrews became a champion of scientific forestry and forest management. He authored the 1916 report of the Minnesota Civil War Monuments Commission that designed, created, placed, and dedicated of all the state's battlefield monuments. Dying in 1923, the general was buried in Oakland Cemetery in Saint Paul.[38]

Col. Hans Mattson returned to his family and law practice in Red Wing, moved to Chicago to edit the *Hemlandet,* then returned to serve as secretary of the Minnesota Board of Immigration. Elected Minnesota's secretary of state in 1870, Mattson afterward turned his attention to recruiting immigrants to the state, traveling repeatedly to Sweden, where his family lived for some time as he forwarded bands of settlers. He published the *Minnesota Stats Tidning* and started the *Swedish Tribune* in Chicago. A Republican presidential elector in 1876, Pres. James Garfield signed his commission as U.S. consul general to India, one of the last four he signed before his assassination in July 1881. Between 1881 and 1883, Mattson traveled widely in Asia, then returned to Minnesota, where he organized the Security Building and Loan Association of Minneapolis. Elected again as secretary of state in 1887, he served until 1891. Mattson died in March 1893.[39]

In contrast, Col. Henry Lester's career lacked diplomatic appointments, newspaper editorships, or mentions in trade publications. The other colonels of the Third were from middle-class origins, but Lester's father had worked "in furnace," so he had known adversity and survival. After being dismissed from the service in December 1862, Lester returned to New York City, where he worked as a lawyer and civil engineer. By 1880 he and his wife rented quarters in Mount Morris, near Geneso. Hired as a research clerk in the Livingstone County Clerk's Office in 1887, he retired in 1899. Lester read and spoke Spanish, French, and German and read Italian. When his alma mater, Hamilton College, established a Phi Beta Kappa chapter, he was among those given honorary membership in recognition of personal scholarship. Noted for his devotion to his wife, who survived him, Lester died of heart disease in April 1902. The sword his officers presented him in Nashville descended within his family before acquisition by the Minnesota Historical Society.[40]

On 3 March 1917, Jesse T. Barrick of Company H, later a second lieutenant in the Fifty-Seventh USCI, received the Medal of Honor. Fifty-four years earlier, while at Snyder's Bluff, Mississippi, Colonel Andrews had recommended several men for recognition, the medal being the only award available at the time. Cited for his bravery in capturing two noted guerrillas singlehandedly, Barrick's honor went unnoticed by the association, though it was one of the last three Medals of Honor awarded for Civil War service. Supposedly a fur trader in Washington State, he was honored with a marker in the Tacoma National Cemetery. But Barrick's body actually lay in an unmarked pauper's grave in the Pasco, Washington, cemetery until 1923, when a police officer learned of his medal and sought his grave. His wife, Sarah, who served as a nurse in the Third Minnesota, was buried in an unmarked grave, presumably at Pasco, but her remains were not recovered. Exhumed, Barrick's body was reburied in the Tacoma National Cemetery with appropriate honors; his wife is memorialized on the obverse of his marker.[41]

NOTES

SPDP   *St. Paul Daily Press*
SPWP   *St. Paul Weekly Press*
SPPD   *St. Paul Pioneer and Democrat*
SRNBA   Stone's River National Battlefield Archives, Murfreesboro, Tenn.
SAFN   *St. Anthony Falls Minnesota State News*
TSLA   Tennessee State Library and Archives, Nashville
UAF   University of Arkansas at Fayetteville, Archives & Special Collections
UALR   University of Arkansas at Little Rock Center for Arkansas History and Culture
UMBHL   University of Michigan, Bentley Historical Library, Ann Arbor
USAMHI   U.S. Army Military History Institute, Carlisle Barracks, Pa.

Introduction: Authorizing the Regiment

1. Fitzharris, "Lizzie Caleff's War"; Fitzharris, "'Our Disgraceful Surrender'"; Fitzharris, "Field Officer Courts."
2. *Annual Report for 1866,* 4, exhibit C, MNAGR.
3. Andrews, "Narrative of the Third."
4. Antiguerrilla operations are military strikes to eliminate guerrillas. Counterguerrilla operations intend to reduce or remove those things that cause people to support guerrillas voluntarily. Mackey, *Uncivil War,* 13–14.
5. Gordon, *Broken Regiment,* develops the idea of "brokenness." Fitzharris examines the collapse of the Third in "'Our Disgraceful Surrender.'"
6. Lombard, *History of the Third*; Andrews, "Narrative of the Third."
7. Gordon, *Broken Regiment,* 3 (unmitigated trash).
8. Gordon, *Broken Regiment,* 3 (building blocks); Musick, "'Little Regiment,'" 151 (primary object of); Cilella, *Upton's Regulars.* Gary Gallagher addresses the motives and reasons for Northerners in *Union War,* 65.
9. Trenerry, "Lester's Surrender," 191–97.
10. Brooksher and Snider, "Surrender or Die," 30–32.
11. Weddle, "Disgraced at Murfreesboro," 12–14 (harassed the enemy; bewildered), 16 (with conflicting messages; criminal), 20–21.
12. Prokopowicz, "Disunion Equals Disaster."
13. Fitzharris, "'Our Disgraceful Surrender.'"
14. Osman, "Audacity, Skill, and Firepower," 24–40; Johnson, "Siege at Fort Abercrombie"; Simon, "Third Minnesota Regiment in Arkansas," 281–92; Christ, "'Hard Little Fight,'" 380–93.
15. Fitzharris, "Field Officer Courts"; Larson, "Private Alfred Gales," 274–83; Foote, *The Gentlemen and the Roughs,* 11, 124, 127, 134–37.
16. Rubinstein, "French Canadians," 26–41.
17. Historical Census Browser, University of Virginia Library (site discontinued); U.S. Census Bureau, *Population of the United States in 1860,* 250–51; Hicks, "Organization of the Volunteer Army in 1861," 328–29. Lass, *Minnesota: A History,* provides a fine overview of the state's history. Atkins, *Creating Minnesota,* has a bit more detail on the Civil War, in which it focuses on the Third Minnesota.
18. Baker, *Lives of the Governors of Minnesota,* 11–14; Haugland, "Ramsey's Rise to Power," 325; Ramsey to Cameron, 14 Apr. 1861, Ramsey Papers, roll 12; Ramsey to Dennison and Acker, 15 Apr. 1861, ibid.

19. Patchin, "Banking in Minnesota," 153–60; Duncan, Sherman, and Company to Andrews, 7 Mar. 1860, C. C. Andrews and Family Papers, MHS.

20. Fisk, "First Fifty Years of Continuous Recorded Weather History in Minnesota," 1861 (across prairies).

21. Miller to Ramsey, 17 Apr. 1861, Ramsey Papers, roll 12; Swanson, "New Hampshire Yankee," 18–26.

22. Cameron to Ramsey, 15 May 1861, Ramsey Papers, roll 12; *St. Paul Weekly Pioneer and Democrat*, 5 July 1861; *MCIW*, 1:3.

23. *MCIW*, 1:6–7; *St. Paul Weekly Pioneer and Democrat*, 12, 19 July 1861.

24. Ramsey Diary, 24 (large patriotic meeting), 25 July 1861, Ramsey Papers, roll 39; *St. Paul Weekly Pioneer and Democrat*, 26 July 1861 (that a Third); *GCR*, 26 July 1861; *MCIW*, 1:14, 52.

25. Miller to Ramsey, 20, 31 (consult with you) July, 22 Aug. (would it not) 1861, Ramsey Papers, roll 12.

26. Gorman to Ramsey, 21 Aug. 1861 (if a vacancy), Ramsey Papers, roll 12; *Winona (Minn.) Daily Republican*, 9 Sept. 1861 (affection for; diligence you have).

27. Ramsey to Cameron, 20 Aug. 1861, OR, ser. 3, 1:465; Ramsey to Cameron, 30 Aug. 1861, MN EXJOU, Ramsey, 408–11; *Mankato (Minn.) Semi-Weekly Record*, 3 Sept. 1861 (for the field; five hundred thousand).

28. Jones to Adj. Gen., 1 Sept. 1861, RGAR, Letters Received, Adjutant General US Army; Jones to Ramsey, 2 Sept. 1861, ibid., Military, Infantry—3rd Regt., General.

29. Ramsey Diary, 24 Aug., 6, 7 (busily engaged in), 11 Sept. 1861, Ramsey Papers, roll 39; *Mankato (Minn.) Semi-Weekly Record*, 12 Sept. 1861.

30. Miller to Ramsey, 12 (talk all these), 14 (you can tell) Sept. 1861, Ramsey Papers, roll 12; Ramsey to Cameron, 14 Sept. 1861, MN EXJOU, Ramsey, 413–14.

31. *Mankato (Minn.) Semi-Weekly Record*, 10, 13 (the harvest is) Sept. 1861; *SPDP*, 18, 22 (these nationalities are) Sept. 1861; *Hastings (Minn.) Independent*, 5 Sept. 1861; *Rochester (Minn.) City Post*, 14 Sept. 1861; *MCIW*, 1:193; Mattson, *Reminiscences*, 60. Information on recruiting comes from newspaper notices; other sources are available only for Company D.

32. Ramsey to Cameron, 17 Sept. 1861 (Shall I call), Ramsey Papers, roll 12; Cameron to Ramsey, 17 Sept. 1861 (adopt measures to), ibid.; Ramsey Diary, 18 Sept. 1861 (unusually hot day), ibid., roll 39; *Winona (Minn.) Daily Republican*, 19 Sept. 1861.

1. Raising the Regiment

1. An excellent reference (out of print) on organization, weapons, etc., is Lord, *They Fought for the Union*. Notesworthy, *Bloody Crucible of Courage*, deals with tactics, weapons, doctrine. A good overview of soldier life is Robertson, *Soldiers Blue and Gray*.

2. Dora Costa and Matthew Kahn argue that homogenous groups from a town or neighboring towns encouraged enlistment and later cohesion in a company, but no company in the Third, including the Scandinavian company, had such homogenous characteristics. *Heroes & Cowards*, 59–62, 162–67.

3. Roos Diary, 1 (became tipsy with), 2 Oct. 1861; Foote, *The Gentlemen and the Roughs*, 10–11; Mattson, *Reminiscences*, 60; Roster of 3rd Regiment, *MCIW*, 1:184; Hans Mattson, Lars Aaker, and Hans Eustrom CMSRs, RG 94; *SPDP*, 24 Oct. 1861; Finnell, *Descendants of Carl Roos*, 1.

4. "Candidates for Offices Third Regiment M.V.," n.d., RGAR, Military, Infantry—3rd Regt., General; Knox to Ramsey, 26 Sept. 1861, ibid.; Hale Diary, 2 Oct. 1861, William D. Hale and Family Papers, MHS.

5. Bowler to Donnelly, 27 May 1861, Ignatius Donnelly and Family Papers, MHS, microfilm, roll 8; "List of Deserters from 3rd Minnesota," 30 Sept. 1863, MNOAG, General Correspondence; Philip Miller and Alonzo Verrill CMSRs, RG 94.

6. *Winona (Minn.) Daily Republican*, 17 Sept. (Messers Upham; young men; we have plenty), 1 Oct. 1861; *Carver (Minn.) Transcript*, quoted in *SPDP*, 19 Sept. 1861 (the war fever).

7. *Winona (Minn.) Daily Republican*, 17 Sept. 1861.

8. Geary, "Civil War Conscription."; *Winona (Minn.) Daily Republican*, 23 Sept. 1861; *St. Paul Weekly Pioneer and Democrat*, 5 July 1861, referencing G.O. no. 15, Adj. Gen. Office, 4 May 1861; *Stillwater (Minn.) Messenger*, 15 July 1861, referencing HQ, State of Minn., G.O. no. 13, repeating the War Department's terms.

9. Shippman to Secretary, 2 Sept. 1920, 3MVVA, *Thirty-Sixth Annual Reunion* (1920), 6 (penniless; walked one hundred); "Levi Butler," Hennepin County Biographies; Simmonds, "George Davis, Wright County Pioneer," MHS; John Berrisford, George Davis, Henry Timms, Peter Shippman, and Ezra Champlin CMSRs, RG 94; Ezra T. Champlin, "President's Address," in 3MVVA, *Nineteenth Annual Reunion* (1903), 14.

10. Osman, *Fort Snelling*, 27–45, 60; *Stillwater (Minn.) Messenger*, 28 Jan. 1862.

11. Christie, "Reminiscences," 44 (old severe man), 45, Thomas and Carmelite Christie and Family Papers, MHS; Roos Diary, 6–7 Oct. 1861; *SPPD*, 3 Nov. 1861; Osman, *Fort Snelling*, 223.

12. Griffin, *Letters Home*, 30 Sept. 1861 (home guards bloody); Donnelly to Ramsey, 10 Oct. 1861 (efforts to jump), RGAR, Letters Received; *SPPD*, 10 Oct. 1861; *SPWP*, 10 Oct. 1861.

13. Hancock to Ramsey, 4 Nov. 1861, RGAR, Military, Infantry—3rd Regt., General; Bertram to Ramsey, [1861], ibid.; Members of Co. H, 3MN to Ramsey, 30 Oct. 1861, ibid.; Andrews to Ramsey, 30 Oct. 1861, ibid.; *SPPD*, 10 Oct. 1861; *SPWP*, 10 Oct. 1861.

14. Shepard to Ramsey, 8 Sept. 1861, RGAR, Military, Infantry—3rd Regt., General.

15. S.O. no. 16, Fort Snelling, 7 Oct. 1861 (appointed Leader of), 3MN Order Books, Co. B, RG 94; Blakely to Donnelly, 15 Oct. 1861 (want the two; refined and high), RGAR, Military, Infantry—3rd Regt., General; Cole to Donnelly, 14 Oct. 1861, Donnelly and Family Papers, roll 9.

16. Frank Redlon, "President's Address," in 3MVVA, *Eighteenth Annual Reunion* (1902), 13 (brass and tallow; old and some; had to be); S.O. no. 94, 3MN, 10 May 1862 (drum major); William L. Cross CMSR, RG 94; Patrick, "History of the Regimental Bands," 67, 81.

17. Heaton to Ramsey, 22, 30 Oct. 1861 (you *will* have; *true Republican*; Steele clique), RGAR, Military, Infantry—3rd Regt., General; Proctor to Ramsey, 19 Sept. 1861 (good medical man), ibid.; Swisshelm to Ramsey, 5 Oct. 1861, ibid.

18. Drs. Gale, Finch, and Rener to Ramsey, 8 Nov. 1861 (fully capable of), RGAR, Military, Infantry—3rd Regt., Chaplains and Surgeons; *Wabashaw (Minn.) County Herald*, 13 Nov. 1861 (one of the); Donnelly to Drs. Gale Finch, and Rener, 1 Nov. 1861, MN EXJOU, Ramsey, 455; G.O. no. 27, 11 Nov. 1861, HQ, State of Minn., Levi Butler, Biographical Collections, MHS; Enlisted Men to Ramsey, 30 Oct. 1861, RGAR, Military, Infantry—3rd Regt., Chaplains and Surgeons.

19. Jones to Ramsey, 15 Oct. 1861 (not strong on), RGAR, Military, Infantry—3rd Regt., Individuals; Howell to Ramsey, 5 Oct. 1861, ibid., General; McLaren to Donnelly, 23 Oct. 1861, Donnelly and Family Papers, roll 9.

20. Scofield to Ramsey, 2 Oct. 1861 (several years experience), RGAR, Military, Infantry—3rd Regt., Chaplains and Surgeons; Swisshelm to Ramsey, 5 Oct. 1861 (his command), RGAR, Military, Infantry—3rd Regt., General; *SPPD*, 1 Nov. 1861 (We can hardly); *Mankato (Minn.) Record,* 5 Nov. 1861 (have not resorted); Nourse to Ramsey, 14 Oct. 1861, RGAR, Military, Infantry—3rd Regt., Chaplains and Surgeons.

21. *St. Paul Weekly Pioneer and Democrat,* 1 Nov. 1861 (The hotels have); *Mankato (Minn.) Semi-Weekly Record,* 8 Nov. 1861 (There are a).

22. Donahower, "Narrative," 144–47, Jeremiah C. Donahower Papers, MHS.

23. Thomas Downs Civil War Diary, 13, 14 (the bonfires of) Oct. 1861, MHS; Donahower, "Narrative," 148 (swinging their hats), Donahower Papers; Aldrich Diary, 13 Oct. 1861, Levi B. Aldrich Papers, MHS; Hale Diary, 13 Oct. 1861, Hale and Family Papers; Beatty to Dear Laura, 13 Oct. 1861, John Reed Beatty Papers, MHS.

24. *Faribault (Minn.) Northern Statesman,* 12 Nov. 1861 (Military etiquette and; Obedience first); S.O. no. 27, 11 Nov. 1861, HQ, State of Minn., Levi Butler, Biographical Collections; *SPPD,* 13 Oct. 1861.

25. Hale to Family, 26 Oct. 1861 (little better than), Hale and Family Papers; *St. Cloud (Minn.) Democrat,* 31 Oct. 1861 (immense pile of; all the trimmings); Donnelly to Ramsey, 28 Oct. 1861 (Men are dirty), MN EXJOU, Ramsey, 451; Canfield to Sister, 5 Nov. 1861, Thomas Canfield Letters, Bruce and George Barnum Family Collection; *Wabashaw (Minn.) County Herald,* 9 Nov. 1861.

26. *GCR,* 1 (They do say), 8 (beautifully mounted sword; very beautiful sword) Nov. 1861.

27. Scott to Ramsey, 29 Oct. 1861 (report to Brig. Genl.), Ramsey Papers, roll 9; G.O. no. 21, 28 Oct. 1861 (General Drill Officer), MNOAG, General Orders.

28. *St. Cloud (Minn.) Democrat,* 4 July 1861 (had the ordinary; white plate); Caleff to Bowler, 2 Nov. 1861, James M. Bowler and Family Papers, MHS; *SPPD,* 3 Nov. 1861; James L. Battey Diary, 3 Nov. 1861, Robert J. Niemela Collection.

29. Ramsey Diary, 3, 4 (making apts), 5 Nov. 1861, Ramsey Papers, roll 39; G.O. no. 25, 5 Nov. 1861, MNOAG; *MCIW,* 1:14, 51; Trenerry, "Lester's Surrender," 194–95. Since Lester appeared in none of the governor's lists of candidates, Minnesota historian Walter Trenerry had questioned the captain's selection. Now we know why.

30. Benjamin F. Smith, Military Record Book, MHS; *SPPD,* 22 Nov. 1861.

31. Officers of 3MN to Ramsey, 3 Nov. 1861 (His Excellency; the want of), RGAR, Military, Infantry—3rd Regt., General; G.O. no. 25, 5 Nov. 1861 (be obeyed and), MNOAG. High commands issue "general orders" to publicize appointments, promotions, assignments, and similar information of broad importance, while "special orders" apply to individuals or small units and require only local distribution.

32. *SPDP,* 7 (a man too), 8 (already made his) Nov. 1861; *SPPD,* 7 Nov. 1861; Tapson, "The Sutler and the Soldier," 176–78; Art. 23, U.S. War Dept., *Revised Regulations,* 85.

33. Hale to Sister Lucie, 10 Nov. 1861 (transformation from the), Hale and Family Papers; Battey Diary, 9 Nov. 1861 (hat and brass; likeness taken); Ramsey Diary, 9 Nov. 1861, Ramey Papers, roll 39; *Wabashaw (Minn.) County Herald,* 9 Nov. 1861.

34. Battey Diary, 10 Nov. 1861 (Orders were read); *Wabashaw (Minn.) County Herald,* 13 Nov. 1861 (did furnish us); *SPWP,* 14 Nov. 1861 (a handsome needle); Redlon, "Presidential Address," 11.

35. *St. Cloud (Minn.) Democrat*, 14 Nov. 1861 (allotted $8 of); *SPWP*, 21 Nov. 1861; *Stillwater (Minn.) Messenger*, 19 Nov. 1861. Russell Johnson takes a dim view of the allotment program; see *Warriors into Workers*, 263–64. See also U.S. Sanitary Commission to Ramsey, Ramsey Papers, roll 9; and "United States Sanitary Commission," USAHEC.

36. Roos Diary, 14 Nov. 1861 (a right proper; a vandalistic business); *Winona (Minn.) Daily Republican*, 15 Nov. 1861; *GCR*, 15 Nov. 1861.

37. Boxell to Wife, 21 Nov. 1861 (up at 3), J[ohn] W. Boxell Civil War Letters and Related Papers, MHS; G.O. no. 13, 3MN, 15 Nov. 1861, 3MN Order Books, Co. B, RG 94; Battey Diary, 16 Nov. 1861; Roos Diary, 16 Nov. 1861.

38. *SPDP*, 4 Dec. 1861 (at least two); Donnelly to Ramsey, 28 Oct. 1861, MN EXJOU, Ramsey, 451; *St. Cloud (Minn.) Democrat*, 31 Oct. 1861.

39. Boxell to Wife, 21 Nov. 1861 (ate hard bread; the hard bread), Boxell Civil War Letters, Roos Diary, 16 Nov. 1861 (display our beautiful); *SPDP*, 17–18, 21 (their needle cases) Nov. 1861; *SPPD*, 17 Nov. 1861.

40. *SAFN*, 7 Dec. 1861 (expresses disappointment at); *St. Paul Weekly Pioneer and Democrat*, 17 (the boys), 22 Nov. 18861. See also Woodworth, "Supporting the Troops," 60. The disappointed soldier was identified in the paper as "JHS," probably Joseph Smith of Company A.

41. *Hastings (Minn.) Independent*, 21 Nov. 1861.

42. *GCR*, 22 Nov. 1861 (each boat was); Ezra T. Champlin, "Response," in 3MVVA, *Twenty-Fourth Annual Reunion* (1908), 187 (a rush was); *SPWP*, 21 Nov. 1861 (two Red Wing); Solon A. Bevans CMSR (suppos[ing] himself discharged), RG 94; Roos Diary, 16 Nov. 1861 (gunshots, hurrahs).

43. *Stillwater (Minn.) Messenger*, 3 Dec. 1861 (two days' rations; was furnished by); *SPWP*, 5 Dec. 1861 (We could eat); *SAFN*, 7 Dec. 1861 (a good share).

44. *Rochester (Minn.) City Post*, 23 Nov. 1861 (soldiers were arrayed); *Winona (Minn.) Daily Republican*, 18 Nov. 1861. For a description of the landing of the Second Minnesota at La Crosse, see Trollope, *North America*, 138–39.

45. Roos Diary, 17 Nov. 1861 (some friends met); *SPDP*, 19 Nov. 1861 (the captains of); *Wabashaw (Minn.) County Herald*, 27 Nov. 1861.

46. *Rochester (Minn.) City Post*, 23 Nov. 1861 (a very elegant); *SPDP*, 4 Dec. 1861 (I must return); Smith to Ramsey, 19 Nov. 1861 (our thanks to), RGAR, Letters Received.

47. Smith to Ramsey, 18 Nov. 1861 (men were served), RGAR, Letters Received; *SPWP*, 5 Dec. 1861 (strong enough to); Roos Diary, 18 Nov. 1861 (were escorted by); *Chicago Tribune*, 21 Nov. 1861, quoted in *SPDP*, 23 Nov. 1861 (the regiment is); *Chicago Times*, 18–19 Nov. 1861.

48. Foote, *The Gentlemen and the Roughs*, chap. 2 passim. Regimental data compiled from CMSRs, RG 94.

49. *MCIW*, 1:178–96, 686–88; 3MN CMSRs, RG 94.

50. Hale to Family, 24 Nov. 1861 (for one half), Hale and Family Papers; Brookins to Thurman Brookins, 24 Nov. 1861 (old Tippecanoe), George W. Brookins and Family Letters, MHS; *SPDP*, 4 Dec. 1861 (plenty of hot); Smith to Ramsey, 18 Nov. 1861, RGAR, Letters Received; Battey Diary, 18 Nov. 1861; Smith to Ramsey, 21 Nov. 1861, Ramsey Papers, roll 9.

2. Learning the Profession of Arms

1. *GCR*, 29 Nov. 1861 (hot coffee, boiled); Roos Diary, 19 Nov. 1861 (almost a continual; Louisville is strong); Andrews, "Narrative of the Third," 148 (cordial expressions

of); Honeywell to Father, 1 Dec. 1861 (woman pok[ed] her; God bless you), Perry Honeywell, Biographical Collections, MHS.

2. Hale to Family, 24 Nov. 1861 (three hours of), William D. Hale and Family Papers, MHS; *Wabashaw (Minn.) County Herald*, 27 Nov. 1861 (Colt's Revolvers); Smith to Ramsey, 21 Nov. 1861 (encamped in regular), Ramsey Papers, roll 9; Boxell to Wife, 21 Nov. 1861, J[ohn] W. Boxell Civil War Letters and Related Papers, MHS; John W. Boxell CMSR, RG 94.

3. Smith to Ramsey, 21 Nov. 1861 (management of troops), Ramsey Papers, roll 9; U.S. War Dept., *Revised Regulations*, 506; Van Buren, *Rules for Preserving the Health of the Solider*, 4, accessed 23 Dec. 2015.

4. Boxell to Wife, 2 Dec. 1861 (good strong coffee), Boxell Civil War Letters; Brookins to Thurman Brookins, 24 Nov. 1861, George W. Brookins and Family Letters, MHS; Bowler to Caleff, 22 Dec. 1861, James M. Bowler and Family Papers, ibid.

5. *Rochester (Minn.) City Post*, 7 Dec. 1861 (no one is); Honeywell to Father, 1 Dec. 1861 (orders to fire), Perry Honeywell, Biographical Collections; Hale to Family, 24 Dec. 1861 (range of liberty), Hale and Family Papers.

6. Buell to McClellan, 30 Nov. 1861 (knew everything about), quoted in Engle, *Don Carlos Buell*, 111; G.O. no. 5, 3MN, 3 Dec. 1861 (understand and perform; responsible for the; deficiencies), 3MN Order Books, Co. B, RG 94; G.O. no. 6, 3MN, 3 Dec. 1861, ibid.; *Rochester (Minn.) City Post*, 7 Dec. 1861; *OR*, 7:461.

7. *Wabashaw (Minn.) County Herald*, 27 Nov. 1861 (good things); Honeywell to Father, 1 Dec. 1861 (the negroes visit; the Boys with; an entire abolishment; the presence of), Perry Honeywell, Biographical Collections; Boxell to Wife, n.d. [24 Nov. 1861], Boxell Civil War Letters. The original transcriber of Boxell to Wife assigned it an incorrect date of 14 January 1862. Matching internal evidence to unit movements and events, however, indicates that the correct date is 24 November 1861.

8. Boxell to Wife, 2, 5 Dec. 1861, Boxell Civil War Letters; Halleran, "Freemasons in the Civil War"; Smith to Ramsey, 27 Nov. 1861, Ramsey Papers, roll 9.

9. *Rochester (Minn.) City Post*, 7 Dec. 1861 (Lieut. W is); *Faribault (Minn.) Central Republican*, 11 Dec. 1861 (if we were); S.O. no. 9, 3MN, 29 Nov. 1861, 3MN Order Books, Co. B, RG 94; Smith to Ramsey, 27 Nov. 1861, Ramsey Papers, roll 9.

10. *GCR*, 20 Dec. 1861 (Our field officers; every inch a gentleman); Smith to Ramsey, 27 Nov. 1861 (a Major was; the order and), Ramsey Papers, roll 9. For the symbolism of the sword, see U.S. War Dept., *Revised Regulations*, 39, sec. 229.

11. G.O. no. 4, Dept. of the Ohio, 22 Nov. 1861, 3MN Order Books, Co. B, RG 94; Griffin, *Letters Home*, 26 Nov. 1861.

12. *Rochester (Minn.) City Post*, 7 Dec. 1861 (a cast off; Such arms were; unsafe for shooting; stacking the worthless); *SAFN*, 7 Dec. 1861 (these weapons).

13. Holt and Owen to Stanton, 1 July 1861 (audit contacts for; as a result), *OR*, ser. 3, 2:191; Edwards, *Civil War Guns*, 92; Shannon, *Organization and Administration*, 1:124–26. A .69-caliber round has a diameter of 0.69 inches.

14. S.O. no. 31, 3MN, 1 Dec. 1861 (declined to perform), 3MN Order Books, Co. B, RG 94; James P. Howlett CMSR, RG 94; Gurnee to Quartermaster, 13 Jan. 1862, MNOAG, General Correspondence; S.O. no. 11, 15 Jan. 1862, Dept. of the Cumberland and the Ohio, General and Special Orders, RG 393, pt. 1, entry 890; Swart, "Military Examination Board," 227.

15. Fry to Commanding Officer, 3MN, 2 Dec. 1861 (against all injury), 3MN Order Books, Co. B, RG 94; *SAFN*, 18 Jan. 1862 (were these bridges); *Rochester (Minn.) City Post*,

14 Dec. 1861. See also "R" in *Mankato (Minn.) Record*, 15 Jan. 1862; and "American Boy" in *GCR*, 10 Jan. 1862.

16. *Rochester (Minn.) City Post*, 21 Dec. 1861 (ankle deep mud; but one feature); *SPWP*, 26 Dec. 1861 (fine grass field); G.O. no. 18, 3MN, 4 Dec. 1861 (as guards or), 3MN Order Books, Co. B, RG 94; *SPDP*, 21 Dec. 1861 (an old muddy).

17. James L. Battey Diary, 6, 8 (Crooked Creek a) Dec. 1861, Robert J. Niemela Collection; *Chatfield (Minn.) Democrat*, 14 Dec. 1861.

18. *SPWP*, 26 Dec. 1861 (a good supper); Jenks to Bowler, 5 Sept. 1907, in 3MVVA, *Twenty-Third Annual Reunion* (1907), 8–9 (a porker of); Smith to Ramsey, 21 Nov. 1861, Ramsey Papers, roll 9; *Stillwater (Minn.) Messenger*, 31 Dec. 1861; Boxell Diary, 9 Dec. 1861, Boxell Civil War Letters; *MCIW*, 1:135.

19. Lester to Fry, 11 Dec. 1861 (not sufficient to), 3MN Papers, RG 94; *Stillwater (Minn.) Messenger*, 31 Dec. 1861 (to be "secesh"); Gurnee to Fry, 9 Dec. 1861, Department of the Cumberland and the Ohio, Telegrams Received, RG 393, pt. 1, entry 885.

20. Ramsey to Wilkinson, 5 Nov. 1861, MN EXJOU, Ramsey, 486; Orrin Smith to Dear Mother, 16 Nov. 1861, Orrin F. Smith and Family Papers, MHS; *SPWP*, 28 Nov. 1861.

21. *Rochester (Minn.) City Post*, 14 Dec. 1861; G.O. no. 21, 3MN, 7 Dec. 1861 (instead of drill), 3MN Order Books, Co. B, RG 94; G.O. no. 25, 3MN, 9 Dec. 1861 (the necessity of; To sentinels in), ibid.

22. Lester to Fry, 11 Dec. 1861 (exceedingly anxious to), 3MN Papers, RG 94; Andrews, *Hints to Company Officers*, 12–13 (A knowledge of); Andrews, "Narrative of the Third," 149 (an unusually high); McClellan, *Regulations and Instructions for the Field Service of the U.S. Cavalry*. The copy of McClellan's *Regulations* owned by the Minnesota Historical Society, charred by fire on its spine and on the edges of its cover, has inscribed on its flyleaf, "Captain Hans Mattson." Sergeants needed to know how to execute commands. To effectively do so, they had to learn when and how to give those commands—in short, sergeants had to be prepared to serve in place of an officer at a moment's notice.

23. Record of Events, Co. E, Dec. 1861 (greatly improved), Company Muster Rolls, 3MN, M594, roll 90; *Winona (Minn.) Daily Republican* quoted in *Rochester (Minn.) City Post*, 29 Mar. 1862 (as a disciplinarian); Theodore Miller (his family were), James [John?] V. Montgomery (fined half months), Richard E. Madden, Francis B. Ide, Henry D. Wakefield, and Lyman J. Barris CMSRs, RG 94; S.O. no. 31, 3MN, 20 Dec. 1861, 3MN Order Books, Co. B, ibid.; S.O. no. 35[?], 3MN, 28 Dec. 1861, ibid.

24. Andrews, "Narrative of the Third," 149 (his uniformly just); Andrews, "Surrender of the Third," 342–43 (luxurious pies); *Stillwater (Minn.) Messenger*, 31 Dec. 1861 (a fine looking; using his best); Bowler to Caleff, 22 Dec. 1861 (camp "Lester" in), Bowler and Family Papers.

25. *SAFN*, 21 Dec. 1861 (a low wet); Honeywell to Sister, 10 Dec. 1861 (a deserted and), Perry Honeywell, Biography Collections; Hale to Family, 18 Dec. 1861 (the curse of), Hale and Family Papers.

26. Hale to Family, 18 Dec. 1861 (a pretty little; a clear stream), Hale and Family Papers; *SPPD*, 11 Feb. 1862 (snug little valley; one mile back); *Wabashaw (Minn.) County Herald*, 15 Feb. 1862.

27. Foster to Ripley, 31 Dec. 1861 (practice firing after; on honor), Foster Collection, Ohio Historical Society, Columbus; *GCR*, 7 Mar. 1862 (commenced the bayonet; We have learned); Lester to Fry, 11 Dec 1861, 3MN Papers, RG 94; Boxell to Wife, 31 Dec. 1861, Boxell Civil War Letters.

28. Battey Diary, 11, 17 (secessionists 350 men) Dec. 1861; *Mankato (Minn.) Record*, 15 Jan. 1862; *Stillwater (Minn.) Messenger*, 31 Dec. 1861; Weitz, "Drill, Training."

29. Mattson to Mrs. Mattson, 8 (asked them at), 19 Dec. 1861, Hans Mattson and Family Papers, MHS; Lester to Ramsey, 18 Dec. 1861 (the men perform), Ramsey Papers, roll 12; Curtis B. Ames CMSR, RG 94; Curtis B. Ames, 3MN, Pension Applications 488918, A729755, C488918, RG 15.

30. Boxell to Wife, 15 Mar. 1862 (a great place; good water), Boxell Civil War Letters; Peter LeClair CMSR, RG 94; Record of Events, Co. C, 31 Dec. 1861, Company Muster Rolls, 3MN, M594, roll 90; Bowler to Caleff, 10 Jan. 1862, Bowler and Family Papers.

31. Roos Diary, 8 Jan. 1862 (a half ration; red-brown mixture; the exercise and); Bowler to Caleff, 10 Jan. 1862, Bowler and Family Papers.

32. Fisk to Lydia Fisk, 2 Feb. 1862 (All of us), James Liberty Fisk and Family Papers, MHS; Mattson to Mrs. Mattson, 9 Jan. 1862 (buried; My Co and), Mattson and Family Papers; Steiner, *Disease in the Civil War*, 12; Joseph Abel CMSR, RG 94; *Stillwater (Minn.) Messenger*, 4 Feb. 1862; *GCR*, 7 Feb. 1862.

33. *SPPD*, 11 Feb. 1862 (interred with martial); *Wabashaw (Minn.) County Herald*, 5 Mar. 1861 (Sergt L. S.); *Lake City (Minn.) Times*, 22 Mar. 1862 (a wife and; that in her; tender to his).

34. Boxell to Wife, 5 Jan. 1862 (Squire Carpenter, a), Boxell Civil War Letters; *SAFN*, 18 Jan. 1862 (the lines are); *Mankato (Minn.) Record*, 15 Jan. 1862 (It is impossible); Andrews, "Surrender of the Third," 341.

35. Mattson to Mrs. Mattson, 19 Dec. 1861, Mattson and Family Papers. Mattson provided several individual examples in this letter—listing name, age, height, complexion, eye color, hair color, residence location, and directions to get to their residences, with remarks. We do not know who ordered the collection and recording of his list, nor when exactly it was created. Based on an extensive discussion of Mattson's letter on the H-CivWar forum in October 1997, provost marshals in many areas infected with guerrillas regularly collected such information, utilizing spies and loyal citizens as sources.

36. Mattson to Mrs. Mattson, 19 Dec. 1861 (greater responsibilities that), Mattson and Family Papers; Bowler to Caleff, 18 Dec. 1861 (without effect; drew their Revolvers), Bowler and Family Papers; Record of Events, Co. C, 31 Dec. 1861, Company Muster Rolls, 3MN, M594, roll 90.

37. Boxell to Wife, 29 Dec. 1861 (the Lieutenant in), Boxell Civil War Letters; Tichenor to Brother, 13 Dec. 1861, Isaac P. Tichenor Letters, Filson Historical Society, Louisville, Ky.

38. Hale to Family, 18 Dec. 1861, Hale and Family Papers.

39. Boxell to Wife, 18 Dec. 1861 (a poor slave), Boxell Civil War Letters; G.O. no. 27, 3MN, 19 Dec. 1861 (colored persons of), 3MN Order Books, Co. B, RG 94; Engle, *Don Carlos Buell*, 49–50.

40. Mattson to Mrs. Mattson, 1 Jan. 1862 (slave auction for), Mattson and Family Papers; William B. Sipes, *7th Pennsylvania*, 14 (but contact with); *Louisville Daily Journal*, 15 Jan. 1862; *Louisville Evening Post*, 7 Feb. 1862, reprinted in *SPPD*, 16 Mar. 1862.

41. Bowler to Caleff, 9 Sept. 1861 (continue until all; desires of my heart), Bowler and Family Papers; Boxell to Wife, 27 Feb. 1862 (most bitter), Boxell Civil War Letters; S.O. no. 10, 3MN, 27 Jan. 1862, John W. Boxell CMSR, RG 94.

42. Boxell to Wife, 29 Dec. 1861 (my shoes and), 7 Jan. 1862 (Lieut Hoit who), Boxell Civil War Letters.

43. Boxell to Wife, 29 Dec. 1861 (the slaves give; an excellent supper), 5 (It is in; We don't admit), 7 Jan. 1862, Boxell Civil War Letters; Roos Diary, 9–10 Jan. 1862.

44. Brookins to Thurman, 15 Jan. 1862 (a house used; very kind &), George W. Brookins and Family Letters, MHS; *GCR*, 24 Jan. 1862 (Our surgeons are).

45. Boxell to Wife, 11 (did not consider), 21 Jan., 22 Feb. (Colonel Lester told; Hoit was very) 1862, Boxell Civil War Letters.

46. Fisk to Lydia Fisk, 2 Feb. 1862 (I shall soon), Fisk Papers; Bowler to Caleff, 13 Feb. 1862 (general hospital for), Bowler and Family Papers; Hale to Family, 4 Mar. 1862 (no care totally), Hale and Family Papers; *Louisville Daily Journal*, 12 Feb. 1862 (soldier's wife from); letter by "Will," 23 Jan. 1862, *GCR*, 7 Feb. 1862.

47. *Louisville Daily Journal*, 5 Feb. 1862.

48. Lester to Ramsey, 14 Feb. 1862 (I AM exceedingly), Ramsey Papers, roll 9; John R. Bennett CMSR (a large and), RG 94; Lester to Ramsey, 26 Feb. 1862 (guided by my), Ramsey Papers, roll 9.

49. Lester to Ramsey, 12 Mar. 1862 (in accordance with), RGAR, Military, Infantry—3rd Regt.–General; Bowler to Donnelly, 16 Mar. 1862 (miserable individual), Ignatius Donnelly and Family Papers, MHS, roll 9.

50. Bowler to Donnelly, 16 Mar. 1862 (in obedience to), Donnelly and Family Papers, roll 9; *SPDP*, 17 Jan. 1862; Cyrene Blakely, Rolin Olin, Levi Phillips, and William Hale CMSRs, RG 94.

51. Aaker to Ramsey, 5 Feb. 1862 (a matter of; They are serious), Ramsey Papers, roll 9; William Webster and Mark Clay CMSRs, RG 94; Lester to Malmros, 11 June 1862, MNOAG, General Correspondence.

52. Mattson to Mrs. Mattson, 11 Jan. 1862 (We have now), Mattson and Family Papers; *Stillwater (Minn.) Messenger*, 14 Jan. 1862 (We have seen); *GCR*, 10 Jan. (our Colonel is), 7 Mar. (We have been) 1862; *SPDP*, 1 Mar. 1862 (Major Thurston, the); *Rochester (Minn.) City Post*, 29 Mar. 1862 (It is as); *Lake City (Minn.) Times*, 22 Mar. 1862 (Of the Colonel's).

53. *Lake City (Minn.) Times*, 22 Mar. 1862 (Lieut. Col Smith); Lester to Ramsey, 26 Feb. 1862 (There is every), Ramsey Papers, roll 9.

54. Bowler to Caleff, 23 Jan. 1862 (Lieutenant Ingman is), Bowler and Family Papers; Bowler to Donnelly, 15 Jan. 1862 (can never pass), Donnelly and Family Papers, roll 9; *Mankato (Minn.) Record*, 18 Jan. 1862 (his greatest fault is); Canfield to Sister, 2 Mar. 1862, Thomas Canfield Letters, Bruce and George Barnum Family Collection.

55. Hokenson to Secretary, 26 Sept. 1916 (over a creek), 3MVVA, *Thirty-Second Annual Reunion* (1916), 18; Mattson to Mrs. Mattson, 30 Jan.[?], 1, 23 Feb. 1862, Mattson and Family Papers; Andrews, "Narrative of the Third," 149.

56. Hobart to Ramsey, 15 Feb. 1862 (Moral Condition), MNOAG, General Correspondence; Lester to Ramsey, 15 Apr. 1862 (services of a), Ramsey Papers, roll 9. Hobart's report was dated the fifteenth but included a notation on discontinuing prayer at dress parade beyond 23 February.

57. Mattson to Mrs. Mattson, 30 Jan.[?], 1 Feb. 1862, Mattson and Family Papers; Weddle, "Ethnic Discrimination."

58. Rice to Father and Mother, 9 Feb. 1862 (charge anyone and), Henry O. Rice Letters, Earl Hess Collection, USAMHI; *Chatfield (Minn.) Democrat*, 22 Feb. 1862 (Col. Lester is); Battey Diary, 6, 8 Feb. 1862; S.O. no. 49, Dept. of the Ohio, 1 Jan. 1862, 3MN Order Books, Co. B, RG 94; Goff, "Evolution of Skirmish Tactics," 4–5; Hardee,

Rifle and Light Infantry Tactics, 33–41; Casey, *Infantry Tactics*, 1:181–223; Duffield, *Camp, Garrison, and Guard Duty*; Mahan, *Elementary Treatise on Advanced-Guard, Out-Post, and Detachment Service*. Earl Hess claims that skirmisher training did not begin until late 1862 in Buell's army. *Rifle Musket*, 125.

59. Halladay to Mother, 8 Feb. 1862 (blacker than a), Sgt. Monroe D. Halladay Letters, Civil War Misc. Collection, USAMHI; *SPPD*, 11 Feb. 1862 (Crooked creek is); Rohrer to Donnelly, 7 Feb. 1862, Donnelly and Family Papers, roll 9; Boxell to Wife, 31 Jan. 1862 (excellent fat mutton), Boxell Civil War Letters; *Chatfield (Minn.) Democrat*, 22 Feb. 1862; Roos Diary, 14 Jan. 1862.

60. *Chatfield (Minn.) Democrat*, 22 Feb. 1862 (Mississippi Tigers); *SPDP*, 25 Feb. 1862 (Heavens! Is this); Roos Diary, 15, 18–20 Feb. 1862.

61. Lester to Fry, 11 Dec. 1861 (wholly worthless), 3MN Papers, RG 94; Ira C. Marlett, Pension Application 809403 (by [the] blowing), RG 15; Ira C. Marlett CMSR, RG 94; *Stillwater (Minn.) Messenger*, 14 Jan. 1862 (scarcely find enough); Ripley to Sanborn, 3 Jan. 1862, MNOAG, General Correspondence.

62. Hale to Lucie, 22 Feb. 1862 (Now is the), Hale and Family Papers; Lester to Waggener, 27 Jan. 1862, 3MN Papers, RG 94.

63. Boxell to Wife, 27 Feb. (new guns appear), 27 Mar. (the blue banner) 1862, Boxell Civil War Letters; Lester to Ramsey, 26 Feb. 1862 (We have received), Ramsey Papers, roll 9; Lester to Ramsey, 3 Jan. 1862, ibid.

64. Roos Diary, 1 Mar. 1862 (snow and sleeting); Hale to Family, 4 Mar. 1862 (the press in), Hale and Family Papers; Barnes to Wife, 27 Feb. 1862, Miller, *Dear Wife*, 35; Andrews, "Sketch of the Third," 7.

65. *GCR*, 7, 21, 28 Feb., 7 Mar. (innumerable dainties for) 1862; *Stillwater (Minn.) Messenger*, 4 Feb., 8 Apr. 1862.

66. Roos Diary, 26 Feb. 1862 (the doctors are); Boxell to Wife, 2 Mar. 1862, Boxell Civil War Letters.

67. S.O. no. 58, Dept. of the Ohio, 3 Mar. 1862 (concentrate his entire), Dept. of the Cumberland and the Ohio, General and Special Orders, RG 393, pt. 1, entry 890; Battey Diary, 7 (1st rate), 8 (likeness taken) Mar. 1862; *Stillwater (Minn.) Messenger*, 1 Apr. 1862 (a little of; a very large; orderlies of company); Roos Diary, 8 Mar. 1862; Boxell to Wife, 9, 15 Mar. 1862, Boxell Civil War Letters; Almon Strickland and Perry Martin CMSRs, RG 94.

68. Roos Diary, 10 Mar. 1862.

69. Boxell to Wife, 15 Mar. 1862 (to the colors; loads felt lighter; advance guard), Boxell Civil War Letters; S.O. no. 63, Dept. of the Ohio, 8 Mar. 1862, Special Orders, Dept. of the Cumberland and the Ohio, General and Special Orders, RG 393, pt. 1, entry 890; Brookins to Thurman and Mary, 11 Mar., in 9 Mar. 1862, Brookins and Family Letters.

70. Wright, *Eighth Regiment Kentucky Volunteer Infantry*, 38–39 (an old personal; saying Colonel Barnes); Boxell to Wife, 15, 27 (7 year old) Mar. 1862, Boxell Civil War Letters; Frank Redlon, "Presidential Address," in 3MVVA, *Eighteenth Annual Reunion* (1902), 11; David Hancock and Joseph Mertz CMSRs, RG 94; Hale to Family, 16 Mar. 1862, Hale and Family Papers; Brookins to Thurman Brookins, 20 Mar. 1862, Brookins and Family Letters.

71. Redlon, "Presidential Address," 11–12 (in column by); Boxell to Wife, 15, 27 ([T]he Colonel [was]) Mar. 1862, Boxell Civil War Letters; *Louisville Democrat*, cited in

Rochester (Minn.) City Post, 29 Mar. 1862 (The men are); Battey Diary, 14, 16 Mar. 1862.

72. Wright, *Eighth Regiment Kentucky Volunteer Infantry*, 39 (the excellent band); Bowler to Caleff, 20 Mar. 1862 (serenade band; five fiddles, 2), Bowler and Family Papers.

3. Mastering Their Trade

1. Boxell to Wife, 29 Mar. 1862 (and full of), J[ohn] W. Boxell Civil War Letters and Related Papers, MHS; Hale to Sister Lucie, 26 Mar. 1862, William D. Hale and Family Papers, MHS.

2. James L. Battey Diary, 22 (signs of energy; look as tho), 23, 24 Mar. 1862, Robert J. Niemela Collection; Hale to Sister Lucie, 26 Mar. 1862 (the unmistakable mark), Hale and Family Papers; Boxell to Wife, 27 Mar. 1862 (several persons remarked), Boxell Civil War Letters; Andrews, "Narrative of the Third," 150; Brookins to Thurman Brookins, 23 Mar. 1862, George W. Brookins and Family Letters, MHS; Bowler to Caleff, 26 Mar. 1862, James M. Bowler and Family Papers, MHS.

3. Hale to Sister Lucie, 26 Mar. 1862 (a rich and), Hale and Family Papers; Tichenor to Friends, 23 Mar. 1862 (gloomy), Isaac P. Tichenor Letters, Filson Historical Society, Louisville, Ky.; *Chicago Times*, 1 Apr. 1862 (bitter, sullen, malignant); *Louisville Daily Journal*, 28 Apr. 1862; Dicey, *Spectator of America*, 187.

4. *Wabashaw (Minn.) County Herald*, 9 Apr. 1862 (are all secesh); *GCR*, 4 Apr., 16 May (basilisks; melodious greeting[s] such) 1862.

5. Boxell to Wife, 27 (the finest camping), 31 Mar. (slops and scraps), 19, 26 Apr. 1862, Boxell Civil War Letters; Brookins to Thurman Brookins, 17 Apr. 1862 (We took pains), Brookins and Family Letters; "H.N.G." to Dear Friend, 1 Apr. 1862 (men out examining), Emery, "Lewis Emery Letters," accessed 22 Apr. 2003.

6. Boxell to Wife, 4 (target shooting and; the rear rank), 19 (We have practiced) Apr. 1862, Boxell Civil War Letters; e-mail, Stephen Osman to the author, 10 Dec. 2013. Upton's fabled 121st New York trained similarly. See Cilella, *Upton's Regulars*, 96. James McPherson claims that target practice was rare. See *Battle Cry of Freedom*, 330.

7. Hobart to Ramsey, 29 Mar. 1862 (reputation for honor), Ramsey Papers, roll 9; Bowler to Caleff, 17 Apr. 1862, Bowler and Family Papers; *St. Paul Weekly Pioneer and Democrat*, 18 Apr. 1862; Battey Diary, 1 Apr. 1862; Durham, *Nashville*, 69–70.

8. Donahower "Reminiscences," 256 (was not disappointed), Jeremiah C. Donahower Papers, MHS; *Wabashaw (Minn.) County Herald*, 9 Apr. 1862 (that he thought); *Louisville Daily Journal*, 28 Apr. 1862 (forced to add); *Chicago Times*, 26 Mar. 1862.

9. *Rochester (Minn.) City Post*, 26 Apr., 3 May (token of their) 1862; Brookins to Thurman Brookins, 16 May 1862 (Col Lesters short), Brookins and Family Letters; *Wabashaw (Minn.) County Herald*, 9 Apr. 1862 (should Minnesota be); Battey Diary, 8 Apr. 1862. See also "Col. Henry C. Lester Civil War Sword," *Minnesota History* (Summer 2005), Minnesota Historical Society, http://www.mnhs.org/collections/upclose/lester.php.

10. Bowler to Caleff, 13 Apr. 1862, Bowler and Family Papers.

11. *Wabashaw (Minn.) County Herald*, 9 Apr. 1862 (absent somewhere in); Hadley to Green, 21 Apr. 1862 (compelt to report), John A. Hadley CMSR, RG 94; *Chatfield (Minn.) Democrat*, 19 Apr. 1862 (compelled to resign); Lester to Green, 13 Apr. 1862, 3MN Muster Rolls, RG 94; *SPDP*, 23 Apr. 1862.

12. *GCR*, 18 Apr. 1862 (unanimously agreed that); Roos Diary, 4 Apr. 1862 (he had limited); Lars Aaker CMSR, RG 94.

13. *Wabashaw (Minn.) County Herald*, 5 (the right man), 9 (unable to do duty) Apr. 1862; S.O. no. 12, Dept. of the Ohio, 8 Apr. 1862, Francis H. Milligan CMSR, RG 94; Boxell to Wife, 26 Apr. 1862, Boxell Civil War Letters.

14. Ramsey to Renner, 7 Apr. 1862 (visit the several), MN EXJOU, Ramsey, 543–44; Lester to Green, 13 Apr. 1862, 3MN Muster Rolls, RG 94. In his report to Ramsey of 28 April 1862, Renner referred to a surgeon from the Third at Park Barracks named Bingham, who perhaps was the New York doctor who had replaced Butler.

15. Boxell to Wife, 30 Mar., 8 Apr. 1862 (magnificent residence owned; quite splendid and; with loaded guns; gentlemanly bearing), Boxell Civil War Letters; Brookins to Thurman Brookins, 17 Apr. 1862 (not to let), Brookins and Family Letters.

16. Canfield to Sister, 4 Apr. 1862 (most all secesh), Thomas Canfield Letters, Bruce and George Barnum Family Collection; Boxell to Wife, 27, 30 Mar., 8, 19 Apr. 1862, Boxell Civil War Letters.

17. Canfield to Sister, 9 Apr. 1862, Canfield Letters.

18. *Louisville Daily Journal*, 28 Apr. 1862 (office of the; Gen. Dumont); Boxell to Wife, 19 Apr. 1862 (at least 40), Boxell Civil War Letters; Brookins to Thurman Brookins, 17 Apr. 1862 (at a full), Brookins and Family Letters; Bowler to Caleff, 13 (the devils), 17 Apr. 1862, Bowler and Family Papers.

19. *Chicago Times*, 31 Mar. 1862 (Michigan Mechanic Fusiliers); S.O. no. 8, Dept. of the Ohio, 22 Mar. 1862, Dept. of the Cumberland and the Ohio, General and Special Orders, RG 393, pt. 1, entry 890; Clay to Vaugh, 13 Apr. 1862, *OR*, 10(2):417 (upon the Nashville); Barnes to Wife, 13 Apr. 1862 (constantly on the), Miller, *Dear Wife*, 38–39. The Fusiliers were the First Regiment of Michigan Engineers and Mechanics.

20. Roos Diary, 14, 20 Apr. 1862; Boxell to Wife, 26 Apr. 1862, J[ohn] W. Boxell Civil War Letters and Related Papers.

21. Boxell to Wife, 19 Apr. 1862 (a green apple; French fiddle; waited on Lieut), Boxell Civil War Letters; Roos Diary, 21 Apr. 1862 (plenty of beer).

22. Boxell to Wife, 19 Apr. 1862 (dress uniforms, with; broad stone terrace; somewhat powdered with), Boxell Civil War Letters; Battey Diary, 16 Apr. 1862; Dicey, *Spectator of America*, 188–89. Dicey, an English travel writer, was present for Johnson's capitol speech to the Third.

23. Hale to Sister Lucie, 24 Apr. 1862 (the citizen soldiers), Hale and Family Papers; Johnson, *Papers of Andrew Johnson*, 5:327 (That's so).

24. *Wabashaw (Minn.) County Herald,* 9 Apr. 1862 (What regiment of); *Nashville Daily Union* quoted in *GCR*, 2 May 1862 (highly respectable citizen); Brookins to Thurman Brookins, 3 (Band Box Regiment), 26 (better drilled, cleaner) Apr. 1862, Brookins and Family Letters; Bowler to Caleff, 4 Apr. 1862 (Gov Andy Johnson), Bowler Letters. Colonel Lester *requested* that the men wear gloves, but they were not issue and could not be required. Most wore them nevertheless, and the officers bought them for those who either could not or would not buy gloves themselves.

25. Brookins to Thurman Brookins, 3, 26 (girls shed tears) Apr. 1862, Brookins and Family Letters; Fry to Green, 23 Apr. 1862, Department of the Cumberland and the Ohio, Telegrams Sent, RG 393, pt. 1, entry 915; Boxell to Wife, 26 Apr. 1862, Boxell Civil War Letters; John A. Spelman CMSR, RG 94.

26. Boxell to Wife, 26 Apr. 1862 (Governor asked what; That cannot be), Boxell Civil War Letters; Hale to Sister Lucie, 24 Apr. 1862 (no sooner did), Hale and Family Papers; Johnson to Maynard, 24 Apr. 1862 (substantially surrendering the), Johnson, Papers

of Andrew Johnson, 5:330; Johnson to Buell, 24 Apr. 1862, ibid.; Buell to Johnson, 24 Apr. 1862, ibid.; Maslowski, Treason Must Be Made Odious, 39.

27. Bowler to Caleff, 24 Apr. 1862 (be discharged before), Bowler and Family Papers; Halver Ockenberg and Amos Lesher (with softening of) CMSRs, RG 94; Roos Diary, 24, 26 Apr. 1862; Boxell to Wife, 26 Apr. 1862, Boxell Civil War Letters.

28. Bowler to Caleff, 28 Apr. 1862 (had to turn; those lazy, blackleg), Bowler and Family Papers; Boxell to Wife, 3 May 1862, Boxell Civil War Letters; Bernard N. McKenna, Morrison M. Allison, and William E. Allison CMSRs, RG 94. William Allison was a hotelkeeper, Morrison Allison a clerk, and McKenna an Irish laborer.

29. Boxell to Wife, 3 May 1862 (the stars shining), Boxell Civil War Letters; Bowler to Caleff, 28 Apr. 1862 (blasting hand of), Bowler and Family Papers; Brookins to Thurman Brookins, 30 Apr. 1862 (burnt some bridges; Our Col is), Brookins and Family Letters.

30. Roos Diary, 28 Apr. 1862 (an alarm at); Bowler to Caleff, 28 Apr. 1862, Bowler Letters.

31. Buell to Mitchel, 27 Mar. 1862, OR, 10(2):71; S.O. no. 1, Dist. of Ohio, Mar. 1862, Dept. of the Cumberland and the Ohio, General and Special Orders, RG 393, pt. 1, entry 890; Maslowski, Treason Must Be Made Odious, 39; Hoffman, "My Brave Mechanics," 59.

32. Parkhurst to Sister Helen, 1 Apr. 1862, John G. Parkhurst Papers, UMBHL; Parkhurst Diary, 3 Apr. 1862, John Gibson Parkhurst Papers, MSUA.

33. Brookins to Thurman Brookins, 16 May 1862 (remonstrated with Col; pitched his tent), Brookins and Family Letters; Record of Events, 9th Michigan, Apr. 1862, ORS, pt. 1, vol. 30, ser. 42, p. 799; Cooley Diary, 1 Apr. 1862, Henry G. Cooley Papers, UMBHL; Mattson to Mrs. Mattson, 27 Apr. 1862, Hans Mattson and Family Papers, MHS; Wright, Eighth Regiment Kentucky Volunteer Infantry, 48–49; Miller, Dear Wife, 38–39.

34. Boxell to Wife, 8 May 1862 (camp is level; a level open), Boxell Civil War Letters; SPDP, 14 May 1862 (this [camp] is).

4. Forged in Murfreesboro

1. Hobgood, "Economic History," 203–28; Tolbert, Constructing Townscapes, 50–62, 247, 262n35; Farley, "Politics of Memory," 25–28.

2. Parkhurst to Helen, 26 Apr. 1862 (one of the), Parkhust Papers, MSUA; Ash, When the Yankees Came, 52; C. Alice Ready Diary, 8, 15 Apr. 1862, University of North Carolina at Chapel Hill, Southern History Collection; 7–8, 10, 12 May 1862, Kate S. Carney Diary, ibid.

3. Carney Diary, 15 June 1862 (I can't bear; what charges no); Ready Diary, 19 Apr. 1862 (The people are); Tolbert, Constructing Townscapes, 123; Barbara Welter, "Cult of True Womanhood"; Murfreesboro Union Volunteer, 20 May 1862.

4. Mattson to Mrs. Mattson, 29 Apr. 1862 (attracted the usual), Hans Mattson and Family Papers, MHS; SPDP, 14 May 1862 (I never was); GCR, 16 May 1862 (brigade-drill, and; the point of); Parkhurst to Sisters, 14 Mar. 1862, John G. Parkhurst Papers, UMBHL; Roos Diary, 30 Apr. 1862; James L. Battey Diary, 1 May 1862, Robert J. Niemela Collection; Bowler to Caleff, 28 Apr. 1862, Bowler Letters.

5. Brookins to Thurman Brookins, 16 May 1862 (to furnish about), George W. Brookins and Family Letters, MHS; Andrews. "Surrender of the Third Regiment," 344 (in street fighting); McClellan, Regulations and Instructions for the Field Service of the U.S. Cavalry, 58, 69 (their interior organization); Wright, Eighth Regiment Kentucky

Volunteer Infantry, 48–49; S.O. no. 16, Dept. of the Ohio, 12 Apr. 1862, Dept. of the Cumberland and the Ohio, General and Special Orders, RG 393, pt. 1, entry 890; Parkhurst Diary, 27 May 1862, John Gibson Parkhurst Papers, MSUA.

6. Duffield to Blayton, 6 May 1862, *OR*, 10(1):885 (strong guards on); Negley to Buell, 1 May 1862, Department of the Cumberland and the Ohio, Telegrams Received, RG 393, pt. 1, entry 929; Matthews to Fry, 3 May 1862, ibid.

7. Bowler to Caleff, 5 May 1862 (two miles from), James M. Bowler and Family Papers, MHS; *SPDP*, 14, 20 May 1862; Boxell to Wife, 3 May 1862, J[ohn] W. Boxell Civil War Letters and Related Papers, MHS; Tarrant, *Wild Riders of the First Kentucky Cavalry*, 80–83; Ames to Nellie, 8 May 1862, Curtis B. Ames Letters, Crandall Collection, Rockford Area Historical Society, Rockford, Minn.

8. Boxell to Wife, 7 May 1862 (on the pike), Boxell Civil War Letters; Mattson to Mrs. Mattson, 5 May 1862, Mattson and Family Papers; Roos Diary, 4–5 May 1862; Bowler to Caleff, 5 May 1862, Bowler and Family Papers.

9. Boxell to Wife, 3 and 7 May 1862 (with 40–60), in 29 Apr. 1862, Boxell Civil War Letters; Mattson to Mrs. Mattson, 9 May 1862 (He felt so), Mattson and Family Papers; Bailey to Father, 21 May 1862 (lay on our), Edward G. Bailey Letters, Ira K. Bailey Correspondence, UMBHL; Parkhurst Diary, 8–9 May 1862, Parkhurst Papers, MSUA; Liljegren to Edblad, 14 May 1862, Swanson, "Civil War Letters of Olof Liljegren," 92; Battey Diary, 4, 5 May 1862.

10. *Murfreesboro Daily Union*, 20 May 1862 (over two hundred); Johnson to Parkhurst, 11 May 1862 (have a proper), Johnson, *Papers of Andrew Johnson*, 5:377; George Brookins to Thurman Brookins, 16 May 1862, Brookins and Family Letters; Parkhurst Diary, 13 May 1862, Parkhurst Papers, MSUA; Carney Diary, 12 May 1862.

11. Boxell to Son, 10 May 1862 (in the enemy's), Boxell Civil War Letters; *SPDP*, 23 May 1862 (picketing is not; country seems to); Mitchell, *Civil War Soldiers*, 132 (bizarre).

12. Cooley Diary, 13, 16 (sergeant of the), 19 May 1862, Henry G. Cooley Papers, UMBHL; Boxell to Son, 10 May 1862, Boxell Civil War Letters; *SPDP*, 23 May 1862; Mitchell, *Civil War Soldiers* 132.

13. Boxell to Son, 3 May in 29 Apr., 10 May 1862, Boxell Civil War Letters; Harrison to Wife, 10 May 1862, "Absolom A. Harrison Civil War Letters," accessed 31 July 2008.

14. Mitchel to Lester, 18 May 1862, Henry C. Lester CMSR, RG 94; Lester to Green 19 May 1862, ibid.; Mitchel to Buell, 27 May 1862, Department of the Cumberland and the Ohio, Telegrams Received, RG 393, pt. 1, entry 929; Fry to Duffield, 21 May 1862, Department of the Cumberland and the Ohio, Telegrams Sent, ibid., entry 915.

15. *St. Paul Daily Press*, 23 May 1862 (the regiment has; as few qualifications); Smith to Lester, 22 May 1862 (utterly incapacitated for), Benjamin F. Smith CMSR, RG 94; Hale to Family, 16 May 1862, Hale Letters.

16. Ash, *When the Yankees Came*, 77; 3MN Regimental Returns, May 1862 (more efficiently), Record of Events, 3MN, RG 94, M594; Boxell to Wife, 10, 20 (very clean and) May 1862, Boxell Civil War Letters; Record of Events, Co. K, 8th Kentucky, May 1863, *ORS*, pt. 2, vol. 22, ser. 34, pp. 292–93.

17. *SPDP*, 3 June 1862 (oven capable of); *Stillwater (Minn.) Messenger*, 10 June 1862 (amid a shower); Boxell to Wife, 20 May 1862, Boxell Civil War Letters; Hale to Family, 16 May 1862, William D. Hale and Family Papers, MHS; Battey Diary, 16 May 1862.

18. Brookins to Thurman Brookins, 16 May 1862 (at the prospect), Brookins and Family Letters; Boxell to Wife, 20 May 1862 (went to sleep), Boxell Civil War Letters;

Pakrhurst to Robertson, 17 May 1862, Records of Michigan, 9th Michigan, Record Group 59-14, Archives of Michigan, Lansing; Roos Diary, 16, 17 May 1862; Battey Diary, 17–18 May 1862.

19. Wedge, "Talk to [Unnamed] Veterans Group," 1910 (was sudden and; keep the men), Mark Jones Collection; Wedge to Ramsey, 19 May 1862, RGAR, Letters Received; *SPDP*, 14 May 1862.

20. *Stillwater (Minn.) Messenger,* 10 June 1862 (Old School Presbyterian); *SPDP*, 3 June 1862 (one complete bed).

21. *SPDP*, 3 June 1862 (cleanliness [w]as one); Bowler to Caleff, 22 May 1862 (a crowd of), Bowler and Family Papers.

22. *SPPD*, 28 May 1862 (it is all); Boxell to Wife, 27 May 1862, Boxell Civil War Letters; Roos Diary, 27 May 1862.

23. Eames to Wife, 27 Mar. 1862 (the old bunks; bunks arranged), William Mark Eames Papers, TSLA, microfilm; Farley, "Politics of Memory," 30–32.

24. Eames to Wife, 24, 29 (like some things) June, 2 (a malicious fellow), 4, 7 July 1862, Eames Papers.

25. Crary to Donnelly, 2 July 1862 (piteously begged for; the kinds of), Ignatius Donnelly and Family Papers, MHS, roll 10.

26. *Wabashaw (Minn.) County Herald,* 21 May 1862 (hard and tedious); *Stillwater (Minn.) Messenger,* 10 Jan. 1862; Lester to Green, 23 May 1862, James P. Howlett, Edgar A. Holcomb, and Francis M. Jerry CMSRs, RG 94.

27. Stanton to Fisk, 23 May 1862 (Superintendent of the), James Liberty Fisk and Family Papers, MHS; Certificate of Discharge, James L. Fisk CMSR, RG 94; S.O. no. 51, Dept. of the Ohio, 19 May 1862, ibid.

28. *SPPD,* 28 May 1862 (since which change); Bailey to Father, 21 May 1862 (We fare little), Bailey Letters; 9th Michigan Regimental Books, RG 94; Edward G. Bailey CMSR, ibid.

29. *Murfreesboro Union Volunteer,* 20 May 1862 (a worthy successor); Parkhurst to Helen, 11 (is not quite), 24 (he is not) May 1862, Parkhurst Letters, UMBHL; Boxell to Wife, 20 May 1862, Boxell Civil War Letters.

30. *SPDP,* 23 May 1862 (considerable fun searching); William H. King Memoirs, 16, University of North Carolina at Chapel Hill, Southern History Collection (suffered much from); *SPPD*, 28 May 1862.

31. Hale to Family, 16 May 1862 (there has been; loss of hope), Hale and Family Papers; *SPDP*, 2 June 1862 (one of those); Speech, 24 May 1862 (the deluded and), Johnson, *Papers of Andrew Johnson,* 5:416–17; Canfield to Sister, 26 May 1862 (they darent say), Thomas Canfield Letters, Bruce and George Barnum Family Collection; Ash, "Sharks in an Angry Sea," 218 (flaunt[ed] contempt for); Carney Diary, 24 May 1862.

32. *Philadelphia Inquirer,* 24 May 1862. There is no other source for this event.

33. *Stillwater (Minn.) Messenger,* 10 June 1862 (highly as we); Carney Diary, 25 May 1862 (met their band); Ash, "Sharks in an Angry Sea," 218 (extension of the).

34. Roos Diary, 26 (thought to be; the negro came), 27 (a Negro came) May 1862; Canfield to Sister, 26 May 1862 (so thick around; better here than), Canfield Letters.

35. Hadley to Fry, n.d. (at the point; the Genne in), James A. Hadley CMSR, RG 94; S.O. no. 59, Dept. of the Ohio, 27 May 1862, ibid.; Hadley to Ramsey, 3 May 1862 (pleas excuse hast), Ramsey Papers, roll 9; *St. Paul Weekly Pioneer and Democrat,* 23 May 1862 (the universal sentiment); Swart, "Military Examination Board."

36. S.O. no. 61, Dept. of the Ohio, 29 May 1862, Benjamin F. Smith CMSR, RG 94; *SPWP*, 5 June 1862. The rosters are all in error on Hoit's, Griggs's, and Mattson's status and commissioning dates in *MCIW*, 1:178–84.

37. Roos Diary, 4 June 1862; *SPDP*, 13, 18 June 1862.

38. Bowler to Caleff, 29 May, 5 June (drawing pigs, chickens) 1862, Bowler Letters; *SPDP*, 10 June 1862 (regiment performs its); Roos Diary, 28 May, 1 June 1862; Record of Events, Co. A, 9th Michigan, May 1862, *ORS*, pt. 2, vol. 30, ser. 42, p. 807.

39. Bowler to Caleff, 5 June 1862, Bowler and Family Papers; Brookins to Thurman Brookins, 8 June 1862, Brookins and Family Letters; *SPDP*, 13 June 1862; Hale to Family, 8 June 1862, Hale Letters.

40. Roos Diary, 8 June 1862 (mess and supplies); *SPWP*, 19 June 1862 (see how we); Brookins to Thurman Brookins, 8 June 1862, Brookins and Family Letters; Mitchel to Buell, 8 June 1862, Department of the Cumberland and the Ohio, Telegrams Received, RG 393, pt. 1, entry 929; *SPDP*, 13 June 1862. To "secure arms" in the school of the soldier, one moves the musket from the right shoulder across the chest and under the left arm, preparatory to shouldering the gun on the left shoulder. Hardee, *Rifle and Light Infantry Tactics*, 11.

41. Owens to Ramsey, 26 June 1862, Ramsey Papers, roll 9; Crary to Ramsey, 13 June 1862, RGAR, Letters Received.

42. Dumont to Buell, 7 June 1862 (an intelligent Frenchman), Department of the Cumberland and the Ohio, Telegrams Received, RG 393, pt. 1, entry 929; Cooper to Johnson, 5 June 1862 (crossed the Mountains), Johnson, *Papers of Andrew Johnson*, 5:441; Mitchel to Halleck 9 June 1862, *OR*, 10(2):283 (I learned that).

43. Buell to Mitchel, 9 June 1862 (the [rail]road to), Department of the Cumberland and the Ohio, Telegrams Sent, RG 393, pt. 1, entry 915; Buell to Stanton, 9 June 1862, *OR*, 10(2):285 (for an active); Mattson to Mrs. Mattson, 10 June 1862 (eastern Tenn, after), Mattson and Family Papers.

44. Crary to Ramsey, 13 June 1862, RGAR, Letters Received; *Mankato (Minn.) Record*, 12 July 1862; *Stillwater (Minn.) Messenger*, 15 July 1862.

45. *Mankato (Minn.) Record*, 12 July 1862 (wash[ed] the dust); Crary to Ramsey, 13 June 1862 (stood the march; a comfortable room), RGAR, Letters Received; *SPDP*, 23 June 1862 (one caisson went); Mattson to Mrs. Mattson, 19, 20 June 1862, Mattson and Family Papers.

46. *Mankato (Minn.) Record*, 12 July 1862 (with our colors); *GCR*, 27 June 1862 (perfect horses on; 'confiscated' chicken, turkies; disturb the property); *Wabashaw (Minn.) County Herald*, 2 July 1862 (the flying infantry); Wright, *Eighth Regiment Kentucky Volunteer Infantry*, 62.

47. Sipes, *7th Pennsylvania*, 25 (impassable for wagons), 26; *SPDP*, 23 June 1862 (you can never); *Wabashaw (Minn.) County Herald*, 2 July 1862 (walk[ing] and push[ing]); Roos Diary, 14 June 1862 (were in danger); *GCR*, 27 June 1862.

48. Roos Diary, 14 June 1862 (clad with a); Hale to Family, 26 June 1862 (*was awful*, at), Hale and Family Papers; *GCR*, 27 June 1862; Sipes, *7th Pennsylvania*, 28.

49. Bowler to Caleff, 22 June 1862, Bowler and Family Papers; Mattson to Mrs. Mattson, 20 June 1862, Mattson and Family Papers; Brookins to Thurman Brookins, 27 June 1862, Brookins and Family Letters; *Mankato (Minn.) Record*, 12 July 1862; *SPDP*, 23 June 1862; Roos Diary, 15–16 June 1862. There is no Floyd on any rosters of the Third, and there is no CMSR for a Floyd. Pvt. Napoleon Steele, a Pikesville farmer, enlisted in Company B on 31 December 1863 in Little Rock. Napoleon Steele CMSR, RG 94.

50. *Wabashaw (Minn.) County Herald*, 2 July 1862 (Our army steals); *GCR*, 24 June 1862 (knapsacks, haversacks, canteens); Hale to Family, 26 June 1862, Hale and Family Papers.

51. Roos Diary, 16, 18–19 June 1862; "H.N.G." to Friend, 1 July 1862 (we gave three), Emery, "Lewis Emery Letters," accessed 22 Apr. 2003; Cave to Wife, 19 June 1862, Emanuel Cave Letter, University of Tennessee–Knoxville.

52. Record of Events, 9th Michigan, June 1862, *ORS*, pt. 2, vol. 30, ser. 42, p. 812 (to procure water); Parkhurst Diary, 19 June 1862 (march to Chattanooga), Parkhurst Papers, MSUA; Roos Diary, 19–20 June 1862.

53. Bowler to Caleff, 22 June 1862 (in front of), Bowler and Family Papers; Parkhurst Diary, 20 (to condense my; the charge was), 21 June 1862, Parkhurst Papers, MSUA.

54. Brookins to Thurman Brookins, 27 June 1862 (a fine shady; a terrible thunderstorm), Brookins and Family Letters; Roos Diary, 23–26 June 1862; *SPWP*, 17 July 1862; Parkhurst Diary, 24 June 1862, Parkhurst Papers, MSUA; Jonah H. Carpenter Diary, 24, 28 June 1862, SRNBA.

55. Andrews, "My Experience in Rebel Prisons," 25 (a moderately high); Officers to Ramsey, "Statement of Facts Concerning Surrender," 12 Dec. 1862 (it was on), MNOAG, General Correspondence; Bowler, "Long-Distance Recollections," 16 (wheeled into column); *SPPD*, 27 Nov. 1862.

56. Roos Diary, 29, 30 June 1862; S.O. no. 89, Army of the Ohio, Order Book, 1 July 1862, Department of the Cumberland and the Ohio, General and Special Orders, RG 393, pt. 1, entry 891; Fry to Duffield or Lester, 8 July 1862 (have you received), Telegrams Sent, ibid., entry 915; Spence, *Diary*, 36–37.

57. Prokopowicz, "Disunion Equals Disaster," 33 (glaring at each); Lytle, *Bedford Forrest*, 92 (a civil war); Roos Diary, 27, 28 (little affair in; in his bashful) June 1862; Bennett, *Ninth Michigan*.

58. *SPDP*, 2 July 1862 (gentlemanly and soldierly); Parkhurst Diary, 2; Parkhurst to Helen, 5 July 1862, Parkhurst Papers, MSUA; Roos Diary, 2 July 1862.

59. Spence, *Diary*, 36 (somewhat the manner); Greene to Fry, 24 June 1862, *OR*, 16(2):59; Fry, *Operations of the Army*, 13–14.

60. *SPWP*, 17 July 1862 (had a very); Eames to Wife, 4 July 1862, Eames Papers; Boxell to Wife, 3–5 July 1862, Boxell Civil War Letters.

61. Daniel, "Special Warfare," 163; Eames to Wife, 7 July 1862, Eames Papers, Negley to Fry, 5 July 1862, *OR*, 16(2):95–96, Negley to Fry, 7 July 1862, ibid., 102; Boxell to Wife, 8 July 1862, Boxell Civil War Letters; Roos Diary, 7 July 1862; King, "Forrest's Attack"; Pittard, "Legends and Stories," 21–22; Carney Diary, 12 July 1862.

62. Faulkner to Johnson, 8 July 1862 (Gov. Harris &), Johnson, *Papers of Andrew Johnson*, 5:534–44; L[ucy] Virginia (Smith) French Diary, 7 July 1862, TSLA (a large cavalry); Cooling, *Fort Donelson's Legacy*, 72–81; Fry to Hambright, 7 July 1862, *OR*, 16(2):102–3; Wright to Thomas, 1 July 1862, ibid., 83–84.

63. Buell to Halleck, 12 July 1862 (but little room), *OR*, 16(2):127; Miller to Lester, 11 July 1862, ibid., 126; Fry to Lester et al., 11 July 1862, Department of the Cumberland and the Ohio, Telegrams Sent, RG 393, pt. 1, entry 915; Green to Fry, 8 July 1862 (I am reliably), Department of the Cumberland and the Ohio, Telegrams Received, ibid., entry 929; Daniel, "Special Warfare," 99.

64. Duffield to Fry, 5 July 1862, Department of the Cumberland and the Ohio, Telegrams Received, RG 393, pt. 1, entry 929; Andrews, "Surrender of the Third," 347.

65. U.S. War Dept., *Revised Regulations*, 11 (turn over to); "Findings of Fact," G.O. no. 4, Army of the Cumberland, 24 Jan. 1863 (consulted fully and), Crittenden Court of Inquiry, LL14, General Courts-Martial, RG 153, entry 15; Lt. W. Williams testimony, ibid.; Carney Diary, 13 July 1862 (had not a); King, "Forrest's Attack," 431, 437 (an iron rule); Parkhurst Diary, 12 July 1862 (Genl Duffield), Parkhurst Papers, MSUA; Hale, untitled paper, in 3MVVA, *Twenty-Ninth Annual Reunion* (1913), 9; Daniel, "Special Warfare," 301.

66. King, "Forrest's Attack," 431; Pittard, "Legends and Stories," 80; Lytle, *Bedford Forrest*, 91; Major Seibert's Statement, 23 Dec. 1862 (that several men; immediately mounted twelve), Crittenden Court of Inquiry, LL14, General Courts-Martial, RG 153, entry 15.

5. The Regiment Broken

1. *Wabashaw (Minn.) County Herald,* 26 July 1862 (instantly at the); "Topographic Sketch . . . Murfreesborough," Subgroup B, T29-5, Records of the Office of the Chief Engineer, RG 77.

2. King, "Forrest's Attack"; *Wabashaw (Minn.) County Herald*, 26 July 1862.

3. Duffield to Fry, 23 July 1862, *OR*, 16(1):800–808; Wright to Duffield, 6 Aug. 1862, ibid., 16(2):267; Blackburn, "Reminiscences of the Terry Rangers," accessed 16 July 2008; Record of Events, 7th Pennsylvania, July 1862, *ORS*, pt. 2, 57:13–38; Crittenden to Garesché, 23 Dec. 1862, Crittenden Court of Inquiry, LL14, General Courts-Martial, RG 153, entry 15; Seibert to Garesché, 23 Dec. 1862, ibid.; Bennett, *Ninth Michigan*, 13.

4. Wedge, "Talk to [Unknown] Veterans Group" (the long roll), Mark Jones Collection; Bennett, *Ninth Michigan*, 14 (heard two guns); Roos Diary, 13 July 1862; U.S. War Dept., *Revised Regulations*, 90–91.

5. William H. King Memoirs, 20 (tyrant and usurper), University of North Carolina at Chapel Hill, Southern History Collection; King, "Forrest's Attack," 437 (summer underwear); Poole, *Cracker Cavaliers*, 22; Scott, "Eighth Texas Cavalry," 64; Henry, *"First with the Most,"* 87; Lytle, *Bedford Forrest*, 95; Bennett, *Ninth Michigan*, 14–17; Parkhurst Diary, 13 July 1862, John Gibson Parkhurst Papers, MSUA; Crittenden Court of Inquiry, LL14, General Courts-Martial, RG 153, entry 15.

6. Pittard, "Legends and Stories," 27 (in a huddle); Bennett, *Ninth Michigan*, 14–17; Duffield to Fry, 23 July 1862 (formed and ready), *OR*, 16(1):800–803; Wilkinson Statement, Crittenden Court of Inquiry, LL14, General Courts-Martial, RG 153, entry 15; Parkhurst Diary, 13 July 1862, Parkhurst Papers, MSUA.

7. Wedge, "Talk to [Unknown] Veterans Group" (German cavalryman); Peaslee to Father, 21 July 1862, 3MVVA, *Thirty-Ninth Annual Reunion* (1923), 5–8; Bowler, "Long-Distance Recollections," 16; Andrews, "Surrender of the Third," 350.

8. Peaslee to Father, 21 July 1862, 3MVVA, *Thirty-Ninth Annual Reunion* (1923), 6 (by platoons, right); Bowler, "Long-Distance Recollections," 16 (at the double); Andrews, "Surrender of the Third," 350 (line extending along; have complete range); Wedge, "Talk to [Unknown] Veterans Group" (a wooded tract).

9. Peaslee to Father, 21 July 1862 (Forward, guide center), 3MVVA, *Thirty-Ninth Annual Reunion* (1923), 7; *Nashville Daily Union*, 29 July 1862 (Keep your line), reprinted in *St. Paul Weekly Pioneer and Democrat*, 1 Aug. 1862; *GCR*, 25 July 1862 (Here we got; loading and firing).

10. Bowler to Caleff, 19 July 1862 (the enemy's bullets), James M. Bowler and Family Papers, MHS; Roos Diary, 13 July 1862 (A Georgia regiment).

11. Bowler, "Recollections of Murfreesboro," 4 (with the same; to one of), 5–6, Bowler and Family Papers; *Rochester (Minn.) City Post*, 2 Aug. 1862 (During the most).

12. Brookins to Thurman Brookins, 20 July 1862 (5 tried to; skulked about the), Brookins Papers; Lawton Report, 17 July 1862 (The enemy sharpshooters), *ORS*, pt. 1, vol. 3, ser. 3, pp. 229–31; *Mankato (Minn.) Record*, 6 Aug. 1862; Roos Diary, 14 July 1862.

13. Lester to Henry Duffield, *MCIW*, 2:116.

14. Lytle, *Bedford Forrest*, 96 (a negro camp); *GCR*, 20 July, 1 Aug. 1862 (the commissary's, hospital); Andrews to Thomas, 12 July 1863, MNOAG, General Correspondence; Lester to Henry Duffield, *MCIW*, 2:116; Hafendorfer, *Died by Twos and Tens*, 129–30; *Nashville Daily Union*, 19 July 1862; Valentine Woodburn, Charles H. Green, and Walter Doyle CMSRs, RG 94; Henry, *"First with the Most,"* 88; Poole, *Cracker Cavaliers*, 24; Brookins to Thurman Brookins, 20 July 1862, Brookins Papers.

15. *St. Cloud (Minn.) Democrat*, 21 Aug. 1862 (begged of the); Griggs, "Fort Snelling to Vicksburg," 20 (he would not); *GCR*, 25 July 1862; *St. Paul Weekly Pioneer and Democrat*, 1 Aug. 1862, citing *Nashville Daily Union*, 19 July 1862; *SPDP*, 27 July 1862.

16. Lester to Henry Duffield, n.d., *MCIW*, 2:116 (sent a scout); Griggs, "Fort Snelling to Vicksburg," 20 (to go to; had he [Lester] acted); Wedge, "Talk to [Unknown] Veterans Group" (We began to); *GCR*, 25 July 1862; Andrews, "Narrative of the Third," 153; Hale to Family, 22 July 1862, William D. Hale and Family Papers, MHS.

17. Lester to Henry Duffield, n.d., *MCIW*, 2:116. Lester apparently understood the applicable principles of war (e.g., concentration of force, mass, and maneuver).

18. *Lake City (Minn.) Times*, 3 Aug. 1862 (a train of); *GCR*, 1 Aug. 1862 (drew rations for); Andrews, "Sketch of the Third," 12 (blackberries, coffee, and); Baker, "Surrender at Murfreesboro," 14 (fired at everything); Miller to Fry, 13 July 1862 (Lester was confident; go carefully &), Department of the Cumberland and the Ohio, Telegrams Received, RG 393, pt. 1, entry 929; Lester to Henry Duffield, n.d., *MCIW*, 2:116; Hafendorfer, *Died by Twos and Tens*, 129–30.

19. *GCR*, 25 July (rested on our), 1 Aug. 1862; Baker, "Surrender at Murfreesboro," 15 (solely to this); Lester to Duffield, *MCIW*, 2:116; Crittenden to Garesché, n.d. (When all was), ibid., 117; Scott, "Eighth Texas Cavalry," 82; Hale to Family, 22 July 1862, Hale and Family Papers; Wedge, "Talk to [Unknown] Veterans Group."

20. Duffield to Fry, 23 July 1862 (fainting from pain), *OR*, 16(1):800–803; Duffield to Maney, 14 Aug. 1862, Lewis M. Maney Papers, University of North Carolina at Chapel Hill, Southern History Collection; W. B. Duffield to Maney, 15 Aug. 1862, ibid.; Parkhurst to Maney, 24 Apr., 1867, ibid.; Robertson, *Michigan in the War*, 299.

21. Baker, "Surrender at Murfreesboro," 15–16 (mention[ed] thus particularly); *GCR*, 1 Aug. 1862; Duffield to Fry, 23 July 1862, *OR*, 16(1):800–803; Poole, *Cracker Cavaliers*, 24.

22. Lester to Duffield, n.d., *MCIW*, 2:116 (interview with the); Baker, "Surrender at Murfreesboro," 16 (remarking that he); Bowler, "Long-distance Recollections," 18; *Lake City (Minn.) Times*, 3 Aug. 1862.

23. *GCR*, 1 Aug. 1862 (quiet and deliberate); Baker, "Surrender at Murfreesboro," 16, 17 (Col. Lester urged); Andrews, "Surrender of the Third," 354 (expressed himself in); Lester to Duffield, n.d., *MCIW*, 2:116.

24. Officers of the Third to Ramsey, 10 Dec. 1862 (fifty to one), MNOAG, General Correspondence; Bowler, "Recollections of Murfreesboro," 10–14; Crary to Donnelly, 4

Aug. 1862, Ignatius Donnelly and Family Papers, MHS, roll 10; *GCR,* 25 July, 1 Aug. 1862; *SPDP,* 10 Aug. 1862.

25. SPPD, 26 July 1862; *GCR,* 25 July 1862; Bowler, "Recollections of Murfreesboro," 10–14; Andrews, "Narrative of the Third," 155.

26. *Lake City (Minn.) Times,* 3 Aug. 1862 (call for volunteers; drew his sword); *GCR,* 25 July 1862; Bowler to Caleff, 31 July 1862, Bowler and Family Papers; Canfield to Sister, 14 Aug. 1862, Thomas Canfield Letters, Bruce and George Barnum Family Collection.

27. *Lake City (Minn.) Times,* 3 Aug. 1862 (that Lester thought); *SPWP,* 21 Aug. 1862.

28. *Lake City (Minn.) Times,* 3 Aug. 1862 (it was with); Spence, *Diary,* 36 (Genl. Duffield sends), 37; Forrest to Cooper, 22 July 1862 (After some parley), *OR,* 16(1):811.

29. Lester to Duffield, n.d., *MCIW,* 2:116 (the matter of); Baker, "Surrender at Murfreesboro," 17.

30. *SPDP,* 31 July 1862; Hale to Family, 22 July 1862, Hale and Family Papers; Boxell to Wife, 17, 23 July 1862, J[ohn] W. Boxell Civil War Letters and Related Papers, MHS; Eames to Wife, 14 July 1862, William Mark Eames Papers, TSLA; Henry, *"First with the Most,"* 90.

31. Boxell to Wife, 23 July 1862 (looked like a), Boxell Civil War Letters; Wedge, "Talk to [Unknown] Veterans Group" (delicacies. . . . [T]hey did); Farley, "Politics of Memory," 38–39.

32. Andrews, "Narrative of the Third," 156; Forrest to Cooper, 22 July 1862, *OR,* 16(1):811; Scott, "Eighth Texas Cavalry," 83.

33. Poole, *Cracker Cavaliers,* 25 (became Captain White's); *New York Herald,* 15 July 1862, cited in *Chicago Times,* 16 July 1862; Lytle, *Bedford Forrest,* 100; Cooling, *Fort Donelson's Legacy,* 87; Boxell to Wife, 17 July 1862, Boxell Civil War Letters; Sipes, *7th Pennsylvania,* 29.

34. 3MVVA, *Eighth Annual Reunion* (1891), 11 (locomotive preceded by; old guard); Nathaniel Parker and John Reeves CMSRs, RG 94; Co. C, 3MN, Record of Events, Aug. 1862, RG 94.

35. Roos Diary, 14 (had shown me), 15 July 1862; Canfield to Sister, 7 Aug. 1862 (road up to), Canfield Letters.

36. *SPPD,* 26 July 1862 (citizen clothes); Smith to Fry, 17 July 1862, Department of the Cumberland and the Ohio, Telegrams Received, RG 393, pt. 1, entry 929; Mattson to Ramsey, 20 July 1862, Ramsey Papers, roll 9.

37. L[ucy] Virginia (Smith) French Diary, 17 July 1862, TSLA.

38. James L. Battey Diary,15 July 1862 (ordered the citizens), Robert J. Niemela Collection; Bowler to Caleff, 31 July 1862 (The officers who), Bowler and Family Papers. Roos Diary, 15 July 1862; 3MVVA, *Thirty-Ninth Annual Reunion* (1923), 5–8; MacMurphy Dairy, 15 July 1862; Mattson to Ramsey, 20 July 1862, Ramsey Papers, roll 9; Rollin C. Olin and Joseph Putnam CMSRs, RG 94.

39. *SPDP,* 31 July 1862 (all order and); Hale to Father and Brother, 21 July 1862 (hired a covered), Hale and Family Papers; *GCR,* 25 July 1862; Roos Diary, 16–17 July 1862.

40. Brookins to Thurman Brookins, 20 July 1862 (taken possession of), Brookins Papers; Eames to Wife, 19, 20 (skedaddle[d] to the) July 1862, Eames Papers; Boxell to Wife, 23 July 1862, J[ohn] W. Boxell Civil War Letters and Related Papers.

41. Roos Diary, 18 (arrested our officers), 19 July 1862; Miller to Fry, 19 July 1862, Department of the Cumberland and the Ohio, Telegrams Received, RG 393, pt. 1, entry 929; Hale to Family, 22 July 1862, Hale and Family Papers; Battey Diary, 18 July 1862.

42. James Boxell to Wife, 23 July 1862, Boxell Civil War Letters.
43. Hale to Family, 22 July 1862, Hale and Family Papers; Roos Diary, 18–19, 21, 23 July 1862; Boxell to Wife, 23 July 1862, Boxell Civil War Letters.
44. *St. Cloud (Minn.) Democrat*, 4 Dec. 1862 (a first class; too dirty for); Foster to Secretary, 26 Aug. 1921 (fresh fish fresh), 3MVVA, *Thirty-Seventh Annual Reunion* (1921), 5; Parkhurst Diary, 17, 20–22 July, 13, 14 Sept. 1862, Parkhurst Papers, MSUA; Andrews, "My Experience in Rebel Prisons," 27–32.
45. *St. Cloud (Minn.) Democrat*, 4 Dec. 1862; Foster to Secretary, 26 Aug. 1921, 3MVVA, *Thirty-Seventh Annual Reunion* (1921), 5; Andrews, *Hints to Company Officers*; Andrews, untitled remarks, in 3MVVA, *Twenty-Sixth Annual Reunion* (1910), 14.
46. Roos Diary, 24 (like swine), 26–30 July 1862; Mattson to Mrs. Mattson, 25 July 1862, Hans Mattson and Family Papers, MHS; Samuel A. Eldridge Letter, 28 July 1862, Filson Historical Society, Louisville, Ky.; Steward S. Bliss, Alonzo Briggs, and Peter LeClair CMSRs, RG 94; Dix to Stanton, 23 July 1862, *OR*, ser. 2, 4:266–68; Brown, "Prisoner of War Parole," 206. Bliss would voluntarily rejoin the Third Minnesota on 30 June 1863 outside Vicksburg.
47. *GCR*, 25 July 1862 (to redeem ourselves); Mattson to Mrs. Mattson, 25 July 1862 (It grieves me), Mattson and Family Papers.

6. Reconstitution and the Quest for Redemption

1. Mattson to Mrs. Mattson, 30 July 1862 (wild with madness), Hans Mattson and Family Papers, MHS; *St. Louis Republican* quoted in *St. Paul Weekly Pioneer and Democrat*, 8 Aug. 1862 (a fine-looking); Roos Diary, 28–29 July 1862; Samuel A. Eldridge Letter, 28 July 1862, Filson Historical Society, Louisville, Ky.; Mattson to Mrs. Mattson, 25 July 1862, Mattson and Family Papers.
2. Brookins to Thurman Brookins, 30 July 1862 (built of rough), Brookins Papers; Tupper to W. Tupper, 27 Mar. 1862 (block; mostly dutch women; a shooting gallery), Francis W. Tupper Letter, Civil War Collection, Missouri Historical Society, St. Louis; Steiner, *Disease in the Civil War*, 20.
3. S.O. no. 300, Camp of Instruction, Benton Barracks, 31 July 1862 (obeyed and respected), 3MN Regimental Papers, RG 94; Swanson, "Civil War Letters of Olof Liljegren," 97, 99 (captain's duty); Olof Liljegren CMSR, RG 94.
4. Crary to Ramsey, 8 Aug. 1862 (mortifying to me), Ramsey Papers, roll 9; Crary to Donnelly, 4 Aug. 1862 (treat[ed him] with), Ignatius Donnelly and Family Papers, MHS, roll 10.
5. *GCR*, 15 Aug. 1862 (to seven day's; in irons at); HQ Benton Barracks to Schofield, 11 July 1862, Abstract—Federal Prisoners of War, 1861–65, RG 249, entry 151; Halleck Endorsement (guard, police, and), ibid.; HQ Benton Barracks to Marsh, 14 July 1862, ibid.; HQ Benton Barracks to Thomas, 28 July 1862, ibid.; Acting Captains of Companies to HQ Benton Barracks, 14 July 1862, ibid.
6. Crary to Donnelly, 4 Aug. 1862 (discouraged and demoralized), Donnelly and Family Papers, roll 10; Brookins to Thurman Brookins, 30 July 1862 (everything goes just), Brookins Papers; Crary to Ramsey, 8 Aug. 1862 (no way to), Ramsey Papers, roll 9; Hunt, the Noncommissioned Officers, and the Privates of the 3MN to Ramsey, 4 Aug. 1862 (Highly Respected Governor; fly to arms), RGAR, Letters Received.
7. Schilplin to Greenleaf, 17 Apr. 1863, Frederick Schilplin CMSR, RG 94; John Pope CMSR, ibid.

8. Canfield to Sister, 7 Aug. 1862 (french leave; got mad and), Thomas Canfield Letters, Bruce and George Barnum Family Collection; Redlon, "Company Cook's Pass," 21 (the bugler); Cyrus F. Redlon, Ezra T. Champlin, Marvin P. Hathaway, and James McGrath CMSRs, RG 94.

9. Roos Diary, 8 Apr. 1862 (in order to); Canfield to Sister, 7 Aug. 1862 (General Muster of), Canfield Letters; Caleff to Bowler, 10 Aug. 1862, James M. Bowler and Family Papers, MHS; Densmore to Dear Father, 16 Aug. 1862, Benjamin Densmore Papers, Goodhue County Historical Society, Red Wing, Minn.

10. Roos Diary, 23 Aug. 1862 (a temple of); Morgan to Provost Marshal, 17 Aug. 1862 (confined in McDowell's), John Wilson CMSR, RG 94; Pierce to Provost Marshal, 17 Aug. 1862 (arrested for Disorderly), Anton Imholt CMSR, ibid.

11. *SPPD*, 1 Aug. 1862; Donald Gray, Francis M. Gerry, David C. Craig, Hadley W. Green, and Edgar A. Holcomb CMSRs, RG 94.

12. Boxell to Ramsey, 3 Aug. 1862 (a place in), Ramsey Papers, roll 9; Mattson to Ramsey, 4 Aug. 1862 (friend Boxell), ibid.; Eames Letters, 31 July, 10, 15 Aug. 1862, William Mark Eames Papers, TSLA; Boxell to Wife, 18 Aug. 1862, J[ohn] W. Boxell Civil War Letters and Related Papers, MHS.

13. Mattson to Mrs. Mattson, 8 Aug. 1862 (smoking cigars and; like an outsider), Mattson and Family Papers; Maslowski, *Treason Must Be Made Odious*, 35; Mattson to Ramsey, 4 Sept. 1862, Ramsey Papers, roll 9; Hodges to Ramsey, 4 Sept. 1862, ibid.

14. *SPDP*, 10 Aug. 1862 (The regiment is); Ramsey Diary, 10 Aug. 1862 (military matters), Ramsey Papers, roll 39; Ramsey to Green, 13 Aug. 1862 (Please send Maj), ibid., roll 13; Mattson to Mrs. Mattson, 14 Aug. 1862, Mattson and Family Papers.

15. Blakely to Nelson, 19 Aug. 1862 (the same bounty), 3MN Regimental Papers, RG 94; Thomas Rice Stewart Memoirs, 1 (until the crops), MHS; *Rochester (Minn.) City Post*, 2 Aug. 1862; *GCR*, 1 Aug. 1862; Malmros to Lincoln, 28 July 1862, Robert Todd Lincoln Papers, MHS.

16. *SPPD*, 10 Aug. 1862 (any person liable; The writ of); Buckingham to Ramsey, 9 Aug. 1862, Ramsey Papers, roll 13; Donnelly to Buckingham, 9 Aug. 1862, ibid.; G.O. no. 25, 10 Aug. 1862, MNOAG; *Hastings (Minn.) Independent*, 14 Aug. 1862; Ramsey Diary, 19–21 Aug. 1862, Ramsey Papers, roll 39.

17. An excellent source is Anderson and Woolworth, *Through Dakota Eyes*.

18. Ramsey Diary, 19 Aug. 1862, Ramsey Papers, roll 39; S.O. no. 20, 19 Aug. 1862 (to be used), MNOAG; G.O. no. 41, 27 Aug. 1862, ibid.; S.O. no. 8, Fort Snelling, 21 Aug. 1862, in Benjamin F. Smith, Military Record Book, MHS.

19. Sibley to Mrs. Sibley, 21 Aug. 1862 (to attend to), Henry H. Sibley Papers, roll 11, MHS; Lincoln to Ramsey, 27 Aug. 1862 (attend to the), Ramsey Papers, roll 13; Buckingham to Ramsey, 23 Aug. 1862, ibid.; Buckingham to Ramsey, 27 Aug. 1862, *OR*, 13:599.

20. Halleck to Schofield, 22 Aug. 1862, *OR*, 13:591; S.O. no. 86, Dist. of Missouri, 23 Aug. 1862 (repair without delay), 3MN Regimental Papers, RG 94; Ramsey to Stanton, 22 Aug. 1862, *OR*, ser. 2, 4:417; Halleck to Ramsey, 23 Aug. 1862, Ramsey Papers, roll 13.

21. *Annual Report for 1863*, 145 (Austrian muskets, complete), MNAGR; Noncommissioned Officers Commanding Companies to Ramsey, 30 Aug. 1862 (respectfully recommend[ing] that), RGAR, Military, Infantry—3rd Regt., General; Hale to Family, 28 Aug. 1862, William D. Hale and Family Papers, MHS; Roos Diary, 27–28 Aug. 1862; G.O. no. 118, Adj. Gen. Office, 27 Aug. 1862, *OR*, ser. 2, 4:445–50.

22. *GCR*, 5 Sept. 1862 (thundering notes of); Roos Diary, 3 Sept. 1862 (found it not); *Hastings (Minn.) Independent*, 28 Aug. 1862 (fight the merciless); Bowler to Caleff, 5 Sept. 1862, Bowler and Family Papers.

23. Sibley to Malmros, 4 Sept. 1862 (in all probability), Sibley Papers, roll 11; *SPPD*, 3 Sept. 1862; S.O. no. 73, 3 Sept. 1862, MNOAG.

24. S.O. no. 78, 4 Sept. 1862 (such other forces), MNOAG; *SPWP*, 4 Sept. 1862 (ammunition from St.); *SPPD*, 5 Sept. 1862 (marched up Third); Hodgson, "Personal Recollections," 5 Sept. 1862 (almost perfect; with them in), Dakota County Historical Society, South St. Paul, Minn.; James Crosby, "Memoirs," 14, SRNBA.

25. Hale to Family, 11 Sept. 1862 (being doctored), Hale and Family Papers; S.O. no. 30, Fort Snelling, 7 Sept. 1862, Benjamin F. Smith, Military Record Book; S.O. no. 32, Fort Snelling, 7 Sept. 1862, ibid.; S.O. no. 35, Fort Snelling, 8 Sept. 1862, ibid.; S.O. no. 36, Fort Snelling, 9 Sept. 1862, Fort Snelling, ibid.; Bowler to Caleff, 5 Sept. 1862, Bowler and Family Papers; Roos Diary, 6–7 Sept. 1862; *Lake City (Minn.) Times*, 6 Sept. 1862;

26. Bowler to Caleff, 10 Sept. 1862 (fighting men and), Bowler and Family Papers; Welch to Ramsey, 9 Sept. 1862 (teams were not), RGAR, Letters Received; *MCIW*, 1:158, 416, 441, 739, 749; David Morgan CMSR, RG 94.

27. Welch to Ramsey, 9 Sept. 1862 (All the able; whom we found), RGAR, Letters Received; Ames to Nellie, 23 Oct. 1862, Curtis B. Ames Letters, Rockford Area Historical Society, Rockford, Minn.

28. Brown to Cathcart, 3 Oct. 1862, William R. Brown Papers, MHS; Gibbon, *The Sioux*, 89, 109–15.

29. Welch to Ramsey, 13 Sept. 1862 (reliable information), RGAR, Letters Received; Hancock, untitled item, in 3MVVA, *Forty-First Annual Reunion* (1925), 7 (the pace was; no camp was); *Minneapolis Tribune*, 8 July 1923 (we were glad); Sibley to Ramsey, 14 Sept. 1862 (Their presence here), RGAR, Letters Received; *MCIW*, 1:334.

30. *SPPD*, 16 Sept. 1862 (the men are); Sibley to Skarr, 16 Sept. 1862, *OR*, 13:644; John Kingsley Wood Diary, 15 Sept. 1862, MHS; Skarr to Sibley, 17 Sept. 1862, Department of the Northwest, Sibley's Indian Expedition, Letters Received, RG 393 pt. 1, entry 3481.

31. Sibley to Skaro[Skarr], 16 Sept. 1862 (saturat[ing] everything), *OR*, 13:644; Hancock, untitled item, in 3MVVA, *Forty-Third Annual Reunion* (1925), 8 (always in the); *OR*, 13:644, 650–51; Thomas Scantlebury and Family Papers, 21 (two lines of), 22 (now and then; sprinkled along in), MHS; James Crosby, "Memoirs," 16.

32. Brookins to Thurman Brookins, 27 Sept. 1862 (threw up earthworks), Brookins Papers; Scantlebury and Family Papers, 21–22.

33. Sibley to Pope, 27 Sept. 1862 (celerity of movement), *MCIW*, 2:254; Sibley to Ramsey, 1 Sept. 1862, Sibley Papers, roll 11; Sibley to Mrs. Sibley, 27 Sept. 1862, ibid.

34. Scantlebury and Family Papers, 23 (and the ducks); Wood Diary, 22 Sept. 1862; Arnott and Maki, "Archeological Investigation of the Wood Lake Battlefield," 45–46.

35. Champlin, "Recollections of the Battle," 245–46 (wholly unauthorized); Carley, "As Red Men Viewed It," 148; Brookins to Thurman Brookins, 27 Sept. 1862, Brookins Papers; Arnott and Maki, "Archeological Investigation of the Wood Lake Battlefield," 48–49. Some modern accounts claim that pioneers also went out to repair the bridge, and these foragers followed them. I have seen no record of such an action.

36. Chanplin, "Battle of Wood Lake," 14; Carley, "As Red Men Viewed It," 148; Brookins to Thurman Brookins, 27 Sept. 1862, Brookins Papers; DeGrove Kimball and William

McGee CMSRs, RG 94. Kimball, also known as Dewitt G Kimball, died of his wounds on 14 October 1862.

37. Brookins to Thurman Brooks, 27 Sept. 1862 (all who want), Brookins Papers; Champlin, "Recollections of the Battle," 246 (shouting Get back); 3MVVA, *Nineteenth Annual Reunion* (1903), 5 (rally on the); Jacob Hamlin to Friends, 24 Sept. 1862, Hamlin Family Papers, MHS; Arnott and Maki, "Archeological Investigation of the Wood Lake Battlefield," 51. Phil Skillman said the bugler was a German with the Seventh Wisconsin, but the soldier might have been from the Seventh Minnesota. 3MVVA, *Nineteenth Annual Reunion* (1903), 5.

38. Bowler to Caleff, 23 Sept. 1862 (dealing death to), Bowler and Family Papers; Champlin, "Recollections of the Battle," *MCIW*, 1:246 (made a wild); 3MVVA, *Third Annual Reunion* (1883), 30; Brookins to Thurman Brookins, 27 Sept. 1862 (out of that), Brookins Papers; Arnott and Maki, "Archeological Investigation of the Wood Lake Battlefield," 53–65. A "2, 40 gait" is a particular pace for a horse race—at least during the 1860s.

39. Bowler to Caleff, 23 Sept. 1862 (Our friendly Indians), Bowler and Family Papers; Riggs to My Dear Wife, 23 Sept. 1862 (scalped most of), Stephen R. Riggs and Family Papers, MHS; "Big Eagle's Account," in Anderson and Woolworth, *Through Dakota Eyes*, 226.

40. Sibley to Ramsey, 30 Sept. 1862, General Correspondence, MNAGR.

41. Riggs to My Dear Wife, 24 Sept. 1862 (exasperated our people; this morning Col.), Riggs and Family Papers; "Big Eagle's Account," 226; *SPDP,* 3 Oct. 1862, in Woolworth and Bakeman, *Camera and Sketchbook.*

42. Champlin, "Recollections of the Battle," *MCIW,* 1:246 (roaring like a); Andrews to Thomas, 20 July 1863 (killed [in battle]), Ramsey Papers, roll 14; Roster of Co. I, 2nd Minnesota, *MCIW,* 1:143; Anthony C. Collins CMSR, RG 94.

43. Champlin, "Recollections of the Battle" *MCIW,* 2:245(redeem in the field); Bowler to Caleff, 27 Sept. 1862, Bowler and Family Papers; Hodgson, "Personal Recollections," 5 Sept. 1862 (protect the people).

44. *Annual Report for 1863,* 55 (so nearly spent), MNAGR; Arnott and Maki, "Archeological Investigation of the Wood Lake Battlefield," 55–61, 72.

45. *SPWP,* 21 Oct. 1862 (cool expertise); Morse to Butler, 11 Oct. 1862 (as soon as), Thomas R. Potts Papers, MHS; Sibley to Ramsey, 23 Sept. 1862, *MCIW,* 2:242.

46. Riggs to Wife, 25 Sept. 1862 (They were as), Riggs and Family Papers; Watson to Father, 24 Sept. 1862, Charles H. Watson Papers, MHS; James T. Ramer Diary, 24 Sept. 1862, MHS.

47. Brookins to Thurman Brookins, 27 Sept. 1862 (We found about), Brookins Papers; Bowler to Caleff, 27 Sept. 1862 (a flag of; The women many), Bowler and Family Papers; Wood Diary, 26 Sept. 1862.

48. Sibley to Mrs. Sibley, 27 Sept. 1862 (unless soon supplied), Sibley Papers, roll 11; Sibley to Mrs. Sibley, 1 Oct. 1862 (We are pretty), ibid.; Wood Diary, 29 Sept., 1 Oct. (all out of) 1862.

49. *SPDP,* 3 Oct. 1862; S.O. no. 60, Draft Rendezvous, Fort Snelling, 29 Sept. 1862, in Smith, Military Record Book; *Rochester (Minn.) City Post,* 4 Oct. 1862; Pope to Sibley, 10 Oct. 1862, Department of the Northwest, Sibley's Indian Expedition, Letters Received, RG 393, pt. 1, entry 3481.

50. Wood Diary, 30 Sept. 1862 (in a double); Olin to Sibley, 2 Oct. 1862 (everything is irregular), Ramsey Papers, roll 9.

51. Bowler to Donnelly, 3 Oct. 1862 (log-rolling for; now if I), Donnelly and Family Papers, roll 11; Men of Co. G, 3MN, to Ramsey, 2 Oct. 1862 (in preference to), RGAR, Letters Received; Hancock to Ramsey, 7 Oct. 1862, ibid.

52. Bowler to Donnelly, 3 Oct. 1862 (what possessed Gov.), Donnelly and Family Papers, roll 11; Sibley to Mrs. Sibley, 1 Oct. 1862 (I believe that), Sibley Papers, roll 11; *SPPD*, 23 Sept. 1862; Ramer Diary, 3 Oct. 1862.

53. S.O. no. 55, Sibley's Indian Expedition, 28 Sept. 1862 (a military commission), Sibley Papers, roll 11; Sibley to Mrs. Sibley, 5 Oct. 1862 (of whom twenty; a hundred or), ibid.; Watson to Father, 27 Sept. 1862, Watson Papers; U.S. War Dept., *Revised Regulations*, 125ff, esp. 505, 509. The 65th and 89th Articles of War were the relevant references by which Sibley could impanel a court but could not approve its sentences; his status as a state militia officer under federal command complicated the issue.

54. Wood Diary, 3 (sugar, flour and), 5 (like a hurricane), 17 (bake a barrel) Oct. 1862; Ramer Diary, 3 Oct. 1862 (quite an excitement); Bowler to Caleff, 9 Oct. 1862, Bowler and Family Papers; *MCIW*, 1:379.

55. *Faribault (Minn.) Central Republican*, 8 Oct. 1862.

56. *MCIW*, 1:255–57.

57. Hale, "Expedition to Fort Abercrombie," 9 (locks or tubes; the tubes would; promised to see; several wagon loads). These Belgian rifles also were issued to at least one company of the new Eighth Minnesota. Houlton, "From Farmboys to Fancy Soldiers," 64.

58. Roos Diary, 11, 13–14, 15 (reorganized as a), 16 Sept. 1862; Hale, "Expedition to Fort Abercrombie," 10; *Annual Report for 1863*, 101–3, MNAGR; *SPDP*, 20 Sept. 1862; Eric Ljunglof CMSR, RG 94.

59. Roos Diary, 16, 17 (lying prone, behind), 18–21 Sept. 1862; Hale, "Expedition to Fort Abercrombie," 10.

60. Roos Diary, 22 (exchange [house] for), 23 (well appointed) Sept. 1862.

61. Roos Diary, 24–26 Sept. 1862; Hale, "Expedition to Fort Abercrombie," 11.

62. Roos Diary, 26 Sept. 1862 (real daredevils—running); Hale, "Expedition to Fort Abercrombie," 11.

63. Roos Diary, 27–28, 29 (with howling and) Sept. 1862; Hale, "Expedition to Fort Abercrombie," 11 (three hundred miles).

64. Hale, "Expedition to Fort Abercrombie," 11 (wagons and teams), 12; Roos Diary, 30 Sept., 1–9 Oct. 1862; *Faribault (Minn.) Central Republican,* 8 Oct. 1862; *SPPD*, 8 Oct. 1862.

65. Olin to Smith, 10 Oct. 1862 (had been better; feel themselves aggrieved; through the kindness), RGAR, Letters Received; Sibley et al. to Ramsey, 25 Oct. 1862, RGAR, Military, Infantry—3rd Regt., General.

66. Smith Endorsement, 14 Oct. 1862, (There is no), RGAR, Letters Received; Riggs to Wife, 9 Oct. 1862 (Although they appear), Riggs and Family Papers; Scantlebury and Family Papers, 27 (of those we).

67. Wood Diary, 15 Oct. 1862; *SPDP*, 21 Oct. 1862; Jonathan Fox CMSR, RG 94.

68. Rogers, "Military Expeditions," 1; Ramer Diary, 16 Oct. 1862; Crosby, "Memoirs," 19; Wood Diary, 13–14 Oct. 1862; *SPDP*, 29 Oct. 1862; Brookins to Thurman, 27 Oct. 1862, Brookins and Family Letters. *Annual Report for 1863*, 65, MNAGR.

69. *Annual Report for 1863*, 65 (27 lodges [were]), MNAGR; *SPDP*, 29 Oct. 1862.

70. Hale to Family, 20 Oct. 1862 (most ruinous to), Hale and Family Papers; Scantlebury and Family Papers, 29–31; *SPPD*, 17 Oct. 1862; S.O. no. 43, Sibley's Indian Expedition, 18 Oct. 1862, 3MN Regimental Papers, RG 94; Wood Diary, 17 Oct. 1862.

71. Donnelly to Wescott, 2 Oct. 1862, James Wescott Papers, MHS; Circular no. 36, Adj. Gen. Office, 25 July 1865, *OR*, ser. 3, 5:96; Soldier's Ballot, Bowler and Family Papers; Trenerry, "Votes for Minnesota's Civil War Soldiers."

72. Ramer Diary, 20 Oct. 1862; Brookins to Thurman Brookins, 27 Oct. 1862 (freezing cold; suffered more with), Brookins and Family Letters; Sibley to Pope, 21 Oct. 1862 (nearly worn out), *OR*, 13:757; *Annual Report for 1863*, 65–66, MNAGR; Scantlebury and Family Papers, 33.

73. Bowler to Caleff, 22 Oct. 1862 (piece of good; to shake hands), Bowler and Family Papers; Hale to Family, 10 Nov. 1862 (trial & execution), Hale and Family Papers; Scantlebury and Family Papers, 33.

74. Scantlebury and Family Papers, 34 (cold northwester); Sibley to Mrs. Sibley, 25 Oct. 1862 (a strong line), Sibley Papers, roll 11; Watson to Father, 24 Oct. 1862, Watson Papers.

75. Roos Diary, 9 (town orders), 10 (unusually cold), 11–12 Oct. 1862.

76. Roos Diary, 15 (transformed into cavalry), 16–26 Oct. 1862; Sofus Rasmussen CMSR, RG 94.

77. Roos Diary, 29 Oct. 1862 (tall and well, plundering . . . the Indian); *SPPD*, 17 Oct. 1862; *SPDP*, 22 Oct.1862.

78. S.O. no. 48, Sibley's Indian Expedition, 27 Oct. 1862 (possession of the), Cyrene H. Blakely CMSR, RG 94; Record of Events, 3MN, 18 Aug. 1862 (Paroled prisoners), *ORS*, pt. 2, 31:743.

79. Roos Diary, 28 Oct., 1 Nov. 1862; Sibley to Mrs. Sibley, 20 Oct. 1862, Sibley Papers, roll 11; Hale to Family, 10 Nov. 1862, Hale and Family Papers.

80. Roos Diary, 2 (on a manure), 3–5, 6 (found the house's), 7 Nov. 1862; Brookins to Thurman Brookins, 28 Nov. 1862 (carving pipes and), Brookins and Family Letters; *Mankato (Minn.) Record*, 8 Nov. 1862; Hale to Family, 10 Nov. 1862, Hale and Family Papers.

81. George W. Doud Diary, 19 Sept. (lowest class), 7 Nov. 1862, MHS; Roos Diary, 7 Nov. 1862; Hodgson, "Personal Recollections," 10 Nov. 1862; Quiner, "Quiner Scrapbooks," vol. 6, 268–71, Wisconsin Historical Society, Madison.

82. Roos Diary, 7 Nov. 1862 (helped themselves, and); Hodgson, "Personal Recollections," 10 Nov. 1862; Doud Diary, 7 Nov. 1862 (the kind treatment).

83. Roos Diary, 9 (steal corn from), 10–11, 12 (devil to ride), 15 (smaller, pretty animal) Nov. 1862; Doud Diary, 7 Nov. 1862; Hale to Family, 10, 16 Nov. 1862, Hale and Family Papers; Densmore to [unknown], 17 Nov. 1862, Densmore Papers; Sibley to Pope, 11 Nov. 1862, RGAR, Letters Received; Skarr to Sibley, 14 Nov. 1862, Department of the Northwest, Sibley's Indian Expedition, Letters Received, RG 393, pt. I, entry 3481.

84. Roos Diary, 14–16 Nov. 1862; Hale to Family, 10, 16 Nov. 1862, Hale and Family Papers.

85. Stewart Memoirs, 4–5 (suffered quite a); Roos Diary, 16 Nov. 1862 (were treated by); *SPDP*, 8, 22 Nov. 1862 (money suddenly gave); Hale to Family, 16 Nov. 1862.

86. Roos Diary, 20, 21 (the red flag) Nov. 1862; *SPDP*, 22 Nov. 1862; 3MN, Record of Events, Nov. 1862, *ORS*, pt. 2, 31:745 (general furlough for).

87. *St. Paul Daily Union*, 22 Nov. 1862 (they reconnoitered the); Orrin Densmore to Brother David, 27 Nov. 1862 (the St. Paullites), Densmore Papers; *SPDP*, 22 Nov. 1862 (rioting and other); *SPPD*, 22 Nov. 1862; Frederick Allis Diary, 23 Nov. 1862, Allis Family Collection; Notation, 21 Nov. 1862, 3MN Order Books, RG 94, 3MN Order Books; Morning Report, Co. C, 3MN, 12 Nov. 1862, RG 94.

88. Roos Diary, 23–24 Nov. 1862.

89. Stewart Memoirs, 11 (threatened repeatedly with), 12 (were rather shy); Wood Diary, 6 Nov. 1862 (there was some); Osman, *Fort Snelling*, 162 (St. Paul newspapers). See also Dahlin, "Words vs. Action."

90. *St. Paul Daily Union*, 22 Nov. 1862 (seized by a); *SAFM*, 29 Nov. 1862 (We have no); *St. Paul Weekly Pioneer and Democrat*, 4 Dec. 1862 (informs us that); *SPPD*, 21 Nov. 1862.

91. Thomas to Ramsey, 15 Oct. 1862 (when original officers), Ramsey Papers, roll 13; Ramsey telegram to Stanton, 14 Oct. 1862, ibid.; Mattson to Mrs. Mattson, 10, 16 Sept., 16 Nov. 1862, Mattson and Family Papers; Malmros to Thomas, 25 Sept. 1862, 3MN Regimental Papers, RG 94; S.O. no. 70, Draft Rendezvous, Fort Snelling, 14 Oct. 1862, in Smith, Military Record Book; Joseph R. Putnam and Benjamin F. Rice CMSRs, RG 94.

92. Parkhkurst Diary, 7–12, 16 (called upon president) Oct. 1862, John Gibson Parkhurst Papers, MSUA; *SPDP*, 22, 24 (experience of Southern) Oct. 1862; Andrews, "My Experiences in Rebel Prisons," 38.

93. Hale to Family, 4 Dec. 1862 (were glad enough), Hale and Family Papers; *Winona (Minn.) Daily Republican*, 21 Dec. 1862 (to demand an); *SPPD*, 30 Nov. 1862 (what we know).

94. S.O. no. 371, Adj. Gen. Office, 1 Dec. 1862, 3MN Regimental Papers, RG 94; *St. Paul Daily Union*, 5 Dec. 1862; *SPDP*, 12 Dec. 1861; Ramsey to Thomas, 5, 16 Dec. 1862, Ramsey Papers, roll 13.

95. Griggs et al. to Selfridge, 20 Nov. 1862 (to advance on), Walter N. Trenerry Papers, MHS; Gurnee to Stanton, 1 Dec. 1862 (court of inquiry), 3MN Regimental Papers, RG 94; Officers of the Regiment to Malmros, n.d., MNOAG, General Correspondence.

96. Preston, Tichenor, and Ingman to Lincoln, 23 Dec. 1862, Trenerry Papers; Norton to Stanton, 22 Aug. 1866, ibid.; Stanton endorsement, 23 Aug. 1866, ibid.; Washburn to Proctor, 21 Feb. 1891, and endorsement, n.d. (dangers of releasing; might operate to), ibid.

97. Citizens of Goodhue County to Ramsey, 12 Dec. 1862 (Mjr. Mattson is), 3MN, MNAGR Meeting of Officers [3MN] to Ramsey, 13 Dec. 1862 (Maj Mattson to), MNOAG, General Correspondence; Andrews to Rice, 8 Dec. 1862, Trenerry Papers; Lester to Olin, 1 Dec. 1862, ibid.; Weddle, "Ethnic Discrimination."

98. Swanson, "Civil War Letters of Olof Liljegren," 101–4; McDonald to Ramey, 7 Dec. 1862, Ramsey Papers, roll 9; McDonald to Rodgers, 7 Dec. 1862 (home to await), ibid.; Rodgers to Ramsey, 15 Dec. 1862, ibid.; *SPPD*, 9 Dec. 1862; Francis H. McDonald CMSR, RG 94.

99. *Rochester (Minn.) City Post*, 20 Dec. 1862; *SPDP*, 21 Dec. 1862; James M. Bowler, Otto Dreher, William F. Morse, David Morgan, and Hiram Gates CMSRs, RG 94.

100. *SPPD*, 18, 21 Dec. 1862; Ramsey to Congressional Delegation, 5 Dec. 1862, Ramsey Papers, roll 13; Buckingham to Ramsey, 16 Dec. 1862, ibid., roll 9; Wilkinson to Ramsey, 11 Dec. 1862, ibid., roll 13, Wilkinson to Ramsey, 20, 24, 26 Dec. 1862, ibid.; Halleck to Sibley, 27 Dec. 1862, *OR*, 22(1):880; *St. Paul Daily Union*, 12, 23 Dec. 1862.

101. *St. Paul Daily Union*, 8 Dec. 1862 (lose largely to); Hale to Family, 4 Dec. 1862, Hale and Family Papers; *St. Cloud (Minn.) Democrat*, 11 Dec. 1862.

102. Roos Diary, 30 Nov., 9 Dec. (Old Man Mattson; a drunken party; with a robust; had much enjoyment) 1862; *SPPD*, 5 Dec. 1862; Hale to Sister, 4 Jan. 1863, Hale and Family Papers.

103. Osman, *Forth Snelling*, 106 (rats as large); *SPDP*, 10 Dec. 1862, 1 Jan. 1863; *SPPD*, 7 Dec. 1862; *St. Paul Daily Union*, 16 Dec. 1862; Warren P. Lincoln CMSR, RG 94.

104. G.O. no. 1, 3MN, 27 Dec. 1862, 3MN Order Books, RG 94; *SPDP*, 27 Dec. 1862.

105. *GCR*, 9 Jan. 1863.

106. Andrews Diary, 8, 11 Jan. 1863, C. C. Andrews and Family Papers, MHS; *Winona (Minn.) Daily Republican*, 10 Jan. 1863; Nathaniel C. Parker Diary, 11–12 Jan. 1863, MHS; Roos Diary, 11–12, 13 (snow and sleet), 14 Jan. 1863.

107. James Boardman Diary, 13–19 Jan. 1863, Civil War Misc. Collection, USAMHI; *Hastings (Minn.) Independent*, 22 Jan. 1863 (to prove ourselves); Bowler to Caleff, 14, 22 (a good supper) Jan. 1863, Bowler and Family Papers.

108. Hoit to Potts, 20 Jan. 1863 (was ruptured at), Potts Papers; Joseph Eigle CMSR, RG 94.

109. Andrews to Ramsey, 17 Jan. 1863, Ramsey Papers, roll 9; Roos Diary, 19–21 Jan. 1863; Parker Diary, 20–21 Jan. 1863; *Winona (Minn.) Daily Republican*, 22–23 Jan. 1863 (some of them); *St. Paul Weekly Pioneer and Democrat*, 23 Jan. 1863.

110. Roos Diary, 23 (roads streamed like), 24 Jan. 1863; *Winona (Minn.) Daily Republican*, 23 Jan. 1863; Parker Diary, 21–23 Jan. 1863; Andrews Diary, 22 Jan. 1863; Boardman Diary, 20–24 Jan. 1863.

7. The Regiment Restored

1. *GCR*, 30 Jan. 1863 (they look hard); *Chicago Times*, 26 (all the appearance), 27 (repaired to the) Jan. 1863; Hale to Family, 29 Jan. 1863 (a splendid dinner), William D. Hale and Family Papers, MHS; Roos Diary, 24–25 Jan. 1863 (the saloons to); Bowler to Caleff, 17 Feb. 1863, James M. Bowler and Family Papers, MHS; John Berrisford [John N. Ford] CMSR, RG 94; "John Berrisford," Minnesota Territorial Pioneers.

2. Roos Diary, 26 (little city square; rushed into the), 27 (a real mud) Jan. 1863; Andrews to Ramsey, 27 Jan. 1863 (reduced to nothing), Ramsey Papers, roll 9; Merrill, "Cairo, Illinois," 243.

3. Andrews to Ramsey, 27 Jan. 1863 (guard . . . saloons), Ramsey Papers, roll 9; Griggs to Ramsey, 29 Jan. 1863 (to [Maj. Gen. William S.] Rosecrans), ibid.; *MCIW*, 2:340; Andrews Diary, 28 Jan. 1863 (an old not), C. C. Andrews and Family Papers, MHS; Bowler to Caleff, 29 Jan. 1863 (in the finest), Bowler and Family Papers; Roos Diary, 28–30, 31 (a whole army) Jan., 1–2 Feb. 1863; Hale to Family, 29 Jan. 1863, Hale and Family Papers.

4. *SPPD*, 8 Feb. 1863 (presented a fine; healthy, cheerful, [and] vigorous; the band has); Patrick, "Regimental Bands of Minnesota," 37 (serenade band).

5. *Winona (Minn.) Daily Republican*, 5 Feb. 1863; Ramsey to Griggs, 14 Jan. 1863, MNOAG, General Correspondence; G.O. no. 3, 3MN, 1 Feb. 1863, 3MN Order Books, RG 94; Walter W. Doyle CMSR, ibid.

6. James Boardman Diary, 3, 5 Feb. 1863, Civil War Misc. Collection, USAMHI; Nathaniel C. Parker Diary, 1–3, 15 Feb. 1863, MHS; Sample to Griggs, 2 Feb. 1863, 3MN Order Books, RG 94; Brookins to Thurman Brookins, 15 Feb. 1863, George W. Brookins and Family Letters, MHS.

7. Roos Diary, 28 Feb. 1863 (the gun carriage); Hale to Family, 3 Mar. 1863, Hale and Family Papers.

8. Roos Diary, 31 Jan., 1–7, 8 (great masses) Feb. 1863; Bowler to Caleff, 17 Feb. 1863 (we can beat), Bowler and Family Papers; SPDP, 13 Mar. 1863 (there is no); Boardman Diary, 15 Feb. 1863; G.O. no. 4, 3MN, 18 Feb. 1863, 3MN Order Books, RG 94; Co. C, 3MN, Morning Reports, 17 Feb. 1863, ibid.

9. Warren McCarter CMSR (some harborers of), RG 94; Warren McCarter, LL777, General Courts-Martial, RG 153, entry 15; McCarter to Andrews, 9 Aug. 1863, 3MN Regimental Papers, RG 94.

10. Marion L. Freeman and Thomas A. Douglas (to allow rebel) CMSRs, RG 94; Boardman Diary, 21 Feb. 1863; Bowler to Caleff, 26 Feb. 1863, Bowler and Family Papers.

11. Hale to Family, 3 Mar. 1863 (at a moments), Hale and Family Papers; SPDP, 13 Mar. 1863; Asboth to Hurlbut, 7 Mar. 1863, OR, 24(3):73; Asboth to Hurlbut, 11 Mar. 1863, ibid., 140; Asboth to Commander U.S. Navy, Columbus, 11 Mar. 1863, ORN, 24:52.

12. Asboth to Pennock, 12 Mar. 1863 (act without regard), ORN, 24:52; Pennock to Asboth, 11 Mar. 1863, OR, 24(3):101.

13. Bowler to Caleff, 12 Mar. 1863, Bowler and Family Papers; Andrews Diary, 12 Mar. 1863; Roos Diary, 12–13 Mar. 1863; Boardman Diary, 12–14 Mar. 1863; Parker Diary, 13 Mar. 1863; Brilliant Decklog, 14 Mar. 1863, vol. 1, RG 24.

14. Roos Diary, 14–15, 16 (a tasty soup) Mar. 1863; Eisterhold, "Fort Heiman," 48–50; Whitesell, "Military Operations in the Jackson Purchase"; SPPD, 22 Mar. 1863; Hale to Family, 16 Mar. 1863, Hale and Family Papers; Boardman Diary, 16 Mar. 1863. Eisterhold incorrectly states that the Federals abandoned Fort Heiman for the rest of the war after the Fifth Iowa Cavalry withdrew.

15. Roos Diary, 17–19, 20 (eternal pork), 21, 27 Mar., 14 Apr. 1863; SPDP, 11 Apr. 1863; Boardman Diary, 28 Mar. 1863.

16. Roos Diary, 22 (14 Negro women), 23–24 Mar. 1863; Boardman Diary, 21 Mar. 1863; Fitch to Porter, 21 Mar. 1863, ORN, 24:62; Stucky, "Joint Operations," 12, 25; Mackey, "Federal Counter-Insurgency Campaign," 3; Mackey, Uncivil War, 166–76; Sutherland, Savage Conflict, 149–60; Birtle, U.S. Army Counterinsurgency . . . Doctrine, 42–44; Croizat, "Naval Forces in River War," 54–55; Kaeuper, "Triumph of the Paw Paw," accessed 20 July 2007; Mills, "Riverine Warfare Conference"; Lang, "Challenging the Union Citizen-Soldier Ideal."

17. Fitch to Porter, 2 Apr. 1863, ORN, 24:63 (reported to be; remov[ed] the running), 64 (brought away about); Hale to Family, 11 Apr. 1863 (transportation free of); GCR, 1 May 1863 (to advance backward); Roos Diary, 27 Mar. 1863; Boardman Diary, 25 Mar. 1863; SPDP, 11 Apr. 1863; Gildrie, "Guerrilla Warfare in the Lower Cumberland," 166–67.

18. Roos Diary, 24, 25 (two cannon boats) Apr. 1863; GCR, 15 (hard ride), 22 May 1863; Parker Diary, 24–25 Apr. 1863; Boardman Diary, 25–27 Apr., 1 May 1863.

19. Densmore to Father, 3 May 1863 (the faculty to), GCR, 22 May 1863; Crary to Donnelly, 4 May 1863 (has gained the), SPDP, 23 May 1863; Mattson to Mrs. Mattson, 5 Apr. 1863 (prejudice . . . to), Mattson and Family Papers; SPWP, 21 May 1863.

20. Roos Diary, 17 (see the comrade), 18 (caught two of; his whole company) May 1863.

21. Baker to Blakely, 28 May 1863, MCIW, 2:337–339.

22. Mattson to Blakely, 2 June 1863, MCIW, 2:336 (scoured the country), 337 (a large rebel; the conduct of); St. Cloud (Minn.) Democrat, 2 July 1863 (notorious Col. Dawson);

Joseph Mertz (meritorious conduct), Jesse Barrick (most distinguished gallantry), John O. Hancock, and Francis M. Jerry CMSRs, RG 94; *St. Paul Weekly Pioneer and Democrat*, 26 June 1863; "List of stores lost," 1 June 1863, Foster Collection, Ohio Historical Society, Columbus.

23. Boardman Diary, 27 (dinner at Williams), 28 May 1863; Hale to Family, 11 Apr. 1863 (a negress what), Hale and Family Papers; Canfield to Sister, 19 May 1863, Thomas Canfield Letters, Bruce and George Barnum Family Collection; *SPDP*, 11 Apr. 1863.

24. Chenoweth and Mock, "Hurricane 'Amanda,'" 1738, accessed 3 July 2018.

25. Roos Diary, 16–19 Apr. 1863; Parker Diary, 13–17, 20 Apr. 1863.

26. Mattson to Mrs. Mattson, 5 Apr. 1863, Hans Mattson and Family Papers, MHS.

27. S.O. no. 15, 3MN, 9 Apr. 1863, 3MN Order Books, Co. B, RG 94; Harrison P. Lowater, Handley B. Richardson, Orrin Case (previous good character), and Ira Marlett CMSRs, ibid.

28. S.O. no. 25, 3MN, 18 Apr. 1863, Order Books, RG 94; David Morgan CMSR (a personal enemy), ibid.; Court-Martial of Capt. James M. Bowler, LL600 (he would have), General Courts-Martial, RG 153, entry 15; Court-Martial of Joseph Pulford (gold breast pin), folder 3, LL777, ibid.; Court-Martial of Joseph Sibley, folder 1, ibid.; Eugene Stone, Johnson R. Truax, Joseph Barker [aka Baker], William E. Allison, James M. Bowler, Joseph Sibley, Joseph Pulford, William F. Grummons, Charles F. Wagner, John McDonald, Joseph Sibley, and Joseph Pulford CMSRs, RG 94; Bowler to Caleff, 30 Apr., 7 May 1863, Bowler and Family Papers.

29. Boardman Diary, 5 Apr. 1863; Jonathan A. Churchill, Donald N. Gray, Marvin P. Hathaway, Louis Littlefield, Simon Meyers, William Alvey, William Bly, Spence Bly, John Knowles, and Joseph Eagle CMSRs, RG 94; Roos Diary, 30 Apr. 1863; 3MN Monthly Return, Apr. 1863, MNOAG, Personnel Records.

30. Roos Diary, 5–6 Apr. 1863 (each third man); Brookins to Thurman Brookins, 5 Apr. 1863 (nearly all rebels), Brookins and Family Letters; Ezra Sargent (offering violence to) CMSR, RG 94; Bowler to Caleff, 7 Apr. 1863 (Detachments are out), Bowler and Family Papers; Boardman Diary, 6 Apr. 1863.

31. Brookins to Thurman Brookins, 5 Apr. 1863 (suffering terribly for), Brookins and Family Letters; Parker Diary, 6, 9–10 Apr. 1863; Roos Diary, 9–10 Apr. 1863; G.O. no. 25, Dept. of the Tennessee, 22 Apr. 1863, *OR*, 24(3):220; Mattson to Mrs. Mattson, 14 Apr. 1863, Mattson and Family Papers.

32. Boardman Diary, 14–15, 16 (two lady nurses), 18–21 Apr. 1863; Parker Diary, 18 Apr. 1863.

33. *GCR*, 15 May 1863 (splendid water, a; half sick, and); Boardman Diary, 10 May 1863; G.O. no. 8, US Forces Fort Heiman, 16 Apr. 1863, 111th Illinois Order Books, RG 94; G.O. no. 5, 111th Illinois, 16 May 1863, ibid.

34. Benjamin F. Crary CMSR, RG 94; Seibel affidavit, Benjamin F. Crary, 3MN, Pension Application 273709, RG 15; Crary, "Catalogue of Contraband," 9 May 1863, Provost Marshal's Files of Papers Relating to Two or More Civilians, Union Provost Marshal General's Bureau, RG 110, entry 4660; Peters, *Underground Railroad*, 55–56; G.O. no. 133, Dist. of Columbus, Dept. of the Tennessee, 4 June 1863, Abraham J. Dearborn, Benjamin Densmore, and Judson B. Shaw CMSRs, RG 94; Griggs to Asboth, 4 June 1863, Francis S. McDonald CMSR, ibid.; S.O. no. 248, Adj. Gen. Office, 8 June 1863, ibid.

35. Parker Diary, 12–13 May 1863 (2 prisoners escaped); S.O. no. 39, US Forces Fort Heiman, 18 May 1863, 111th Illinois Order Books, RG 94; Roos Diary, 13 May 1863.

36. Receipt for Ordnance Stores, 20 May 1863 (two Enfield rifle), Foster Collection OHS; Clothing Issue, 22 May 1863 (flannel sack coats), ibid.; Canfield to Sister, 19 May 1863, Canfield Letters; Bowler to Caleff, 24 May 1863, Bowler and Family Papers; Boardman Diary, 20 May 1863.

37. Grant to Hurlbut, 25 May 1863 (reduce the garrison), Letters Sent, RG 39, pt. 1, entry 4709; Hurlbut to Oglesby, 28 May 1863 (no tents except), OR, 24(3):358; Grant to Hurlbut, 31 May 1863, ibid., 368; S.O. no. 48, US Forces Fort Heiman, 30 May 1863, 3MN Order Books, RG 94; S.O. no. 49, US Forces Fort Heiman, 30 May 1863, 111th Illinois Order Books, ibid.; Hurlbut to Asboth, 29 May 1863, MCIW, 2:346; Bowler to Caleff, 30 May 1863, Bowler and Family Papers; Parker Diary, 31 May 1863; Roos Diary, 31 May 1863; Walker to Asboth, 4 July 1863, OR, 23:629–30.

38. Roos Diary 30–31 May 1863.

39. Phelps to Porter, 24 July 1863 (in a stampede), ORN, 25:823; "List of stores lost," 1 June 1863, Foster Collection, OHS; Boardman Diary, 3 June, 1863; Bowler to Caleff, 4 June 1863, Bowler and Family Papers; Roos Diary, 3 June 1863.

40. SPPD, 11 June 1863 (hundreds of citizens; thoroughly posted in); SPWP, 21 May 1863 (guerrillas cannot exist). "Gill" was probably Cpl. Owen E. Gillen of Company B, Fifth Iowa Cavalry. See MCIW, 1:588.

41. SPDP, 23 May 1863 (The men are); SPWP, 21 May 1863 (I hazard nothing).

42. Bowler to Caleff, 4 June 1863 (laid in an), Bowler and Family Papers; Parker Diary, 3 June 1863; Lewis S. Hancock and Joseph L. Mertz CMSRs, RG 94.

43. GCR, 12 June 1863 (the bully Third; like a gambler; No one could); Roos Diary, 4, 5 (language limitations) June 1863; Boardman Diary, 4–5 June 1863; Levi Butler, William W. Webster, and John Wilson CMSRs, RG 94; MCIW, 1:189.

44. Roos Diary, 5, 6 (Vasa boys; welcomed . . . with) June 1863; Brookins to Thurman Brookins, 9 June 1863, Brookins Papers; Griggs et al. to Asboth, 6 June 1863, Benjamin Densmore Papers, Goodhue County Historical Society, Red Wing, Minn.; Crary to Harris, 6 June 1863, Benjamin Densmore CMSR, RG 94; Boardman Diary, 6 June 1863; Wabashaw (Minn.) County Herald, 9 July 1863.

45. Roos Diary, 8 June 1863 (mass of transport); Brookins to Thurman Brookins, 9 June 1863 (gave the rebels; hear the mortars), Brookins Papers; Bowler to Caleff, 12 June 1863 (light artillery sounded), Bowler and Family Papers; Roesch, "Memorandum," 5 June 1863, 7; Grant to Porter, 10 June 1863, ORN, 25:67–68; Porter to Welles, 20 May 1863, ibid., 6; Grant to Kimball, 3 June 1863, Department of Tennessee, Letters Sent, RG 393, pt. 1, entry 4709; G.O. no. 4, Montgomery's Brig., 12 June 1863, 40th Iowa Order Books, RG 94; J. C. Whitehill, "Extracts from the Report of the Chief Medical Officer of Kimball's Provisional Division for June, 1863," MSHCW, 1(1):app., 334; Boardman Diary, 7–9 June 1863; Parker Diary, 7–9 June 1863.

46. Roos Diary, 8 (the warriors might), 9, 10 (tenacious red clay), 11–13 June 1863; Boardman Diary, 12 (to support a), 13 June 1863; SPWP, 2, 9 July 1863 (fourteen head of); Mattson, Reminiscences, 68–69 (quiet, orderly, cheerful); SPDP, 3 July 1863; James Crosby, "Memoirs," 21, SRNBA; Andrews to Malmros, 24 July 1863, MCIW, 2:343; Parker Diary, 12–13 June 1863.

47. Roos Diary, 13–14 (life and appeared), 15 (pitch darkness), 18, 22 June 1863; Sherman to Rawlins, 16 June 1863 (well adapted to), OR, 24(3):415; Boardman Diary, 11, 13 June 1863; Whitehill, "Extracts from the Report of the Chief Medical Officer," MSHCW, 1(1):app, 334; Andrews to Malmros, 24 July 1863, MCIW, 2:343.

48. Andrews Diary, 19 June 1863 (army & works); Bowler to Caleff, 26 June 1863, Bowler and Family Papers; Andrews to Malmros, 24 July 1863, Roth, *Well Mary*, 18–20.

49. Parker Diary, 23 June 1863 (the Adjutant General); Bowler to Caleff, 17 June 1864 (the colored business), Bowler and Family Papers; Oren Densmore to David Densmore, 1 July 1863 (systematizing the contraband), Densmore Papers; Boardman Diary, 23 June 1863; *SPWP*, 2 July 1863; S.O. no. 151, Dist. of Columbus, Dept. of the Tennessee, 22 June 1863, Densmore Papers; S.O. no. 230, XVI Corps, 27 July 1863, Benjamin Densmore CMSR, RG 94; S.O. no. 169, Dept. of the Tennessee, 23 June 1863, Henry C. Collins CMSR, ibid.

50. Whitehill, "Extracts from the Report of the Chief Medical Officer," *MSHCW*, 1(1):app., 334 (the most stringent; very miasmatic locality; inferior quality of); John E. Summers, "Extract from a Report of the Inspection of Camp and Field Hospitals . . . in the Rear of Vicksburg, . . . June, 1863," ibid., 1(2):95 (with lime and; extremely filthy conditions; general indifference to); Brookins to Thurman Brookins, 13 July 1863 (It requires all); John D. Ripley CMSR (congestive fever on), RG 94; Parker Diary, 15 July 1863; G.O. no. 6, Kimball's Div., 7 July 1863, Co. D, 61st Illinois, Order Books, RG 94; *St. Paul Weekly Pioneer and Democrat*, 31 July 1863; Steiner, *Disease in the Civil War*, 26–33.

51. Bowler to Caleff, 28 June, 1 (three 'darkes' [to be]), 4 July (a death-like; a national salute; the rebs replaced; out in line; Hail Columbia, Dixie) 1863, Bowler and Family Papers; Folsom to Mary Jane Folsom, 4 July 1863 (by the Report; held Divine services), W. H. C. [Philander] Folsom and Family Papers, MHS; Boardman Diary, 1–2 July 1863; Roos Diary, 2–4 July 1863.

52. Bowler to Caleff, 5 (in 10 min[utes]), 6 (slaying cattle, pigs; a fine residence) July 1863, Bowler and Family Papers; Brookins to Thurman Brookins, 13 July 1863 (at least 3), Brookins Papers; Roos Diary, 5 July 1863 (leaf huts and); Parker Diary, 5, 6 (found good water) July 1863; Sherman to Grant, 4 July 1863, *OR*, 24(3):474; S.O. no. 28, Kimball's Div., 5 July 1863, MNOAG, General Correspondence.

53. Hale to Family, 10 July 1863 (many evinced a), Hale and Family Papers; G.O. no. 10, HQ Kimball's Division, 11 July 1863 (on guard and; be done right), Department of Arkansas and VII Army Corps, Letters, Reports, and Telegrams, RG 393, pt. 1, entry 272; *St. Paul Weekly Pioneer and Democrat*, 31 July 1863; *SPPD*, 21 July 1863; Parker Diary, 9, 15 July 1863; Boardman Diary, 15 July 1863; G.O. no. 5, Kimball's Div., 7 July 1863, Bowler and Family Papers; Bowler to Caleff, 5 July 1863, ibid.; G.O. no. 6, Kimball's Div., 7 July 1863, Co. D, 61st Illinois, Order Books, RG 94; Andrews Diary, 10 July 1863.

54. Surgeon's Certificate, 9 July 1863 (done no duty), Myron Putnam CMSR, RG 94; Hoit to Morse, 19 July 1863 (be restored without), Steward S. Bliss CMSR, ibid.; Griggs to Fry, 11 July 1863 (released . . . and), 3MN Letter Book, ibid.; Andrews to Fry, 23 July 1863, with endorsements and travel requisitions (on 14 Aug. endorsed, "under guard"), 3MN Regimental Papers, ibid.; *St. Paul Pioneer and Democrat*, 15, 28 July 1863; Co. C Morning Report, 1 July 1863, 3MN Order Book, RG 94; S.O. no. 285, Dist. of Minn., 10 July 1863, Cyrene H. Blakely CMSR, ibid.; S.O. No 273, Adj. Gen. Office, 20 June 1863, Joseph R. Putnam, John Conrad, Lucien Q. Allen, John Pope, and Frederick Schilplin CMSRs, ibid.; Scott to Commanding Officer, 3MN, 23 July 1863, 3MN Regimental Papers, ibid.

55. Griggs to Ramsey, 12 July 1863 (in this I; Rev. Mr. [Simon] Putnam), 3MN Letter and Endorsement Book, RG 94; Simon Putnam CMSR, ibid.

56. Andrews Diary, 12, 15 (Gen Grant's adjutant), 16–18 July 1863; G.O. no. 7, 3MN, 17 July 1863 (distinguished themselves in), Order Books, RG 94; Andrews to Thomas, 20 July 1863 (captured one of), Ramsey Papers, roll 14 (copy in MNOAG, General Correspondence, dated 12 July; Andrews Diary dates this as happening on 20 July 1863); Griggs speech, 16 July 1863, 3MN Order Books, RG 94; Andrews to Officers and Men, 16 July 1863, ibid.; Parker Diary, 16 July 1863; *SPDP*, 29 July 1863; Boardman Diary, 16 July 1863; *SPWP*, 30 July 1863.

57. Roos Diary, 19 July 1863 (small red blisters); Parker Diary, 20 July 1863; G.O. no. 8, 3MN, 19 July 1863, Order Books, RG 94; Bowler to Caleff, 19 July 1863, Bowler and Family Papers; 3MN Monthly Return, July 1863, MNOAG, Personnel Records; Lars E. Bringen CMSR, RG 94.

58. Grant to Washburn, 20 July 1863 (up river as), *OR*, 24(3):536; Grant to Schofield, 21 July 1863 (division [was] to), ibid., 22(1):21; Grant to Hurlbut, 24 July 1863 (the only troops), Department of the Tennessee, Letters Sent, RG 393, pt. 1, entry 4709; Grant to Washburn, 22 July 1863, *ORN*, 25:319; Parker Diary, 21 July 1863; Andrews Diary, 21 July 1863; G.O. no. 7, 3MN, 22 July 1863, 3MN Order Books, RG 94 (G.O. no. 8 was issued out of order on 19 July); Kimball to Richmond, 23 July 1863, Department of Arkansas and VII Army Corps, Letters, Reports, and Telegrams, RG 393, pt. 1, entry 272; Boardman Diary, 24 July 1863.

8. The Arkansas Expedition and Little Rock

1. Schofield to Hurlbut, 6 Aug. 1863 (the rebel [Sterling Price's] army), *OR*, 22(1):22–23; Christ, *Civil War Arkansas*, 5–8; Sude, "Federal Military Policy," 155–62.

2. Hurlbut to Steele, 31 July 1862, *OR*, 22(2):413; Schofield to Hurlbut, 6 Aug. 1863, ibid., 22(1):22–23; Folsom to Mary Jane Folsom, 5 Aug. 1863, W. H. C. [Philander] Folsom and Family Papers, MHS; Hale to Lucie, 3 Aug. 1863, William D. Hale and Family Papers, MHS; James Boardman Diary, 26–28 July 1863, Civil War Misc. Collection, USAMHI; Roos Diary, 26–28 July 1863; S.O. no. 32, 3MN, 30 July 1863, 3MN Order Books, RG 94; Steiner, *Disease in the Civil War*, 217–25; G.O. no. 105, XVI Corps, 5 Aug. 1863, *OR*, 24(3):577; Kohl, "'This God-Forsaken Town.'"

3. Bowler to Caleff, 30 July 1863 (gobbled about 100), James M. Bowler and Family Papers, MHS; Roos Diary, 31 July, 2, 12 Aug. 1863; Andrews Diary, 29 July, 3 Aug. 1863, C. C. Andrews and Family Papers, MHS.

4. Andrews to Ramsey, 11 Aug. 1863 (best regiment he), Ramsey Papers, roll 14; *SPWP*, 24 Sept. 1863 (fine military appearance); Hale to Lucie, 3 Aug. 1863 (fully regained the), Hale and Family Papers; S.O. no. 8, 2nd Div., Ark. Exp., 12 Aug. 1863, Department of Arkansas and VII Army Corps, Letters, Reports, and Telegrams, RG 393, pt. 1, entry 270; Andrews Diary, 12 Aug. 1863; Andrews to Malmros, 31 Aug. 1863, *MCIW*, 2:183.

5. G.O. no. 3, 2nd Div., Ark. Exp., 6 Aug. 1863 (5 spades and), Department of Arkansas and VII Army Corps, Letters, Reports, and Telegrams, RG 393, pt. 1, entry 270; Circular, 1st Brig., 3rd Div., Ark. Exp., 11 Aug. 1863, ibid.; 3MN Tri-Monthly Return, 30 July 1863, MNOAG, Personnel Records; Kimball to Graves, 27 July 1863, Department of Arkansas and VII Army Corps, Letters, Reports, and Telegrams, RG 393, pt. 1, entry 272; G.O. no. 2, Ark. Exp., 5 Aug. 1863, *OR*, 22(2):432–33; Kimball to Graves,

27 July 1863, Department of Arkansas and VII Army Corps, Letters, Reports, and Telegrams, RG 393, pt. 1, entry 272.

6. Stillwell, *Story of a Common Soldier*, 151 (too feeble to); Kimball to Graves, 27 July 1863, Department of Arkansas and VII Army Corps, Letters, Reports, and Telegrams, RG 393, pt. 1, entry 272; Circular, 1st Brig., 2nd Div., Ark. Exp., 11 Aug. 1863, ibid.; S.O. no. 7, 2nd Div., Ark. Exp., 11 Aug. 1863, ibid.; Isaac Taylor CMSR, RG 94.

7. Roos Diary, 4 Aug. 1863; Andrews Diary, 31 July 1863; Report, July 1863, 3MN Regimental Papers, RG 94; Alfred P. Parks, Harry P. Lowater, and Olof Liljegren CMSRs, ibid.

8. S.O. no. 21, Ark. Exp., 31 Aug. 1863, 3MN Order Books, RG 94; Nathaniel C. Parker Diary, 29 Aug. 1863, MHS.

9. S.O. no. 183, XVI Corps, 9 Aug. 1863 (on special service), James P. Howlett CMSR, RG 94; Bowler to Caleff, 9 Aug. 1863, Bowler and Family Papers; Foster, "Certification of Loss," 8 Aug. 1863, Foster Collection, Ohio Historical Society, Columbus; John Devereaux CMSR, RG 94.

10. Schofield to Hurlbut, 6 Aug. 1863 (the natural line), *OR*, 22(1):22–23; Stone, "Brother against Brother," 24–25 (a glorified drainage), 30; Davidson to Schofield, 9 Aug. 1863 (since 1844, 4), *ORN*, 25:357; Bache to Porter, 9 Aug. 1863, ibid.; Bache to Porter, 16 Aug. 1863, ibid., 354–55; Bache to Porter, 16 Aug. 1863, ibid., 356.

11. Andrews Diary, 13 Aug. 1863 (honor and health); G.O. no. 4, Ark. Exp., 10 Aug. 1863 (straggling, marauding, and), *OR*, 22(2):440; *Chicago Times*, 20 Aug. 1863.

12. Hale to family, 15 Aug. 1863 Hale and Family Papers; Steele to Hurlbut, 16 Aug. 1863, *OR*, 22(2):454; Stevens, *"Dear Carrie . . . ,"* 148; *Chicago Times*, 28 Aug. 1863.

13. Roos Diary, 15 (only white females; fat pork), 18 (green-yellow grease) Aug. 1863; *Chicago Times*, 28 Aug. 1863 (nectar); Shea, "Semi-Savage State," 88–89.

14. George F. Gregg, OO16 (halt on the; to whip said; court martial and; conduct Prejudicial), General Courts-Martial, RG 153, entry 15; G.O. no. 15, HQ Kimball's Div., 29 Nov. 1863, George Gregg CMSR, RG 94.

15. Sperry, *33d Iowa Infantry*, 50 (the very home); Roos Diary, 16–20 Aug. 1863; Hale to Family, 19 Aug. 1863, Hale and Family Papers; Mattson to Mrs. Mattson, 20 Aug. 1863, Mattson and Family Papers; Andrews Diary, 20 Aug. 1863; Popchock, *Soldier Boy*, 80–81; *St. Paul Weekly Pioneer and Democrat*, 18 Sept. 1863; Grant endorsement on Hurlbut to Grant, 21 Aug. 1863, *OR*, 22(2):465.

16. Bowler to Caleff, 22 Aug. 1863 (grabbed), Bowler and Family Papers; Parker Diary, 20–21 Aug. 1863.

17. Roos Diary, 23 Aug. 1863 (India Rubber); Reddington to Mary, 20 Aug. 1863, Edward S. Reddington Papers, MHS; Parker Diary, 21–22 Aug. 1863; Record of Events, 126th Illinois, Aug. 1863, *ORS*, pt. 2, vol. 14, ser. 26, p. 672.

18. *SPWP*, 22 Oct. 1863 (many crawled out); Roos, Diary, 24 Aug. 1863; Record of Events, Co. B, 126th Illinois, Aug. 1863, *ORS*, pt. 2, vol. 14, ser. 26, p. 167; Lockney Diary, 24–25 Aug. 1863, James Browne Lockney Papers, Wisconsin Historical Society, Madison.

19. Lockney Diary, 24 (to do the), 25–27 Aug. 1863; Roos Diary, 26 (laid out in), 28 Aug. 1863; *SPWP*, 22 Oct. 1863; Mattson to Mrs. Mattson, 26 Aug. 1863, Hans Mattson and Family Papers, MHS; S.O. no. 15, 2nd Div., Ark. Exp., 25 Aug. 1863, Department of Arkansas and VII Army Corps, Letters, Reports, and Telegrams, RG 393, pt. 1, entry 279; *SPWP*, 22 Oct. 1863; Stevens, *"Dear Carrie . . . ,"* 159; Bowler to Caleff, 26 Aug. 1863, Bowler and Family Papers; Albert Wedge CMSR, RG 94; Ellis to "Aunty," 27 Aug. 1863, Henry Ellis Letters, UALR.

20. Mattson to Mrs. Mattson, 26 Aug. 1863 (real wilderness), Mattson and Family Papers; *Chicago Times*, 2 Sept. 1863; Steele to Hurlbut, 23, 26 Aug. 1863, *OR*, 22(1):472–73; Stevens, *"Dear Carrie . . . ,"* 161; Parker Diary, 28 Aug. 1863.

21. Folsom to Mary Jane, 31 Aug. 1863, Folsom and Family Papers; Andrews Diary, 30 Aug. 1863; Parker Diary, 30 Aug. 1863; Roos Diary, 30 Aug. 1863; Lockney Diary, 28, 30 Aug. 1863.

22. Mattson to Mrs. Mattson, 26, 29 Aug. 1863, Mattson and Family Papers.

23. Bowler to Caleff, 26 Aug. 1863 (with all the), Bowler and Family Papers; Andrews to Steele, 3 Aug. 1863, Department of Arkansas and VII Army Corps, Letters, Reports, and Telegrams, RG 393, pt. 1, entry 266; Hardie to Ramsey, 24 Aug. 1863, 3MN Regimental Papers, RG 94.

24. Roos Diary, 30 Aug. (not entered the), 1 (muddy and stagnant), 2–3 Sept. 1863; G.O. no. 7, 2nd Div., Ark. Exp., 31 Aug. 1863, Department of Arkansas and VII Army Corps, Letters, Reports, and Telegrams, RG 393, pt. 1, entry 270; Jed F. Fuller CMSR, RG 94; Lockney Diary, 1–2 Sept. 1863; Sperry, *33d Iowa Infantry*, 270n32.

25. Hale to Family, 9 Sept. 1863, Hale and Family Papers; Circular, 1st Brig., 2nd Div., Ark. Exp., 8 Sept. 1863, Department of Arkansas and VII Army Corps, Letters, Reports, and Telegrams, RG 393, pt. 1, entry 270; G.O. no. 16, 5 Sept. 1863, ibid.; Christ, *Civil War Arkansas*, 175ff; Parker Diary, 5–8 Sept. 1863; Lockney Diary, 7–8 Sept. 1863; Bowler to Caleff, 9 Sept. 1863, Bowler and Family Papers; Mattson to Mrs. Mattson, 9 Sept. 1863, Mattson and Family Papers.

26. Mattson to Mrs. Mattson, 15 Sept. 1863 (pop went a; up in the), Mattson and Family Papers; Andrews Diary, 10 Sept. 1863; Andrews to Malmros, 11 Sept. 1863, *MCIW*, 2:379; Parker Diary, 10 Sept. 1863.

27. Mattson to Mrs. Mattson, 15 Sept. 1863 (strong rebel fortifications; corn dodgers), Mattson and Family Papers; Hale to Family, 15 Sept. 1863 (small arms, cooking), Hale and Family Papers; Andrews to Malmros, 11 Sept. 1863, *MCIW*, 2:379.

28. Mattson to Mrs. Mattson, 15 Sept. 1863 (a large room; an elegant room), Mattson and Family Papers; G.O. no. 1, Post of Little Rock, 11 Sept. 1863, 3MN Order Books, RG 94; Andrews Diary, 12 Sept. 1863; Swanson, "Civil War Letters of Olof Liljegren," 108; Stevens, *"Dear Carrie . . . ,"* 174.

29. *St. Paul Weekly Pioneer and Democrat*, 16 Oct. 1863; Sperry, *33d Iowa Infantry*, 57; Swanson, "Civil War Letters of Olof Liljegren," 108; Reddington to Mary, 13 Sept. 1863, Reddington Papers; Richards, *Story of a Rivertown*, 56; Hale to Family, 15 Sept. 1863, Hale and Family Papers; Lockney Diary, 15 Sept. 1863.

30. Andrews to Malmros, 11 Sept. 1863, *MCIW*, 2:379–81.

31. Moneyhon, *Impact of the Civil War*, 162–63; Boulden, "So Long as Strangers Are the Rulers," 18–19.

32. G.O. no. 4, Post of Little Rock, 16 Sept. 1863 (temperate in their), MNOAG Personnel Records; G.O. no. 6, Post of Little Rock, 24 Sept. 1863, ibid.; Phelps to Porter, 27 Sept. 1863, *ORN*, 25:435–36; Elder, *Love Amid the Turmoil*, 225; Lockney Diary, 16–17 Sept., 17 Oct. 1863.

33. Richards, *Story of a Rivertown*, 64 (for two or); Bunch, "Confederate Women of Arkansas," 178–79; O'Donnell, *Civil War Quadrennium*, 52; Boulden, "So Long as Strangers Are the Rulers," 18–22; James Crosby, "Memoirs," 21, SRNBA; Andrews Diary, 11 Jan. 1864; G.O. no. 3, Post of Little Rock, 16 Sept. 1863, MNOAG, Personnel Records; G.O. no. 6, Post of Little Rock, 24 Sept. 1863, ibid.; Circular, Headquarters, Army of Arkansas, 15 Sept. 1863, Civil War Records, A-5, UALR.

34. *SPPD*, 8 Oct. 1863 (esprit de corps; charmed him); G.O. no. 5, Kimball's Div., 18 Sept. 1863, Department of Arkansas and VII Army Corps, Letters Sent, RG 393, pt. 2, entry 4729.

35. Popchock, *Soldier Boy*, 85 (good service as); Bowler to Caleff, 3 Oct. 1863 (If these things), Bowler and Family Papers; Parker Diary, 17–18 Nov. 1863; Elder, *Love Amid the Turmoil*, 234.

36. Stevens, *"Dear Carrie . . . ,"* 182–83 (platform cars . . . with); Swanson, "Civil War Letters of Olof Liljegren," 108–9.

37. Lockney Diary, 19–20 (guarded and non-committal), 27 Sept., 4 Oct. 1863; Stevens, *"Dear Carrie . . . ,"* 193 (responded audibly to); Mattson to Mrs. Mattson, 20 Sept. 1863, Mattson and Family Papers; Hale to Family, 15 Sept. 1863, Hale and Family Papers; O'Donnell, *Civil War Quadrennium*, 52; Urwin, "'The Lord Has Not Forsaken Me,'" 333.

38. Steele to Hurlbut, 31 Oct. 1863, *OR*, 22(2):685; Strong, *Diary of the Civil War*, 382; Boulden, "So Long as Strangers Are the Rulers," 21–26; Moneyhon, *Impact of the Civil War*, 159–61; Sutherland, "Guerrillas," 144; Andrews Diary, 19 Jan. 1864; S.O. no. 33, VII Corps, 2 Mar. 1864, Department of Arkansas and VII Army Corps, Special Orders, RG 393, pt. 1, entry 282.

39. Wilson to William Wilson, 2 Nov. 1863, Wilson Letters; Parker Diary, 20–21, 23 Nov. 1863; Miller to Mother, 12 Nov. 1863, Minos Miller Letters, UAF.

40. Sutherland, "Guerrillas," 168 (forbearance, justice, and); *St. Paul Weekly Pioneer and Democrat*, 25 Dec. 1863 (the ladies of); Popchock, *Soldier Boy*, 102.

41. Field-Officer Court, 3 Oct. 1863 (a poor lazy), Charles Thomas CMSR, RG 94; Field-Officer Court, 1 Oct. 1863 (damned SOBs), Thomas Doig CMSR, ibid.; Regimental Court-Martial, 20 Oct. 1863 (unless he was), Joseph Sibley CMSR, ibid.; S.O. no. 52, 3MN, 19 Oct. 1863, ibid.; Boardman Diary, 1 Dec. 1863; G.O. no. 7, Dept. of Ark., 19 Sept. 1863, Civil War Records, A-5, ser. 2, UALR.

42. G.O. no. 45, Dept. of Ark., 25 Nov. 1863, Stephen Rhoads CMSR, RG 94.

43. Grover Landing and Warren McCarter CMSRs, RG 94; Fitzharris, "Field Officer Courts," 55–56.

44. Kimball, "Instructions to Guards," 24 Sept. 1863, Department of Arkansas and VII Army Corps, Letters, Reports, and Telegrams, RG 393, pt. 1, entry 272; G.O. no. 6, Post of Little Rock, 24 Sept. 1863, MNOAG, Personnel Records; Mackey, *Uncivil War*, 60–61.

45. Mackey, "Federal Counter-Insurgency Campaign," 10 (political citizens); Stillwell, *Story of a Common Soldier*, 183; G.O. no. 2, Army of Arkansas, 7 Jan. 1864, Department of Arkansas and VII Army Corps, Special Orders, RG 393, pt. 1, entry 282; Andrews Diary, 8 Jan. 1864; *St. Paul Weekly Pioneer and Democrat*, 29 Jan. 1864; "David O. Dodd," *Encyclopedia of Arkansas*, accessed 11 May 2016.

46. Steiner, *Disease in the Civil War*, 223–25; *Chicago Times*, 22 Sept. 1863; J. R. Smith, "Extracts from the Sanitary Reports of the Department of Arkansas," *MSHCW*, 1(1):app., 343–44; ibid., 1(3):963; Elijah Evan Edwards Civil War Journals, 16, 24 Sept. 1864, MHS; Boardman Diary, 17 Sept., 2, 5 Oct. 1863.

47. Roos Diary, 24–28 Sept., 1–4, 8, 17 (a thick cotton), 20–23, 28, 31 (prescribed Lager beer) Oct., 3 Nov. (night chairs; equipped with all) 1863; Smith, "Extracts from the Sanitary Reports of the Department of Arkansas," *MSHCW*, 1(1):app., 343–44; ibid., 1(3):963; Edwards Civil War Journals, 16, 24 Sept. 1864.

48. Boardman Diary, 3, 24, 26–27 Nov., 25 Dec. 1863.
49. Roos Diary, 10, 24 Oct., 10–15, 21, 27–29 Nov. 1863; Carl Roos CMSR, RG 94; S.O. no. 97, Army of Arkansas, 28 Nov. 1863, 3MN Order Books, ibid.; Parker Diary, 28 Nov.–2 Dec. 1863.
50. Andrews, "Narrative of the Third," 169–70; Instructions to Recruiting Officers for Veteran Volunteer Corps, Minnesota Governor, Records of Gov. Henry A. Swift, State Archives, MHS; Murdock, *One Million Men*, 17.
51. Andrews Diary, 5 Jan. 1864 (worth more to; they would not; that for the); Bowler to Caleff, 23 Dec. 1863, Bowler and Family Papers.
52. Canfield to Sister, 22 Dec. 1863 (being a veteran), Thomas Canfield Letters, Bruce and George Barnum Family; Andrews Diary, 6, 7 Jan. 1864; G.O. no. 376, Adj. Gen. Office, 21 Nov. 1863, *OR*, ser. 3, 31084; *St. Paul Weekly Pioneer and Democrat*, 4 Mar. 1864; *Rochester (Minn.) City Post*, 13 Feb. 1864.
53. Robertson, "Re-enlistment Patterns," 17–24.
54. *SPDP*, 4–5, 28 Feb. 1864; Record of Events, Co. K, 3MN, Apr. 1864, RG 94; Andrews Diary, 4, 8 Jan. 1864.
55. Andrews Diary, 26 Jan. (treat this evening), 6–7 Feb. 1864; Circular, 24 Feb. 1864, 2nd Div., VII Corps, Department of Arkansas and VII Army Corps, Letters, Reports, and Telegrams, RG 393, pt. 1, entry 272; S.O. no. 8, VII Corps, 6 Feb. 1864, Special Orders, ibid., entry 282; S.O. no. 24, VII Corps, 21 Feb. 1864, ibid.; Willis Cowan CMSR, RG 94; *SPDP*, 20 Feb. 1864; G.O. no. 96, Adj. Gen. Office, 10 Mar. 1864, *OR*, ser. 3, 4:161.
56. Foster to Mattson, 21 Jan. 1864, Mattson and Family Papers; Andrews Diary, 20 Jan. 1864.
57. Charles W. Moon (accepted new recruit), Joshua Burton, and William Sears [called Warren Sears in some records] CMSRs, RG 94; e-mail, Lore Gibson to the author, 8 Aug. 2002; *St. Paul Weekly Pioneer and Democrat*, 4 Mar. 1864; Record of Events, Co. K, 3MN, Apr. 1864, RG 94; S.O. no. 24, VII Corps, 21 Feb. 1864, Department of Arkansas and VII Army Corps, Special Orders, RG 393, pt. 1, entry 282.
58. Slatter to Sibley, 26 Mar. 1864, George F. Baker CMSR, RG 94.
59. Field-Officer Court, 31 May 1864, David L. Morgan CMSR, RG 94; Mattson to Mrs. Mattson, 6, 16 Apr. 1864, Mattson and Family Papers; Morning Report, Co. D, 3MN, 7, 13 Apr. 1864, RG 94.
60. Henry Glass (so Drunk as), Michael Stahler, Henry Coil (so drunk that) CMSRs, RG 94; Grummons to Sherwood, 15 Apr. 1864, MNOAG, Personnel Records; Andrews Diary, 11 Mar. 1864; Inspection Report, Feb. 1864, Department of Arkansas and VII Army Corps, Inspector General, RG 393, pt. 1, entry 323; G.O. no. 4, Post of Little Rock, 8 Mar. 1864, 3MN Order Books, RG 94.
61. Andrews Diary, 16 Mar. 1864.
62. Steele to Sherman, 10 Mar. 1864, *OR*, 34(2):547; Steele to Banks, 10 Mar. 1864, ibid., 542; Grant to Steele, 15 Mar. 1864, ibid., 616; Steele to Banks, 5 Feb. 1864, ibid., 246; Steele to Sherman, 27 Mar. 1864, ibid., 34(1):659; Steele to Banks, 28 Feb. 1864, U.S. Congress Joint Committee, *Report . . . on the Conduct of the War*, 2:155–56; Steele to Kimball, 23 Mar. 1864, *OR*, 34(2):704; Circular, 3rd Div., VII Corps, 12 Mar. 1864, ibid., 577; Andrews Diary, 23–24 Mar. 1864.
63. Kimball to Steele, 30 Mar. 1864, *OR*, 34(2):784; Andrews Diary, 30–31 Mar. 1864.

9. Fighting Guerrillas and Disease at Pine Bluff

1. Andrews to Thomas, 2 Apr. 1864 (lurking about the), *OR*, 34(1):863; Knight, "Fitzhugh's Woods," 18 (through darkness, rain); Andrews Diary, 30–31 Mar. 1864, C. C. Andrews and Family Papers, MHS; Christ, "'Hard Little Fight,'" 387–93.
2. Andrews to Thomas, 2 Apr. 1864, *OR*, 34(1):864.
3. *OR*, 34(1):864.
4. Knight, "Fitzhugh's Woods," 19–20 (a shower of); Andrews to Thomas, 2 Apr. 1864, *OR*, 34(1):865 (poured forth a).
5. Andrews to Thomas, 2 Apr. 1864 (Down with the), *OR*, 34(1):866; Swanson, "Civil War Letters of Olof Liljegren," 111 (about being a); Foster to Peetz, 3 Apr. 1864, *OR*, 34(1):867–68; Knight, "Fitzhugh's Woods," 21.
6. Mattson to Mrs. Mattson, 16 Apr. 1864 (to take their), Hans Mattson and Family Papers, MHS; Orrin Case, 3MN, Pension Application 872442 (rendered him almost), RG 15; Canfield to Sister, 16 Apr. 1864 (We have heard), Thomas Canfield Letters, Bruce and George Barnum Family; Putnam to Thomas, 31 May 1864, RGSM, Appointments, Military—Units, 1864; Andrews to Thomas, 2 Apr. 1864, *OR*, 34(1):863–66; Corydon Bevans, Henry Farnsworth, Albert G. Hunt, Orrin Case, Benjamin Sanderson, and Albert R. Pierce CMSRs, RG 94.
7. Knight, "Fitzhugh's Woods," 21 (the hardest lot); Garner to Henrietta, 2 Apr. 1864, Mary Hope Moose Papers, UAF; Christ, "'Hard Little Fight,'" 393; Statement of R. I. Holcombe, 3MVVA, *Fourteenth Annual Reunion* (1898), 22–23.
8. Gottfried Hauser CMSR (proof [was] not), RG 94; S.O. no. 22, 3MN, 14 Apr. 1864 (a school for), 3MN Order Books, ibid.; Franklin Skillman and Thomas J. Canfield CMSRs, ibid.; Canfield to Sister, 16 Apr. 1864, Canfield Letters.
9. Philip Miller, 9 Apr. 1864 (do his duty), LL1917, General Courts-Martial, RG 153, entry 15; G.O. no. 18, VII Corps, 21 Apr. 1864, Philip Miller CMSR, RG 94.
10. Andrews Diary, 14 (it was more), 19–23 Apr. 1864; Canfield to Sister, 16 Apr. 1864, Canfield Letters; Stillwell, *Story of a Common Soldier*, 191–93; Record of Events, 61st Illinois, Apr. 1864, *ORS*, pt. 2, vol. 12, ser. 24, p. 486; Geiger to Mason, 22 Apr. 1864, *OR*, 34(3):253; Kimball to Geiger, 19 Apr. 1864, ibid., 223; Andrews to Livingston, 21 Apr. 1864, ibid., 248; Livingston to Green, 25 Apr. 1864, *OR*, 34(1):899. Andrews's date of rank was 5 January 1864.
11. Mattson to Mrs. Mattson, 20/24 Apr. 1864 (had to cross), Mattson and Family Papers; Andrews to Mason, 24 Apr. 1864 (75 able-bodied), *OR*, 34(1):898.
12. George N. Godfrey (left with several), Alfred P. Parks (that he had), and Francis A. Hamlin (being a recruit) CMSRs, RG 94.
13. William McGee CMSR, RG 94.
14. Andrews Diary, 25–26 [marked 27] Apr. 1864; Charles Oscar Torrey Diary, 25 Apr. 1864, Torrey Papers, Library of Congress, Washington, DC; West to Andrews, 26 Apr. 1864, *OR*, 34(3):297–98.
15. Mattson to Mrs. Mattson, 26 Apr. 1864 (to march with), Mattson and Family Papers; Andrews Diary, 25–27 Apr. 1864; S.O. no. 22, VII Corps, 25 Apr. 1864, 3MN Order Books, RG 94; Lockney Diary, 26–27 Apr. 1864, James Browne Lockney Papers, Wisconsin Historical Society, Madison; Record of Events, Co. F, 12th Michigan, 26 Apr. 1864, *ORS*, pt. 2, , vol. 31, ser. 43, p. 97.
16. Andrews Diary, 28 (merely to get) Apr. 1864; Green to Sherman, 28 Apr. 1864 (loaded

with scant), *OR*, 34(3):321; Record of Events, Co. F, 12th Michigan, 26 Apr. 1864, *ORS*, pt. 2, vol. 31, ser. 43, p. 97.

17. Swanson, "Civil War Letters of Olof Liljegren," 114 (some negro Soldiers); Mattson to Mrs. Mattson, 1 May 1864, Mattson and Family Papers.

18. Lockney Diary, 11, 14–16 Nov., 6, 25, 28 Dec. 1863, 8, 14–16, 27 May 1864; Lockney to Brother Matt, 8 May in 6 May 1864, Lockney Papers; Stevens, *"Dear Carrie . . . ,"* 199.

19. James Crosby, "Memoirs," SRNBA, 23 (a yellowish scum); Mattson to Malmros, 1 Nov. 1864, MN EXDOC, Miller; Lockney Diary, 23, 25 May 1864; Mattson to Mrs. Mattson, 24 May 1864, Mattson and Family Papers.

20. George Cook Diaries, 4–6 May 1864 (Rebel mail and), Wisconsin Historical Society, Madison; Andrews Diary, 5–8 May 1864; Lockney Diary, 6–7 May 1864.

21. Lockney Diary, 12, 16 (worst and most), 21–22 May 1864; Cook Diaries, 22 May 1864.

22. Lockney Diary, 12 May 1864; Field-Officer Court for Michael Farrell, William E. Hale and Michael Farrell CMSRs, RG 94.

23. Putnam to Thomas, 31 May 1864 (such as becomes), RGSM, Appointments, Military–Units, 1864; Mattson to Mrs. Mattson, 20 May 1864, Mattson and Family Papers; Harrington to Clayton, 28 May 1864, Department of Arkansas and VII Army Corps, Inspector General, RG 393, pt. 1, entry 324; Andrews to Green, 21 June 1864, *OR*, 34(4):485; G.O. no. 18, VII Corps, 24 June 1864, ibid., 533.

24. Mattson to Mrs. Mattson, 18 June 1864 (fairly good), Mattson and Family Papers; Erskine to Carr, 11 June 1864, *OR*, 34(4):310; Putnam to Thomas, 15 July 1864, RGSM, Appointments, Military—Units, 1864; Lockney Diary, 6, 19–20 June 1864; Clayton to Dyer, 17 June 1864, *OR*, 34(1):1025.

25. Lockney Diary, 19 June 1864 (lost females); Hiram D. Gates CMSR, RG 94.

26. Asst. Insp. Gen. VII Corps, Reports, 20 July 1864 (camp [was] thoroughly), Military Division of the West Mississippi, 1864–65 Inspector General's Office, RG 393, pt. 1, entry 5543; Lockney Diary, 20, 22, 24 June 1864; Stevens, *"Dear Carrie . . . ,"* 227–28; Canfield to Sister, 29 June 1864, Canfield Letters.

27. Stevens, *"Dear Carrie . . . ,"* 235–36 (chain guard); Chambers to Brother, 20 July 1864, Milton P. Chambers Papers, UAF; Lockney Diary, 21–22 July 1864; Phelps to Porter, 22 July 1864, *ORN*, 26:484; Stevens, *"Dear Carrie . . . ,"* 234–35; Charles J. Strand, "Four Years with a Minnesota Soldier in the Civil War," 20, MHS.

28. Clayton to Dyer, 26 June 1864, *OR*, 34(4):521; Phelps to Porter, 27 June 1864, *ORN*, 26:428; Bache to Phelps, 28 June 1864, ibid., 423; Phelps to Porter, 1 July 1864, ibid., 422; Stevens, *"Dear Carrie . . . ,"* 228; Cook Diaries, 28 June 1864; Lockney Diary, 28, 30 June 1864.

29. Ryan to Dyer, 3 Aug. 1864, *OR*, 41(2):503; Carr to Dyer, 3 Aug. 1864, ibid.; Etheridge to Miller, 25 Oct. 1864, MN EXDOC, Miller, 624–25; Lockney Diary, 2, 5 Aug. 1864; Canby to Rosecrans, 19 June 1864, *OR*, 34(4):456; Messmer, "Louisville during the Civil War," 227; Bell, *Mosquito Soldiers*; *MSHCW*, 1(3):693–705; Charles Bolander CMSR, RG 94.

30. Mattson to Malmros, 27 Aug. 1864 (to put the), MNOAG, General Correspondence; Mattson to Malmros, 27 Aug. 1864 (no man in; it becomes absolutely; there being no), ibid., 253; Miller to Grummons, 7 June 1864, MN EXJOU, Miller, B:253; Miller to Mattson, 12 Aug. 1864, ibid., 386; Grummons to Miller, 30 June 1864, RGSM

Appointments, Military—Units, 1864; William F. Grummons, Thomas Hunter, and Bonde Olson CMSRs, RG 94.

31. Mattson to Mrs. Mattson, 18, 29 June, 3 Aug. 1864 (longing for Poppa; entire upper wing), Mattson and Family Papers; Clayton to Dyer, 19 July 1864, *OR*, 41(2):265; Clayton to Dyer, 20 July 1864, ibid., 287; Gordon to Canby, 19 July 1864, *ORN*, 26:482; Phelps to Steele, 20 July 1864, ibid., 482.

32. Mattson to Mrs. Mattson, 3 Aug. 1864 (it is fearfully), Mattson and Family Papers; Mattson, "Early Days of Reconstruction," 326 (brought to that); Mattson to Malmros, 1 Nov. 1864, MN EXDOC, Miller, 583.

33. *SPDP*, 22 July 1864 (fine body of); Miller to Averrill, 28 June 1864, MN EXJOU, Miller, B:282.

34. Emery to Ursula Emery, 6, 11, 17, 20 July, 9 Aug. 1864, Emery, "Lewis Emery Letters," accessed 22 Apr. 2003; Canfield to Sister, 9 Aug. 1864, Canfield Letters; Levi Emery, George Moore, and Thomas Canfield CMSRs, RG 94.

35. Mattson to Mrs. Mattson, 29 June (own quick regiment), 4 Aug. 1864, Mattson and Family Papers; Anderson to Sobalski, 10 Aug. 1864 (standing Picket Guard), Department of Arkansas and VII Army Corps, Other Records, RG 393, pt. 1, entry 296.

36. Andrews Diary, 14 Aug. 1864 (nice fresh roasted; they have suffered); Strand, "Four Years," 20 (were in such); Mattson to Malmros, 1 Nov. 1864, MN EXDOC, Miller, 582.

37. Clayton to Steele, 20 Aug. 1864, *OR*, 41(2):784; Pratt to Chesley Pratt, 25 Aug. 1864, (horses and carbines), Chesley Pratt and Family Papers, MHS; Skillman to Bowler, 28 Aug. 1912, 3MVVA, *Twenty-Eighth Annual Reunion* (1912), 10.

38. Skillman to Bowler, 28 Aug. 1912 (started back), ibid., 11; Co. D, 3MN, Morning Report, 25 Aug. 1864, RG 94.

39. Trego to Wife, 7 Aug. 1864, in Langsdorf, "Letters of Joseph H. Trego," 398; Canfield to Sister, 9 Aug. 1864, Canfield Letters; Stevens, *"Dear Carrie...,"* 19 Aug. 1864, 241; Dyer to Commanding Officer, Brownsville, 19 Aug. 1864, *OR*, 41(2):772; Andrews to Steele, 20 Aug. 1864, ibid., 783.

40. Lockney Diary, 12 (infamous character noted), 20, 21 (the lady of), 23 Aug. 1864; Reddington Diary, 17 July, 15 Aug. 1864, Edward S. Reddington Papers, MHS; Stevens, *"Dear Carrie...,"* 251.

41. Clayton to Steele, 25 Aug. 1864, *OR*, 41(2):854; Carlock to Clayton, 26 Aug. 1864, ibid., 878; Orville Gillet Diary, 24 Aug. 1864, File 123, UAF; Carr to Clayton, 26 Aug. 1864, *OR*, 41(2):877.

42. Butler to Miller, 8 Aug. 1864, MN EXDOC, Miller, 615; Miller to Surgeon General, 11 Aug. 1864, ibid., 382; Crary to Miller, 18 Aug. 1864, in *Rochester (Minn.) City Post*, 3 Sept. 1864.

43. Miller to Mattson, 12 Aug. 1864 (temporary supply of), MN EXJOU, Miller, B:483; Miller to Wren, 26 Aug. 1864 (Surgical Commissioner on), ibid.; G.O. no. 295, Adj. Gen. Office, 15 Aug. 1864, ibid., 430; Miller to Wood, 27 Sept. 1864 (all possible relief), ibid., 501; Miller to Mattson, 18 Sept., 1864, ibid.; Miller to F. B. Etheridge, 16 Sept. 1864, ibid., 480; Miller to Briston, 16 Sept., 1864, ibid., 472; Mattson to Miller, 26 Aug. 1864, MNOAG, General Correspondence; *SPDP*, 27 Aug. 1864; Canfield to Sister, 9 Aug. 1864, Canfield Letters.

44. Asst. Insp. Gen. Dept. of Ark. to Insp. Gen. Mil. Div. of the West Miss., 6 Oct. 1864 (filthy; The regiment has), Military Division of the West Mississippi, 1864–65, Inspector General's Office, RG 393, pt. 1, entry 5543.

45. Etheridge to Miller, 25 Oct. 1864, *Annual Report for 1864*, 624–25, MNAGR; Bowler to Caleff, 2, 6 Oct. 1864, James M. Bowler and Family Papers, MHS; Alpheus Bulen CMSR, RG 94.

46. Geene to Clayton, 9 Oct. 1864 (a sanitary measure), *OR*, 41(3):723; Miner Monroe (no effects) and Robert Fulton CMSRs, RG 94; Etheridge to Miller, 25 Oct. 1864, *Annual Report for 1864*, 624–25, MNAGR; Elijah Evan Edwards Civil War Journals, 7 Oct. 1864, MHS.

47. Charles W. A. Nudd, 3MN, Pension Application 84558 (a congestive chill), RG 15; *SPWP*, 25 Aug. 1864; Charles W. Nudd and Simon Putnam CMSRs, RG 94; Wedge, "Address," 10–11.

48. Akers to Malmros, 27 Aug. 1864, General Correspondence, MNAGR; *St. Paul Weekly Pioneer and Democrat*, 30 Sept. 1864 (well officered, and); Peterson Diary, 24 Aug. 1864, Andrew Peterson and Family Papers, MHS; Levi Debel, John Galter, Andrew Norelius, and Lewis Norelius CMSRs, RG 94; Coleman to the author, 22 Apr. 2001; Coleman, "History of the Swedes."

49. *Hastings (Minn.) Independent*, 21 Sept. 1864 (all the soldier); *SPDP*, 28 Aug. 1864 (Unfortunately, in nearly; was found guilty); Peter LeClair CMSR, RG 94.

50. Mattson to Mrs. Mattson, 14 Oct. 1864, Mattson and Family Papers.

51. Emery to Ursula Emery, 17 Oct. 1864 (Mr. A. V.; looked ragged and), Emery, "Lewis Emery Letters"; Mattson to Malmros, 18 Oct. 1864 (it was painful), 3MN Letter Book, RG 94; S.O. no. 255, Dept. of Ark., 17 Oct. 1864, Department of Arkansas and VII Army Corps, Special Orders, RG 393, pt. 1, entry 282; Andrews, "Narrative of the Third," 175 (erroneously claiming that the Third left on 10 October); Lockney Dairy, 16 Oct. 1864, Lockney Papers; A. V. Hamlin, Edward R. Williams, and Peter Moobeck CMSRs, RG 94.

10. Recovery at DeVall's Bluff

1. *SPDP*, 14 Oct. 1864 (a military post; the necessity of); McConnell, "Up in Arkansas," 238 (Hay, hard-tack).

2. Mattson to Mrs. Mattson, 22 (I shall build), 26 Oct. 1864, Hans Mattson and Family Papers, MHS; Andrews to Dyer, 6 Nov. 1864, *OR*, 41(4):451; S.O. no. 152, 2nd Div., VII Corps, 13 Oct. 1864, Department of Arkansas and VII Army Corps, Letters, Reports, and Telegrams, RG 393, pt. 1, entry 270; James Crosby, "Memoirs," 24, SRNBA.

3. Madison Coleman, Seldon Coleman, Addison Coleman, Chauncey D. Gibbs, and Louis B. Littlefield CMSRs, RG 94; Miller to Thomas, 22 Dec. 1864, MN EXJOU, Miller, C:60; Mattson to Malmros, 30 Nov. 1864, MN EXDOC, Miller, 585.

4. George W. Brookins CMSR (broken down in), RG 94; *SPDP*, 18 June 1864 (ready and willing); George W. Brooks, 3 MN, Pension Application 359756 (see Certificate 275121), RG 15.

5. *SPPP*, 22 (there are few), 23 (does not talk), 25 Dec. 1864; *SPDP*, 22 Dec. 1864; Miller to McLaren, 22 Dec. 1864, MN EXJOU, Miller, C:60.

6. John Cochran, Kleber Wilkerson, Lewis Kimball, and Arne Arneson CMSRs, RG 94.

7. Marples to Dear Wife, 23 Jan. 1865, Charles Marples and Family Papers, MHS; Averill to Marples, 24 Jan. 1865, ibid.; Franklin W. Chapin, Henry Graham, Tallef Halverson, Ola Larson, James F. Ortney, and Host Schindler CMSRs, RG 94; Muster and Descriptive Roll for Charles Simon, 3MN, MNOAG.

8. *SPPD*, 29 Oct. (the bull-pen), 2 Nov. 1864; *SPDP*, 25 Oct. 1864.

9. *SPDP*, 17 Nov. 1864; John Barnes and Frank Brunell CMSRs, RG 94; Muster Roll, U.S. General Hospitals, St. Louis, 1 Dec. 1864, MNOAG, Misc. Reports.

10. Reynolds to Steele, 8 Nov. 1864, *OR*, 41(4):485; Popchock, *Soldier Boy*, 161–62; Crosby, "Memoirs," 24.

11. Wilson to Christensen, 15 Nov. 1864, *OR*, 41(3):569–71.

12. Andrews to Goodspeed, 20 Nov. 1864, *OR*, 41(4):628; Andrews to Green, 18 Nov. 1864 (Lieutenant Oliphant, a), ibid., 41(1):921; Canfield to Sister, 6 Dec. 1864 (what chickens and), Thomas Canfield Letters, Bruce and George Barnum Family Collection; Emery to Ursula Emery, 17 Dec. 1864, Larson, "Lewis Emery Letters," accessed 22 Apr. 2003.

13. Marion L. Freeman CMSR, RG 94; Andrews to Dyer, 23 Nov. 1864, *OR*, 41(4):655.

14. S.O. no. 283, Dept. of Ark., 15 Nov. 1864 (military duty), *OR*, 41(4):579; Andrews to Steele, 22 Nov. 1864, ibid.; Circular, 2nd Div., VII Corps, 23 Nov. 1864, Department of Arkansas and VII Army Corps, Letters, Reports, and Telegrams, RG 393, pt. 1, entry 272.

15. S.O. no. 197, 2nd Div., VII Corps, 29 Nov. 1864 (according to the), 3MN Order Books, RG 94; Steele to Reynolds, 27 Nov. 1864, *OR*, 41(4):696–97; Steele to Canby, 9 Nov. 1864, ibid., 498–99; Andrews to Moore, 27 Nov. 1864, ibid., 699.

16. Canfield to Sister, 6 Dec. 1864 (paraded out to), Canfield Letters; Andrews to Graves, 8 Dec. 1864 (in great need), *OR*, 41(4):983; Andrews to Graves, 7 Dec. 1864, ibid., 983; Andrews to Mattson, 6 Dec. 1864, Department of Arkansas and VII Army Corps, Letters, Reports, and Telegrams, RG 393, pt. 1, entry 272.

17. Emery to Ursula Emery, 17 Dec. 1864 (for firearms, rebs), Larson, "Lewis Emery Letters"; Monroe to Mattson, 12 Dec. 1864, *OR*., 41(4):835; Andrews to Graves, 13 Dec. 1864, ibid., 848; Mattson to Monroe, 15 Dec. 1864, ibid., 41(1):989–91.

18. Asst. Insp. Gen. Dept. of Ark., Report, 10 Dec. 1864 (awkward and not), Military Division of the West Mississippi, 1864–65, Inspector General's Office, RG 393, pt. 1, entry 5543; Asst. Insp. Gen. Dept. of Ark., Report, 5 Jan. 1865 (eighty prisoners, including; the picket duty), ibid.; Stith, "Guerrilla Warfare," 205–8.

19. Bowler to Caleff, 11 Dec. 1864 (has not done), James M. Bowler and Family Papers, MHS; Reynolds to Christensesn, 19 Dec. 1864, *OR*, 41(4):887; Harris to Father, 15 Jan. 1865, Albert Harris Collection, UAF; Sperry, *33d Iowa Infantry*, 66.

20. G.O. no. 49, Dept. of Ark., 24 Dec. 1864 (Tomorrow being Christmas), Dept. of Ark. Department of Arkansas and VII Army Corps, Special Orders, RG 393, pt. 1, entry 282; Bowler to Caleff, 27 Dec. 1864, Bowler and Family Papers; Popchock, *Soldier Boy*, 171; Sperry, *33d Iowa Infantry*, 66.

21. Andrews to Lincoln, 22 Dec. 1864, *OR*, 41(4):916; S.O. no. 318, Dept. of Ark., 27 Dec. 1864, ibid., 943; Circular no. 3, 2nd Div., VII Corps, 28 Dec. 1864, ibid., 950–51; Bowler to Caleff, 27 Dec. 1864, Bowler and Family Papers.

22. G.O. no. 6, 2nd Div., VII Corps, 14 Jan. 1865(refuse matter of), Department of Arkansas and VII Army Corps, Letters, Reports, and Telegrams, RG 393, pt. 1, entry 270;

G.O. no. 5, 2nd Div., VII Corps, 12 Jan. 1865, ibid.; G.O. no. 3, 2nd Div., VII Corps, 6 Jan. 1865, ibid.; G.O. no. 4, 2nd Div., VII Corps, 11 Jan. 1865, ibid.; G.O. no. 8, 2nd Div., VII Corps, 17 Jan. 1865, ibid.; G.O. no. 9, 2nd Div., VII Corps, 18 Jan. 1865, ibid.; Crosby, "Memoirs," 24.

23. Upham to Henry Upham, 16, 19 Apr. 1865 (there is money), D[aniel] P. Upham Collection, UALR; Canfield to Dear Sister, 5 Feb. (two or three), 21 Apr. 1865, Canfield Letters.

24. Mattson, *Reminiscences*, 77; Applegarth to Cousin Cordelia, 6 Jan. 1865, Henry W. Applegarth Letters, J. David Johnson Collection; Circular, 2nd Div., VII Corps, 20 Jan. 1865 (the work is), *OR*, 48(1):592–93; G.O. no. 9, 2nd Div., VII Corps, 18 Jan. 1865, Department of Arkansas and VII Army Corps, Letters, Reports, and Telegrams, RG 393, pt. 1, entry 270.

25. U.S. Military Telegraph to Shaler, 13 Jan. 1865, Department of Arkansas and VII Army Corps, Letters, Reports, and Telegrams, RG 393, pt. 1, entry 270; Conrad Reineke Letter, 24 Jan. 1865, Buelow Brothers Collection; Emery to Ursula Emery, 1 Jan. 1865, Emery, "Lewis Emery Letters," accessed 22 Apr. 2003; Co. D, 3MN, Morning Report, 24 Jan. 1865, RG 94; Anthony Wilford CMSR, ibid.

26. Miller to Stanton, 24 Feb. 1865 (This is discreditable), MN EXJOU, Miller, C:154; Ezra Champlin voucher, 3 Mar. 1865 (voucher for the), MNOAG, Civil War Muster Rolls, 3MN; Reynolds to Halleck, 10 Jan. 1865 (much dissatisfaction and), *OR*, 48(1):472; Applegarth to Cousin Cordelia, 6 Jan. 1865, Applegarth Letters; Mattson to Smith, 7 Jan. 1865 and endorsement by Brown on 17 Jan. 1865, Department of Arkansas and VII Army Corps, Letters, Reports, and Telegrams, RG 393, pt. 1, entry 259; Muster-out roll for William G. F. Akers, 6 Feb. 1865, Civil War Records, A-5, UALR; G.O. no. 31, Mil. Div. of the West Mississippi, 4 Mar. 1865, Department of Arkansas and VII Army Corps, Letters, Reports, and Telegrams, RG 393, pt. 1, entry 270.

27. Mattson to Green, 10 Jan. 1865, with endorsements, James M. Bowler CMSR, RG 94; Bowler to Levering, 14 Jan. 1865, ibid.; Mattson to Miller, 14 Feb. 1865, RGSM, Appointments, Military–General; Exhibit of Infantry, Dept. of Ark., 6 Feb. 1865, *OR*, 48(1):756–58.

28. John C. White (Detective [in the] Provost), John Spellman, Levi Emery, John O. Crummett, Nathaniel Olds, and Simeon Olds CMSRs, RG 94; Matson to Asst. Adj. Gen. VII Corps, and endorsement, 1 Jan. 1865, Department of Arkansas and VII Army Corps, Letters, Reports, and Telegrams, RG 393, pt. 1, entry 262; Forster to Asst. Adj. Gen. 2nd Div., 20 Jan. 1865, ibid.

29. William B. Day, Peter LeClair (girls he had), and Charles E. Bradish CMSRs, RG 94; G.O. no. 5, 1st Brig., 2nd Div., VII Corps, 4 Mar. 1865 (police and fatigue), 3MN Order Books, ibid.

30. Patrick Tammany CMSR, RG 94; Ireland to Mattson, and endorsements, 21 Mar. 1865, Department of Arkansas and VII Army Corps, Letters, Reports, and Telegrams, RG 393, pt. 1, entry 259.

31. S.O. no. 129, Dept. of Ark., Letters, Reports, 31 Jan. 1865 (to accept the), Department of Arkansas and VII Army Corps, Letters, Reports, and Telegrams, RG 393, pt. 1, entry 270; Lewis S. Hancock CMSR, RG 94; Mattson to Malmros, 13 Mar. 1865 (much improved in), MNOAG, General Correspondence; Lewis Hancock, carte de visite, Wayne Jorgenson Collection; e-mail, Stephen Osman to the author, 3 June 2016.

32. Mattson to Miller, 14 Feb. 1865 (a reasonable share), RGSM, Appointments, Military—General; *Rochester (Minn.) City Post*, 25 Feb. (improperly stricken from), 18 Mar. (Excitement in the) 1865; Reynolds to Christensen, 9 Feb. 1865 (a party of), *OR*, 48(1):788; Mattson to Malmros, 26 Mar. 1865, MNOAG, General Correspondence; Caleff to Bowler, 19 Feb. 1865, Bowler and Family Papers.

33. Emery to Ursula Emery, 20, 27 Mar. 1865, Larson, "Lewis Emery Letters."

34. S.O. no. 48, Dept. of Ark., 23 Feb. 1865 (capacity and fitness), Department of Arkansas and VII Army Corps, Special Orders, RG 393, pt. 1, entry 282; e-mail, Joseph Glattharr to the author, 5 Aug. 2018 (may have been); Godfrey to Asst. Adj. Gen. VII Corps, 1 Mar. 1865, Department of Arkansas and VII Army Corps, Letters, Reports, and Telegrams, RG 393, pt. 1, entry 262; Clark to Asst. Adj. Gen. VII Corps, 6 Mar. 1865, ibid.; Pyburn to Asst. Adj. Gen. VII Corps, 28 Mar. 1865, ibid.; Bowler to Caleff, 24 Mar. 1865, Bowler and Family Papers; Eugene W. Stone, George N. Godfrey, Justus R. Clark, and Andrew J. Pyburn [Ryburn?] CMSRs, RG 94.

35. David Sesser, "113th United States Colored Infantry," *Encyclopedia of Arkansas History & Culture*, last updated 29 Apr. 2016, http://www.encyclopediaofarkansas.net /encyclopedia/entry-detail.aspx?entryID=8703, accessed 17 Jan. 2019; G.O. no. 84, Dept. of Ark., 6 Apr. 1865 (train of cars), Foster Collection, Ohio Historical Society, Columbus; Bowler to Caleff, 24 Mar. 1865, Bowler and Family Papers; S.O. no. 80, Dept. of Ark., 1 Apr. 1865, Civil War Records, A-5, UALR.

36. Marples to Dear Wife, 12 Apr. 1865 (sell the sheep), Marples and Family Papers; Bowler to Caleff, 14 Apr. 1865 (two hundred guns; an illumination), Bowler and Family Papers; *SPDP*, 13 Apr. 1865.

37. Bowler to Caleff, 15 Apr. 1865 (abstain from all; This fills the), Bowler and Family Papers; Mattson *Reminiscences*, 78 (wild with grief; man by the); Felix B. Stark CMSR, RG 94.

38. Canfield to Sister, 21 Apr. 1865 (quite a gloom), Canfield Letters; Mattson to Mrs. Mattson, 23 Apr. 1865, Mattson and Family Papers.

39. Phileo to Lincoln, 1 Apr. 1865, with endorsements, Edward B. Phileo CMSR, RG 94.

40. Emery to Ursula Emery, 28 Apr. 1865 (to hold on), Larson, "Lewis Emery Letters"; William T. Flora CMSR, RG 94; G.O. No 12, 1st Brig., 2nd Div., VII Corps, 28 Apr. 1865, 3MN Order Books, ibid.; G.O. no. 56, 2nd Div., VII Corps, 29 Apr. 1865, Peter LeClair CMSR, ibid.

41. Field-Officer Court, 18 Apr. 1865 (clean mud off), Nicholas Gross CMSR, RG 94; Joseph Cayou, OO907, General Courts-Martial, RG 153, entry 15; Joseph Cayou CMSR, RG 94.

42. Upham to Henry Upham, 21 Apr. 1865 (Bushwhackers, Gorillas &c), Upham Collection; Wenzel, "Freedmen's Farm Letters," 169 (in many places); Reynolds to Fagan, 24 Apr. 1865 (alleviating as far), *OR*, 48(2):177; Grant to Reynolds, 30 Apr. 1865 (lay down their), ibid., 248; Shaler to Levering, 20 Apr. 1865, ibid., 140; Shaler to Levering, 25 Apr. 1865, ibid., 190; Bliff to VII Corps, 30 Apr. 1865, ibid., ser. 3, 5:300; Hughes, "Wartime Gristmill Destruction," 182.

11. Pacifying Arkansas

1. *SPPD*, 5, 28 (exposure of our) May 1865; Vincent to Stanton, 1 May 1865, *OR*, ser. 3, 5:1; G.O. no. 101, Adj. Gen. Office, 30 May 1865, ibid., 43; G.O. no. 114, Adj. Gen. Office, 15 June 1865, in 2nd Div. to U.S. Forces White River, 22 June 1865, Department of

Arkansas and VII Army Corps, Letters, Reports, and Telegrams, RG 393, pt. 1, entry 272; Miller to Paymaster General, 29 May 1865, MN EXJOU Miller, C:291.

2. *SPPD*, 1 July 1865 (committee of ladies); *St. Paul Weekly Pioneer and Democrat*, 2 June 1865; *SPDP*, 4 June 1865; Osman, *Fort Snelling*, 267–69; Trenerry, "When the Boys Came Home," 289–91.

3. Canfield to Sister Cordelia, 10 May 1865 (everything is in), Thomas Canfield Letters, Bruce and George Barnum Family Collection; Thomas to Stanton, 1 May 1865, *OR*, ser. 3, 5:1; Mattson to Mrs. Mattson, 4 May 1865, Hans Mattson and Family Papers, MHS.

4. Mattson to Malmros, 2 May 1865, MNOAG, General Correspondence; Reynolds to Ball, 12 May 1865 (to Mexico to), *OR*, 48(2):416–17; Howe to Commander, 11 May 1865, ibid., 49(2):402–4; Canfield to Sister Cordelia, 10 May 1865, Canfield Letters; Co. C, 3MN, Morning Report, 8 May 1865, RG 94; Mattson to Mrs. Mattson, 8 May 1865, Mattson and Family Papers.

5. Mattson to Mrs. Mattson, 12 July 1865, Mattson and Family Papers; Coles to Esme, 26 May 1865, Coles Letters, UAF; George Herber and Charles Marples CMSR, RG 94; S.O. no. 181, Dept. of Ark., 2 Aug. 1865 Department of Arkansas and VII Army Corps, Special Orders, RG 393, pt. 1, entry 282; Strugy to Miller, 8 Aug. 1865, MNOAG, General Correspondence; 3MN Monthly Return, July 1865, ibid., Personnel Records; Durant to Miller, 11 July 1865, RGSM, Letters Received.

6. Howe to Mattson, 16 May 1865 (scour[ing] the country; encourage agriculture; approval from higher), *OR*, 48(2):466–67; S.O. no. 114, Dept. of Ark., ibid., 417; Mattson to Mrs. Mattson, 8, 14 May 1865, Mattson and Family Papers; Mattson, "Early Days of Reconstruction," 323.

7. Emery to Ursula Emery, 20 May 1865 (a pretty place), Emery, "Lewis Emery Letters," accessed 22 Apr. 2003; Mattson to Mrs. Mattson, 26 May 1865, Mattson and Family Papers; Mattson, "Early Days of Reconstruction," 327–28.

8. Pope to Reynolds, 22 May 1865 (the whole country), *OR*, 48(2):541; Mattson, "Early Days of Reconstruction," 323–24, 327–29 (unlimited power to; a government mule); Hans Mattson, "Address," 3MVVA, *Third Annual Reunion* (1883), 26 (to know how; perfect ladies but); G.O. no. 1, U.S. Forces Batesville, 20 May 1865, Mattson and Family Papers.

9. Mattson to Mrs. Mattson, 26, 30 (low—not near) May, 5 June (awful rebels) 1865, Mattson and Family Papers; Howe to Mattson, 26 May 1865, Department of Arkansas and VII Army Corps, Letters, Reports, and Telegrams, RG 393, pt. 1, entry 269.

10. Mattson, "Early Days of Reconstruction," 324 (avoid political discussions), 332, 333 (Many of you); Mattson to Mrs. Mattson, 5 June 1865, Mattson and Family Papers.

11. Mattson to Howe, 25 June 1865 (Capt. Gleason), Department of Arkansas and VII Army Corps, Letters, Reports, and Telegrams, RG 393, pt. 1, entry 269; S.O. no. 129, Dept. of Ark., 31 May 1865, *OR*, 48(2):701; Witt to Dreher, 10 June 1865, ibid. 844–45; Mattson to Howe, 31 May 1865, 3MN Letter Book, RG 94; Mattson to Mrs. Mattson, 5, 8 June 1865, Mattson and Family Papers.

12. Hodges to Levering, 15 June 1865 (Independent Feds; robbed of all), Department of Arkansas and VII Army Corps, Letters, Reports, and Telegrams, RG 393, pt. 1, entry 269; Levering to Ryan, 1 June 1865, *OR*, 48(2):721.

13. Mattson to Mrs. Mattson, 11 (Our work here), 24 (regarded as a; the citizens especially) June 1865, Mattson and Family Papers; Mattson, "Early Days of Reconstruction," 330 (pensmen and accountants), 331.

14. Mattson, "Early Days of Reconstruction," 335–36.
15. Emery to Ursula Emery, 26 July, 6 Aug. 1865, Emery, "Lewis Emery Letters."
16. Mattson, "Early Days of Reconstruction," 330 (an old-fashioned); Mattson to Mrs. Mattson, 12 July (very pleasant visit; everybody is so), 2 Aug. 1865, Mattson and Family Papers; Reynolds Endorsement, 18 Aug. 1865 (This regiment cannot), on Mattson to Reynolds, 15 July 1865, Department of Arkansas and VII Army Corps, Letters, Reports, and Telegrams, RG 393, pt. 1, entry 259; Emery to Ursula Emery, 9 July 1865, Emery, "Lewis Emery Letters."
17. Mattson to Mrs. Mattson, 7 (mutiny—lay down; D-A-H), 9 (the prospects for), 15 (the soldiers had) Aug. 1865, Mattson and Family Papers; Emery to Ursula Emery, 19 Aug. 1865 (tried to kick), Emery "Lewis Emery Letters."
18. John H. King (driving a US; drunkenness is not) and Joseph Kester CMSRs, RG 94.
19. G.O. no. 84, 2nd Div., VII Corps, 17 Aug. 1865 (disgraceful language to), Department of Arkansas and VII Army Corps, Letters, Reports, and Telegrams, RG 393, pt. 1, entry 272; Dreher to Folsom, 2 Sept. 1865 (quick and orderly), Orville Golden CMSR, RG 94; David E. Petty and James H Malloy CMSRs, ibid.
20. Mattson, "Address," 3MVVA, *Third Annual Reunion* (1883), 26–27 (imposing sight, good); Mattson to Mrs. Mattson, 21 Aug. 1865, Mattson and Family Papers.
21. Mattson to Mrs. Mattson, 30 Aug., 1 Sept. 1865, Mattson and Family Papers.
22. S.O. no. 207, Dept. of Ark., 1 Sept. 1865 (Col. Hans Mattson), Department of Arkansas and VII Army Corps, Special Orders, RG 393, pt. 1, entry 282; Miller to Adjutant General, 29 Aug. 1865, MN EXJOU, Miller, C:424; Wagner to Shaler, 25 Aug. 1865, Department of Arkansas and VII Army Corps, Letters, Reports, and Telegrams, RG 393, pt. 1, entry 256.
23. "Muster out of a detachment of Co. G," 2 Sept. 1865 (detachment of Co. G), Civil War Records, A-5, UALR; "Muster out of a detachment of Co. I," 2 Sept. 1865 (detachment of Co. I), ibid.; William I. Flora, William A Logan, Charles W. Lombard, and John Spellman CMSRs, RG 94.
24. *SPPD*, 10 (to receive and), 12 Sept. 1865 (I have the); *SPDP*, 12 Sept. 1865.
25. *SPDP*, 13 Sept. 1865 (for the very); Hancock, "Address," 3MVVA, *Thirty-Fourth Annual Reunion* (1918) 14 (loyal ladies of).
26. *SPDP*, 12 Sept. 1865 (that the ladies; Colonel Mattson will); *SPDP*, 12 Sept. 1865 (this was considered).
27. Trenerry, "When the Boys Came Home," 292 (unexplained incivility); Hancock, "Address," 3MVVA, *Thirty-Fourth Annual Reunion* (1918) 14 (an article appeared); Mattson to Mrs. Mattson, 12 Sept. 1865 (we had a), Mattson and Family Papers.
28. *Hastings (Minn.) Conserver*, 12 Sept. 1865.
29. Mattson to Mrs. Mattson, 12 Sept. 1865, Mattson and Family Papers; Osman, *Fort Snelling*, 267–69; Mattson to Peller, 13 Sept. 1865, MNOAG, General Correspondence.
30. G.O. no. 16, 3MN, 16 Sept. 1865 (its bone and; from the northwestern), 3MVVA, *Forty-Third Annual Reunion* (1927), 10–11; James Crosby, "Memoirs," 26, SRNBA.
31. Mattson to Mrs. Mattson, 15 Sept. 1865, Mattson and Family Papers.
32. *Hastings (Minn.) Conserver*, 12 Sept. 1865.

Epilogue: The Regiment in Memory

1. Marten, "Exempt from the Ordinary Rules," 57–61, 69–70; Marten, *Sing Not War*, 1–6, chap. 1.

2. Marten, "Exempt from the Ordinary Rules," 57–61, 69–70; Jordan, *Marching Home*, chap. 1.

3. Martin, "Exempt from the Ordinary Rules," 57–61, 69–70; Lee, "Military Position and Post Service Occupational Mobility," 12–19.

4. 3MVVA, *Sixth Annual Reunion* (1889), 8–9, 24–25; *St. Paul Daily Globe*, 16 Sept. 1887.

5. 3MVVA, *Seventh Annual Reunion* (1890), 9 (J. W. Green); 3MVVA, *Fifteenth Annual Reunion* (1899), 6 (Reuben Griggs), 16.

6. 3MVVA, *Seventeenth Annual Reunion* (1901), 8–14; 3MVVA, *Twenty-First Annual Reunion* (1905), 2–6, 10–11, 13; 3MVVA, *Thirty-Ninth Annual Reunion* (1923), 11.

7. 3MVVA, *Twenty-First Annual Reunion* (1905), 12–13; 3MVVA, *Twenty-Second Annual Reunion* (1906), 2–4, 13–15.

8. Champlin to W. D. Hale, 12[?] Oct. 1906 (brute), Buelow Brothers Collection; comments by W. D. Hale and W. E. Hale, courtesy Eugene Buelow to author, 6 Sept. 2005; 3MVVA, *Thirty-Third Annual Reunion* (1917), 14–15; MHS, *Minnesota State Capitol Art*, 3, accessed 23 Aug. 2016 (copy in author's possession).

9. 3MVVA, *Twenty-Third Annual Reunion* (1907), 2, 7; 3MVVA, *Twenty-Fourth Annual Reunion* (1908), 4, 10, 12.

10. Shipman to Secretary, 1 Sept. 1917, 3MVVA, *Thirty-Third Annual Reunion* (1917), 8, 18–20; 3MVVA, *Thirtieth Annual Reunion* (1914), 1; 3MVVA, *Thirty-Fourth Annual Reunion* (1918), 1; 3MVVA, *Thirty-Fifth Annual Reunion* (1919), 10–14.

11. 3MVVA, *Thirty-Seventh Annual Reunion* (1921), 1; 3MVVA, *Thirty-Eighth Annual Reunion* (1922), cover; 3MVVA, *Thirty-Ninth Annual Reunion* (1923), cover, 3MVVA, *Forty-Second Annual Reunion* (1926), 1; 3MVVA, *Forty-First Annual Reunion* (1925), 1.

12. 3MVVA, *Forty-Third Annual Reunion* (1927), 5–6 (in honor of); 3MVVA, *Forty-Second Annual Reunion* (1926), 1.

13. 3MVVA, *Forty-Fifth Annual Reunion* (1929), 3 (assurances of the); 3MVVA, *Forty-Second Annual Reunion* (1926), 1; 3MVVA, *Forty-Third Annual Reunion* (1927), inside back cover; 3MVVA, *Forty-Seventh Annual Reunion* (1931), 1; Roster of Attendees, Forty-Eighth Reunion, 1932, Third Minnesota Veteran Volunteers Association Records.

14. Lee, "Military Position and Post Service Occupational Mobility," 12–19.

15. 3MVVA, *Sixth Annual Reunion* (1889), 16 (Our Fools; sporting house); 3MVVA, *Thirty-Eighth Annual Reunion* (1922), 9; George W. Brookins CMSR, RG 94; George W. Brookins, 3MN, Pension Application 359756, Certificate 275121, RG 15; Bernard McKenna CMSR, RG 94; McKenna Filing, 2 Aug. 1865, Department of Arkansas and VII Army Corps, Letters, Reports, and Telegrams, RG 393, pt. 1, entry 266.

16. Mattson, "Early Days of Reconstruction," 335 (the most bitter); Foster, "Our Fools," 13, 14 (klukluxed; when he fired), 15 (the terror of).

17. 3MVVA, *Sixth Annual Reunion* (1885), 16–17; Benjamin F. Rice and James H. Swan CMSRs, RG 94.

18. 3MVVA, *Sixth Annual Reunion* (1885), 17; 3MVVA, *Thirty-Eighth Annual Reunion* (1922), 2, 7, 9.

19. 3MVVA, *Sixth Annual Reunion* (1885), 17–18; James L. Hodges CMSR, RG 94.

20. Foster to Mosher, 1 Sept. 1917, Third Infantry Regiment Minnesota Volunteer Association Records, MHS; Foster to Law, 24 Aug. 1919, ibid.; 3MVVA, *Sixth Annual Reunion* (1885), 8, 16.

21. 3MVVA, *Sixth Annual Reunion* (1885), 13–14; *Thirty-First Annual Reunion* (1916), 7–8; Marquis, *Book of Minnesotans*, 206.

22. Bradish to Secretary, 28 Aug. 1916, 3MVVA, *Thirty-Second Annual Reunion* (1916), 13–14; Charles E. Braddish CMSR, RG 94; Curtiss-Wedge, *Dakota and Goodhue Counties*, 2:667; Marquis, *Book of Minnesotans*, 83; Castle, *St. Paul and Vicinity*, 734–45.

23. Curtiss-Wedge, *Dakota and Goodhue Counties*, 2:708–9, Marquis, *Book of Minnesotans*, 123.

24. 3MVVA, *Thirty-Sixth Annual Reunion* (1920), 15; Curtiss-Wedge, *Dakota and Goodhue Counties*, 2:667.

25. Marquis, *Book of Minnesotans*, 83; "Minnesota Legislators Past & Present," accessed 27 Aug. 2016.

26. Upham and Dunlap, *Minnesota Biographies*, 211, 807.

27. 3MVVA, *Thirty-Third Annual Reunion* (1917), 7–8 (dance all night); Chamberlain Obituary, Third Infantry Regiment Minnesota Volunteer Association Records.

28. *Portrait and Biographical Record, Jasper . . . Iowa*, 590–591,books.google.com, accessed 16 Aug. 2016; "James W. Crosby (1844–1931)," WikiTree, last updated 29 May 2016, http://www.wikitree.com/wiki/Crosby-2320, accessed 16 Aug. 2016.

29. William Sears and Clark L. Angell CMSRs, RG 94; "The G. A. R.," accessed 28 Aug. 2016.

30. Larson, "Private Alfred Gales," 280–83.

31. Upham and Dunlap, *Minnesota Biographies*, 68.

32. 3MVVA, *Twenty-Seventh Annual Reunion* (1911), 8; "Adolphus Elliot," accessed 27 Aug. 2016.

33. Thilgen, "Man of His Time," 8 (fierce pitcher), 9–12.

34. Blakely Family Biographical File, Olmstead County Historical Society, Rochester, Minn.

35. Curtiss-Wedge, *Dakota and Goodhue Counties*, 2:1024; Upham and Dunlap, *Minnesota Biographies*, 148; *San Francisco Call*, 18 Mar. 1895, California Digital Newspaper Collection, UCR Center for Bibliographical Studies and Research, https://cdnc.ucr.edu/?a=d&d=SFC18950318&e=-------en--20--1--txt-txIN--------1, accessed 11 Aug. 2016; Manuscript Schedule, 1880 U.S. Census for Minnesota, Ancestry.com, accessed 11 Aug. 2016.

36. Atwater and Stevens, *History of Minneapolis*, 906–7, 969; Marquis, *Book of Minnesotans*, 541.

37. *St. Louis (Mo.) Lumberman*, 1 Nov. 1910, Google books, https://books.google.com /books?, accessed 11 Aug. 2016.

38. Swanson, "New Hampshire Yankee," 18–25.

39. 3MVVA, *Tenth Annual Reunion* (1894), 7–10; Upham and Dunlap, *Minnesota Biographies*, 496; Mattson to Foster, 29 Aug. 1919, 3MVVA Records, MHS.

40. Gilmore to Trenerry, 16 July 1963, Walter N. Trenerry Papers, MHS; New York Certificate and Record of Death for Henry C. Lester, ibid.; Tolles to Trenerry 1 Aug. 1963, ibid.

41. Jesse T. Barrick CMSR, RG 94; "Grave Rededication for Jessie T. Barrick," http://home.comcast.net/~suvcw1/events/barrick/barrick.html, accessed 10 June 2007 (site discontinued).

BIBLIOGRAPHY

Archives

Archives of Michigan, Lansing

Record Group 59-14: Records of the Michigan Military Establishment, 1831–1920, Box 102, 9th Michigan Infantry, Folder 4, Letters Relating to the Regiment, 1861–65.

Dakota County Historical Society, South St. Paul, Minn.

Thomas C. Hodgson. "Personal Recollections of the Sioux War, No. 7." *Dakota County Tribune*, 12 October 1889.
"Travels of Co. F [8th Minnesota] as Related by a Veteran, Reminiscence."

Filson Historical Society, Louisville, Ky.

Samuel A. Eldridge Letter.
Isaac P. Tichenor Letters.

Goodhue County Historical Society, Red Wing, Minn.

Benjamin Densmore Papers.
Lewis Johnson Diaries.

Indiana State Archives

Oliver P. Morton. Morton Telegram Book No. 4, Department & General Telegrams, from June 11th 1862 to July 31st 1862. Also available at http://ulib.iupuidigital.org/cdm/ref/collection/Telegraph/id/1005.

Library of Congress, Washington, D.C.
Charles Oscar Torrey Papers.

Michigan State University Archives, East Lansing

John Gibson Parkhurst Papers.

Minnesota Historical Society, St. Paul

George R. Adams Papers.
Levi B. Aldrich Papers.
C. C. Andrews and Family Papers.
Barrick Family Civil War Materials. Candace Barrick, comp.
George T. Bartlett Papers.
John Reed Beatty Papers.
Biographical Collections: Levi Butler, George Davies, Perry Honeywell, Robert Lumsden.
Judson Wade Bishop and Family Papers.
James M. Bowler and Family Papers.
J[ohn]. W. Boxell Civil War Letters and Related Papers. Robert A. Boxell, comp.
George W. Brookins and Family Letters.
William R. Brown Papers.
Benjamin J. Butler and Family Papers.
Samuel D. Carrell and Family Papers.
Thomas and Carmelite Christie and Family Papers.
Dakota Conflict of 1862 Manuscripts Collection.
Jeremiah C. Donahower Papers.
Ignatius Donnelly and Family Papers. Microfilm.
George W. Doud Diary.
Thomas Downs Civil War Diary and Related Papers.
Durand Family Papers.
Elijah Evan Edwards Civil War Journals.
Hubert N. Eggelston Papers.
Charles J. Fisk. "The First Fifty Years of Continuous Recorded Weather History in Min-
    nesota (1820–1869): A Narrative Chronology." Typescript, 1994. Also available at
    https://www.climatestations.com/minnesota-weather-history-1820-to-1869/.
James Liberty Fisk and Family Papers.
W. H. C. [Philander] Folsom and Family Papers.
William D. Hale and Family Papers.
Hamlin Family Papers.
John Jones and Family Papers.
Robert Todd Lincoln Papers.
Charles Marples and Family Papers.
Eugene Marshall. "Narrative of the Civil War."
Ebenezer Brewer Mattocks & Family Papers.
Hans Mattson and Family Papers.
Minnesota. Adjutant General Records.
        Annual Reports.
        General Correspondence.
        3rd Regiment Volunteer Infantry.
Minnesota Commission on the Wood Lake Battlefield. Report on the Battle of Wood
    Lake and Map. Typescript, 1907.
Minnesota. Governor. Executive Documents of the State of Minnesota (1861–62: Ramsey;
    1863: Swift, Miller; 1864–65: Miller).
Minnesota. Governor. Executive Journals. (vol. A. 1858–62: Sibley, Ramsey; vol. B. 1863–64:
    Swift, Miller; vol. C. 1864–66: Miller).

Minnesota. Governor (1860–63: Ramsey). Records of Gov. Alexander Ramsey. State
    Archives.
        Copies of Letters Sent, 1861–63.
        Letters Received.
        Military. General, 1860–63; Infantry—3rd Regiment, General (1861–63), Individuals
            (1861), and Chaplains and Surgeons (1861–63); Infantry—3rd or 4th Regiment,
            General, Chaplains and Surgeons (1861); Medical and Hospital (1861–63).
Minnesota. Governor (1862–63: Ramsey, Swift). Memorandum Books.
Minnesota. Governor (1863–64: Swift). Records of Gov. Henry A. Swift. State Archives.
Minnesota. Governor (1864–66: Miller). Records of Gov. Stephen Miller. State Archives.
        Appointments, Military. General (1864–65); Medical (1864–65); Other (1864–65);
            Units (1864–65).
        Letters Received.
        Letters Sent, 1864–65.
Minnesota. Office of the Adjutant General Records.
        Civil War Muster Rolls, Third Minnesota Volunteer Infantry.
        General Correspondence.
        General Orders, 1858–63, 1863–73.
        Miscellaneous Reports.
        Military Service Records, Civil and U.S.–Dakota Wars.
        Personnel Records.
John Henry Mitchell and Family Papers.
John Nelson Papers.
Nathaniel C. Parker Diary.
Andrew Peterson and Family Papers.
Eli K. Pickett Correspondence.
Thomas R. Potts Papers.
Chesley Pratt and Family Papers.
James T. Ramer Diary.
Alexander Ramsey and Family Personal Papers and Governor's Records, Correspondence,
    and Miscellaneous Papers. Microfilm.
Edward S. Reddington Papers.
Stephen R. Riggs and Family Papers.
Henry Ristine and Family Papers.
Carl Roos and Family Papers.
        Charles J. LaVine, trans., "Carl Roos' War Diary, 1861–1863."
Thomas Scantlebury and Family Papers.
Henry H. Sibley Papers. Microfilm.
Claude E. Simmonds. "George Davis, Wright County Pioneer." 1946. Typescript.
Orrin F. Smith and Family Papers.
Benjamin F. Smith, Military Record Book.
Henry J. Snyder Letters.
Thomas Rice Stewart Memoirs.
Charles J. Strand. "Four Years with a Minnesota Soldier in the Civil War." (Typescript
    of Charles E. Hunt diary.)
Third Infantry Regiment Minnesota Volunteer Association Records, 1870–1935.
Walter N. Trenerry Papers.

Horatio P. Van Cleve and Family Papers.
Henry Wadsworth. "Reminiscence [of the Dakota Conflict of 1862]."
Jesse A. and Luman P. Washburn Papers.
Charles H. Watson Letters.
Abraham Edward Welch and Family Papers.
James Wescott Papers.
Edwin and Wilfred J. Whitefield Papers.
John Kingsley Wood Diary.
Works Progress Administration. Minnesota. Writers' Project. Annals of Minnesota.

Missouri Historical Society, St. Louis

Francis W. Tupper Letter. Civil War Collection.

National Archives and Records Administration, Washington, D.C.

RG 15: Records of the Veteran's Administration.
    Pensions.
RG 24: Records of the Bureau of Naval Personnel.
    Decklogs.
RG 77: Records of the Office of the Chief Engineer.
    Subgroup B, T29-5.
RG 92: Records of the Office of the Quartermaster General.
    Station Book, 1861–67. Entry 1138.
RG 94: Office of the Adjutant General, U.S. Army, 1780–1917.
    Compiled Military Service Records, 3rd Minn.
    Generals' Papers. Entry 159.
    Company Muster Rolls, Record of Events and Regimental Returns, 3rd Reg't Minn. Inf.
    Regimental Books and Papers, Order Books, Letter Books, Muster Rolls, Morning Reports.
    Returns from U.S. Volunteer Regiments, 1861–65.
    State Organization Records: Illinois (18th, 61st, 106th, 111th Inf.), Iowa (40th Inf.), Kentucky (23rd Inf.), Michigan (9th, 12th Inf.), Minnesota (3rd Inf.), Wisconsin (27th Inf.).
RG 110: Records of the Provost Marshal General's Bureau (Civil War).
    Files of Papers Relating to Two or More Civilians. Entry 4660.
RG 153: Records of Office of the Judge Advocate General (Army).
    General Courts-Martial. Entry 15.
RG 159: Records of the Office of the Inspector General (Army).
    Letters Received, Register of Letters Received. Microfilm M474.
RG 249: Records of the Commissary General of Prisoners.
    Abstracts and Copies of Orders, Letters, and Telegrams Relating to Paroled and Exchanged Federal Prisoners of War, 1861–65. Entry 151.
    Consolidated Morning Reports of Detachments, Battalions, and Companies of Paroled and Exchanged Federal Prisoners of War, 1862–65. Entry 154.
    Consolidated Morning Reports of Paroled Federal Prisoners of War, 1862–65. Entry 155.

RG 393: U.S. Army Continental Commands, 1821–1920, Pt. 1.
    Department of Arkansas and VII Army Corps.
        General Orders and Circulars. Entries, 274, 276, 278.
        Inspector General. Entries 323–24.
        Letters, Reports, and Telegrams. Entries 256, 259, 262, 266, 269–70, 272, 279.
        Other Records. Entry 296.
        Provost Marshal. Entries 342–43.
        Special Orders. Entries 282–83.
    Departments of the Cumberland and the Ohio.
        General and Special Orders. Entries 890–91, 911, 944.
        Letters and Telegrams. Entry 885.
        Telegrams Received. Entry 929.
        Telegrams Sent. Entry 915.
    Department of the Northwest.
        Sibley's Indian Expedition, Letters Received. Entry 3481.
    Department of Tennessee.
        Letters Sent. Entry 4709.
    Military Division of the West Mississippi, 1864–65.
        Inspector General's Office. Entry 5543.
RG 393: U.S. Army Continental Commands, 1821–1920, Pt. 2.
    Department of Arkansas and VII Corps.
        Letters and Telegrams Sent. Entry 4729.
RG 393: U.S. Army Continental Commands, 1821–1920, Pt. 5.
    Fort Snelling (Minn.).
        General Orders, Special Orders, and Circulars. Entry 12 (vol. 1).
        Letters and Endorsements. Entry 2 (vols. 1 and 2).

Olmstead County Historical Society, Rochester, Minn.

Alpheus W. Belen & Family Biographical Files.
Blakely Family Biographical File.
John Vosburgh Biographical File.

Ohio Historical Society, Columbus

Everett W. Foster Collection.

Private Collections

Allis Family Collection.
    Frederick Allis Diary.
Bruce and George Barnum Family Collection. Lake City, Minn.
    Thomas Canfield Letters.
Buelow Brothers Collection. Vernon Center, Minn.
    Ezra Champlin Letter.
    Conrad Reineke Letter.
J. David Johnson Collection. Lake City, Minn.
    Henry W. Applegarth Letters.
    Carte de Visite Collection.

Mark Jones Collection. Owatonna, Minn.
    Albert C. Wedge. "Talk to [Unnamed] Veteran's Group." Typescript. 1910.
Wayne Jorgenson Collection. Eden Prairie, Minn.
    Carte de Visite Collection.
Robert J. Niemela Collection. White Bear Lake, Minn.
    James L. Battey Diary. Typescript.
Stephen E. Osman Collection. Minneapolis.
    Carte de Visite Collection.
    Olin Collection.
    Vasa Illustrata Collection.
Alan Woolworth Collection.
    Elwin Rogers, "Military Expeditions." Typescript, n.d.

Rockford Area Historical Society, Rockford, Minn.

Curtis B. Ames Letters. Crandall Collection.

St. Olaf College Archives, Northfield, Minn.

Norwegian-American Historical Association, Civil War Papers.

Stone's River National Battlefield Archives, Murfreesboro, Tenn.

Jonah H. Carpenter Diary.
James Crosby "Memoirs of James Crosby."
Patrick M. Hill. "Dancing with the Devil: General N. B. Forrest & Minnesota at Murfreesboro." Typescript.

Tennessee State Library and Archives, Nashville

William Mark Eames Papers. Microfilm MF.1306.
L[ucy] Virginia (Smith) French Diary.

U.S. Army Military History Institute, Carlisle Barracks, Pa.

Civil War Miscellaneous Collection.
    James Boardman Diary.
    Robert N. Diver Civil War Diary.
    Sgt. Monroe D. Halladay Letters.
Earl Hess Collection.
    Henry O. Rice Letters.

University of Arkansas at Fayetteville, Archives & Special Collections

Milton P. Chambers Papers.
Danford D. Cole Letters.
Orville Gillet Diary, 1861–1865.
Albert Harris Collection.
Robert and Sephronia McCollom Papers.
Minos Miller Letters.
Mary Hope Moose Papers.

Frederick Steele. Selected Documents, 1863–1865. Microfilm.
Arabella Lanktree Wilson Letters.

University of Arkansas at Little Rock, Center for Arkansas History and Culture

James A. Campbell Papers.
Civil War Records. A-5.
Henry Ellis Letters.
Charles H. Lake Papers.
Report, Arkansas County Governments, 1865.
D[aniel] P. Upham Collection, 1865–1883. MS.0158.

University of Michigan, Bentley Historical Library, Ann Arbor

Amos W. Abbott Letters.
Edward G. Bailey Letters. Ira K. Bailey Correspondence.
Henry G. Cooley Papers.
DeLand Family Papers.
Arthur B. Hathaway Papers.
A. H. Kelley Letters.
John C. Love Papers.
John G. Parkhurst Papers.
Wellington White Diary.

University of Memphis Special Collections

William Vermillion—[Charles W.] Kittredge Letters.

University of North Carolina at Chapel Hill, Southern History Collection

Kate S. Carney Diary.
William H. King Memoirs.
Lewis M. Maney Papers.
C. Alice Ready Diary. Typescript.

Wisconsin Historical Society, Madison

George Cook Diaries.
James Browne Lockney Papers.
Edwin B. Quiner, comp., "Quiner Scrapbooks: Correspondence of the Wisconsin Volunteers, 1861–1865," vol. 6.

Government Publications

U.S. Army. Corps of Engineers, Nashville District. *Summary Report, Flood Plain Information Survey, Murfreesboro, Tennessee (West Fork Stones River and Lytle and Sinking Creeks)*. . . . Nashville, Tenn., 1966.
———. Surgeon General's Office. *The Medical and Surgical History of the War of the Rebellion (1861–65)*. 2 vols. in 6 pts. Washington, D.C.: Government Printing Office, 1870–88. Reprint, Wilmington, N.C.: Broadfoot, 1990–91.
U.S. Census Bureau. *Population of the United States in 1860: Compiled from the Original Returns of the Eight Census*. 2 vols. Washington, D.C.: Government Printing Office, 1864.

U.S. Congress. Joint Committee on the Conduct of the War. *Report of the Joint Committee on the Conduct of the War, at the Second Session, Thirty-Eighth Congress.* . . . Vols. 2–3. Washington, D.C: Government Printing Office, 1865.

U.S. Navy Department. *Official Records of the Union and Confederate Navies in the War of the Rebellion.* 31 vol. Washington, D.C.: Government Printing Office, 1884–1922.

U.S. War Department. *Atlas of the War of the Rebellion.* . . . New York: Atlas, 1892.

———. *General Orders of the War Department, Embracing the Years 1861, 1862, & 1863.* . . . Compiled by Thomas M. O'Brien and Oliver Diefendorf. New York: Derby & Miller, 1864.

———. *Revised Regulations for the Army of the United States, 1861.* Philadelphia: J. G. L. Brown, 1861. Reprint, Harrisburg, Pa.: National Historical Society, 1980.

———. *The War of the Rebellion: A Compilation of the Official Records of the Union and Confederate Armies.* 128 vols. Washington, D.C.: Government Printing Office, 1880–1921.

Newspapers

Army and Navy Official Gazette
Chatfield (Minn.) Democrat
Chicago Times
Chicago Tribune
Faribault (Minn.) Central Republican
Faribault (Minn.) Northern Statesman
Goodhue County Republican (Red Wing, Minn.)
Hastings (Minn.) Independent
Lake City (Minn.) Times
Louisville Daily Journal
Mankato (Minn.) Record
Mankato (Minn.) Semi-Weekly Record
Murfreesboro Daily Union
Murfreesboro Union Volunteer
Nashville Daily Union
Rochester (Minn.) City Post
St. Anthony Falls Minnesota State News
St. Cloud (Minn.) Democrat
St. Paul Daily Press
St. Paul Daily Union
St. Paul Weekly Press
St. Paul Pioneer and Democrat
St. Paul Weekly Pioneer and Democrat
Stillwater (Minn.) Messenger
Wabashaw (Minn.) County Herald
Winona (Minn.) Daily Republican

Published Primary Sources

Abbott, John S. C. "Heroic Deeds of Heroic Men, XIV, The Wilds of Arkansas." *Harper's New Monthly Magazine* 33, no. 197 (1866): 581–601.

Bailey's St. Paul Directory for 1863. Vol. 1. St. Paul, Minn.: A. Bailey, 1863.

Anderson, Gary C., and Alan R. Woolworth, eds. *Through Dakota Eyes: Narrative Accounts of the Minnesota Indian War of 1862.* St. Paul: Minnesota Historical Society Press, 1988.

Andrews, Christopher C. *Hints to Company Officers on Their Military Duties.* New York: Van Nostrand, 1863.

———. "My Experience in Rebel Prisons." In *Glimpses of the Nation's Struggle: A Series of Papers Read before the Minnesota Commander of the Military Order of the Loyal Legion of the United States*, 4th ser., 24–40. St. Paul, Minn.: H. L. Collins, 1898.

———. "Narrative of the Third Regiment." In Board of Commissioners, *Minnesota in the Civil and Indian Wars*, 1:147–97.

———. "Sketch of the Third Regiment." in Third Minnesota Veteran Volunteer Association, *Third Annual Reunion of the Third Regiment Minnesota Veteran Volunteers*, 7. Minneapolis: Harrison and Smith Printing, 1886.

———. "The Surrender of the Third Regiment." In *Glimpses of the Nation's Struggle: A Series of Papers Read before the Minnesota Commander of the Military Order of the Loyal Legion of the United States,* [1st ser.], 337–68. St. Paul, Minn.: St. Paul Book and Stationery, 1883.

Baker, Edward L. "Surrender at Murfreesboro." In Third Minnesota Veteran Volunteer Association, *Seventh Annual Reunion of the Third Regiment Minnesota Veteran Volunteers*, 11–20. Minneapolis: Harrison and Smith Printing, 1890.

Bennett, Charles W. *Historical Sketches of the Ninth Michigan Infantry.* Coldwater, Mich.: Daily Courier Print, 1913.

Board of Commissioners, comp. *Minnesota in the Civil and Indian Wars.* 2 vols. St. Paul, Minn.: Pioneer, 1893.

Bowler, James M. "Some Long-Distance Recollections and Near-by Thoughts Concerning the Murfreesboro Disaster." In Third Minnesota Veteran Volunteer Association, *Eighteenth Annual Reunion of the Third Regiment Minnesota Veteran Volunteers*, 15–20. Minneapolis, 1902.

Brown, Alonzo L. *History of the Fourth Regiment of Minnesota Infantry Volunteers during the Great Rebellion, 1861–1865.* St. Paul, Minn.: Pioneer, 1892. Facsimile reprint, Salem, Mass.: Higginson, 1995.

Buck, Daniel. "Battle of Wood Lake." In Third Minnesota Veteran Volunteer Association, *Twenty-first Annual Reunion of the Third Regiment Minnesota Veteran Volunteers*, 17–20. Minneapolis, 1905.

Carley, Kenneth. ed. "As Red Men Viewed It: Three Indian Accounts of the Uprising, Chief Big Eagle's Story." *Minnesota History* 38, no. 3 (1962): 129–43.

———. "The Sioux Campaign of 1862: Sibley's Letters to His Wife." *Minnesota History* 38, no. 3 (1962): 99–114.

Casey, Silas. *Infantry Tactics for the Instruction, Exercise, and Manoeuvres of the Soldier, a Company, Line of Skirmishers, Battalion, Brigade, or Corps d'Armée.* Vols. 1–2. New York: D. Van Nostrand, 1862.

Chamberlain, H. E. *Commercial Advertiser: Directory for Saint Anthony and Minneapolis to which Is Added a Business Directory, 1859–1860.* St. Anthony, Minn.: Croffut & Clark, 1859.

Champlin, Ezra T. "Battle of Wood Lake." In Third Minnesota Veteran Volunteer Association, *Twenty-First Annual Reunion of the Third Regiment Minnesota Veteran Volunteers*, 14. Minneapolis, 1905.

———"Recollections of the Battle." In *Minnesota in the Civil and Indian Wars*, 2:245–48.

Cooke, Chauncey H. *A Badger Boy in Blue: The Civil War Letters of Chauncey H. Cooke.* Detroit: Wayne State University Press, 2007.

Dicey, Edward. *Spectator of America.* Edited Herbert Mitgang. Athens: University of Georgia Press, 1989.

"Document 124. Battle near Little Rock, Arkansas: A National Account." *Rebellion Record,* 7:417–25.

Duffield, William W. *Camp, Garrison, and Guard Duty, with a Modified Manual of Arms for the Officers and Soldiers of the Michigan Infantry.* Detroit: Wm. B. Howe, 1861.

Eisendrath, Joseph L., Jr., comp. *The Story of Sergeant Robert G. Ardrey, 111th Illinois, Inf., 1862–1865.* St. Louis: Genealogical Research and Publications, 1980.

Elder, Donald C., III, ed. *Love Amid the Turmoil: The Civil War Letters of William and Mary Vermillion.* Iowa City: University of Iowa Press, 2003.

Forman, Jacob G. *The Western Sanitary Commission: A Sketch of Its Origin, History, Labors for the Sick and Wounded of the Western Armies, and Aid Given to Freedmen and Union Refugees, with Incidents of Hospital Life.* St. Louis: R. P. Studley, 1864.

Foster, Everett. "Our Fools." In Third Minnesota Veteran Volunteer Association, *Sixth Annual Reunion of the Third Regiment Minnesota Veteran Volunteers,* 10–18. Minneapolis: Harrison and Smith Printing, 1889.

Fry, James B. *Operations of the Army under Buell from June 10th to October 30th, 1862, and the "Buell Commission."* New York: Van Nostrand, 1884.

Giles, L. B. *Terry's Texas Rangers.* Austin, TX: Van Boeckman-Jones, 1911. Reprint, Austin, TX: Pemberton, 1967.

Gill, John C. "An Ohio Doctor Views Campaigning on the White River, 1864." Edited by Harry F. Lupold. *Arkansas Historical Quarterly* 34 (1975): 333–51.

Gould, Benjamin Apthorp. *Investigations into the Military and Anthropological Statistics of American Soldiers.* New York: Hurd & Houghton for the U.S. Sanitary Commission; Cambridge, Mass.: Riverside, 1869.

Griffin, David B. *Letters Home to Minnesota: 2nd Minnesota Volunteers.* Compiled by Joan W. Albertson. Spokane, Wash.: P. D. Enterprises, 1992.

Griggs, Chauncey D. "Fort Snelling to Vicksburg." In Third Minnesota Veteran Volunteer Association, *Third Annual Reunion of the Third Regiment Minnesota Veteran Volunteers,* 20. Minneapolis: Harrison and Smith Printing, 1886.

Hale, William D. [Opening Remarks]. In Third Minnesota Veteran Volunteer Association, *Twenty-Fifth Annual Reunion of the Third Regiment Minnesota Veteran Volunteers,* 3–4. Minneapolis, 1909.

———. "Remarks [Regarding the Surrender]." In Third Minnesota Veteran Volunteer Association, *Twenty-Ninth Annual Reunion of the Third Regiment Minnesota Veteran Volunteers,* 9–10. Minneapolis, 1913.

Hale, William E. "Expedition to Fort Abercrombie." In Third Minnesota Veteran Volunteer Association, *Fourth Annual Reunion of the Third Regiment Minnesota Veteran Volunteers,* 7–11. Minneapolis: Harrison and Smith Printing, 1887.

Hewett, Janet, ed. *Supplement to the Official Records of the Union and Confederate Armies.* 100 vols. Wilmington, N.C.: Broadfoot, 1994–2001.

Hill, Alfred J. *History of Company E of the Sixth Minnesota Regiment of Volunteer Infantry.* St. Paul, Minn.: Pioneer, 1899.

Holcombe, R. I. "Statement [of Travel to Arkansas in 1895 and Meeting General McRae]." In Third Minnesota Veteran Volunteer Association. *Fourteenth Annual Reunion of the Third Regiment Minnesota Veteran Volunteers* 22–24. Minneapolis: Elander Stadder, 1898.

Johnson, Andrew. *The Papers of Andrew Johnson*. Vols. 5–6, edited by Leroy P. Graf and Ralph W. Haskins. Knoxville: University of Tennessee Press, 1979, 1983.

Knight, G. W. "Third Minnesota at Fitzhugh's Woods." In Third Minnesota Veteran Volunteer Association, *Fourteenth Annual Reunion of the Third Regiment Minnesota Veteran Volunteers*, 18–21. Minneapolis: Elander Stadder, 1898.

Langsdorf, Edgar, ed. "The Letters of Joseph H. Trego, 1857–1864, Linn County Pioneer: Part Three, 1863, 1864—Concluded." *Kansas Historical Quarterly* 19, no. 4 (1951): 381–400.

Lombard, Charles W. *History of the Third Regiment Infantry Minnesota Volunteers with the Final Record of the Original Regiment*. Faribault, Minn., 1869.

McClellan, George B. *Regulations and Instructions for the Field Service of the U.S. Cavalry in Time of War*. Philadelphia: J. B. Lippincott, 1861.

McConnell, G. M. "Up in Arkansas." *United States Service Magazine* 5, no. 3 (1866): 234–41.

Mahan, Alfred T. *An Elementary Treatise on Advanced-Guard, Out-Post, and Detachment Service of Troops*. N.p., 1861.

Mattson, Hans. "Early Days of Reconstruction in Northeastern Arkansas." In *Glimpses of the Nation's Struggle: A Series of Papers Read before the Minnesota Commander of the Military Order of the Loyal Legion of the United States*, 2nd ser., 322–37. St. Paul, Minn.: St. Paul Book and Stationery, 1890.

———. *Reminiscences: The Story of an Emigrant*. St. Paul, Minn.: D. D. Merrill, 1892.

Miller, Maude B. *Dear Wife: Letters from a Union Colonel*. Ann Arbor, Mich.: Sheridan Books, 2001.

Moneyhon, Carl H., ed. "Life in Confederate Arkansas: The Diary of Virginia Davis Gray, 1863–1865, Part I." *Arkansas Historical Quarterly* 42 (Spring 1983): 47–85; "Part II." 42 (1983): 47–85.

North, Eben. [Speech regarding Company C after Murfreesboro]. In Third Minnesota Veteran Volunteer Association, *Eighth Annual Reunion of the Third Regiment Minnesota Veteran Volunteers*, 11. Minneapolis: Harrison and Smith Printing, 1891.

Nydahl, Theodore L. "The Diary of Ignatius Donnelly, 1859–1884." Ph.D. dissertation, University of Minnesota, 1941.

Popchock, Barry, ed. *Soldier Boy: The Civil War Letters of Charles O. Musser, 29th Iowa*. Iowa City: University of Iowa Press, 1995.

Rea, Ralph R., ed. "Diary of Private John P. Wright, USA, 1864–1865." *Arkansas Historical Quarterly* 16 (1957): 304–18.

Redlon, Frank. "The Company Cook's Pass." In Third Minnesota Veteran Volunteer Association, *Seventh Annual Reunion of the Third Regiment Minnesota Veteran Volunteers*, 21–22. Minneapolis: Harrison and Smith Printing, 1890.

Robertson, John. *Michigan in the War*. Rev. ed. Lansing, Mich.: W. S. George, 1882.

Roesch, Philip. *"Memorandum of Philip Roesch, Co. H., 25th Regiment, Wisconsin Volunteers: Kept All during My Service, August 6, 1862, to June 11, 1865."* Midland, Mich.: Richard K. Long, 1979.

Roth, Mary Brobst, ed. *Well Mary: Civil War Letters of a Wisconsin Volunteer*. Madison: University of Wisconsin Press, 1960.

Sipes, William B. *The 7th Pennsylvania Volunteer Cavalry*. Pottsville, Pa.: Miners Journal Print, [1905?].

Skillman, Phil. "Letter to Member, 5 August 1903." In Third Minnesota Veteran Volunteer Association, *Nineteenth Annual Reunion of the Third Regiment Minnesota Veteran Volunteers*, 5–6. Minneapolis, 1903.

———. "Pine Bluff, Ark." In Third Minnesota Veteran Volunteer Association, *Fifth Annual Reunion of the Third Regiment Minnesota Veteran Volunteers*, 8–12. Minneapolis: Harrison and Smith Printing, 1888.

Spence, John C. *A Diary of the Civil War.* Murfreesboro, Tenn.: Rutherford County Historical Society, 1993.

Sperry, A. F. *History of the 33d Iowa Infantry Volunteer Regiment, 1863–6.* Edited by Gregory J. W. Urwin and Cathy K. Urwin. Fayetteville: University of Arkansas Press, 1999.

Stevens, Thomas N. *"Dear Carrie. . . .": The Civil War Letters of Thomas N. Stevens.* Edited by George M. Blackurn. Mount Pleasant: Clarke Historical Library, Central Michigan University, 1984.

Stillwell, Leander. *The Story of a Common Soldier of Army Life in the Civil War, 1861–1865.* 2nd ed. Erie, [Kans.?]: Franklin Hudson, 1920.

Strong, George T. *Diary of the Civil War, 1861–1865.* Edited by Allan Nevins. New York: Macmillan, 1962.

Swanson, Alan, ed. "The Civil War Letters of Olof Liljegren," *Swedish Pioneer Historical Quarterly* 31, no. 1 (1980): 86–121.

Third Minnesota Veteran Volunteers Association. *Annual Reunion of the Third Regiment Minnesota Veteran Volunteers.* 3rd to 47th reunions. Minneapolis: Harrison and Smith Printing, 1886–95; Erlander Stadder, 1896–1900; no publisher listed, 1901–31.

Trimble, Sarah R., ed. "Behind the Lines in Middle Tennessee, 1863–1865: The Journal of Bettie Ridley Blackmore." *Tennessee Historical Quarterly* 12, no. 1 (1953): 48–80.

Trollope, Anthony. *North America.* Edited by Donald Smalley and Bradford Allen Booth. New York: Alfred A. Knopf, 1951.

Wedge, Albert C. "Address." In Third Minnesota Veteran Volunteer Association, *Tenth Annual Reunion of the Third Regiment Minnesota Veteran Volunteers*, 3–4. Minneapolis: Harrison and Smith Printing, 1894.

Wenzel, Carol N. "Freedmen's Farm Letters of Samuel and Louisa Mallory to 'Our Absent but Ever Remembered Boy' in McHenry County, Illinois." *Journal of the Illinois State Historical Society* 75, no. 3 (1980): 162–76.

Wright, Thomas J. *History of the Eighth Regiment Kentucky Volunteer Infantry.* St. Joseph, Mo.: St. Joseph Steam Printing, 1880.

Secondary Sources

Alpert, Cady, and Kyle D. Kauffman. "The Economics of the Union Draft: Institutional Failure and Government Manipulation of the Labor Market during the Civil War." *Essays in Economic and Business History* 17, no. 1 (1999): 89–107.

Arnott, Sigrid, and David Maki. "Results of a Phase 1 Archeological Investigation of the Wood Lake Battlefield, Yellow Medicine County, Minnesota." American Battlefield Protection Program, GA-2287-14-021. Sigrid Arnott Consulting, November 2016.

Ash, Stephen V. *Middle Tennessee Society Transformed, 1860–1870: War and Peace in the Upper South.* Baton Rouge: Louisiana State University Press, 1988.

———. "Sharks in an Angry Sea: Civilian Resistance and Guerrilla Warfare in Occupied Middle Tennessee, 1862–1865." *Tennessee Historical Quarterly* 45 (1986): 217–29.

———. *When the Yankees Came: Conflict and Chaos in the Occupied South, 1861–1865*. Chapel Hill: University of North Carolina Press, 1995.

Atkins, Annette. *Creating Minnesota: A History from the Inside Out*. St. Paul: Minnesota Historical Society, 2007.

Atwater, Isaac, and John H. Stevens. *History of Minneapolis and Hennepin County*. New York: Munsell, 1895.

Bailey, Anne J., and Daniel E. Sutherland, eds. *Civil War Arkansas: Beyond Battles and Leaders*. Fayetteville: University of Arkansas Press, 2000.

———"The History and Historians of Civil War Arkansas." *Arkansas Historical Quarterly* 53, no. 3 (1999): 232–63.

Bakeman, Mary H., and Antona M. Richardson, eds. *Trail of Tears: Minnesota's Dakota Indian Exile Begins*. Roseville, Minn.: Park Genealogical Books, 2008.

Baker, James M. *The Lives of the Governors of Minnesota*. St. Paul: [Minnesota Historical] Society, 1908.

Bell, Andrew M. *Mosquito Soldiers: Malaria, Yellow Fever, and the Course of the American Civil War*. Baton Rouge: Louisiana State University Press, 2010.

Birtle, Andrew J. *U.S. Army Counterinsurgency and Contingency Operations Doctrine, 1860–1941*. Washington, D.C.: U.S. Army Center for Military History, 1997.

Boulden, Benjamin. "So Long as Strangers Are the Rulers: General Frederick Steele and the Politics of Wartime Reconstruction in Arkansas." Master's thesis, University of Arkansas, 1992.

Brooksher, William, and David Snider. "Surrender or Die." *Military History* 1, no. 4 (February 1985): 30–32.

Brown, Gary D. "Prisoner of War Parole: Ancient Concept, Modern Utility." *Military Law Review* 156 (1998): 200–223.

Bunch, Clea L. "Confederate Women of Arkansas Face 'the Fiends in Human Shape.'" *Military History of the West* 27 (1997): 173–87.

Burns, Ken. *The Civil War*. Florentine Films, 1990.

Burton, William L. "'Title Deed to America': Union Ethnic Regiments in the Civil War." *Proceedings of the American Philosophical Society* 124, no. 6 (1980): 455–63.

Castle, Henry A. *History of St. Paul and Vicinity: A Chronicle of Progress and a Narrative Account of the Industries, Institutions, and People of the City and Its Tributary Territory*. Vol. 2. Chicago: Lewis, 1912.

Christ, Mark K. *Civil War Arkansas, 1863: The Battle for a State*. Norman: University of Oklahoma Press, 2011.

———. "'A Hard Little Fight': The Battle of Fitzhugh's Woods, April 1, 1864." *Arkansas Historical Quarterly* 64, no. 4 (2005): 380–93.

———, ed., *Rugged and Sublime: The Civil War in Arkansas*. Fayetteville: University of Arkansas Press, 1994.

Cilella, Salvatore G., Jr. *Upton's Regulars: The 121st New York Infantry in the Civil War*. Lawrence: University Press of Kansas, 2009.

Clinton, Catherine, and Nina Silber, eds. *Divided Houses: Gender and the Civil War*. New York: Oxford University Press, 1993.

Clodfelter, Michael, *The Dakota War: The United States Army Versus the Sioux, 1862–1865*. Jefferson, N.C.: McFarland, 1998.

Coggins, Jack. *Arms and Equipment of the Civil War*. Mineola, N.Y.: Dover, 1990.

Coleman, Leslie F. "History of the Swedes from Isanti Township, Isanti County, in the 3rd Minnesota Regiment." Typescript, 2001.

Collett, Chris. "Countering Irregular Activity in Civil War Arkansas—A Case Study." Strategic Research Project, U.S. Army War College, 2007.

Cooling, Benjamin F. *Fort Donelson's Legacy: War and Society in Kentucky and Tennessee, 1862–1863*. Knoxville: University of Tennessee Press, 1997.

———. "A People's War: Partisan Conflict in Tennessee and Kentucky." In Sutherland, *Guerrillas, Unionists, and Violence*, 113–32.

Costa, Dora L., and Matthew E. Kahn. *Heroes & Cowards: The Social Face of War*. Princeton, N.J.: Princeton University Press, 2008.

Cotterill, R. S. "The Louisville and Nashville Railroad, 1861–1865." *American Historical Review* 29, no. 4 (1924): 700–715.

Cray, Loren. "Experiences in Southwestern Minnesota, 1859 to 1867." *Minnesota History Collections* 15 (1915): 435–54.

Croizat, Victor J. "Naval Forces in River War." *Proceedings of the United States Naval Institute* 92, no. 10 (1966): 52–61.

Curtiss-Wedge, Franklyn, ed. *History of Dakota and Goodhue Counties, Minnesota*. 2 vols. Chicago: H. C. Cooper, 1910.

Dahlin, Curtis. "Words vs. Action." In *Trails of Tears: Minnesota's Dakota Indian Exile Begins*, edited by Mary H. Bakeman and Antonia M. Richardson, 44–48. Roseville, Minn.: Prairie Echoes/Park Genealogical Books, 2008.

Daniel, John S., Jr. "Special Warfare in Middle Tennessee and Surrounding Areas, 1861–1862." M. A. thesis, University of Tennessee at Knoxville, 1971.

Dean, Eric T., Jr. "'A Scene of Surpassing Terror and Awful Grandeur': The Paradoxes of Military Service in the American Civil War." *Michigan Historical Review* 21, no. 2 (1995): 37–61.

———. "'We Will All Be Lost and Destroyed': Post-Traumatic Stress Disorder and the Civil War." *Civil War History* 37, no. 2 (1991): 138–53.

DeBlack, Thomas A. "1863: 'We Must Stand or Fall Alone.'" In Christ, *Rugged and Sublime*, 59–104.

Dougan, Michael B. *Confederate Arkansas: The People and Politics of a Frontier State in Wartime*. University: University of Alabama Press, 1976.

Durham, Walter T. *Nashville, the Occupied City: The First Seventeen Months—February 16, 1862 to June 30, 1863*. Nashville: Tennessee Historical Society, 1988.

Edwards, William B. *Civil War Guns: The Complete Story of Federal and Confederate Small Arms: Design, Manufacture, Identification, Procurement, Issue, Employment, Effectiveness, and Postwar Disposal*. Gettysburg, Pa.: Thomas, 1997.

Eisterhold, John A. "Fort Heiman: Forgotten Fortress." *West Tennessee Historical Society Papers* 28 (1974): 43–54.

Engle, Stephen D. *Don Carlos Buell: Most Promising of All*. Chapel Hill: University of North Carolina Press, 1999.

Farley, Miranda. "The Politics of Memory: Remembering the Civil War in Rutherford County, Tennessee." Ph. D. dissertation, Indiana University, 2004.

Faust, Drew G. *This Republic of Suffering: Death and the American Civil War*. New York: Knopf, 2008.

Finnell, Arthur A. *Descendants of Carl Roos and Clara Sophia Persdotter: From Varmland, Sweden, to Vasa, Goodhue County, Minnesota, the First Five Generations*. Bloomington, Minn.: A. L. Finnell, 1992.

Fitzharris, Joseph C. "Field Officer Courts and Civil War Justice: The 3rd Minnesota as a Case Study, 1863–1865." *Journal of Military History* 68 (2004): 47–72.

———. "Going to War with the 25th Wisconsin—in Minnesota! Post–Dakota Uprising Service in 1862." Paper presented to the University of Wisconsin River Falls History Alumni, 20 April 2012.

———. "Lizzie Caleff's War of the Rebellion." Paper presented to the Twin Cities Civil War Round Table, 21 March 1995.

———. "'Our Disgraceful Surrender': The Third Minnesota Infantry's Disintegration and Reconstruction in 1862–1863." *Military History of the West* 30 (2000): 1–20.

Foote, Lorien. *The Gentlemen and the Roughs: Violence, Honor, and Manhood in the Union Army.* New York: New York University Press, 2010.

Frank, Lisa T. *Women in the American Civil War.* 2 vols. Santa Barbara, Calif.: ABC-CLIO, 2007.

Gallagher, Gary W. *The Union War.* Cambridge, Mass.: Harvard University Press, 2012.

Geary, James W. "Civil War Conscription in the North: A Historiographical Review." *Civil War History* 23, no. 3 (1986): 208–28.

Gibbon, Guy. *The Sioux: The Dakota and Lakota Nations.* Hoboken, N.J.: Wiley-Blackwell, 2002.

Gibson, Charles D., and E. Kay Gibson. *Assault and Logistics: Union Army Coastal and River Operations, 1861–1865.* Camden, Maine: Ensign, 1995.

Gildrie, Richard P. "Guerrilla Warfare in the Lower Cumberland River Valley, 1862–1865." *Tennessee Historical Quarterly* 48, no. 3 (1990): 161–76.

Gordon, Lesley J. *A Broken Regiment: The 16th Connecticut's Civil War.* Baton Rouge: Louisiana State University Press, 2014.

Gray, Lewis C. *A History of Agriculture in the Southern United States to 1860.* 2 vols. New York: Peter Smith, 1940.

Grimsley, Mark. *The Hard Hand of War: Union Military Policy toward Southern Civilians, 1861–1865.* New York: Cambridge University Press, 1995.

Hackemer, Kurt. "Response to War: Civil War Enlistment Patterns in Kenosha County, Wisconsin." *Military History of the West* 29, no. 1 (1999): 31–62.

Hafendorfer, Kenneth A. *Nathan Bedford Forrest, the Distant Storm: The Murfreesboro Raid of July 13, 1862.* Louisville, Ky.: KH Press, 1997.

———. *They Died by Twos and Tens: The Confederate Cavalry in the Kentucky Campaign of 1862.* Louisville, Ky.: KH Press, 1995.

Hagerman, Edward. "Field Transportation and Strategic Mobility in the Union Armies." *Civil War History* 34, no. 2 (1988): 143–71.

Halleran, Michael A. "Freemasons in the Civil War." *North & South* 12, no. 5 (January 2011): 52–57.

Hallock, Judith. "The Role of the Community in Civil War Desertion." *Civil War History* 29, no. 3 (1983): 123–34.

Haugland, John C. "Politics, Patronage, and Ramsey's Rise to Power, 1861–1863." *Minnesota History* 37 (1961): 324–34.

Hawkins, Susan. "Forts Henry, Heiman, and Donelson: The African American Experience." Master's thesis, Murray State University, n.d.

Henry, Robert S. *"First with the Most" Forrest.* Indianapolis: Bobbs-Merrill, 1944.

Hess, Earl J. *Civil War Infantry Tactics: Training, Combat, and Small-Unit Effectiveness.* Baton Rouge: Louisiana State University Press, 2015.

————. *The Rifle Musket in Civil War Combat: Reality and Myth*. Lawrence: University Press of Kansas, 2008.

Hicks, John D. "The Organization of the Volunteer Army in 1861 with Special Reference to Minnesota." *Minnesota History Bulletin* 2 (1918): 324–68.

Hobgood, Baxter E. "Economic History of Rutherford County." In *A History of Rutherford County*, edited by Carlton C. Sims, 201–30. Murfreesboro, Tenn., 1947.

Hoffman, Mark *"My Brave Mechanics": The First Michigan Engineers and Their Civil War*. Detroit: Wayne State University Press, 2007.

Holmes, Richard. *Acts of War: The Behavior of Men in Battle*. New York: Free Press, 1989.

Houlton, Caitlin. "From Farmboys to Fancy Soldiers: The Tale of the 8th Regiment Volunteer Infantry of Minnesota in the Dakota Uprising of 1862." Papers from the Civil War Seminar, Fall 2010, University of St. Thomas, Minn., pp. 62–81.

Huff, Leo E. "Guerrillas, Jayhawkers, and Bushwhackers in Northern Arkansas during the Civil War." *Arkansas Historical Quarterly* 24 (1965): 127–48.

————. "The Memphis and Little Rock Railroad during the Civil War." *Arkansas Historical Quarterly* 23 (1964): 260–70.

————. "The Union Expedition against Little Rock, August–September 1863." *Arkansas Historical Quarterly* 22 (1963): 224–37.

Hughes, Michael A. "Wartime Gristmill Destruction in Northwest Arkansas and Military-Farm Colonies." *Arkansas Historical Quarterly* 46, no. 2 (1987): 167–86.

Hughes, Thomas. "History of Steamboating on the Minnesota River." *Minnesota History Collections* 10, no. 1 (1905): 131–63.

Huston, James A. "Logistical Support of Federal Armies in the Field." *Civil War History* 7 (1961): 36–47.

Jarchow, Merrill E. *The Earth Brought Forth: A History of Minnesota Agriculture to 1885*. St. Paul: Minnesota Historical Society, 1949.

Johnson, Roy. "The Siege at Fort Abercrombie." *North Dakota History* 24, no. 1 (1957): 4–79.

Johnson, Russell L. *Warriors into Workers: The Civil War and the Formation of Urban-Industrial Society in a Northern City*. New York: Fordham University Press, 2003.

Jones, James B., Jr. "Negley's Raid, May 31–June 9, 1862." *North & South* 11, no. 2 (December 2008): 84–87.

Jordan, Brian M. *Marching Home: Union Veterans and Their Unending Civil War*. New York: Liveright, 2014.

Kohl, Rhonda M. "'This Godforsaken Town': Death and Disease at Helena, Arkansas, 1862–1863." *Civil War History* 50 (2004): 109–44.

Lang, Andrew F. "Challenging the Union Citizen-Soldier Ideal." In McKnight and Myers, *The Guerrilla Hunters*, 305–34.

Larson, Douglas E. "Private Alfred Gales: From Slavery to Freedom." *Minnesota History* 57 (2001): 274–83.

Lass, William. *Minnesota: A History*. 2nd ed. New York: W. W. Norton, 1998.

Lee, Chulhee. "Military Position and Post Service Occupational Mobility of Union Army Veterans, 1861–1880." Working Paper 12416. Cambridge, Mass., NBER, July 2006.

Leslie, James W. *Land of Cypress and Pine*. Little Rock: Rose, 1976.

Leonard, William E. "Early Days in Minneapolis." *Minnesota History Collection* 15 (1915): 497–514.

Linderman, Gerald F. *Embattled Courage: The Experience of Combat in the American Civil War*. New York: Free Press, 1987.

———. "Military Leadership and the American Experience." *Military Review* 70, no. 4 (1990): 24–32.

Lord, Francis A. *They Fought for the Union*. New York: Bonanza Books, 1960.

Lytle, Andrew N. *Bedford Forrest and His Critter Company*. New York: G. P. Putnam's Sons, 1931.

Mackey, Robert R. "Bushwhackers, Provosts, and Tories: The Guerrilla War in Arkansas." In Sutherland, *Guerrillas, Unionists, and Violence*, 171–85.

———. "The Federal Counter-Insurgency Campaign in Arkansas, 1862–1865." Paper presented to the Northern Great Plains History Conference, St. Cloud, Minn., October 1999.

———. *The Uncivil War: Irregular Warfare in the Upper South, 1861–1865*. Norman: University of Oklahoma Press, 2004.

Manning, Chandra Miller. "'Like a Handle on a Jug': Union Soldiers and Abraham Lincoln." *North & South* 9, no. 4 (August 2006): 34–46.

Marquis, Albert N., ed. *The Book of Minnesotans: Biographical Dictionary of Leading Living Men of the State of Minnesota*. Chicago: A. N. Marquis, 1907.

Marten, James. "Exempt from the Ordinary Rules of Life: Researching Postwar Adjustment Problems of Union Veterans." *Civil War History* 47 (2001): 57–70.

———. *Sing Not War: The Lives of Union & Confederate Veterans in Gilded Age America*. Chapel Hill: University of North Carolina Press, 2011.

Maslowski, Peter. "A Study of Morale in Civil War Soldiers." *Military Affairs* 34, no. 4 (1970): 122–26.

———. *Treason Must Be Made Odious: Military Occupation and Wartime Reconstruction in Nashville, Tennessee, 1862–1865*. Millwood, N.Y.: KTO, 1978.

McDowell, Robert Emmett. *City of Conflict: Louisville in the Civil War, 1861–1865*. Louisville, Ky.: Louisville Civil War Roundtable, 1962.

McKnight, Brian D., and Barton A. Myers, eds. *The Guerrilla Hunters: Irregular Conflicts during the Civil War*. Baton Rouge: Louisiana State University Press, 2017.

McPherson, James M. *Battle Cry of Freedom*. New York: Oxford, 2003.

———. *For Cause and Comrades: Why Men Fought in the Civil War*. New York: Oxford University Press, 1997.

Merrill, James M. "Cairo, Illinois: Strategic Civil War River Port." *Journal of the Illinois State Historical Society* 76 (1983): 242–56.

Messmer, Charles. "Louisville during the Civil War." *Filson Club History Quarterly* 52, no. 2 (1978): 206–33.

Mills, Eric. "Riverine Warfare Conference Final Wrap-Up: Lessons from the Civil War." Paper presented at the Applied Naval History Conference, Riverine Warfare: Back to the Future, Annapolis, Md., 6–7 April 2006.

Mitchell, Reid. *Civil War Soldiers*. New York: Penguin, 1988.

Moneyhon, Carl H. "From Slave to Free Labor: The Federal Plantation Experiment in Arkansas." *Arkansas Historical Quarterly* 53, no. 2 (1994): 137–60.

———. *The Impact of the Civil War and Reconstruction on Arkansas: Persistence in the Midst of Ruin*. Baton Rouge: Louisiana State University Press, 1994.

———. "1865: 'A State of Perfect Anarchy.'" In Christ, *Rugged and Sublime*, 145–61.

Moran, Nathan K. "Military Government and Divided Loyalties: The Union Occupation of Northwest Tennessee, June 1862–August 1862." *West Tennessee Historical Society Papers* 48 (1994): 91–106.

Mountcastle, Clay. *Punitive War: Confederate Guerrillas and Union Reprisals*. Lawrence: University Press of Kansas, 2009.

Murdock, Eugene C. *One Million Men: The Civil War Draft in the North*. Madison: State Historical Society of Wisconsin, 1971.

———. *Patriotism Limited, 1862–1865: The Civil War Draft and the Bounty System*. Kent, Ohio: Kent State University Press, 1967.

Musick, Michael P. "'The Little Regiment': Civil War Units and Commands." *Prologue* 27, no. 2 (1995): 151–71.

Nelson, James Lynn. "Intrepid Gray Warriors: The 7th Texas Infantry, 1861–1865." Ph.D. dissertation, Texas Christian University, 1995.

Noe, Kenneth W. "Jigsaw Puzzles, Mosaics, and Civil War Battle Narratives." *Civil War History* 53 (2007): 236–43.

Notesworthy, Brent. *Bloody Crucible of Courage: Fighting Methods and Combat Experience of the Civil War*. New York: Carroll & Graf, 2003.

O'Donnell, William W. *The Civil War Quadrennium*. Little Rock: Civil War Round Table of Arkansas, 1985.

Osman, Stephen E. "Audacity, Skill, and Firepower: The Third Minnesota's Skirmishers at the Battle of Wood Lake." *Minnesota's Heritage* 3 (January 2011): 24–40.

———. *Fort Snelling and the Civil War*. St. Paul, Minn.: Ramsey County Historical Society, 2017.

Parrish, William E. "The Western Sanitary Commission." *Civil War History* 36 (1990): 17–35.

Patchin, Sydney A. "The Development of Banking in Minnesota." *Minnesota History Bulletin* 2 (1917): 111–68.

Patrick, Stewart G. "A History of the Regimental Bands of Minnesota during the Civil War." Ph.D. dissertation, University of North Dakota, 1972.

Peters, Pamela R. *The Underground Railroad in Floyd County, Indiana*. Jefferson, N.C.: McFarland, 2001.

Pittard, Homer P. "Legends and Stories of Civil War Rutherford County." Master's thesis, George Peabody College for Teachers, 1940.

Poole, John Randolph. *Cracker Cavaliers: The 2nd Georgia Cavalry under Wheeler and Forrest*. Macon, Ga.: Mercer University Press, 2000.

Prokopowicz, Gerald. "All for the Regiment: Unit Cohesion and Tactical Stalemate in the Army of the Ohio, 1861–1862." Ph.D. dissertation, Harvard University, 1994.

———. "Disunion Equals Disaster." *America's Civil War* 15, no. 1 (March 2002): 30–36, 72.

Reardon, Carol. "Writing Battle History: The Challenge of Memory." *Civil War History* 53 (2007): 252–63.

Richards, Ira D. *Story of a Rivertown: Little Rock in the Nineteenth Century*. Benton, Ark., 1969.

Robertson, James I., Jr. *Soldiers Blue and Gray*. Columbia: University of South Carolina Press, 1988.

Robertson, John. "Re-enlistment Patterns of Civil War Soldiers." *Journal of Interdisciplinary History* 32, no. 1 (2001): 15–35.

Rodgers, Thomas E. "Billy Yank and G.I. Joe: An Exploratory Essay on the Sociopolitical Dimensions of Soldier Motivation." *Journal of Military History* 69 (2005): 93–121.

Rubinstein, Sarah P. "The French Canadians and French." In *They Chose Minnesota: A Survey of the State's Ethnic Groups*, edited by June D. Holmquist, 26–41. St. Paul: Minnesota Historical Society, 1981.

Russ, William. "Administrative Activities of the Union Army during and after the Civil War." *Mississippi Law Journal* 17 (1945): 71–89.

Saperstein, Dana, and Roger Saperstein. "The Emotional Wounds of War." *Military Review* 72, no. 1 (1991): 54–61.

Schiller, Laurence D. "Two Tales of Tennessee: The Ups and Downs of Cavalry Command." *North & South* 4, no. 4 (April 2001): 78–86.

Scott, Paul R. "Eighth Texas Cavalry Regiment, CSA." Master's thesis, University of Texas at Arlington, 1977.

Shannon, Fred A. "The Life of the Common Soldier in the Union Army." *Mississippi Valley Historical Review* 13, no. 4 (1927): 465–82.

———. *The Organization and Administration of the Union Army, 1861–1865.* Cleveland: Arthur H. Clark, 1928.

Shea, William L. "A Semi-Savage State: The Image of Arkansas in the Civil War." In Bailey and Sutherland, *Civil War Arkansas,* 85–99.

Simon, Don. "The Third Minnesota Regiment in Arkansas, 1863–1865." *Minnesota History* 40 (1967): 281–92.

Slotkin, Richard. "Unit Pride: Ethnic Platoons and the Myths of American Nationality." *American Literary History* 13, no. 3 (2001): 469–98.

Steiner, Paul E. *Disease in the Civil War: Natural Biological Warfare in 1863–1865.* Springfield, Ill.: Charles C. Thomas, 1968.

Stith, Matthew M. "Guerrilla Warfare and the Environment in the Trans-Mississippi Theater." In McKnight and Myers, *Guerrilla Hunters,* 192–212.

Stone, Jayme L. "Brother against Brother: The Winter Skirmishes along the Arkansas River, 1864–1865." *Military History of the West* 25 (1995): 23–49.

Stucky, Scott W. "Joint Operations in the American Civil War." Master's thesis, National War College, 1993.

Sude, Barry R. "Federal Military Policy and Strategy in Mississippi an Arkansas, 1861–1863: A Study of Command and Conflict." Ph.D. dissertation, Temple University, 1986.

Sutherland, Daniel E. "1864: 'A Strange, Wild Time.'" In Christ, *Rugged and Sublime,* 105–44.

———. "Afterward." In McKnight and Myers, *Guerrilla Hunters,* 354–64.

———. "Guerrillas: The Real War in Arkansas." In Bailey and Sutherland, *Civil War Arkansas,* 133–53.

———, ed. *Guerrillas, Unionists, and Violence on the Confederate Home Front.* Fayetteville: University of Arkansas Press, 1999.

———. *A Savage Conflict: The Decisive Role of Guerrillas in the American Civil War.* Chapel Hill: University of North Carolina Press, 2009.

Swart, Stanley L. "The Military Examination Board in the Civil War: A Case Study." *Civil War History* 16 (1970): 227–45.

Swanson, Evadene B. "A New Hampshire Yankee in King Oscar's Court." *Swedish Pioneer Historical Quarterly* 16, no. 1 (1965): 18–26.

Tapson, Alfred J. "The Sutler and the Soldier." *Military Affairs* 23, no. 4 (1957): 176–78.

Thilgen, Dean R. "A Man of His Time: A Chronology of Events during Dr. Rollin C. Olin's Life." 2000. Unpublished typescript in author's possession.

Tolbert, Lisa C. *Constructing Townscapes: Space and Society in Antebellum Tennessee.* Chapel Hill: University of North Carolina Press. 1999.

Trenerry, Walter N. "Lester's Surrender at Murfreesboro." *Minnesota History* 39 (1965): 191–97.

———. "Votes for Minnesota's Civil War Soldiers." *Minnesota History* 36 (1959): 167–72.

———. "When the Boys Came Home." *Minnesota History* 38 (1963): 287–97.

Upham, Warren, and Rose B. Dunlap. *Minnesota Biographies, 1655–1912*. St. Paul: Minnesota Historical Society, 1912.

Urwin, Gregory J. W. "'The Lord Has Not Forsaken Me and I Won't Forsake Him': Religion in Frederick Steele's Union Army, 1863–1864." *Arkansas Historical Quarterly* 52, no 3 (1993): 318–40.

Watson, Bruce A. *When Soldiers Quit: Studies in Military Disintegration*. Westport, Conn.: Praeger, 1997.

Way, Frederick, Jr., comp. *Way's Packet Directory, 1848–1983: Passenger Steamboats of the Mississippi River System since the Advent of Photography in Mid-continent America*. Athens: Ohio University Press, 1983.

Weber, Jennifer L. "The Neighbors' War." *North & South* 9, no. 7 (February 2007): 32–48.

Weddle, Kevin J. "Disgraced at Murfreesboro, the 3rd Minnesota Recovered to Forge a Proud Fighting Record." *America's Civil War* 4, no. 2 (May 1991): 12, 14, 16, 20, 60–61.

———. "Ethnic Discrimination in Minnesota Volunteer Regiments during the Civil War." *Civil War History* 35 (1989): 239–59.

Weitz, Mark A. "Drill, Training, and the Combat Performance of the Civil War Soldier: Dispelling the Myth of the Poor Soldier, Great Fighter." *Journal of Military History* 62 (1998): 263–89.

Welcher, Frank J. *The Union Army, 1861–1865: Organization and Operation*. Vol. 2, *The Western Theater*. Bloomington: Indiana University Press, 1993.

Welter, Barbara. "The Cult of True Womanhood." *American Quarterly* 18, no. 2 (1966): 151–74.

Wesbrook, Stephen D. "Morale, Proficiency, and Discipline." *Journal of Political and Military Sociology* 8, no. 1 (Spring 1980): 43–54.

White, Helen M. "Captain Fisk Goes to Washington." *Minnesota History* 38 (1963): 216–30.

Whitesell, Hunter B. "Military Operations in the Jackson Purchase Area of Kentucky, 1862–1865." *Register of the Kentucky Historical Society* 63, no. 2 (1965): 141–67.

Wiley, Bell Irwin. *The Life of Billy Yank, the Common Soldier of the Union*. Indianapolis: Bobbs-Merrill, 1952.

Williams, Charles G. "Houses Used by the Union Army in the City of Little Rock, Arkansas." *Pulaski County Historical Review* 33 (1985): 48.

Wilson, Mark R. *The Business of Civil War: Military Mobilization and the State, 1861–1865*. Baltimore: Johns Hopkins University Press, 2006.

Woolworth, Alan, and Mary H. Bakeman, eds. *Camera and Sketchbook: Witnesses to the Sioux Uprising of 1862*. Roseville, Minn.: Prairie Echoes/Park Genealogical Books, 2004.

Woodworth, Steven E. "Supporting the Troops: The Bond between Civilians and Soldiers in the Civil War." *North & South* 9, no. 2 (May 2006): 56–63.

Internet Sources

The Abraham Lincoln Association. "The Collected Works of Abraham Lincoln." Updated 11 September 2008. http://quod.lib.umich.edu/l/lincoln/.

"Absolom A. Harrison Civil War Letters." Updated 28 February 2002. Letters about the Civil War. American Civil War Homepage. http://www.civilwarhome.com.

"Adolphus Elliot." Academic Health Center History Project. University of Minnesota. http://editions.lib.umn.edu/ahcarchives/? s=adolphus+elliot.

Blackburn, J. K. P. "Reminiscences of the Terry Rangers." *Southwestern Historical Quarterly* 22 (1918): 38–77. Internet Archive. Uploaded 20 March 2013. https://archive.org/details/jstor-30234772.

Chenoweth, Michael, and C. J. Mock. "Hurricane 'Amanda': Rediscovery of a Forgotten U.S. Civil War Florida Hurricane." *Bulletin of the American Meteorological Society* (November 2013): 1735–42. https://journals.ametsoc.org/doi/pdf/10.1175/BAMS-D-12-00171.1.

Cowan 's Auctions. "Civil War Tiffany Presentation Sword, Lot 375." 2002 Historical Americana. http://www.cowanauctions.com/auctions/item.aspx?id=2207 (page discontinued; printout in author's possession).

Duffield, William W. *School of the Brigade, and Evolutions of the Line; or, Rules for the Exercise and Manoeuvres of Brigades and Divisions. Designed as a Sequel to the United States Infantry Tactics, Adopted May 1, 1862.* Philadelphia: J. B. Lippincott, 1862. Internet Archive. Uploaded 7 October 2008. http://archive.org//details/schoolbrigadeanooduffgoog/page/n5.

Emery, Lewis. "Lewis Emery Letters." Compiled by Glen Larson. http://www.geocities.com/glenallanlarson/civilwarletters/intro.html (site discontinued; printouts in author's possession).

The Encyclopedia of Arkansas History & Culture. http://www.encyclopediaofarkansas.net/.

"The G. A. R." Meeker County Historical Society. http://www.garminnesota.org/#!blank/xpm48.

Goff, Kent J. "The Evolution of Skirmish Tactics in the U.S. Civil War." Skirmish Doctrine. Papers. Resources. Mississippi Valley Educational Programs. http://www.mvep.org/skirmishold.htm.

Hardee, William J. *Rifle and Light Infantry Tactics.* Memphis: E. G. Kirk, 1861. http://books.google.com/books.

Hennepin County, Minnesota, Biographies. Genealogy Trails. http://genealogytrails.com/minn/hennepin/bioindex.html.

Historical Census Browser. University of Virginia Library. http://mapserver.lib.virginia.edu (site discontinued).

Iowa GenWeb Project. http://iagenweb.org.

Kaeuper, Richard W. "The Forgotten Triumph of the Paw Paw." *American Heritage Magazine* 46, no. 6 (October 1995). http://www.americanheritage.com/content/forgotten-triumph-paw-paw.

King, William H. "Forrest's Attack on Murfreesboro, July 13, 1862." *Confederate Veteran* 32, no. 11 (November 1924): 430–31, 437. Internet Archive, http://archive.org/details/confederateveter3219conf/page/n5.

MacMurphy, Gilbert L. "[Diary of G. L. MacMurphy]." https://texashistory.unt.edu/ark:/67531/metapth619490/.

Martin, James B. *Third War: Irregular Warfare on the Western Border, 1861–1865.* Fort Leavenworth, Kans.: Combat Studies Institute Press, 2012. Ike Skelton Combined Arms Research Library Digital Library. http://cgsc.contentdm.oclc.org/cdm/singleitem/collection/p16040coll3/id/159/rec/1.

Minnesota Historical Society. *Minnesota State Capitol: Overview of the Fine Art.* 2015. https://mn.gov/admin/assets/ 2015-03-23-overview-fine-art-in-capitol-MNHS_tcm36-225814.pdf.

"Minnesota Legislators Past & Present." Minnesota Legislative Reference Library. https://www.leg.state.mn.us/legdb/.

Minnesota Territorial Pioneers—Biographical Sketches of Territorial Pioneers. http://www.pressenter.com/~gregboeminnesota_territorial_pioneers_biographies.htm (site discontinued; printouts in author's possession).

Portrait and Biographical Record of Jasper, Marshall, and Grundy Counties, Iowa: Containing Biographical Sketches of Prominent and Representative Citizens of the Counties, together with Biographies and Portraits of the Presidents of the United States. Chicago: Biographical Publishing, 1894. http://books.google.com/books.

Tarrant, Eastham. *The Wild Riders of the First Kentucky Cavalry: A History of the Regiment in the Great War of the Rebellion, 1861–1865, Telling of Its Origin and Organization, a Description of the Material of Which It Was Composed, Its Rapid and Severe Marches, Hard Service, and fierce conflicts . . . a Regimental Roster. . . .* Louisville, Ky.: Published by a Committee of the Regiment, 1894. Uploaded 12 June 2008. Internet Archive. http://archive.org/details/wildridersoffirsootarr/page/n7.

U.S. National Park Service. "Troop Movement Maps." Stones River National Battlefield. Updated 14 April 2015. https://www.nps.gov/stri/learn/historyculture/troopmaps.htm.

——. *Stones River National Battlefield, Tennessee: Draft General Management Plan, Development Concept Plan, Environmental Impact Statement.* [Denver]: Resource Planning Group, Denver Service Center, 1997. https://babel.hathitrust.org/Record/003200185.

——. Soldiers and Sailors Database. Updated 14 May 2015. https://www.nps.gov/civilwar/soldiers-and-sailors-database.htm.

U.S. Navy. Naval History Division. "Riverine Warfare: The U.S. Navy's Operations on Inland Waters." Washington, D.C.: Naval History Center, 2006. https://www.history.navy.mil/content/history /nhhc/research/library/online-reading-room/title-list-alphabetically/r/riverine-warfare-us-navys-operations-inland-waters.html.

"United States Sanitary Commission." U.S. Army Heritage and Education Center. https://ahec.armywarcollege.edu/exhibits/CivilWarImagery/Sanitary_Commissionl.cfm.

Van Buren, W. H. *Rules for Preserving the Health of the Soldier.* 5th ed. [Washington, D.C.: U.S. Sanitary Commission, 1861.] Digital Collections. U.S. National Library of Medicine. https://collections.nlm.nih.gov/catalog/nlm:nlmuid-101523993-bk.

Index

Page numbers in *italics* indicate illustrations.

Lesher, Amos, 63
Lester, Henry C., 12, 61, *138*, 147;
    appointment to Third, 25; assumption
    of command of the Third, 37;
    assumption of command of the
    Twenty-Third Brigade, 68, 69; on
    camp security, 37; dismissal of,
    132; "flag of truce" narrative and,
    94–95; on medical care quality,
    58–59; as military disciplinarian,
    38, 45; Murfreesboro battle and,
    81, 84, 85–86, 87, 90, 91, 92–93;
    on Murfreesboro security, 77;
    Murfreesboro surrender and, 95–97,
    99; officer training and, 37–38; post-
    war career, 234; promotions and, 58;
    reputation of, 38–39, 47, 57, 74, 99, 132;
    rivalry with Parkhurst, 74, 83–84; on
    runaway slaves, 43; surrender effect
    and, 3, 4; as tactician, 93; training
    and, 49, 53; unit histories' depiction
    of, 7–9; on weapons' condition, 50–51
"Lester's Surrender at Murfreesboro"
    (Trenerry), 7
Lewis, Albert, 91
Libby Prison, 131
Liljegren, Olof, 60, 68, 104, 128, 133, 151,
    167, 186, 189
Lincoln, Abraham, 108, 120, 132, 165, 168,
    174, 176, 183, 212–13
Lincoln, Warren, 135
Lindall, James, 160
Linderman, Gerald, 181
Lindquist, Rev., 126
Little Crow, 4–5, 8, 115, 118, 120
Littlefield, Louis, 91, 92, 102, 104, 154, 155,
    158, 201. *See also* "American Boy"
Little Rock, Ark.: Confederate
    withdrawal from, 172; discharged men
    returning to, 228–29; hospitals in, 179;
    pacification policies in, 174–77, 184;
    religious services in, 175–76; telegraph
    line in, 208; Third as provost guard
    in, 172–80
Little Rock Quartermaster Depot, 214
Lockney, James, 175, 190
Logan, William, 221

Lombard, Charles, 221, 225
looting, 80, 128, 130
Louisville, Ky., 33
Louisville & Nashville Railroad, 32, 51
Louisville Daily Journal, 43, 57, 60
Louisville Democrat, 53
Louisville Journal, 53, 56
Lowater, Harry, 153, 167
Lower Sioux Agency, 108
Lowry, Sylvanus, 11
loyalty oaths, 66, 74–75, 157, 175, 178, 214, 217
lumbering firms, 233
Lytle, Andrew, 98

"M" (soldier correspondent), 47, 50, 52
Madden, Richard, 38
Mader, Cincinatus V., 176
major, competition for appointment as, 22
Malloy, James, 220
Malmros, Oscar, 106, 107, 109, 131, 194, 197,
    198, 200, 217
Maney House, 81, 89, 94
Mankato Record, 23
Mankato Semi-Weekly Record, 23
Manter, Francis, 176
marine brigade, 152–53
Mark's Mills action, 189
Marlett, Ira, 50, 153
Marples, Charles, 203, 212, 216
Marshall, William, 120, 124, 125, 130, 131
martial law: in Chicago, 105; in Louisville,
    33; in Murfreesboro, 65–66, 86; over
    draft-eligible men, 107
Martin, Perry, 41, 52, 151
Masons, 34, 41, 44, 51, 69, 72, 218, 232
Matthews, Stanley, 79, 84
Mattson, Cherstie, 171, 207
Mattson, Edgar L., 227
Mattson, Hans, 5, 14, 18, 24, 27, 28, 38, 40,
    41, 42, 43, 44, 47, 48, 49, 51, 55, 57, 66,
    67–68, 70, 76–77, 78–79, 80, 100, 101,
    102, 103, 106, 107, 127, 131, 133, 134, 135,
    140, 147, 150–52, 151, 160, 162, 167, 168,
    171, 172, 173, 180, 181, 182, 186, 187, 191,
    193, 194, 195, 198, 199, 200, 201, 202,
    204, 205, 208, 209, 210, 212, 213, 216,
    217, 218, 219, 221, 222, 223, 225, 233–34